REASSESSING THE ROGUE TORY

REASSESSING THE ROGUE TORY
Canadian Foreign Relations in
the Diefenbaker Era

Edited by Janice Cavell and Ryan M. Touhey

UBCPress · Vancouver · Toronto

27 26 25 24 23 22 21 20 19 18   5 4 3 2 1

Printed in Canada on FSC-certified ancient-forest-free paper (100% post-consumer recycled) that is processed chlorine- and acid-free.

Library and Archives Canada Cataloguing in Publication

Reassessing the rogue Tory: Canadian foreign relations in the Diefenbaker era / edited by Janice Cavell and Ryan M. Touhey.

Includes bibliographical references and index.
Issued in print and electronic formats.
ISBN 978-0-7748-3813-9 (hardcover). – ISBN 978-0-7748-3815-3 (PDF). –
ISBN 978-0-7748-3814-6 (softcover). – ISBN 978-0-7748-3816-0 (EPUB). –
ISBN 978-0-7748-3817-7 (Kindle)

1. Diefenbaker, John G., 1895–1979.   2. Canada – Foreign relations – 1945–.
I. Touhey, Ryan, editor   II. Cavell, Janice, editor

FC616.D53R43 2018   971.064'2   C2018-904712-7
                                                              C2018-904713-5

Canadä

UBC Press gratefully acknowledges the financial support for our publishing program of the Government of Canada (through the Canada Book Fund), the Canada Council for the Arts, and the British Columbia Arts Council.

This book has been published with the help of a grant from the Canadian Federation for the Humanities and Social Sciences, through the Awards to Scholarly Publications Program, using funds provided by the Social Sciences and Humanities Research Council of Canada.

Printed and bound in Canada by Friesens
Set in Warnock Pro by Apex CoVantage, LLC
Copy editor: Joanne Richardson
Proofreader: Carmen Tiampo
Indexer: Cheryl Lemmens

UBC Press
The University of British Columbia
2029 West Mall
Vancouver, BC V6T 1Z2
www.ubcpress.ca

Contents

Acknowledgments / viii

Abbreviations / x

Introduction / 3
Janice Cavell

Part 1: The Commonwealth

1 A New Vision for the Commonwealth: Diefenbaker's
Commonwealth Tour of 1958 / 25
Francine McKenzie

2 Different Leader, Different Paths: Diefenbaker
and the British, 1957–63 / 45
Norman Hillmer

Part 2: Canadian-American Relations

3 The Spirit of '56: The Suez Crisis, Anti-Americanism,
and Diefenbaker's 1957 and 1958 Election Victories / 67
Janice Cavell

4 When the Chips Are Down: Eisenhower,
Diefenbaker, and the Lebanon Crisis, 1958 / 85
Greg Donaghy

5 The Problem Child: Diefenbaker and Canada in the
Language of the Kennedy Administration / 103
Stephen Azzi

Part 3: Nuclear Weapons

6 The Defence Dilemma, 1957–63: Reconsidering the
Strategic, Technological, and Operational Contexts / 123
Isabel Campbell

7 "I Would Rather Be Right": Diefenbaker and
Canadian Disarmament Movements / 143
Nicole Marion

Part 4: The Developing World

8 A Limited Engagement: Diefenbaker, Canada, and
Latin America's Cold War, 1957–63 / 167
Asa McKercher

9 The Diefenbaker Government and Foreign Policy
in Africa / 186
Kevin A. Spooner

10 Tilting the Balance: Diefenbaker and Asia, 1957–63 / 209
Jill Campbell-Miller, Michael Carroll, and Greg Donaghy

11 The Winds of Change: Ellen Fairclough and the
Removal of Discriminatory Immigration Barriers / 227
Robert Vineberg

Part 5: The Role of the Foreign Minister

12 Sidney Smith, Howard Green, and the Conduct of Canadian
Foreign Policy during the Diefenbaker Government, 1957–63 / 249
Michael D. Stevenson

Part 6: The End of the Diefenbaker Era

13 A Complex Reckoning: A Personal Reflection on the 1963
Election / 271
Hugh Segal

Conclusion / 279
Ryan M. Touhey

Contributors / 287

Index / 289

Acknowledgments

Some of the chapters in this book were first presented in two back-to-back sessions at the 2015 Canadian Historical Association meeting. The sessions, followed by a reception, marked the publication of the 1962–63 volume in the series, *Documents on Canadian External Relations*. These events were jointly sponsored by the CHA's Political History Group and the Historical Section, Foreign Affairs and International Trade Canada (now Global Affairs Canada). Thanks are due to Penny Bryden of the Political History Group; Michel Duquet at the CHA; Jordan Zed, director of the Policy Research Division at Foreign Affairs and International Trade Canada; and to the session chairs, Lisa Pasolli and Laura Madokoro.

The contributors to this collection were wonderful to work with. Their hard work, enthusiasm, and superb research more than fulfilled our hopes for the volume.

At UBC Press, Emily Andrew and Darcy Cullen gave early encouragement, then Randy Schmidt expertly steered the manuscript through the review process. The two anonymous peer reviewers made constructive and very helpful suggestions. Finally, Holly Keller and her team ensured that production of the book went smoothly.

The Awards to Scholarly Publications Program generously provided a grant, while funding for the index came from St. Jerome's University at the University of Waterloo.

Several colleagues were exceptionally helpful. Greg Donaghy not only contributed to the contents of the book, he advised on various matters from beginning to end. John English, Norman Hillmer, Ken McLaughlin, Andrew Burtch, Tim Cook, Dan Gorman, David Meren, and Whitney Lackenbauer also offered words of wisdom that were much appreciated.

Finally, we wish to acknowledge the steadfast support of our families: Breanna Touhey and newborn son, James; Alex, Cecily, and Ben Cavell, plus the latest addition, Cedric Cavell-Blaine.

Abbreviations

CCCRH	Canadian Committee for the Control of Radiation Hazards
CCOS	Chairman, Chiefs of Staff
CDC	Cabinet Defence Committee
CIA	Central Intelligence Agency
CPC	Canadian Peace Congress
CRO	Commonwealth Relations Office (UK)
CUCND	Combined Universities Campaign for Nuclear Disarmament
DEA	Department of External Affairs
DRVN	Democratic Republic of Viet Nam (North Vietnam)
EEC	European Economic Community
FAC	Foreign Assets Control (US)
FTA	free trade area (EEC)
ICBM	Intercontinental Ballistic Missile
ICC	International Control Commission
JBMDS	Joint Ballistic Missile Defence Staff
MAAG	Military Assistance Advisory Group (US)
NATO	North Atlantic Treaty Organization
NORAD	North American Air Defence Command
OAS	Organization of American States
ONUC	Opération des Nations Unies au Congo
PRC	People's Republic of China
RCAF	Royal Canadian Air Force

RCN	Royal Canadian Navy
SSEA	Secretary of State for External Affairs
UAR	United Arab Republic (Egypt and Syria)
UAW	United Auto Workers
UNEF	United Nations Emergency Force (Suez Crisis)
UNESCO	United Nations Educational, Scientific and Cultural Organization
UNOGIL	United Nations Observation Group in Lebanon
USSEA	Undersecretary of State for External Affairs
VOW	Voice of Women

REASSESSING THE ROGUE TORY

Introduction

JANICE CAVELL

It is now over half a century since John Diefenbaker's Progressive Conservative government was defeated in the election of 1963. Diefenbaker came to power with a minority government in 1957, after more than two decades of Liberal rule; quickly returned to the hustings in 1958 and won the largest parliamentary majority up to that time in Canada (208 out of 265 seats); then was reduced again to a minority in mid-1962 and lost power in April of the next year. By 1962, his government was beset by controversies, many of them related to foreign policy. The events of early 1963 were, quite simply, unprecedented in Canadian history.

With his government crumbling from within as cabinet ministers questioned his leadership, Diefenbaker also faced a direct attack from Washington when the State Department issued a press release that in effect called him a liar. On 5 February 1963 he lost a non-confidence vote in the House of Commons, having been formally accused of "lack of leadership" and "confusion and indecision in dealing with national and international problems."[1] During the ensuing tumultuous election, Diefenbaker campaigned with passion, using openly anti-American rhetoric to win back some of the support he had lost. Liberal leader Lester B. Pearson was confronted by demonstrators who burned an American flag and denounced him as Washington's "stooge."[2] Pearson could do no better than another minority government, a result that was repeated in the 1965 election. Diefenbaker clung to his position as Conservative leader until 1967 and then stayed on as a member of Parliament until his death in 1979.

Understandably, Diefenbaker remains one of the most controversial prime ministers in Canadian history. His record in international affairs, and particularly his handling of Canada-United States relations, has always been the major focus of his critics, and the enduring image of Diefenbaker's foreign policy is one of disastrous indecision. In this view, Diefenbaker's election victory marked the end of a "golden age" in Canadian foreign relations, and his tenure as prime minister was an embarrassingly amateurish interlude between the more impressive Liberal regimes of Louis St. Laurent and Lester Pearson.

The Conservatives' foreign policy failures have long been attributed mainly to Diefenbaker's personality traits, particularly his indecisiveness, paranoia, and excessive fear of losing power. That Diefenbaker often showed poor judgment, emotional instability, and a partisan concern for domestic political advantage is unquestionable,[3] and many contemporaries responded to these characteristics with distaste even if they did not entirely disagree with the prime minister's views. For example, the cosmopolitan and erudite diplomat Charles Ritchie, who was appointed as Canada's ambassador to Washington in 1962, often bristled with annoyance when US officials ridiculed Canadian foreign policy initiatives. Nevertheless, in 1963 Ritchie wrote that "there should be prayers of thanksgiving in the churches" for the Conservative electoral defeat so far as it concerned Diefenbaker himself.[4]

Basil Robinson, who acted as a liaison between Diefenbaker and the Department of External Affairs from 1957 to 1962, recorded numerous gaffes and rash decisions in his memoir, *Diefenbaker's World*. Yet Robinson was also careful to note that Diefenbaker handled many foreign policy issues well, particularly during his government's early years. Robinson concluded by remembering that in 1963, although he was relieved by the change in government, he knew enough about Diefenbaker's record in international affairs to be "sceptical of wholesale condemnations."[5]

Not only did the Diefenbaker government have several foreign policy successes to its credit, but after 1963 thorny issues such as anti-Americanism in Canada continued to plague Pearson and his ministers, occasionally causing embarrassing diplomatic fiascos. For example, in 1965 Pearson was harshly taken to task by President Lyndon B. Johnson over Canada's stance on the Vietnam War. Diefenbaker's oversized ego and his colourful outspokenness make it easy to place factors of personality front and centre when evaluating his government's foreign policy performance.[6] However, even in the immediate aftermath of his defeat, some well-informed observers pointed instead to the broad underlying shifts in world affairs between 1957 and 1963. Both the geopolitical scene and Canada's place in it were changing at an unprecedented rate, making the task that confronted first Diefenbaker and then Pearson exceptionally challenging. Indeed, the contrast between Pearson's successes during the 1950s and his sometimes floundering efforts at statesmanship during the 1960s demonstrates that even a politician with far more experience of international affairs than Diefenbaker found it impossible to maintain his former stature amid the turmoil of the '60s.

In 1965 Marcel Cadieux, then the undersecretary of state for external affairs (as the deputy minister of Canada's foreign ministry was called before 1993), addressed the question of how the breach in Canada-United States relations could be repaired. He began not by blaming the Diefenbaker government but by offering an overview of the past two decades. Cadieux noted that Canada's international stature was considerably enhanced by the Second World War; in the immediate postwar era, many other Western nations were still struggling to recover from the conflict, but Canada prospered. In foreign policy, "the circumstances were propitious for Canadian initiatives" through the United Nations (UN) and the North Atlantic Treaty Organization (NATO). This period ended with the Suez Crisis. In the early Diefenbaker years, Cadieux wrote, "the international environment had begun to change," particularly through decolonization and "the increasing complexity of the nuclear problem." At the same time, "rightly or wrongly, the potential threat to Canadian independence from mounting United States investment began to be seriously felt." Cadieux pointed out that Washington was "not without fault in its attitude toward Canada" and tended "to make rather irrational demands" of its allies. He cautioned that these worrisome conditions "still exist, if anything in greater magnitude."[7] The mere removal of Diefenbaker from office, then, would not be enough to set matters right.

The Diefenbaker Government and Foreign Policy

As Cadieux observed, the Suez Crisis of November 1956 marked both the high point and the end of a period when Canadian diplomacy met with great success and high international respect. On the domestic front, from 1945 until 1956 external policy was rarely, if ever, a matter of partisan debate. Indeed, if there was such a thing as a golden age it was Suez, rather than the victory of Diefenbaker's Progressive Conservatives seven months later, that marked its end. For the first time the policies of Canada's two main allies, the United Kingdom and the United States, diverged sharply. The domestic consensus on international issues was shattered; the Liberals' support for the American rather than the British position gained them as much criticism as praise, and anti-American sentiment increased markedly. The next decade brought frequent questions about Canada's place in North America and in the Western alliance.

It also brought a greater awareness of the need for Canada to engage with the global south. Decolonization was among the most important of the shifts in the Diefenbaker era. During the Suez Crisis, the Conservatives had seemed fixated on support for the United Kingdom, ignoring the effect that Britain's neo-imperial aggression had on the new Asian and potential African members of the Commonwealth. St. Laurent attempted to use this stance against Diefenbaker during the 1957 election campaign. An editorial in the Liberal *Toronto Star* agreed that the Conservatives were "living in an age that is past." The election was set for 10 June; a Commonwealth prime ministers' meeting would follow shortly afterwards in London. Another Liberal journalist argued that, while St. Laurent could play a constructive role at this meeting, with Diefenbaker as Canada's representative the outlook would be far less promising.[8]

Such predictions seemed reasonable enough: Diefenbaker was of Scottish descent on his mother's side, and he had an unusually strong dedication to the United Kingdom. The new prime minister did indeed revel in the traditional British connection during his triumphant visit to London. However, Diefenbaker was a dedicated upholder of human rights, and the German component in his ancestry made him sensitive to the concerns of those from non-British backgrounds. Once in office, he was quick to demonstrate his belief in the New Commonwealth. His 1958 world tour began with another visit to Europe and ended in the predominantly white dominions of Australia and New Zealand, but the main focus was on India, Pakistan, Ceylon, and Malaya.

Francine McKenzie leads off the collection with a carefully nuanced chapter that examines Diefenbaker's vision of the future multiracial Commonwealth through a case study of the tour. She points out the contradictions in and limitations of this vision, but at the same time she demonstrates that Diefenbaker's political philosophy was broadly aligned with the new era of decolonization and, thus, was innovative and forward-looking rather than nostalgic. McKenzie's contribution also shows that Diefenbaker's character traits did not always stand in the way of effective diplomacy.

Like McKenzie's piece, Kevin Spooner's chapter on the Conservative government and Africa demonstrates Canada's growing attunement to the developing world during the Diefenbaker years, as do Asa McKercher's contribution on Latin America and the chapter on Asia by Jill Campbell-Miller,

Michael Carroll, and Greg Donaghy. McKenzie suggests that Diefenbaker was more of a liberal internationalist than previous historians have given him credit for, and his government's relations with Commonwealth countries in Africa and Asia do much to confirm her hypothesis. Outside the Commonwealth, Ottawa found the prospect of increased trade alluring and moved towards greater involvement, particularly in such episodes as the 1960 and 1961 wheat sales to the People's Republic of China. Yet, at the same time, potential Cold War flashpoints in the Congo, Cuba, and Indochina demonstrated the need for caution. Diefenbaker and his colleagues nevertheless made preliminary advances that would be followed up by later governments: for example, Diefenbaker was the first Canadian prime minister to make an official visit to a Latin American country (Mexico) and also the first to make such a visit to Japan.

While the studies of Africa, Latin America, and Asia offer broad overviews of the Diefenbaker government's policies in key areas of the Third World, Robert Vineberg's contribution is more tightly focused. Vineberg shows how Canada's first female cabinet minister, Ellen Fairclough, brought immigration policy in line with the evolution of foreign policy, easing the long-standing restrictions on non-white immigration. The prime minister himself did little except to let Fairclough have her way. This chapter demonstrates that, when Diefenbaker's own interest in the decolonizing world reached its limits, his ministers could step forward on their own to initiate major changes. In this way, the Conservative government's policy agenda gained a coherence that the leader would not have achieved alone.

Diefenbaker's liberal internationalism may have wavered at times, but it was strong enough to create unexpected difficulties. Ironically, his very dedication to the New Commonwealth brought the Canadian leader into conflict with the "mother country" to which he had initially felt such devotion. As Norman Hillmer's chapter explains, Diefenbaker became prime minister just when, in the aftermath of the Suez debacle, Harold Macmillan's government decided to turn away from imperial dreams and Commonwealth associations. Macmillan preferred to move towards Europe, which by then had not only recovered from its postwar malaise but was in a period of economic boom. Many in Whitehall viewed Canadian aspirations to world influence as (to borrow the term employed by a British diplomat in 1958) "tiresome" at the best of times.[9] At this juncture, Diefenbaker's efforts to promote stronger ties with the New Commonwealth were especially inconvenient and unwelcome to Macmillan.

As Spooner's chapter shows, Diefenbaker's decision at the 1961 Commonwealth prime ministers' meeting to side with India's Jawaharlal Nehru and other New Commonwealth leaders against South Africa's apartheid regime (he was the only white prime minister to do so) was a principled stand that won him well-deserved applause. Hillmer, however, argues cogently that, from the perspective of Canada's bilateral relations with the United Kingdom, the move was disastrous. A wiser statesman might have satisfied New Commonwealth aspirations while keeping Britain's goodwill; as it was, Diefenbaker's relations with Macmillan were soured just when Canada could have benefited most from British advice and support in other areas.

Despite his reverence for Britain, Diefenbaker refused to change course. Many New Commonwealth leaders felt serious apprehension about the Macmillan government's application to join the European Economic Community. Throughout 1962, Diefenbaker acted as the spokesman for those who opposed the British move, thus alienating Macmillan even further.[10] As Hillmer sums it up, the story of Anglo-Canadian relations during the Diefenbaker years is "not a happy one."

The story of Canada-United States relations in the same period is, of course, unhappier still: by 1963 the situation had deteriorated to the point where it can credibly be argued that President John F. Kennedy and members of his administration deliberately helped to bring about the fall and electoral defeat of the Conservative government. Here again, the Suez Crisis of 1956 marked an important change. As my own chapter demonstrates, Canadian public opinion about the invasion of Egypt was mixed. However, there was intense and widespread resentment of Washington for the humiliation it inflicted on the United Kingdom and France through its blunt insistence that their forces be withdrawn. Given this demonstration of just how powerful the United States had become, Canadians' nationalist aspirations increasingly seemed to be on a collision course with the forces of American political, economic, and cultural domination.

Diefenbaker deftly used these aspirations and resentments to his advantage in the election campaigns of 1957 and 1958, while holding back from the strongest excesses of popular anti-Americanism. Opposition to communism was one of Diefenbaker's most firmly held political convictions, making him unlikely to oppose the United States on substantive Cold War issues. As Greg Donaghy's chapter shows, Diefenbaker's good relationship with President Dwight D. Eisenhower owed as much to the prime minister's own efforts as to Eisenhower's. By the end of 1958 Eisenhower was convinced that, when the "chips were down," Ottawa could be relied on to stand with Washington.

At the same time, however, the outgoing Liberal government had left some difficult issues unresolved. First there was the agreement for an integrated approach to continental defence through the North American Air Defence Command (NORAD). Told by top military leaders that the agreement had already been negotiated and only awaited approval, Diefenbaker (who was temporarily acting as his own secretary of state for external affairs) and the minister of national defence, George Pearkes, signed in July 1957 without any discussion by the full cabinet. But, in fact, concerns previously raised by the Department of External Affairs about the need to protect Canadian sovereignty through ongoing political consultation had not been met.

In an episode proving that the non-partisan era in Canadian foreign policy was indeed over, the Liberals used their pre-election inside knowledge to embarrass Diefenbaker. Despite the strong military logic behind integrated continental defence, then, NORAD gave rise to serious and justified concerns. Eisenhower was sympathetic to the prime minister's plight, and a more satisfactory agreement was substituted on 12 May 1958. This agreement provided for "the fullest possible consultation" at the political level whenever circumstances seemed to warrant placing forces on alert.[11] Although the Liberal attack did Diefenbaker no lasting political harm, he became more leery about controversial foreign policy decisions.

It was not long before the Americans suggested that the new arrangements should include Canada's acquisition of nuclear weapons. This question was entwined with another difficult issue left unresolved by the Liberals: the fate of the CF-105 (Avro Arrow) supersonic interceptor aircraft. In August 1958, Pearkes recommended cancelling the Arrow program because of its ever-escalating cost and the seeming certainty that, for all their technological sophistication, the planes would soon be obsolete. The Arrow was designed to destroy Soviet nuclear bombers, but it appeared evident that bombers would be phased out and replaced by intercontinental ballistic missiles (ICBMs). As a far less expensive replacement for the Arrow in the interval before the end of the bomber era, Pearkes recommended the Boeing CIM10-B Bomarc defensive ground-to-air missile, which carried a nuclear warhead.

On this occasion, there was a full cabinet debate. However, the ministers focused mainly on the agonizing Arrow decision, knowing that cancellation would hurt both national pride and the Canadian aircraft industry.[12]

Acquisition of the Bomarc was approved in September 1958. The decision was announced along with the news that the Arrow might be cancelled. In February 1959 Diefenbaker confirmed the cancellation; he also stated that Canada intended to acquire nuclear warheads for the Bomarc and for another missile system, the Lacrosse, which would be obtained for the Canadian NATO brigade in Europe. In May 1959 a further step was taken when cabinet approved a nuclear strike role for Canadian aircraft serving with NATO. For this purpose, cabinet selected the Lockheed F-104G (Starfighter), which could be manufactured in Canada, helping to offset the Arrow loss.

As Isabel Campbell points out in her chapter, the momentous decisions of 1958 and 1959 opened a period when defence policy became a "political minefield" in a way it had never been before. Not only were the chosen weapons systems soon revealed to have serious flaws, but broad strategic concepts were in constant flux. Canadian military leaders, especially those in the Royal Canadian Air Force (RCAF), were stubbornly set on their nuclear choices, which they saw as essential to Canada's prestige and influence within the Western alliance. They did nothing to promote awareness that, with the development of Polaris, Minuteman, and other ICBMs, the US nuclear deterrent was rapidly becoming strong enough to make a Soviet first strike all but impossible, rendering the potential Canadian tactical nuclear contributions to North American defence ever less significant.[13]

The Bomarc and Lacrosse systems (as well as the Honest John, which was later chosen to replace the unsatisfactory Lacrosse) were still under development when they were selected, while the F-104 required redesign for its new role. There was, accordingly, a lengthy period before the warheads would be required. Between 1959 and 1962, Campbell argues, there was time to formulate an approach that took new strategic developments into consideration. However, the Department of National Defence refused to work with the Department of External Affairs on a coordinated plan, with the result that the government received contradictory advice. With the publication of new and alarming facts about fallout, public opposition to the weapons was on the rise, and a well-organized disarmament movement soon formed. Moreover, by January 1960, Diefenbaker had concluded that not enough was being done to safeguard Canadian sovereignty. Nicole Marion contends that this realization, rather than fear of the disarmers' influence on public opinion and voting outcomes, was the main cause of the prime minister's notorious prevarications and delays on nuclear policy.

Another factor was the influence of Howard Green, who became secretary of state for external affairs in June 1959. In September 1957, Diefenbaker had assigned the external affairs portfolio to Sidney Smith, the president of the University of Toronto. Although Smith lacked political experience, he had long-standing ties to the Progressive Conservative Party and, indeed, he had been urged by those who most strongly opposed Diefenbaker's leadership bid in 1956 to run for the position himself[14] – a fact of which Diefenbaker was undoubtedly aware, and which casts an interesting light on both the prime minister's decision to offer Smith the external affairs post and the inability of the two men to work harmoniously together after Smith had accepted it. As Michael Stevenson's chapter demonstrates, despite a few successes Smith was generally a disappointment in his new role.

Following Smith's sudden and unexpected death in March 1959, Green was chosen as his replacement. While Green did not initially question the nuclear choices the government had already made, his attitude soon changed. Green was an experienced parliamentarian, respected by his colleagues from all parties, but nothing in his background seemed to qualify him for the external affairs portfolio. However, unlike Smith, he had strong support from the prime minister, and he was exceptionally well informed about nuclear technology. Green was quick to grasp the implications of the new fallout studies, which showed that, because of global weather patterns, a disproportionate amount of radioactive debris fell in Canada.[15] By late 1959, Green had dedicated himself to the cause of disarmament; a year later, Diefenbaker stated that there would be no nuclear acquisition "while progress towards disarmament continues."[16]

The disarmament crusade was consistent with Green's broad plan for Canadian foreign policy. He argued that it was time for Canada to drop the Liberals' "honest broker" model and take a more activist approach to world affairs. In Green's view, Canada needed to put forward more initiatives at the UN and elsewhere, thereby demonstrating that it had views and a voice of its own.[17] In other words, Green feared that Canada was sliding ever closer to the position of an American satellite, and he sought above all to counter both the reality and the perception of such a development.

For all the harmonious relations between Ottawa and the Eisenhower administration, there was reason for Canadians to feel that Washington indeed often expected acquiescence rather than discussion. Following the Cuban revolution of January 1959 and the formation of a new government dominated by Fidel Castro, policy on Cuba was the cause of numerous disagreements. By mid-1960 Washington's anger against Castro's regime was intense. At the meeting of the Canada-US Ministerial Joint Committee on Defence in Montebello, Quebec, the Americans put forward proposals for an economic embargo of Cuba; Canada declined to participate. The Canadian ambassador in Washington, Arnold Heeney, recorded that Green was badly shaken by the US officials' aggressive attitude. Heeney afterwards identified the Montebello meeting as the point at which Canada-US relations began to deteriorate.[18]

This was the situation when John F. Kennedy was elected as the new US president in November 1960. Diefenbaker had formed the opinion that Kennedy was "courageously rash" and set on reinforcing Washington's position of leadership within the Western alliance.[19] Stephen Azzi's chapter demonstrates that Diefenbaker was not wrong: the general ethos of the Kennedy administration valorized extreme toughness, with opposing views frequently being dismissed as weak or ill-informed. The president and his officials used then common metaphors – heavily influenced by the jargon of Freudian psychology and by gender stereotypes – to express this attitude, describing the representatives of other nations as irrational women or children. These tropes had insidious power when employed by the many journalists (not all of them American) who supported Kennedy. Washington insiders used an even more extreme form of this language among themselves, and such rhetoric made overbearing behaviour appear justified in the Americans' own eyes.[20] As Azzi's chapter details, Kennedy displayed insensitivity throughout his May 1961 visit to Ottawa; in this context, the discovery that the president had left behind a memo by his advisor W.W. Rostow, in which Rostow listed the issues on which the US should "push" Canada, was particularly galling to Diefenbaker.

Campbell points out that Kennedy and his secretary of defence, Robert McNamara, were interested in the increased use of conventional forces. Yet the president concentrated on getting Canada to accept the nuclear warheads, and, despite the lack of any real strategic need for Canada to have these weapons, he was determined to secure quick Canadian compliance. Economic advantages were offered in the form of a deal whereby Canada would build F-104s for NATO partners and receive McDonnell F-101 (Voodoo) interceptors from the United States.

The crisis caused that summer by the erection of the Berlin Wall, along with the resumption of Soviet nuclear tests, added urgency to Kennedy's request. Diefenbaker, as ready as he had been in the Eisenhower era to cooperate with the Americans at moments of heightened Cold War tension, substantially increased the Canadian NATO contingent. On the nuclear front, Kennedy wrote to urge an agreement on the warheads as a means to demonstrate NATO solidarity.[21] Diefenbaker was apparently on the verge of action when the correspondence was leaked to journalists, quite possibly by Kennedy himself.

The chapters by Azzi, Campbell, and Marion all attest to the importance of this episode. Such heavy-handed intervention was the worst possible way to deal with Diefenbaker. Kennedy gave a speech to the UN General Assembly on 25 September in which he unveiled a new disarmament plan and stated that there should be no expansion of the "nuclear club" – meaning the group of nations with independent nuclear capability, which France had recently joined. Diefenbaker seized on the speech as an excuse to claim that the president had made it impossible for Canada to accept nuclear weapons.[22] In the following month, a massive anti-nuclear demonstration on Parliament Hill provided another pretext for delay. There was little movement on the nuclear issue in early or mid-1962; as Azzi recounts, frustrated American officials concluded that Canadians suffered from a collective mental illness.

By the spring of 1962, the government was in serious trouble on economic issues such as unemployment and the falling value of the Canadian dollar. It was clear that Diefenbaker could not proceed without a renewed mandate, and he therefore called an election he was not sure he could win. In late April Kennedy hosted a White House dinner for Nobel laureates; Pearson was the only non-American in attendance. The State Department had advised against inviting him, but Kennedy not only went ahead, he agreed to Pearson's request for a private meeting. Afterwards, Pearson let it be known that he and Kennedy had talked for forty minutes.

Diefenbaker was understandably angered that Kennedy seemed bent on giving his rival favourable publicity at such a critical time. However, the prime minister's response was excessive by any standard. Diefenbaker informed US ambassador Livingston Merchant that he would make Canada-US relations a campaign issue, using the Rostow memo to demonstrate Washington's arrogant attitude. Although Merchant was appalled and infuriated by Diefenbaker's threat, he seemed to believe that the president might be at least somewhat in the wrong. The ambassador suggested a careful strategy to establish US neutrality in the election, involving a public, friendly encounter between Kennedy and his Canadian counterpart. But Kennedy furiously declared he would never see or speak to Diefenbaker again – a resolution to which he adhered for over six months.[23] The 1962 election, then, not only reduced the Conservatives to a precarious minority government, it brought Canada-US relations to a new low.

Throughout 1961 and 1962, Cuba continued to be the cause of frequent irritation between the two countries. As McKercher's chapter demonstrates, Diefenbaker and Green drew back from Latin American involvement once it became clear that Castro was aligning himself with the Soviet bloc. Nevertheless, during the Cuban Missile Crisis of October 1962 Kennedy and his officials were in no mood to observe the niceties of the 1958 NORAD agreement. The president avoided even speaking to Diefenbaker on the telephone, and this lack of communication or consultation exacerbated Diefenbaker's resentment, although it did not stop him from taking several measures in support of the Americans.[24] Following the crisis, public opinion shifted towards greater (although still far from universal) approval for the acquisition of nuclear warheads. There was broad agreement among media commentators that, with the weapons systems now in place, the time had come for a definite decision one way or the other.[25]

Diefenbaker opened negotiations at last, but in the face of critical comments by the retiring NATO commander, General Lauris Norstad, he defended his delays. In contrast, Pearson sought political advantage by shifting to support for acquisition. Even within Pearson's own party, not everyone was convinced; for example, the Liberal *Toronto Star* continued to firmly oppose nuclear weapons for Canada.[26] As Campbell explains, there was much truth in the prime minister's arguments about the need for careful reconsideration of the entire issue. Nevertheless, following a State Department press release that cast doubt on Diefenbaker's veracity and was intended as shock therapy for the supposed "essentially neurotic" Canadian worldview,[27] the government fell. In the book's concluding chapter, Hugh Segal explores both the appeal of Diefenbaker's nationalist message during the election campaign and the doubts that prevented voters from giving Pearson's Liberals a majority mandate.

Diefenbaker and the Historians: Assessing (and Reassessing) the Rogue Tory

Two lines of interpretation for the Diefenbaker era were set out within a few years of its end. Philosopher George Grant's *Lament for a Nation* described Diefenbaker and Green as the last defenders of traditional Canadian nationalism, fighting a hopeless yet necessary battle. Grant's powerful polemic did much to inspire the "new nationalists" of the 1960s, but Diefenbaker himself, with his old-fashioned style of political oratory, was not well suited to become a hero among the younger generation.[28] Moreover, Peter Newman's *Renegade in Power* put forward a view that was starkly opposed to Grant's, highlighting Diefenbaker's poor judgment and indecisiveness as the explanation for his government's failures.[29]

Newman's basic premise was developed in a more academic vein through survey histories by Robert Bothwell, J.L. Granatstein, Norman Hillmer, and others.[30] Their case against Diefenbaker was most succinctly presented by Granatstein in 2011. In his view, good relations with the United States were the most basic factor contributing to Canada's national interest, and any prime minister who lost sight of this essential truth deserves condemnation.[31] While these historians are sometimes critical of Kennedy, they assign by far the largest portion of blame for the breakdown in relations to Diefenbaker. Granatstein, for example, states that Kennedy's initial tolerance of Diefenbaker's antics "can only be described as remarkable."[32] According to Bothwell, by early 1963 these antics were "more than could be borne," and the Americans were justified in deciding it was "high time to put Diefenbaker in his place."[33]

On the other side of the argument, Jocelyn Maynard Ghent cast a critical light on the Canadian defence establishment and on the Kennedy administration. According to Ghent, Canadian military leaders felt more loyalty to their US counterparts than to their own civilian colleagues and political masters, and much of the confusion in the Diefenbaker era was caused by their determination to push forward with their defence agenda through the creation of NORAD and the acquisition of nuclear weapons. Ghent also produced evidence to substantiate long-standing suspicions about excessive US interference in Canadian affairs.[34] With regard to the personal clashes between the two leaders, she argued that, because the prime minister was willing to mend the relationship after the 1962 election while the president was not, Kennedy should bear the greater part of the blame.[35] On the NORAD issue, Ghent's conclusions were refined and expanded by Joseph Jockel, who demonstrates that the Canadian military chiefs of staff were even more enthusiastic about operational integration than their US counterparts; that they did not share the sovereignty concerns felt by many politicians and the general public; and that they deliberately misled the new Conservative government in 1957.[36]

In 1995, Denis Smith's magisterial biography of Diefenbaker and the second volume of the official history of the Department of External Affairs, co-authored by John Hilliker and Donald Barry, provided thoroughly researched and well-balanced general accounts.[37] These works, along with the release of documents through the *Foreign Relations of the United States* and the *Documents on Canadian External Relations* series and the expanded

declassification of government files, opened the way for numerous special-
ized studies. There has, in fact, been an upsurge of interest in the Diefenbaker era, characterized by a strong revisionist trend. Among the historians
who have used the wealth of new primary source material since 2000, a
favourable (though never entirely uncritical) attitude is often apparent, particularly on what once seemed to be the weakest point in the Diefenbaker
government's foreign policy record: its performance on the nuclear weapons issue. On this topic, revisionism was encouraged by Don Munton's 1996
article, in which he shrewdly questioned several widely accepted but erro-
neous beliefs.[38] Among those who followed Munton's lead in disputing the
anti-Diefenbaker consensus, the work of Patricia McMahon, Daniel Heidt,
Erika Simpson, and Michael Stevenson is particularly noteworthy.[39] Other
key areas of study are Canada-UK relations and decolonization. Following
the growth of imperial history and postcolonial theory, Canada's relations
with Britain and with the global south (especially the New Commonwealth)
have taken on fresh interest and are the focus of innovative works
by Asa McKercher, Ryan Touhey, and others.[40] Finally, Daniel Macfarlane
and Asa McKercher offer positive assessments of Diefenbaker's diplomatic
performance during the Berlin and Cuban crises.[41]

Perhaps the key overall theme – sometimes explicit and sometimes
implicit – in recent writing is the inadequacy of the "golden age" periodization. Greg Donaghy, Adam Chapnick, and Hector Mackenzie all point out
the flaws of this approach, which in its most extreme form involves two
broad assertions: first, that the genius for foreign policy demonstrated by
Pearson and his subordinates in the Department of External Affairs was
the main cause of Canada's increasing international stature between 1945
and 1957 and, second, that Diefenbaker's election marked the end of the
era.[42] The golden age concept was first outlined by retired diplomat Escott
Reid in 1967, but in Reid's view it extended roughly from 1941 until 1951,
and the era's end came as Canada became ever more closely tied to US
Cold War policies.[43] Using Reid's chronology, it is possible to consider the
Suez Crisis, the Diefenbaker government's difficulties over defence and
other Cold War issues such as Cuba, and the anti-American protests of
the Pearson years as parts of an ongoing process. Diefenbaker had the
misfortune to gain office at a time when this process was entering a period
of acute crisis. As Chapnick points out, his underlying philosophy on international affairs did not differ in any essential way from that of the Liberals.[44] Chapnick's analysis makes clear the need to study the continuities
between the Liberal and Conservative periods and to account for their

differences by considering broader factors than Diefenbaker's personal quirks and failings.

The historiography of the Diefenbaker period stands at the point where a general reassessment is warranted. Not only are there conflicting interpretations to be considered, but the periodization that underpinned some major works of the late twentieth century must be called into question. *Reassessing the Rogue Tory* offers innovative studies of the well-known themes that have long concerned historians, while also extending into newer areas of scholarly interest. The contributors address the wider issues that affected Canadian foreign policy throughout the 1950s and 1960s, carefully analyzing the domestic and international pressures with which the Conservative government had to deal. They avoid generalizations and instead examine the factors that led to success or failure, decision or indecision, on specific issues. Although Diefenbaker inevitably plays a major role in many chapters, the aim of the volume is to consider the foreign policy of his government as a whole and to place its achievements and shortcomings within a broad context. Together, the contributions demonstrate that underlying structural changes were indeed largely responsible for the extraordinary tumultuousness of the Diefenbaker era. Diefenbaker has often been criticized for failing to "master" his times,[45] but it may well be questioned whether any Canadian politician could have done so.

NOTES

1 Canada, House of Commons, *Debates*, 1962–63, vol. 3, 3409.

2 John A. Munro and Alex I. Inglis, eds., *Mike: The Memoirs of the Right Honourable Lester B. Pearson*, vol. 3 (Toronto: University of Toronto Press, 1975), 82.

3 For a detailed and often devastating critique of Diefenbaker's foreign policy methods from a former professional diplomat, see Peyton V. Lyon, *The Policy Question: A Critical Appraisal of Canada's Role in World Affairs* (Toronto: McClelland and Stewart, 1963), 91–113, 116–18. Despite their general validity, Lyon's points are put forward with a superciliousness that does much to explain Diefenbaker's distrust of the Department of External Affairs, where Lyon worked from 1953 to 1959. On Diefenbaker and the department, see John Hilliker, "The Politicians and the 'Pearsonalities': The Diefenbaker Government and the Conduct of Canadian External Relations," *Canadian Historical Association Historical Papers* 19, 1 (1984): 151–67; and Asa McKercher, "No, Prime Minister: Revisiting Diefenbaker and the 'Pearsonalities,'" *Canadian Journal of History* 52, 2 (2017): 264–89.

4 Charles Ritchie, *Storm Signals: More Undiplomatic Diaries, 1962–1971* (Toronto: Macmillan, 1983), 47.

5 H. Basil Robinson, *Diefenbaker's World: A Populist in Foreign Affairs* (Toronto: University of Toronto Press, 1989), 311.

6 Factors of personality can, of course, also be studied in the context of broad trends: both British prime minister Harold Macmillan and US president John F. Kennedy had adopted varieties of masculinity in which Diefenbaker's histrionic style was viewed with suspicion, making his relations with them more difficult. See Martin Francis, "Tears, Tantrums, and Bared Teeth: The Emotional Economy of Three Conservative Prime Ministers, 1951–1963," *Journal of British Studies* 41 (July 2002): 354–87; and Robert D. Dean, *Imperial Brotherhood: Gender and the Making of Cold War Foreign Policy* (Amherst: University of Massachusetts Press, 2001).

7 Marcel Cadieux, draft memo for Paul Martin, 4 January 1965, Library and Archives Canada (hereafter LAC), MG30 E144, Arnold Heeney Papers, vol. 4, file Canada-US Relations 1943–65. The first draft of this memo was written by Paul Bridle, who did include several negative comments about the Diefenbaker government. These comments were removed by Cadieux. A.E. Ritchie also believed that "it would be a mistake to make too much" of the contrasts between the Diefenbaker and Pearson governments. See changes by Cadieux to Bridle's draft, 23 December 1964, and Ritchie to Bridle, 29 December 1964, both in LAC, RG 25, vol. 8795, file 202–1-2-USA pt. 1.

8 "Two Commonwealths," *Toronto Star*, 8 May 1957; H.H. Guest, "Mr. Pearson's Commonwealth Policy," *Winnipeg Free Press*, 6 June 1957.

9 See Francine McKenzie (Chapter 1, this volume).

10 The British application was ultimately unsuccessful due to the opposition of French president Charles de Gaulle.

11 Joseph T. Jockel, *Canada in NORAD, 1957–2007: A History* (Montreal and Kingston: McGill-Queen's University Press, 2007), 36.

12 There is no substance to the popular theory that the Arrow's cancellation was caused by a conspiracy emanating from Washington. See Donald C. Story and Russell Isinger, "The Origins of the Cancellation of Canada's Avro CF-105 Arrow Fighter Program: A Failure of Strategy," *Journal of Strategic Studies* 30, 6 (2007): 1025–50.

13 The Bomarc and other defensive nuclear weapons were intended to protect Strategic Air Command bases in the United States so that, in the event of a Soviet first strike, retaliation would still be possible. They offered little protection to the civilian population and were effective only against bombers. There were no defensive systems to counter the ICBM threat. However, the new US offensive intercontinental missiles could be launched from submarines and protected underground sites. The certainty of strong US retaliation was accordingly enough to deter any Soviet attempt at a first strike.

14 Party members such as Grattan O'Leary, Donald Fleming, and George Nowlan considered Smith as "the only individual we could see across the country who might be successful against Diefenbaker" – a judgment that appears questionable in the light of subsequent events. Smith was tempted, but ultimately declined. Interview with R.A. Bell, in Peter Stursberg, *Diefenbaker: Leadership Gained, 1956–62* (Toronto: University of Toronto Press, 1975), 12–13.

15 Daniel Heidt, "'I Think That Would Be the End of Canada': Howard Green, the Nuclear Test Ban, and Interest-Based Foreign Policy, 1946–1963," *American Review of Canadian Studies* 42, 3 (2012): 347–50.

16 John Diefenbaker, "Foundations of Canadian External Policy," Canadian Club of Ottawa, 24 November 1960, Canada, Department of External Affairs, *Statements and Speeches*, No. 60–41.

17 Canada, House of Commons, *Debates*, 1960, vol. 1, 929–40.

18 Arnold Heeney, *The Things That Are Caesar's: Memoirs of a Canadian Public Servant* (Toronto: University of Toronto Press, 1972), 162–63.

19 Robinson memo for Green, 9 November 1960, Janice Cavell, ed., *Documents on Canadian External Relations*, vol. 27, *1960* (Ottawa: Foreign Affairs and International Trade Canada, 2007), doc. 239.

20 For a different view, see Asa McKercher, *Canada and Camelot: Canadian-American Relations in the Kennedy Era* (New York: Oxford University Press, 2016), 18.

21 See Dean Rusk to Livingston Merchant, forwarding Kennedy to Diefenbaker, 3 August 1961, *Foreign Relations of the United States, 1961–1963*, vol. 13, *Western Europe and Canada*, ed. Charles S. Sampson and James E. Miller (Washington, DC: US Government Printing Office, 1994), doc. 426 (hereafter *FRUS*).

22 Robinson, *Diefenbaker's World*, 231–32. In support of Diefenbaker's position, it should be noted that the term "nuclear club" was often used in popular discourse to mean all nations with nuclear weapons, whether independently produced or obtained from the United States.

23 See Jocelyn Maynard Ghent, "Canadian-American Relations and the Nuclear Weapons Controversy, 1958–1963" (PhD diss., University of Illinois at Urbana-Champaign, 1976), 132, 133, citing memo by Letitia Baldrige, 2 April 1962, and memo by Fred Holborn, 29 April 1962. Ghent's dissertation, which, unfortunately, was never published, gives the best account of this crucial episode. See also "Mike, JFK in 40-Min. Private Talk," *Toronto Star*, 30 April 1962; Livingston Merchant to George Ball, 5 May 1962, *FRUS, 1961–1963*, vol. 13, *Western Europe and Canada*, doc. 433; Knowlton Nash, *Kennedy and Diefenbaker: Fear and Loathing across the Undefended Border* (Toronto: McClelland and Stewart, 1990), 160–62. At Harold Macmillan's urging, the president reluctantly had a short, awkward meeting with the prime minister in Nassau in late December 1962.

24 On these measures, see Asa McKercher, "A 'Half-hearted Response'? Canada and the Cuban Missile Crisis, 1962," *International History Review* 33, 2 (2011): 335–52.

25 For example, see "Define the Objectives," *Winnipeg Free Press*, 10 December 1962.

26 For example, see, "Militarily Useless, Even Perilous," *Toronto Star*, 20 February 1963. The *Star* gave its editorial endorsement to Pearson as the party leader most likely to provide stable, effective government, but remained critical of his new pro-nuclear policy throughout the 1963 election campaign. For example, see "The Basic Issue Remains," 6 April 1963. The *Vancouver Sun*, *Ottawa Citizen*, and *Le Devoir* also opposed acquisition. For an overview, see Mark A. Eaton, "Canadian Editorial Opinion and the 1963 Nuclear Weapon Acquisition Debate," *American Review of Canadian Studies* 35, 4 (2005): 641–66.

27 See Stephen Azzi (Chapter 5, this volume).

28 George Grant, *Lament for a Nation: The Defeat of Canadian Nationalism* (Toronto: McClelland and Stewart, 1965).

29 Peter C. Newman, *Renegade in Power: The Diefenbaker Years* (Toronto: McClelland and Stewart, 1963).

30 See Robert Bothwell, *Canada and the United States: The Politics of Partnership* (Toronto: University of Toronto Press, 1992); Robert Bothwell, *Alliance and Illusion: Canada and the World, 1945–1984* (Vancouver: UBC Press, 2007); Robert Bothwell, *Your Country, My Country: A Unified History of the United States and Canada* (New York: Oxford University Press, 2015); Robert Bothwell, Ian Drummond, and John English, *Canada since 1945: Power, Politics, and Provincialism* (Toronto: University of Toronto Press, 1981); J.L. Granatstein, *Canada 1957–1967: The Years of Uncertainty and Innovation* (Toronto: McClelland and Stewart, 1986); Norman Hillmer and J.L. Granatstein, *For Better or For Worse: Canada and the United States to the 1990s* (Toronto: Copp Clark Pitman, 1991); Norman Hillmer and J.L. Granatstein, *Empire to Umpire: Canada and the World to the 1990s*, 1st ed. (Toronto: Copp Clark Longman, 1994), rev. ed. (Toronto: Nelson, 2008); and Norman Hillmer and J.L. Granatstein, *For Better or For Worse: Canada and the United States into the Twenty-First Century* (Toronto: Nelson, 2007). For a critique of this approach, see Phillip Buckner, "How Canadian Historians Stopped Worrying and Learned to Love the Americans!," *Acadiensis* 25, 2 (1996): 117–40, on 126–31.

31 J.L. Granatstein, "When the Department of External Affairs Mattered – And When It Shouldn't Have," in *In the National Interest: Canadian Foreign Policy and the Department of Foreign Affairs and International Trade, 1909–2009*, ed. Greg Donaghy and Michael K. Carroll (Calgary: University of Calgary Press, 2011), 69–79, on 70, 75–77.

32 J.L. Granatstein, *Yankee Go Home? Canadians and Anti-Americanism* (Toronto: HarperCollins, 1996), 131–32.

33 Bothwell, *Canada and the United States*, 86. See also Buckner, "How Canadian Historians," 127, 130; and Bothwell, *Alliance and Illusion*, 173, 176–77. Some of Granatstein's and Bothwell's views have recently been upheld in McKercher, *Canada and Camelot*.

34 Ghent, *Canadian-American Relations*. See also her "Did He Fall or Was He Pushed? The Kennedy Administration and the Collapse of the Diefenbaker Government," *International History Review* 1, 2 (1979): 246–70, and "Canada, the United States, and the Cuban Missile Crisis," *Pacific Historical Review* 48, 2 (1979): 159–84; and Kevin J. Gloin, "Canada-US Relations in the Diefenbaker Era: Another Look," in *The Diefenbaker Legacy: Canadian Politics, Law and Society Since 1957*, ed. D.C. Story and R. Bruce Shepard (Regina: Canadian Plains Research Centre, 1998), 1–14.

35 Ghent, *Canadian-American Relations*, 282.

36 Joseph T. Jockel, "The Military Establishments and the Creation of NORAD," *American Review of Canadian Studies* 12, 3 (1982): 1–15; and Joseph T. Jockel, *No Boundaries Upstairs: Canada, the United States, and Origins of North American Air Defence, 1945–1958* (Vancouver: UBC Press, 1987).

37 John Hilliker and Donald Barry, *Canada's Department of External Affairs: Coming of Age, 1946–1968* (Montreal and Kingston: McGill-Queen's University Press, 1995); Denis Smith, *Rogue Tory: The Life and Legend of John G. Diefenbaker* (Toronto: Macfarlane, Walter and Ross, 1995). A third work from the 1990s, Knowlton Nash's

Kennedy and Diefenbaker, should be used with caution, but contains valuable information on the journalism of the time.

38 Don Munton, "Going Fission: Tales and Truths about Canada's Nuclear Weapons," *International Journal* 51, 3 (1996): 506–28.

39 Heidt, "'I Think That Would Be the End of Canada'"; Patricia McMahon, *Essence of Indecision: Diefenbaker's Nuclear Policy, 1957–1963* (Montreal and Kingston: McGill-Queen's University Press, 2009); Erika Simpson, *NATO and the Bomb: Canadian Defenders Confront Critics* (Montreal and Kingston: McGill-Queen's University Press, 2001); Michael D. Stevenson, "'A Very Careful Balance': The 1961 Triangular Agreement and the Conduct of Canadian American Relations," *Diplomacy and Statecraft* 24, 2 (2013): 291–311; and Michael D. Stevenson, "'Tossing a Match into Dry Hay': Nuclear Weapons and the Crisis in US-Canadian Relations, 1962–1963," *Journal of Cold War Studies* 16, 4 (2014): 5–34. Diefenbaker is viewed much less favourably in Andrew Richter, *Avoiding Armageddon: Canadian Military Strategy and Nuclear Weapons, 1950–1963* (Vancouver: UBC Press, 2002); and Sean Maloney, *Learning to Love the Bomb: Canada's Nuclear Weapons during the Cold War* (Washington, DC: Potomac Books, 2007).

   On Canada-US relations generally, see Donald Barry and Duane Bratt, "Defense against Help: Explaining Canada-US Security Relations," *American Review of Canadian Studies* 38, 1 (2008): 63–89; Brian Bow, *The Politics of Linkage: Power, Interdependence, and Ideas in Canada-US Relations* (Vancouver: UBC Press, 2009); Janice Cavell, "'Like Any Good Wife': Gender and Perceptions of Canadian Foreign Policy, 1945–1975," *International Journal* 63, 2 (2008): 385–403; and Asa McKercher, "Dealing with Diefenbaker: Canada-US Relations in 1958," *International Journal* 66, 4 (2011): 1043–60.

40 Philip Buckner, ed., *Canada and the End of Empire* (Vancouver: UBC Press, 2005); Janice Cavell, "Suez and After: Canada and British Policy in the Middle East, 1956–1960," *Journal of the Canadian Historical Association* 18, 1 (2007): 157–78; Asa McKercher, "Southern Exposure: Diefenbaker, Latin America, and the Organization of American States," *Canadian Historical Review* 93, 1 (2012): 57–80; Asa McKercher, "The Centre Cannot Hold: Canadian, Colonialism and the 'Afro-Asian Bloc' at the United Nations, 1960–62," *Journal of Imperial and Commonwealth History* 42, 2 (2014): 329–49; Asa McKercher, "Sound and Fury: Diefenbaker, Human Rights, and Canadian Foreign Policy," *Canadian Historical Review* 97, 2 (2016): 165–94; Kevin A. Spooner, "Just West of Neutral: Canadian 'Objectivity' and Peacekeeping during the Congo Crisis, 1960–61," *Canadian Journal of African Studies* 43, 2 (2009): 303–36; Kevin A. Spooner, *Canada, the Congo Crisis and UN Peacekeeping, 1960–1964* (Vancouver: UBC Press, 2009); Ryan Touhey, "Dealing in Black and White: The Diefenbaker Government and the Cold War in South Asia 1957–1963," *Canadian Historical Review* 92, 3 (2011): 429–54; and Ryan Touhey, *Conflicting Visions: Canada and India in the Cold War World, 1946–76* (Vancouver: UBC Press, 2015).

41 McKercher, "Half-hearted Response"; and Daniel Macfarlane, "Courting War over a Rubber Stamp: Canada and the 1961 Berlin Wall Crisis," *International Journal* 63, 3 (2008): 751–68. For a different evaluation of the Berlin crisis, see Timothy Andrews

Sayle, "Canada, NATO, and the Berlin Crisis, 1961–1962: 'Slow-boil' or 'Pressure Cooker'?," *International Journal* 68, 2 (2012–13): 255–68.

42 Greg Donaghy, "Coming off the Gold Standard: Re-assessing the 'Golden Age' of Canadian Diplomacy" (lecture, Saskatchewan Institute of Public Policy, 26 October 2005), http://www.suezcrisis.ca/pdfs; Adam Chapnick, "The Golden Age: A Canadian Foreign Policy Paradox," *International Journal* 64, 1 (2008–9): 205–21; Hector Mackenzie, "Golden Decade(s)? Reappraising Canada's International Relations in the 1940s and 1950s," *British Journal of Canadian Studies* 23, 2 (2010): 179–206. On the varying temporal definitions of the golden age, see Mackenzie, "Golden Decade(s)," 180–82. For the most specific identification of Diefenbaker's 1957 victory as the end of the age, see Bothwell, *Canada and the United States*, 71. Bothwell's analysis is challenged in Cara Spittal, "The Diefenbaker Moment" (PhD diss., University of Toronto, 2011), 251.

43 Chapnick, "Golden Age," 206–9.

44 Adam Chapnick, "Peace, Order, and Good Government: The 'Conservative' Tradition in Canadian Foreign Policy," *International Journal* 60, 3 (2005): 635–50. See also Asa McKercher and Galen Roger Perras, "Introduction: Lester Pearson and Canadian External Affairs," in *Mike's World: Lester B. Pearson and Canadian External Affairs*, ed. McKercher and Perras (Vancouver: UBC Press, 2017), 13.

45 For example, see Newman, *Renegade in Power*, 333; Smith, *Rogue Tory*, xii–xiii; Bothwell, *Alliance and Illusion*, 134.

PART 1

The Commonwealth

1

A New Vision for the Commonwealth
Diefenbaker's Commonwealth Tour of 1958

FRANCINE McKENZIE

Five days after John Diefenbaker was sworn in as the thirteenth prime minister of Canada, he attended a meeting of Commonwealth prime ministers in London. It was fitting that this should be his first diplomatic foray. Diefenbaker had "nailed his colours to the Commonwealth mast" while in Opposition.[1] His attachment went beyond simple enthusiasm. Basil Robinson, his principal foreign policy advisor, explained that when Diefenbaker was first elected in 1957, the only "vision in international affairs" that he might be said to have "fell within the Commonwealth framework."[2] Officials in the Department of External Affairs subsequently confirmed that the Commonwealth was a high foreign policy priority for him: "From the time he assumed office, the Prime Minister has continually spoken of the value of the Commonwealth association and has sought to strengthen its ties and to improve relations between its members."[3] Diefenbaker was keen to strengthen an institution that he believed had an honourable past and an important future but that had come under attack internationally and was strained from within following the Suez Crisis of 1956. His belief in the Commonwealth as a leader and model in world affairs and as a focus for Canadian international activity persisted throughout his time as prime minister despite shifts in British orientation towards Europe, the breakdown of his relationship with British prime minister Macmillan, and an ever more global engagement for Canada in the world.

Few prime ministers have been as harshly criticized as Diefenbaker for their handling of foreign policy. Indeed, his election in 1957 is linked to the end of the so-called golden era of Canadian foreign policy when Canada's standing in the international community had surpassed its middle power status.[4] Diefenbaker himself is at the centre of explanations about the floundering of Canadian foreign policy. His relevant failings include impulsive decision making, crass politicization of foreign policy, and a hubristically personalized approach to diplomacy. Even scholars with nuanced analyses still conclude that ultimately he was "the architect of his own demise" and "the author of his own misfortunes."[5] Basil Robinson endorsed such a reading of his foreign policy failures. As he put it, "for those who wanted a creative, resourceful role for Canada in the world, Diefenbaker was not the answer."[6] But in recent revisionist accounts, some historians have praised his judgment and diplomatic skills.[7] This opens the door to a thorough review, and possible re-assessment, of Diefenbaker's diplomacy and ideas.

Diefenbaker's enthusiasm for the Commonwealth in general, and the conduct of relations with Britain in particular, has contributed to the overall critical view of his handling of foreign policy.[8] Any reassessment of his foreign policy record must take the Commonwealth into account. This chapter therefore focuses on Diefenbaker's seven-week world tour of 1958, which was primarily a tour of Asian Commonwealth members, plus Britain. The Commonwealth tour is also important to study because it was well regarded at the time. According to Joe Garner, the British high commissioner in Ottawa, the tour was "an outstanding success."[9] Diefenbaker received "excellent press" in London, Malaya, Pakistan, and Wellington. Reports from Australia even went so far as to suggest that there was a "spontaneous love affair between John Diefenbaker and the hard-to-impress Aussie public."[10] Diefenbaker himself was credited with deftly managing difficult issues and sparking renewed enthusiasm for the Commonwealth. His speeches elicited less praise; they were described as histrionic, evangelical, incoherent, naïve, formless, and shallow.[11] But overall he was judged to have been an adept ambassador for the Commonwealth, eliciting enthusiasm where little existed, creating new connections that strengthened its base, and, in general, making a case for its enduring relevance.

The Tour

Shortly after the 1958 election, Diefenbaker decided he wanted to go on a world tour. In August, he asked the Department of External Affairs to prepare an itinerary.[12] One month later, plans were being finalized for a tour that would start in Britain, followed by several brief stops in Western Europe, before turning to Commonwealth countries in Asia (Pakistan, India,

Ceylon, Malaya, Singapore, Australia, and New Zealand) as well as Indonesia.[13] Prime ministerial globe-trotting was new, but not unprecedented. Prime Minister Louis St. Laurent had taken a tour in 1954, and Diefenbaker followed a similar route.[14] The stated purpose of Diefenbaker's tour was to better acquaint him with the pressing global issues of the day, to enable him to see for himself what was happening in Europe and Asia, and to forge closer personal relations with other leaders.[15] Although he explained his goals for the tour in laudable but general terms (not dissimilar to St. Laurent) he had more specific objectives for the Commonwealth leg. Diefenbaker wanted to promote "Commonwealth friendship and solidarity" and strengthen the ties that unified the member countries.[16]

There was need for improvement following the Suez Crisis debacle of 1956. Diefenbaker had criticized the way that St. Laurent and Lester Pearson had handled the crisis, accusing them of turning their backs on Britain. Diefenbaker was determined to show his support. British officials nonetheless wondered about Diefenbaker's motivations. J.B. Johnston of the Commonwealth Relations Office asked if Diefenbaker was jockeying for a co-leadership position within the Commonwealth. Did he resent British leadership? Was he trying to be like Mackenzie King or Nehru?[17] F.E. Cumming-Bruce, who was posted to the high commission in Ottawa, reassured his colleague that there was no "sinister" intention behind the tour and that there were "no signs whatever of Mr. Diefenbaker wishing to supplant United Kingdom leadership."[18]

In contrast to Johnston's suspicions, many British officials welcomed the tour as an opportunity to tutor Diefenbaker in diplomacy, warn him about trouble spots, and curb his "propensity" to make rash and ill-considered statements, a tendency that showed "no signs of abating." Because Diefenbaker held Harold Macmillan in such high regard, the British leader could encourage him to be more prudent and thoughtful.[19] In fact, Diefenbaker was not inexperienced in foreign policy. He had followed Canadian involvement in world affairs since his parliamentary debut in 1940. He had been the Conservative critic on foreign policy. He even served as his own secretary of state for external affairs for several months in 1957 before appointing Sidney Smith. The patronizing tone that came across in British preparations for Diefenbaker's visit was not reserved for the new Canadian prime minister. It informed a wider scepticism about Canada's middle power activism, which Cumming-Bruce described as "tiresome" and a product of "national ego."[20] The mistrustful reaction also revealed an enduring conception in London of the Commonwealth as British-centred and led.

Members of the Department of External Affairs were also anxious about the tour. There was an uneasy rapport between career diplomats and the prime minister, a situation made worse by Diefenbaker's mistrust of civil servants, especially those in the Department of External Affairs.[21] Basil Robinson, who had moved to the Prime Minister's Office as his principal policy advisor, was the only diplomat included on the tour, although the group met with Canadian diplomats along the way. Other members of the party included Diefenbaker's wife Olive, his brother Elmer, and his personal physician. As Robinson noted, preparations for the tour were more like "a family preparing for a tourist excursion" than a carefully planned diplomatic mission.[22]

The tour began on 28 October. The prime minister's party stopped briefly in New York, where Diefenbaker met with Dag Hammarskjöld, secretary general of the United Nations. Then it was off to Britain for one week where he met with Macmillan and other senior British officials and made time for a family pilgrimage to Scotland. Brief meetings followed with French president Charles de Gaulle and West German chancellor Konrad Adenauer. Diefenbaker met with NATO leaders in Brussels and squeezed in a visit with the pope in Rome before travelling to Pakistan, where a military coup had recently brought Ayub Khan to power, followed by visits to India, Ceylon, Singapore, Malaya, Indonesia, and then final stops in Australia and New Zealand. Diefenbaker met with heads of state and prominent politicians; received honorary degrees and was made an honorary Maori chief; visited development projects; paid respect at shrines, cemeteries, and memorials; and attended teas, lunches, and dinners. There was a tiger hunt in India (no tiger was spotted), an elephant ride in Ceylon, and a fishing expedition in New Zealand. He gave speeches everywhere he went. He returned home in mid-December, a little earlier than planned because of his mother's ill health.

Throughout the tour Diefenbaker sang the praises of the Commonwealth. His enthusiastic boostering elicited some amused commentary. In part this was a result of his rhetorical style: as Cara Spittal observes, his language was old-fashioned. But as she also helpfully points out, his ideas were forward-looking and new, particularly his advocacy of its ethnic pluralism.[23] More than an unexamined Commonwealth champion, Diefenbaker had articulated a vision for a "changed Commonwealth" that addressed current global conditions.[24] In particular, he emphasized three roles for the Commonwealth: as an anti-communist force; as a proponent of social justice and racial equality; and as a forum within which to promote trade. Diefenbaker's reimagining of the Commonwealth was timely because the "improbable alliance" needed an updated purpose and identity that all members could endorse.[25]

Despite its contemporary relevance, Diefenbaker's vision was not easy to put into practice. The causes that he believed transcended individual interests were in fact divisive, or at least they revealed that interests were not compatible across the Commonwealth. Moreover, his confidence that the Commonwealth should act as a leader and model in world affairs rested on a selective understanding of its history. Although he was not simply old fashioned or nostalgic, not all Commonwealth leaders endorsed Diefenbaker's understanding of the past and its relation to the future.

The Cold War

Diefenbaker's conception of the Commonwealth and its role in world affairs took shape in relation to the dominant geopolitical forces and priorities of the day, starting with the Cold War. Diefenbaker's anti-communist views were long-standing and entrenched. Despite some relaxation of international tensions following the death of Stalin in 1953 and Khrushchev's endorsement of peaceful co-existence in 1956, Diefenbaker remained alive to the threat of communism. He was sceptical of Soviet support for détente and policies meant to minimize East-West tensions, for example on disarmament.[26] His meetings in London at the start of the tour reinforced his concerns. Both the British foreign minister and prime minister emphasized that the Cold War had once again become hot: "The Russians were being hostile; the Chinese communists were truculent and aggressive; and the dangers of a weakening of the anti-Communist position in the Far East were much greater."[27] Diefenbaker's tour of Asian Commonwealth countries heightened his concern about communist expansion. The threat emanated not only from the Soviet Union but also from China, which he described as "forging ahead."[28] Diefenbaker believed that the Commonwealth had a vital role to play in containing the expansion of communism, a role to which it was especially well suited because newly independent countries were particularly susceptible to communist advances. However, he did not imagine the Commonwealth as an independent actor in the global Cold War conflict; rather, it was part of the Western bloc, led by the United States.[29] Diefenbaker set out to strengthen the anti-communist purpose of the Asian Commonwealth.

In most places – including Pakistan, Malaya, Indonesia, and Australia – Diefenbaker was reassured that leaders were on guard against communism.

But he detected weaknesses in the anti-communist orientation of some Commonwealth members, especially India. India was a leader of the non-aligned movement that had formed at the Bandung Conference of 1955; in Diefenbaker's eyes, non-alignment had pro-communist overtones. Moreover, Nehru had recently visited the Soviet Union. In several discussions with Nehru, Diefenbaker set out his concerns about communist threats and the dangers of policies that supported or endorsed communist countries. In particular, he discussed the Sino-American conflict that had recently flared up over the contested islands of Quemoy and Matsu and talked of the need to find a face-saving solution that would prevent the United States from retreating into isolationism. If that happened, he feared "the results would be disastrous" as Asian nations would likely fall under the sway of communism, starting with Japan.[30] Diefenbaker subsequently defended the United States in an address to the Indian Parliament. He insisted that the United States "has no aggressive designs, and is dedicated to peace." According to a Canadian journalist, this picture refuted a widespread view in India of the US as plotting and dominating.[31] Diefenbaker asked Nehru to use his influence to persuade China to "adopt a less aggressive and more conciliatory attitude calculated to ease tensions and prevent the situation form worsening." Despite Diefenbaker's efforts, Nehru remained unalarmed by communism, sympathetic to the Soviet Union, and critical of the United States.[32]

Although Diefenbaker spoke of the growing strength and dangers of China, he nonetheless sent mixed signals on the controversial question of recognition. During the tour, he made several statements that implied he was moving towards recognition of the People's Republic of China (PRC). When asked about these statements in Canberra, he said that a country of over 600 million inhabitants "cannot be ignored," and he discussed the benefits of contact with China. He ended by saying that the question was under "constant review."[33] But other statements suggested that recognition could not happen immediately lest it be interpreted as an "approbation of communism,"[34] or lest it "damage our Commonwealth sister nations and other friends in Asia."[35] Diefenbaker's inconsistency on recognition did not mean that his anti-communist views were shifting: he remained a convinced and outspoken opponent of communism throughout his career.[36] But it revealed a pragmatic strand to his thinking as well as his difficulty with making a real decision. There might also have been a hint of anti-Americanism present. In discussion with Harold Macmillan, Diefenbaker had explained that President Eisenhower "got more excited than he had ever seen him" at the possibility of Canadian support for recognition of the PRC in the United

Nations. Eisenhower had told Diefenbaker that if that happened, the United States might leave the United Nations.[37]

Despite this hint of his own anti-American feelings, the anti-communist credentials of Commonwealth leaders strongly influenced Diefenbaker's reaction to them. This was particularly evident in Pakistan and Ceylon. He lavished praise on the dictator Ayub Khan, who had come to power in Pakistan through a coup d'état and was strongly anti-communist. Diefenbaker was highly impressed with Khan, whom he described as "most Western minded" and "the Saviour of the Nation." He believed Khan's explanation that the democratically elected government that he had ousted was corrupt and that he would restore democracy as soon as possible.[38] Diefenbaker repeated this conviction to the Australian cabinet later in the tour, describing Khan as "perfectly honest" about stepping down "as soon as order and good government had been restored."[39]

In contrast to Khan, S.W.R.D. Bandaranaike, the democratically elected leader of Ceylon, made "an exceptionally bad impression on Diefenbaker." Diefenbaker was shocked when Bandaranaike threatened to seek development aid from the Soviet bloc in what Diefenbaker understood to be "a blatant attempt to blackmail Canada." He subsequently toyed with the idea of cutting off all aid to Ceylon.[40] Diefenbaker described Bandaranaike critically as a "semi-intellectual leftist" who had converted from Christianity to Buddhism for political reasons,[41] from which Diefenbaker concluded that he lacked integrity. His negative impression was generalized to the entire country. Diefenbaker reported to his ministers that he had been appalled at "a complete lack of principle in Ceylon, not only in public life, but also in private affairs."[42] Although he claimed to have had a long-standing interest in Ceylon and to have been impressed at the enthusiasm for the Commonwealth there, this stop marked the lowest point in the tour.

For Diefenbaker, the strongest rejoinder to communism was the defence of freedom, which he defined in terms of legally protected individual freedoms that were a hallmark of democratic societies. Diefenbaker believed that the Commonwealth had a special role to play as a proponent of freedom in a Cold War world. He claimed that it had "a mission and a mandate of freedom."[43] He even went so far in his memoirs as to call it "the greatest instrument for freedom that the world has ever seen."[44] Such claims revealed his idealized reading of the history of the British Empire and Commonwealth, a version not all would accept.[45] But his association of the Commonwealth with freedom also showed that he had adapted his views of the past to suit contemporary global conditions.

The intersection of two global forces – the Cold War and decolonization – heightened the Commonwealth's relevance as a promoter of political systems that upheld individual freedoms and the rule of law. Diefenbaker believed the desire for independence was unstoppable and that the Commonwealth could act as a "dynamic incubator of new nations,"[46] promoting stable democratic systems in newly decolonized countries that were particularly vulnerable to communist advances. During the tour he visited parliaments and courts, institutions that upheld individual freedoms and democratic political orders. He remarked on the importance of these institutions as a unifying bond across the Commonwealth: "I could go into any of the countries in Asia. I could feel at home in their Parliament – the same rules in effect, the same attachment to the principles of parliamentary government that we have. I could go into the courts, really start to argue a case there, whether successfully or not, none the less, argue it."[47] His enduring belief in the Commonwealth as a relevant world leader rested on his understanding of institutional and constitutional legacies and infrastructure that upheld democratic systems. This role was even more urgent at a time of sudden and dramatic global change associated with the end of formal empires. And yet his conviction that the Commonwealth should be closely aligned with the United States and should inculcate democratic political values was not easily endorsed by newly independent Commonwealth countries. Commonwealth leaders like Nehru and Bandaranaike understood global dynamics and defined foreign policy priorities in terms of a postcolonial logic, something Diefenbaker only partly grasped.

Race and the New Commonwealth

Just as Diefenbaker envisioned a Commonwealth that strengthened a democratic political order, so, too, he believed the Commonwealth was an essential instrument of social justice, particularly with regard to the elimination of racial prejudice. This was central to his vision of the Commonwealth and, he believed, essential to international peace and stability. It represented a more idealistic strand of his foreign policy, yet, as a result of decolonization, there was an urgency to it. And, as with its Cold War role, the Commonwealth's supposed ability to promote racial equality depended on Diefenbaker's selective and idealistic reading of its past and glossing over the racist policies of some of its members.

After the Second World War, UNESCO had challenged the belief that there was a biological basis to race, thus seeming to inaugurate a post-racial era.[48] Nonetheless many people, including Diefenbaker, continued to believe in race and spoke openly about it. Diefenbaker identified people by a variety of racial categories, including biology; hence the emphasis he placed upon physical features like skin colour as well as upon religion, nation, language, and culture. Perhaps it was Diefenbaker's candour that led the Indian high commissioner in Ottawa to suspect that his enthusiasm for the Commonwealth would manifest itself in terms of greater support for the white dominions.[49] Certainly Diefenbaker believed that the dominions had a common heritage, and he did not want to turn against another dominion; however, in his vision of the future Commonwealth he did not privilege the white dominions. Instead, he appreciated the new Commonwealth in ways his predecessors had not. Basil Robinson recorded that when Diefenbaker attended the 1957 meeting of Commonwealth prime ministers he had been struck by the presence of Kwame Nkrumah, the president of Ghana, and the imminent membership of Malaya, something that Robinson did not think either St. Laurent or Pearson would have remarked on.[50] During the tour Diefenbaker explained that the future of the Commonwealth rested with its prospective Asian and African members. He hoped to tour the African Commonwealth members next, but this never happened.

Diefenbaker regarded racial diversity as a global and eternal fact. For him, it was also one of the "traditional barriers," along with religion, language, geography, and economic interest, that had had a divisive effect on international relations.[51] According to Diefenbaker, the Commonwealth's transformation into a multiracial association showed how differences could become a unifying bond. He explained that integration reflected the "essential spirit of the Commonwealth in which differing races, religions and cultures are able to live in peace together."[52] But tolerating racial differences was not enough. Diefenbaker insisted that there must be no discrimination on the basis of race and that there had to be opportunity for all people. As he said at the end of the tour: "[this is] the number one thing, the principle that I derive from this visit to the Commonwealth."[53]

During the tour, Diefenbaker discussed Canada's recent history as proof that racial divisions and prejudices could be overcome. He understood his own election (he was the first prime minister "of other than purely British or French origin") as a testament to the opportunities now available to all people living in Canada. He boasted that the Conservative government included members from "13 different racial origins." Voters in the Vancouver Centre riding, which he described as "90 per cent English speaking," had elected a member of Parliament of "Chinese origin." He was referring to Douglas Jung, the first elected MP of Chinese heritage. Diefenbaker also noted his recent appointment of a First Nations man to the Senate. (As he explained to his audience in Australia, they "would call it the red Indian race."[54]) The senator was James Gladstone, a member of the Blood Tribe of the Blackfoot Nation.

Even though he denounced discrimination on the basis of race and insisted on both tolerance and opportunity for all, Diefenbaker did not always call out racial prejudices and practices. Indeed, in some cases he seemed to be an apologist for racism. For example, he reassured Australian cabinet ministers that Australia's white immigration policy aroused little opposition in Asian Commonwealth countries. He even went so far as to claim that Malaya and Singapore did not want Australia to be "inundated with Chinese."[55] When asked about apartheid in South Africa, he said that he would not criticize "the policies of other countries."[56] Diefenbaker did not confront persistent white supremacist policies, practices, and worldviews because he wanted to avoid division within the Commonwealth. Promoting racial equality and upholding the solidarity of the new Commonwealth were not always compatible goals. But during his tour, he got away with simultaneously combatting and enabling racial discrimination.

Trade and Aid

Diefenbaker believed that trade was not only an important link among Commonwealth members but also that it was an area of Commonwealth cooperation in need of renewal. He had been taken aback by the lack of interest in Commonwealth trade at the 1957 meeting of prime ministers. After that meeting, determined to strengthen the ties that bound Commonwealth members, and with Canada's own trade imbalance in mind, the prime minister made a startling impromptu policy announcement about shifting 15 percent of Canadian trade away from the United States to Britain. This is usually included in lists of his foreign policy gaffes. As Michael Hart has written, the proposal "smacked of naïveté and nostalgia."[57] Even so, there was a follow-up Commonwealth economic meeting in Montreal, but it yielded few tangible results. Ever since the Ottawa Imperial Economic Conference of 1932, the proportion of Commonwealth trade had been decreasing relatively. Although the British market was still essential for South Africa, New Zealand, and Australia in 1958,[58] the declining trend was clear. This was partly because Commonwealth members competed for markets and there was limited complementarity between their exports and imports. But, from a Canadian point of view, trade diversification made sense as a way of offsetting the preponderance of the United States as a trading partner. Future prime ministers would also try to diversify Canada's trade. Nonetheless, Diefenbaker's belief that Commonwealth trade could grow contradicted the opinion of other Commonwealth leaders, and his efforts to promote trade – particularly with regard to Canada's agricultural exports – strained the very relations he hoped to strengthen.

Diefenbaker began the 1958 tour with a strong plug for Commonwealth trade. In an address to five thousand members of the Commonwealth and Empire Industries Association at the Royal Albert Hall in London, he suggested that the main purpose of the Commonwealth was to promote trade and aid.[59] The *Globe and Mail* reported that he received a standing ovation and noted that "his vigorous faith in the Commonwealth" had impressed, and possibly even embarrassed, his British hosts.[60] The *Economist*, on the other hand, described the speech as "really rather dreadful" and concluded that Diefenbaker had been swayed by "the heady brew with which the Beaverbrook newspapers had regaled their readers before and during the visit."[61] Joe Garner was equally unimpressed, describing his speech as "so flocculent and high-flown that it was difficult to draw any coherent message from it. His ringing tones went down well with the more emotional and unthinking, but I don't think it did him very much good in more informed circles."[62]

Harold Macmillan was not pleased. The British government had recently opted out of the Treaty of Rome, which had established the European common market. This decision was fraught with questions about British identity, sovereignty, and standing in world affairs, but it did not mean the British saw much future in Commonwealth trade, a point Macmillan made in his memoirs in one of his few references to Diefenbaker: "He is a fine man – sincere and determined; but I fear he has formed a picture of what can and cannot be done with the Commonwealth today which is rather misleading."[63] In their discussions, Macmillan emphasized the need for trade to expand (which was not happening within the Commonwealth), and Diefenbaker claimed to agree that expansion was the key point: he "was rather apologetic about his occasional lapses from his proper theory."[64] But neither the economic nor the political message sank in.

Diefenbaker continued to plug Commonwealth trade throughout the tour. He insisted that the 1958 Montreal economic meeting had elicited "a new spirit" that could somehow increase Commonwealth trade. He also linked the expansion of Commonwealth trade to the security of democratic states in the Western alliance. Commonwealth trade could counter the "communist world trade offensive" spearheaded by the Soviet Union and, to a lesser extent, China.[65]

The prime minister's interest in Commonwealth trade did not disguise his particular interest in promoting Canadian exports. This was especially apparent in his visit to New Zealand. New Zealand exported a small number of agricultural exports and, as a result, was vulnerable to international economic forces. To reduce its vulnerability, the government controlled access to its market through quotas. This interventionist approach worked in that, in the 1950s, New Zealanders enjoyed one of the highest standards of living in the world. In his discussions with Prime Minister Walter Nash, himself an advocate of controlling access to New Zealand's market, Diefenbaker nonetheless broached the possibility of expanding Canadian markets in New Zealand, asking where there was room to increase Canadian exports. Nash, in turn, probed the possibility of token dairy imports – then and now a highly protected and politicized area of trade in Canada – and Diefenbaker was quick to rebuff him.[66] Thus, although Diefenbaker used the Commonwealth as leverage on trade matters, both Canada and New Zealand defined trade policies in relation to national priorities. As a result, Diefenbaker's attempts to advance Canadian trade opportunities under the guise of Commonwealth spirit came to nothing in New Zealand.

When Commonwealth sentiment and Cold War issues did not parlay into expanded market opportunities, Diefenbaker tried using development assistance as leverage. He insisted that wealthier members of the Commonwealth had a duty to assist the economic development of those who were less well off. At one level, he believed that overcoming poverty was essential to the future of the Commonwealth; it could not survive "half prosperous and half starving."[67] He made clear that Canada was a strong supporter of the Colombo Plan, the Commonwealth's main development initiative. The plan was set up in 1950, and members extended technical and financial aid to countries in South and Southeast Asia in the hope of preventing the expansion of communism to the region.[68] But he also pushed for improved access to the markets of developing Commonwealth members in return for continued or increased aid. For instance, in Pakistan, under the Colombo Plan, he proposed increased wheat purchases. Pakistan's officials replied that, if they agreed to this, they would have to cut back on purchases of other items. Diefenbaker was candid in explaining that Canadians' willingness to support aid depended "to a large extent on the willingness and capacity of the recipient countries to increase the proportion of agricultural products which they accepted under Canadian aid programmes."[69] In Malaya, Diefenbaker again tied Canada's aid to the purchase of Canadian products. Here his efforts were rewarded: in return for slight increase in

Colombo Plan funds, Malaya announced a relaxation of import controls affecting many Canadian products.[70]

When Australian journalists asked about the link between trade and Colombo Plan aid, Diefenbaker explained that, while surplus products could not be forced on aid recipients – that would be inconsistent with market forces and contrary to the free basis of their association with one another – recipient countries nonetheless had an obligation to purchase as much as possible, consistent with their needs. He suggested that if they did not, donor countries would find themselves in the untenable position of having "agricultural products pile up" at home while the recipients procured agricultural commodities elsewhere "on terms better than we could give in direct purchase or sale."[71] If Diefenbaker's support for the Commonwealth as an agent of freedom in a Cold War context suggests that he was an imperial-internationalist,[72] his pushing for trade opportunities reveals well-defined national instincts and priorities to which the Commonwealth was instrumental. For this he made no apologies. As he admitted in his memoirs, "where I could, I advanced specific Canadian interests during my tour."[73]

Fast Forward and a Conclusion

Although Britain was gradually reorienting itself by moving closer to Europe, the enthusiasm that Diefenbaker elicited for the Commonwealth pleased British officials. While some thought Diefenbaker's conception of the Commonwealth was sentimental and simplistic, British high commissioners from every stop on the tour reported favourably on the boost his visit gave to the Commonwealth. For example, in Malaya there was not usually much press comment on the Commonwealth, but during Diefenbaker's visit references "abounded." His visit did "a service to the Commonwealth at large" and additional aid showed practical benefits of Commonwealth membership that offset "to some extent the more emotional but less rewarding attraction of the Afro-Asian influences."[74] In India, where the Commonwealth was viewed with considerable scepticism, the British high commissioner reported that his visit "stimulated much friendly comment on the nature of the Commonwealth."[75] Diefenbaker's enthusiasm helped to shore up "the Commonwealth spirit" in Pakistan.[76] In Australia, where the attachment was not in doubt, Diefenbaker was credited with broadening the base of Australia's attachment beyond Britain. The high commissioner reported: "I believe that this will have a small but valuable enduring effect."[77] Diefenbaker was an effective Commonwealth ambassador when it came to boosting general enthusiasm. But that enthusiasm was not subsequently channelled into support for the three roles he advocated for a changed Commonwealth.

The three policy areas in which Diefenbaker believed the Commonwealth had its most important roles – those relating to the Cold War, racial equality, and trade – imploded a few years after his 1958 tour. During the Cuban Missile Crisis of 1962, Diefenbaker questioned American handling of the crisis and held back Canadian support for NORAD, a move that imperiled continental security and permanently soured his relations with American president John F. Kennedy. In stark contrast, Britain defended American action at the UN and Kennedy consulted with Macmillan on a daily basis during the crisis. Thus, with regard to Cold War issues, Diefenbaker contributed to the factionalization of the Commonwealth. Although he had wanted to evade a discussion of racial inequality, he could not do so when South Africa applied for readmission to the Commonwealth in 1961 following its decision to become a republic in 1960. Diefenbaker's worst fears were realized: Britain, Australia, and New Zealand wanted South Africa to remain, whereas Asian and African members wanted it expelled. Diefenbaker proposed that the meeting end with a resolution endorsing racial equality, hoping that this would be unacceptable to South Africa and lead to its withdrawing its application. This was what happened. Diefenbaker stopped a mass walkout but left the door open for South Africa's return, and he was showered with praise for his efforts.[78] However, this success did not resolve the disagreement over race and the racial policies and practices that weakened Commonwealth unity. As for the issue of Commonwealth trade, it finally came to a head in 1961, when the Macmillan government decided to make a formal application to join the European Economic Community (EEC). Diefenbaker spoke out against it. Macmillan was having enough trouble over EEC membership without Diefenbaker stoking nativist Commonwealth feelings in Britain. He was livid with Diefenbaker and avoided him at later meetings.[79] The decline of Commonwealth trade would not be reversed.

The dramatic implosions of the Commonwealth in the early 1960s on issues of security, trade, and racism raise questions about the nature of Diefenbaker's confidence in the Commonwealth as a centre of Canadian foreign policy and as a leader in world affairs. Was it all rosy retrospective delusion? Did it reflect his own unexamined anglophilia? Did he mishandle later events? He knew that not everyone shared his opinion of a bright future for the Commonwealth. He acknowledged this openly when he observed that some people predicted that it was "approaching its end."[80] His private reflections outlined a long list of concerns, including anti-American sentiment, communist advances, the weakness of parliamentary democracy, poverty, and nationalism. The "Commonwealth concept" did not animate "the masses of Asians." But, as Garner reported, rather than giving up on the Commonwealth, Diefenbaker's faith in its future had "only been sharpened."[81]

Diefenbaker applied his vision across the Commonwealth but it was a vision that reflected Canada's experience as a settler colony. As a result, not all Commonwealth countries agreed with his reading of the past or his prescriptions for the future. For example, his support for a new Commonwealth that was based on British institutions was paternalistic; his belief in the Commonwealth as a force for freedom could not be endorsed by former colonies; his anti-communist convictions reflected a Western ideology that could not be imposed on a Commonwealth whose members had diverse political cultures. That the Commonwealth was made up of many centres, all of which defined their priorities and interests according to their own readings of the past and hopes for the future, was especially evident on questions of trade. Diefenbaker was himself guilty of promoting Canadian commercial interests first and foremost, using the Commonwealth connection as leverage. What was clear was that Diefenbaker's own internationalist convictions were comfortably expressed through the Commonwealth, even though there were contradictions between and among its national, imperial, and international manifestations. These characteristics might make his vision appear to be incoherent: certainly there were contradictions that he did not appear to grasp and that he did not have to confront during the tour, when enthusiasm papered over tensions and made contradictions appear compatible.

Any review of the foreign policy of the Diefenbaker years has to grapple with Diefenbaker himself. He was impossible to ignore during the tour because he put himself front and centre. This raises questions about his diplomatic skills, his understanding of global affairs, and his mark on the substance of Canadian policies. Many of the elements that contributed to his later failures were evident on the 1958 tour: hints of anti-Americanism, an overly personalized approach to diplomacy, lack of nuance, mistrust of civil servants, and the politicization of foreign policy. The tour is a reminder that such personality traits need not result in diplomatic disasters. Diefenbaker's influence on the substance of Canadian foreign policy also requires consideration. While security had dominated the international agenda since the end of the Second World War, Diefenbaker's emphasis on racial equality and his support for the establishment of new democratic states expanded the scope of Canadian foreign policy. He was innovative. He was also consistent with his predecessors, for example in linking the Commonwealth to the anti-communist cause. The importance that Diefenbaker attached to the Commonwealth outlasted his time in office. When Lester Pearson became prime minister in 1963, he also continued to value the Commonwealth, as did Pierre Trudeau, who remarked on its dynamism and the candour that was possible among its members. Diefenbaker's promotion of the Commonwealth as a relevant and constructive force in world affairs cannot be read only as proof of nostalgia. The 1958 Commonwealth tour therefore suggests a need to reconsider whether or not Canada's liberal internationalism came to an end with Diefenbaker's election, for his brand of internationalism both extended and added to Canadian engagement in world affairs in enduring ways.

NOTES

1 J.J.S. Garner, High Commissioner (hereafter HC) Ottawa, to Secretary of State for Commonwealth Relations (hereafter SSCR), 14 January 1959, DO35/10847, The National Archives, UK (hereafter TNA).

2 H.B. Robinson, *Diefenbaker's World: A Populist in Foreign Affairs* (Toronto: University of Toronto Press, 1989), 4.

3 Memorandum from Information Division to Undersecretary of State for External Affairs (hereafter USSEA), 11 September 1958, in M.D. Stevenson, ed., *Documents on Canadian External Relations*, vol. 24, *1957–1958*, pt. 1 (Ottawa: Canadian Government Publishing, 2003) (hereafter *DCER*, vol. 24), doc. 388, 880.

4 When Pearson and the Liberals were re-elected in 1963, Donaghy notes, they set out to "restore the diplomatic credibility that Diefenbaker had squandered." See Greg Donaghy, *Grit: The Life and Politics of Paul Martin Sr.* (Vancouver: UBC Press, 2015), 191.

5 McMahon explains that Diefenbaker believed that Canada should honour its nuclear weapons obligations but feared that doing so would lead to his political demise. See Patricia McMahon, *Essence of Indecision: Diefenbaker's Nuclear Policy, 1957–1963* (Montreal and Kingston: McGill-Queen's University Press, 2009), x, xii, 175. Bothwell suggests that fundamental changes, along with the nature and complexity of the issues that he had to confront, explain his failures; "the issues ... overwhelmed the institutions." See Robert Bothwell, *Alliance and Illusion: Canada and the World 1945–1984* (Vancouver: UBC Press, 2007), 136, 147.

6 Robinson, *Diefenbaker's World*, 103.

7 For example, see Asa McKercher, "Southern Exposure: Diefenbaker, Latin America and the Organization of American States," *Canadian Historical Review* 93, 1 (2012): 57–80.

8 Peter C. Newman, *Renegade in Power: The Diefenbaker Years* (Toronto: McClelland and Stewart, 1963), 254. According to Newman, Diefenbaker's "deep emotional

attachment to Great Britain" and his desire to make Canada "ALL BRITISH" (as he said in 1926) were the "true roots of his foreign policy." Newman was critical of this concept and claimed the flipside of his pro-British attitude was "profound suspicion of the United States."

9 Garner to SSCR, 14 January 1959, DO35/10847, TNA.

10 "Best since Sinatra: Australians Are Agog over Canadian PM," *Globe and Mail*, 6 December 1958.

11 For examples of comments on his style of public speaking, see UK HC, Karachi to SSCR, 12 December 1958, or Office of the High Commissioner, Ottawa to SSCR, 14 January 1959, both in DO35/10847, TNA. Newman claimed his speeches "defied proper syntax" (*Renegade in Power*, 6). Diefenbaker explained that he valued spontaneity and a rapport between speaker and audience. "To read a prepared text to an audience is to miss it all." See John G. Diefenbaker, *One Canada: Memoirs of the Right Honourable John G. Diefenbaker – The Years of Achievement, 1957–1962* (Toronto: Macmillan of Canada, 1976), 18.

12 Memorandum from special assistant to secretary of state for External Affairs (hereafter SSEA) to USSEA, 11 August 1958, *DCER*, vol. 24, doc. 388, 880–81.

13 Memorandum from Information Division to USSEA, 11 September 1958, *DCER*, vol. 24, doc. 388, 880.

14 For a description of St. Laurent's tour, see Dale C. Thomson, *Louis St. Laurent, Canadian* (Toronto: Macmillan of Canada, 1967), 357–71.

15 Denis Smith, *Rogue Tory: The Life and Legend of John G. Diefenbaker* (Toronto: MacFarlane, Walter and Ross, 1995), 296, 297.

16 Memorandum from Information Division to USSEA, 11 September 1958, *DCER*, vol. 24, doc. 388, 880.

17 Johnston to Cumming-Bruce, 10 October 1958, DO35/10846, TNA.

18 Ottawa to Commonwealth Relations Office (hereafter CRO), Cumming-Bruce to Johnston, Telegram 1141, 20 October 1958, DO35/10846, TNA.

19 Mr. Diefenbaker's visit: background brief, n.d., DO35/10847, TNA.

20 Cumming-Bruce to Johnston, Telegram 1141, 20 October 1958, DO35/10846, TNA.

21 Diefenbaker reflected on civil servants in his memoirs and admitted his mistrust of their loyalty. See Diefenbaker, *One Canada*, vol. 2, 52–54.

22 Smith, *Rogue Tory*, 297.

23 Cara Spittal, "The Diefenbaker Moment" (PhD diss., University of Toronto, 2011), 245, 265, 279.

24 Diefenbaker, State Luncheon Speech, Wellington, 10 December 1958, DO35/10847.

25 Ibid.

26 Robinson, *Diefenbaker's World*, 11.

27 Record of conversation between the secretary of state and Mr. Diefenbaker on 4 November 1958, PREM 11/2606, TNA.

28 Garner, HC Ottawa, to Laithwaite, 9 January 1959, CRO, DO35/10847, TNA.

29 HC Karachi to SSCR, 12 December 1958, DO35/10847. He denied that the Commonwealth could act as an independent or third force on Cold War questions.

30 Record of prime minister's conversation with Mr. Nehru, New Delhi, 19 November 1958, *DCER*, vol. 24, doc. 397, enclosure 1, 910–15; Prime Minister Diefenbaker's

conversation with Mr. Nehru on Offshore Islands, New Delhi, 23 November 1958, *DCER*, vol. 24, doc. 397, enclosure 2, 915–16.

31 Elie Abel, "Diefenbaker Predicts Test in Asia," *Globe and Mail*, 22 November 1958.

32 Record of prime minister's conversation with Mr. Nehru, New Delhi, 19 November 1958, *DCER*, vol. 24, doc. 397, enclosure 1, 910–15; Prime Minister Diefenbaker's conversation with Mr. Nehru on Offshore Islands, New Delhi, 23 November1958, *DCER*, vol. 24, doc. 397, enclosure 2, 915–16.

33 Press conference given by the Canadian prime minister, the Right Honourable John Diefenbaker, at Parliament House, Canberra, 3 December 1958, in HC Canberra to SSCR, December 1958, DO35/10847, TNA.

34 "PM Hopeful of Aiding New Lands," *Globe and Mail*, 15 November 1958.

35 Diefenbaker, *One Canada*, vol. 2, 115.

36 See, for example, his angry retort to Khrushchev at the UN in 1960 in Diefenbaker, *One Canada*, vol. 2, 129–34.

37 Note by the prime minister of his conversation with Mr. Diefenbaker, 31 October 1958, PREM 11/2606, TNA. There is a summary of the meeting between Diefenbaker and Eisenhower in *DCER*, vol. 25, *1957–58*, pt. 2 (Ottawa: Department of Foreign Affairs and International Trade, 2004), doc. 9, 26–27.

38 Diefenbaker to Macmillan, 15 November 1958, PREM 11/2606, TNA; HC Karachi to SSCR, 12 December 1958, annex: visit of the Canadian prime minister to Pakistan, note of a meeting on November, DO35/10847.

39 Mr. Diefenbaker's discussion with the Australian cabinet, n.d., DO35/10847, TNA.

40 R.H. Scott, Commissioner General for the United Kingdom in Southeast Asia, to Gilbert Laithwaite, CRO, 5 December 1958, DO35/10847, TNA.

41 Diefenbaker, *One Canada*, vol. 2, 110. His visit to Ceylon began badly when Bandaranaike showed the sensitive Diefenbaker a picture of Pearson and praised C.D. Howe. Reported in HC Ceylon to SSCR, 6 December 1958, DO35/10847, TNA. Diefenbaker did not mention this in his memoirs.

42 Extract from Cabinet Conclusions, report by prime minister on his world tour, *DCER*, vol. 24, doc. 400, 921.

43 "PM Hopeful of Aiding New Lands," *Globe and Mail*, 15 November 1958.

44 Diefenbaker, *One Canada*, vol. 2, 111.

45 Bothwell notes that "he had a strong sense of the past, if not of history" (*Alliance and Illusion*, 135).

46 HC New Delhi to SSCR, 4 December 1958, DO35/10847.

47 Diefenbaker, State Luncheon Speech, Wellington, 10 December 1958, DO35/10847.

48 UNESCO, 1950 statement on race in "Four Statements on the Race Question," booklet (Paris: UNESCO 1969), 33, http://unesdoc.unesco.org/images/0012/001229/122962eo.pdf.

49 Ryan Touhey, "Dealing in Black and White: The Diefenbaker Government and the Cold War in South Asia, 1957–1963," *Canadian Historical Review* 92, 3 (2011): 441.

50 Robinson, *Diefenbaker's World*, 12–13.

51 Abel, "Diefenbaker Predicts Test."

52 W.A.C. Goode, Governor of Singapore, to Alan Lennox-Boyd, Secretary of State for the Colonies, No. 135, 6 December 1958, DO35/10847.

53 Diefenbaker, State Luncheon Speech, Wellington, 10 December 1958, DO35/10847.
54 Press conference given by the Canadian prime minister, the Right Honourable John Diefenbaker, at Parliament House, Canberra, 3 December 1958, in HC Canberra to SSCR, December 1958, DO35/10847, TNA.
55 Mr. Diefenbaker's discussion with the Australian cabinet, n.d., DO35/10847, TNA.
56 Press conference given by the Canadian prime minister, the Right Honourable John Diefenbaker, at Parliament House, Canberra, 3 December 1958, in HC Canberra to SSCR, December 1958, DO35/10847, TNA. Asa McKercher also explains his unwillingness to criticize apartheid because it was a domestic practice of a sovereign state. See Asa McKercher, "Sound and Fury: Diefenbaker, Human Rights, and Canadian Foreign Policy," *Canadian Historical Review*, 97, 2 (2016): 176–77.
57 Michael Hart, *A Trading Nation: Canadian Trade Policy from Colonialism to Globalization* (Vancouver: UBC Press, 2002), 208.
58 In 1958, 27.1 percent of Australian exports, 55.6 percent of New Zealand exports, 27 percent of South African exports, and 15.8 percent of Canadian exports went to Britain.
59 George Bain, "Commonwealth's Potential Stressed by Diefenbaker," *Globe and Mail*, 5 November 1958.
60 "A Commonwealth Champion," *Globe and Mail*, 6 November 1958.
61 "'Dief's' Better Half," *The Economist*, 15 November 1958, 585.
62 Letter from Garner, HC in Ottawa, 17 November 1958, CRO, DO35/10847, TNA.
63 Harold Macmillan, *Riding the Storm, 1956–1959* (London: Macmillan, 1971), 377.
64 Note by the prime minister of his conversation with Mr. Diefenbaker on 31 October 1958, PREM 11/2606, TNA.
65 Press conference given by the Canadian prime minister, the Right Honourable John Diefenbaker, at Parliament House, Canberra, 3 December 1958, in HC Canberra to SSCR, December 1958, DO35/10847, TNA.
66 Note of a discussion between Mr. Diefenbaker and Mr. Nash, n.d., DO35/10847, TNA.
67 "Half-and-Half Commonwealth," *Globe and Mail*, 8 December 1958.
68 For a thorough account of the establishment of the Colombo Plan – with a focus on Australia – see Daniel Oakman, *Facing Asia: A History of the Colombo Plan* (Acton: ANU E Press, 2010).
69 Note, memorandum, prime minister's conversation with President Ayub Khan, Karachi, 15 November 1958, *DCER*, vol. 24, doc. 396, 906–7.
70 HC Kuala Lumpur to SSCR, 15 December 1958, DO35/10847, TNA.
71 Press conference given by the Canadian prime minister, the Right Honourable John Diefenbaker, at Parliament House, Canberra, 3 December 1958, in HC Canberra to SSCR, December 1958, DO35/10847, TNA.
72 Spittal, "Diefenbaker Moment," 245.
73 Diefenbaker, *One Canada*, vol. 2, 115.
74 HC Kuala Lumpur, 15 December 1958, DO35/10847, TNA.
75 HC New Delhi to SSCR, 4 December 1958, DO35/10847, TNA.
76 HC Karachi to SSCR, 12 December 1958, DO35/10847, TNA.
77 HC Canberra to SSCR, December 1958, DO35/10847, TNA.

78 Newman, *Renegade in Power*, 259. McKercher argues that Diefenbaker played an important but "supporting role" in the events that led to South Africa's withdrawal from the Commonwealth. Even so, Hendrik Verwoerd complained that he had butted up against an "Afro-Asian-Canadian bloc." See McKercher, "Sound and Fury," 179, 180.
79 The briefing notes for their visit in 1963 began: "I do not suppose you will wish to say very much to Mr. Diefenbaker but I attach summaries of a few defensive points prepared by the C.R.O." See Mr. Diefenbaker, 22 February 1963, PREM11/4121, TNA.
80 Diefenbaker, State Luncheon Speech, Wellington, 10 December 1958, DO35/10847, TNA.
81 Garner to SSCR, 14 January 1959, C.R.O., DO35/10847, TNA. He repeated many of these concerns in his briefing of the cabinet. See extract from Cabinet Conclusions, 15 December 1958, *DCER*, vol. 24, doc. 400, 921–24.

Different Leader, Different Paths
Diefenbaker and the British, 1957–63

NORMAN HILLMER

High on the list of John Diefenbaker's enthusiasms were the British connection that had mothered Canada from colony to independent country, the young Queen Elizabeth, and a commonwealth of nations that was transforming an old empire. It was exhilarating to stand before a Canadian Club dinner audience at the Savoy Hotel in London on 1 July 1957, two weeks after unexpectedly becoming prime minister and in the midst of a meeting of Commonwealth leaders. There he was, Diefenbaker exulted, "in the shadow of the Mother of Parliaments" alongside "other creators and guardians of those traditions of freedom that are based on the concept of the dignity of the human person, the respect for the rule of Law and all those things which under Her Majesty the Queen unite us in whatever part of this Commonwealth is our home."[1]

But on the other side of enthusiasm lies disappointment, and disappointment came quickly. Britain and Canada were on divergent international paths by the late 1950s, even as their long histories together and mutual usefulness still had so much resonance for so many. Diefenbaker and his supporters looked longingly to the British to stem the Americanization of Canada, while the United Kingdom government led by Harold Macmillan increasingly moved towards Europe as the British Empire inevitably faded away. The Commonwealth was an arena in which the two countries could and did hope for shared Good Things – in vain, as it turned out. The story is not a happy one, and the trail of evidence in British and Canadian archives does not justify a revision of John Diefenbaker's reputation as a deeply flawed international leader. His rehabilitation can be sought or found in other chapters of this book, but not here, in the Anglo-Canadian relationship about which Diefenbaker cared so deeply.

The British welcomed Diefenbaker's 1957 election victory. Louis St. Laurent's Liberal government, led at the United Nations by the foreign minister, L.B. Pearson, had refused to support the Anglo-French military action against Egypt during the Suez Crisis only months before. London felt badly let down and so, declared the UK Commonwealth Relations Office (CRO), did a large majority of Canadians of British origin, "possibly as many as 90%." As the CRO saw it, the Liberals had tilted their policies away from the Commonwealth and towards the US and "the somewhat isolationist French-Canadian element in Quebec." Diefenbaker and his colleagues, on the other hand, would "wish to show that they can take an independent line from the United States and broadly they will be anxious to maintain the closest relations with the United Kingdom and to support Commonwealth projects."[2]

The CRO's respected chief diplomat in Canada, High Commissioner Sir Saville Garner, augmented his department's analysis. Diefenbaker's Conservatives were a grouping quite unlike the Liberals: "most of the leaders of the Conservative Party and much of its rank and file are of British stock and feel towards Britain strong emotional and sentimental ties." They believed that "the Liberal Government unnecessarily trailed behind Washington and, without attempting any remedial measures, watched a situation arise in which United States interests secured an economic foothold in the country to an extent which could threaten the independence of Canada." The new government would not be foolish enough to toss the US to one side, or unsubtle enough not to see the value of manipulating the Commonwealth connection to demonstrate to the Americans that Canada had other friends to whom it could turn. Diefenbaker's policies would not "always be in the direct interests of the United Kingdom," Garner predicted, "but their disposition to be helpful to Britain will be stronger than in any other Canadian Government for a long time past."[3]

Diefenbaker eased comfortably into the 1957 meeting of Commonwealth prime ministers, his first – and he always said his favourite – of the four that he attended. He loved meeting the Queen and claimed to have been inspired by the frank discussion and spirit of give-and-take. Americans were close neighbours, but in London he was among family.[4] In his conference interventions, he hewed to the Cold War internationalism of the previous

Canadian government and extolled the Commonwealth as a potential "instrument of dynamic freedom." His greatest concern was economic. Advisors had warned him that the trade front was not a promising avenue to pursue, but he vigorously pitched a Commonwealth summit meeting in Ottawa on the subject. He also encouraged investment in the Canadian economy, by way of making a complaint resonating with the recent election campaign: as he put it to his conference colleagues, the "extent to which the determination of her economic development was passing into USA hands" was a threat to the "independence of Canada."[5] The argument seems to have made an impression on the meeting's delegates, and that, in turn, might have reinforced Diefenbaker's belief that he was on the right track in arguing that the Commonwealth could act as a counterweight to the power of American markets and money. However, at least some (and maybe all) of his counterparts would have liked those US dollars for themselves.[6]

The British prime minister, Harold Macmillan, an old charmer, poured it on to considerable effect. The Suez Crisis had damaged the relationship with the United States and split the Commonwealth. The prime ministers' conference was an opportunity to bring the Commonwealth together again, and Diefenbaker was welcome as the sympathetic new leader of an important member of the association whose stance over Suez had disappointed Macmillan. Diefenbaker reported to his cabinet that Macmillan had given him "real help and support" at the meeting and had guaranteed that Britain's proposed participation in a free trade area (FTA) arrangement with the just established European Economic Community (EEC) would not be allowed to interfere with the privileged position of Canadian agricultural products in the UK market.[7]

Macmillan's private reaction to Diefenbaker was mixed. The Canadian was "strong," "modest, but quite impressive," and "a man," unlike Louis St. Laurent, who, in Macmillan's opinion, was a "stuffed shirt." However, Diefenbaker was also naïve and still caught up in his election oratory: "I fear that he has formed a picture of what can and cannot be done with the Commonwealth today wh[ich] is rather misleading."[8] Diefenbaker beat the drum hard for his prime ministers' trade conference, eventually acceding to a compromise that would see the Commonwealth finance ministers consider the matter further later that year. That, however, did not happen before Diefenbaker (in Macmillan's words at the time) "looked first puzzled, then pained, then indignant" when he encountered vociferous opposition to his plan. Macmillan took credit in his diary for extricating "poor Mr D" from the hole into which he had dug himself.[9] Macmillan believed, with good reason, that he had Diefenbaker's confidence, and he probably thought that the Canadian leader would not need his concentrated attention.

Macmillan would have preferred to avoid Ottawa on his way back from a trip to Washington at the end of 1957. He suggested a visit nonetheless, because he had seen Diefenbaker's predecessor in the Canadian capital and did not want anyone to draw the conclusion "that a Liberal Prime Minister was taken into confidence more than a Conservative one." Once the Canadians made the idea public, he told his foreign secretary, "I agree with you that we cannot escape."[10] The meeting went smoothly, helped by the fact that it was very brief. Macmillan was easily bored, particularly, his biographer claims, by Diefenbaker.[11]

Macmillan's, and Britain's, international position was a delicate one, even putting Suez aside. Citing a mid-1950s Macmillan statement to Parliament as foreign secretary in the Anthony Eden government, the historian David Dilks states that "Britain felt the pull of three distinct forces: the Commonwealth tie, on which no small part of Britain's economic and financial strength depended; the geographical and cultural link with Europe; the alliance with the United States." Macmillan "argued that the British must try to find a way of supporting greater unity in Europe, but without running counter to their other interests." Dilks makes explicit the role the Commonwealth then held "at the forefront of political business in Britain and ... the general consciousness."[12] The Commonwealth, however, changed radically during Macmillan's tenure as prime minister, and British opinion changed with it.[13]

Macmillan promised Diefenbaker at the 1957 London meeting, and continued to promise him, that Britain's FTA negotiators would protect Canadian agricultural producers. If "it came to a choice between the Commonwealth and the European arrangements the UK would undoubtedly choose the Commonwealth."[14] The British prime minister hoped for no choices. He was spearheading the ultimately unsuccessful FTA initiative, thinking in characteristically large terms, and wondering if it would not be possible to "retain the leadership of the Commonwealth world and at the same time seize the leadership of Europe."[15]

The Saskatchewan government's representative in the British capital described the splash Diefenbaker made at the Commonwealth gathering. Graham Spry wrote that the prime minister impressed with "his energy and directness. He is, of course, being welcomed here in all Conservative circles with enormous rejoicing and to read some of the cheaper newspapers one would think that Canada had not only rejoined the Commonwealth, but was almost going to amalgamate with the United Kingdom."[16]

High Commissioner Garner reported to Macmillan that Diefenbaker "found his visit to London a most exciting and stimulating experience. He was delighted with the warmth of his reception and undoubtedly felt that his visit had been a great personal success. He returned elated."[17] A contemporary academic observer remembered the light in Diefenbaker's eyes: "The warmth of the welcome convinced him that it was his destiny to revive the Commonwealth."[18] Blown on the winds of his conference performance, the prime minister alighted at the Ottawa airport with an improvised promise to divert 15 percent of Canadian trade from the United States to the United Kingdom. Diefenbaker always watched the newspapers, and they were approving, if sceptical, about his trade initiative.[19]

The 15 percent solution was no solution at all, as the prime minister's officials did not hesitate to inform him. A 15 percent shift meant that the British share of the Canadian market would have to increase a staggering 130 percent. A glance at Canada's trade tables over the past decades demonstrated that British exports to Canada had been slowing and American exports had been galloping, so that the latter now dominated the field at more than 70 percent of the total imports into Canada. That was Diefenbaker's complaint, and he was far from alone in making it, but what was to be done? Canadians only needed and wanted some of Britain's exports, and it was not within the capacity of UK industry to expand production of these goods sufficiently to create a significant movement of Canadian trade away from the US and towards Britain.[20] A Canadian trade mission to Britain in late 1957 discovered that businesspeople in the two countries were divided by more than the Atlantic Ocean. The Canadians irritated the British with their constant talk of the 15 percent diversion, which was accompanied by a taunt: "You show us; give us priority on delivery, good service and spare parts guarantees and then we'll decide if we can do business."[21]

Diefenbaker's cabinet, inexperienced and facing a minority Parliament, trembled at the hint of controversy. The minister of finance, the sober Donald Fleming, told Garner that the 15 percent promise was "his biggest headache," an embarrassment that was not going to go away soon.[22] Fleming publicly transformed his chief's diversion scheme into a long-term aspiration to alleviate the heavy dependence of the Canadian economy on the United States.[23] Diefenbaker retreated, implicitly (but only that) admitting that his enthusiasm had got the better of him, and concentrated attention on his hope for the Commonwealth finance ministers' meeting.[24] He had consulted no one before his grand gesture. Garner remarked that the prime minister was purposely dominant: "he has succeeded in maintaining complete ascendancy in the public eye." Diefenbaker was constantly on the move, preventing him "from devoting time to the development of policy and he does not appear to be giving much thought to the more distant future or indeed to the implementation of such policies as he has announced."[25] The 15 percent gambit revealed the lack of discipline and collegiality that Macmillan had observed at the prime ministers' meeting. Diefenbaker was a one-man operation: gregarious on the surface but living inside himself, almost devoid of empathy, a much better talker than listener.[26]

The Macmillan government forcefully reminded Diefenbaker, in Garner's words, that "his 15 per cent statement had created a difficult political situation for United Kingdom Ministers, who were under equal pressure to find an effective way of achieving the objective Mr. Diefenbaker had laid down."[27] The reminding was done with a sweeping proposal for a Canada-UK free trade area. The UK government "should – if anything – overbid Mr Diefenbaker," said Macmillan, who thought an Anglo-Canadian trade agreement "very important, both politically and for economic reasons."[28] The approach had many advantages from London's point of view. An FTA, unlike tinkerings with existing preferential tariffs, was consistent with the obligations both countries had undertaken under the General Agreement on Tariffs and Trade. It would, moreover, be helpful in trade talks with the Europeans to let them know that Britain had other lines of inquiry under way, and useful at home to let the Commonwealth constituency in Parliament and outside know that its government was not neglecting that part of the world.[29] British officials acknowledged that the bargain would be better for the UK than it would be for their negotiating partner, but this was not unreasonable: "given the imbalance of trade there was no case for an exactly balanced move by both countries, and, as regards tariffs, Canada already enjoyed duty-free entry for most of her exports to us." Canadian industries would lose their tariff protection, but the process would be gradual and there would be safeguards built into the agreement. The optimistic conclusion was that an FTA was sure to "catch the imagination of people in both countries."[30]

The British decided in the late summer of 1957 to make their FTA appeal to Diefenbaker personally as a means to get around the opposition that understandably mounted in Ottawa, but the Canadian leader would have none of it. Garner was sympathetic to Diefenbaker's political situation, with an election possible at any time and jobs on the line in Ontario and Quebec, but the high commissioner and his colleagues found the prime minister "mercurial," unable to make up his mind, and possessing neither economic expertise nor the will to acquire the basic vocabulary needed to carry on an intelligent discussion about trade. The UK proposal was declared to have produced in Diefenbaker and his circle "a combination of paralysis and alarm."[31]

Garner and the British were miffed at not having got what they wanted, but their criticisms of Diefenbaker went deeper, to his competence and capacity to manage the government. It is striking that the still-new prime minister's relationship with the UK government had lost its shine so quickly. Perhaps it had never shone at all. Diefenbaker suffered by comparison to the St. Laurent-Pearson Liberals. He did not have their polish, style, and connections. Nor did Diefenbaker's scattered working habits and his chaotic approach to decision making change, even after he won a stunning victory in the 1958 election. Garner's reports portrayed to his home government the paradox of a leader who consulted his cabinet to his ministers' exhaustion but insisted on being the last word on all things major and too many things minor.[32]

The prime minister's election triumph meant that his would be the government to preside over the Montreal conference of Commonwealth finance ministers in 1958. His advisors repeated that the prospects for notable advances in Anglo-Canadian or Commonwealth trade were dismal. A pre-conference meeting of top officials concluded that "the Commonwealth involved a clash between form and substance." As to form, the Commonwealth was widely regarded as "a good thing" that could function as "a bridge between the West and the newly emergent countries of Asia and Africa." However, as to substance, there were only the remnants of a Commonwealth economy, "and the trend was for member countries to back away from such economic links as had at one time existed."[33] The conference was earnestly prepared for and engaged in by the Canadian government, and by no one more earnestly than Minister of Finance Fleming.[34] Ottawa went out of its way to inform the United States that it was not the target of Commonwealth collaboration. The precaution was unnecessary. The trumpets blared and the rhetoric soared in Montreal, yet the concrete results were meagre and little was done to advance trade. The inauguration of a Canadian-initiated Commonwealth Scholarship program is regularly cited as the highlight in academic descriptions of the Montreal meeting.[35]

The Canadian government addressed the conference's theme of an expanding Commonwealth with a promise to increase development assistance under the rubric of the Colombo Plan from $35 million to $50 million. Diefenbaker was determined to make the sale of Canadian wheat part of Colombo Plan aid, and he did so, although he was never as successful in convincing his colleagues in developing countries that his domestic priorities were as important as he thought they were. The connection of internal interests, particularly those of his prairie home base, to external policy writ larger was a prominent and unchanging theme in Diefenbaker's world.[36]

But so was the Commonwealth itself. It was the institutional lens through which Diefenbaker most readily saw international affairs and his role in them. It was a link to the United Kingdom, a pathway to Africa and Asia, a bulwark of freedom against communism, and a counterweight to American power. With his government secure, the prime minister set off on a Commonwealth tour – not just of the old Commonwealth but of the new one as well. Coming back from the 1957 prime ministers' conference, he had commented favourably to his cabinet, in a way that was unusual for a Canadian leader at the time, about the increasingly multiracial composition of what had so recently been a white man's club.[37] He launched the tour at the Royal Albert Hall in London on 4 November 1958, introduced by Prime Minister Macmillan. Diefenbaker called the Commonwealth "a bright beacon in the black clouds of man's folly, inhumanity and pride ... shining forth from Westminster to all parts of the world, casting its light everywhere, without respect to colour, or race, or creed – or even form of government." The Diefenbaker Commonwealth was not carefully thought through or conceptually sophisticated, and it was paternalistic in its attitudes towards newcomers, but his summoning up of the association's "spiritual things on which all free men must lean" and "guiding principles of good conduct in government" was heartfelt.[38]

Rapidly accelerating decolonization was transforming the Commonwealth into a crowded place. Canada joined eight other former colonies at the 1957 meeting, Diefenbaker noting in particular the presence of Kwame Nkrumah of Ghana. In 1962, at the Canadian prime minister's final Commonwealth conference, sixteen member countries were represented. On that occasion, Diefenbaker began the first meeting by welcoming the prime ministers of newly independent Sierra Leone, Tanganyika, Jamaica, and Trinidad and Tobago, and "he felt that he could do so fittingly as Prime Minister of a country which had in her time been a colonial territory."[39]

Commonwealth proceeded alongside empire, the one waxing as the other waned. Britain's resources were sorely stretched over a still vast empire, but the Macmillan government believed that its overseas interests were indispensable to the United Kingdom's survival as a Great Power, and to holding up its end of the Cold War struggle against the Soviet Union and maintaining the respect of the United States. The Commonwealth could be thought to serve a similar purpose, but the bigger, more diverse, and more unruly it became, the less likely it was to retain its collegiality and credibility. Macmillan compared Britain to "a great land-owner who, faced with high taxation and heavy death duties, declined to give up the old house even though he had to close some of the wings and cut down some of the trees." He moved cautiously, not wishing to be at the head of an exploding Commonwealth he could not control. Outside events and the internal dynamics of government drew him away from the status quo he preferred.[40]

Within the new Commonwealth, tensions bubbled over apartheid, South Africa's brutal doctrine of race separation that kept the majority black population in the grip of privileged white descendants of European settlers. Commonwealth practice was that a member's domestic life was its own affair, but South Africa's racial policies forced their way on to the agenda when it gave notice that it wished to remain in the association after cutting ties with the monarchy and making itself into a republic. That required the Commonwealth's approval. How could a multiracial grouping of states abide a racist regime in its midst? The answer seemed obvious.

Canada and Britain shared common ground on the issue. Opinion in both countries condemned apartheid. By 1959, officials in the UK government and Commonwealth Relations Office minister Lord Home were talking about the damage that Britain's connection to South Africa was inflicting on international relationships and Commonwealth cohesion.[41] Harold Macmillan, speaking in the South African Parliament in early 1960, described the "wind of change" that "African national consciousness" was blowing over that continent. He said that Britain wanted to give South Africa, as a member of the Commonwealth, support and encouragement, but that was "impossible for us to do ... without being false to our own deep convictions about the political destinies of free men to which in our own territories we are trying to give effect."[42] Priding himself on his support for human rights and racial equality, Diefenbaker was about to launch a bill of rights for Canadians that he saw as a statement against discrimination wherever it existed in the world.[43]

Yet both leaders had no intention, as Diefenbaker put it, of throwing South Africa out of the Commonwealth. There was "no merit in such action," the Canadian prime minister told the House of Commons on 27 April 1960, one month after the killing of sixty-nine black protesters by South African police at Sharpeville reverberated in condemnatory headlines around the world. South Africa's expulsion from the Commonwealth, said Diefenbaker, "would respond to natural feelings of distaste for racial policy; it may commend itself for its purgatory effect. What would it solve? Would it bring relief to the 10 million blacks in that country?"[44]

With that, Diefenbaker was off to the Commonwealth Prime Ministers Meeting of 1960, his human rights principles less prominent than his anxiety to avoid a showdown over South Africa.[45] It horrified him that Canada might be held responsible for bold action that drove South Africa out of the Commonwealth. The Canadian leader lay low, in his mind balancing support for multiracialism with fears about a disrupted or dismembered Commonwealth if multiracialism was pushed too far or the new countries took control of the organization. He warned South Africa that it must show some flexibility if Canada's "moderate line" was to continue, but he saw the "plausibility" of the case the South African chief representative at the conference made to him on behalf of apartheid.[46]

Diefenbaker was annoyed at and suspicious of Macmillan. He believed that the British prime minister had brought the Commonwealth to the brink by whipping up criticism of South Africa with his "wind of change" speech, but he was now blithely preaching Commonwealth solidarity. Macmillan countered with displeasure of his own. Of the major leaders at the 1960 meeting, Diefenbaker was for Macmillan the least helpful – personally agreeable, but over-sensitive to slights, preoccupied by domestic party politics, his partial deafness preventing him from entering fully into the discussion. So said Macmillan's memoirs.[47] His diary added "ignorant, and little more than a 'tub-thumper.'"[48] The Australian prime minister, Robert Menzies, seen by Diefenbaker as a rival (for Macmillan's affections, among other things), helped the British bring the South Africans to accept a conference communiqué that, for now, squared the circle. It stipulated that the Commonwealth was a multiracial organization, but delayed any final decision about South Africa's future in the Commonwealth until it returned as a republic wishing to carry on its membership in the organization. The Canadian prime minister had what he wanted: putting things off was a Diefenbaker habit. A sympathetic cabinet minister characterized it as "deliberate indecisiveness." Other colleagues were less generous.[49]

Home from London, Diefenbaker's back seemed to stiffen against South Africa, very unhelpfully from Macmillan's point of view and driving a further wedge between the two prime ministers. South Africa's white population voted narrowly in favour of a republic on 5 October 1960, but their government let it be known that it would wait until after another Commonwealth meeting to declare the country's new constitutional status. Diefenbaker was often unable to divorce the personal from the political.

He was not, he believed, receiving sufficient respect from Macmillan and the British. They preferred the advice of Menzies, and they were scheming behind his back to keep South Africa in the Commonwealth. Diefenbaker asserted himself with a message that he insisted be placed in Macmillan's hands directly, bypassing officials in both countries as well as Canada's foreign minister.[50] "I feel obliged," Diefenbaker wrote, "to let you know that unless significant changes occur in the Union Government's racial policies, Canada cannot be counted on to support South Africa's readmission to the Commonwealth." Macmillan sighed: "John Diefenbaker is going to be troublesome about S Africa. He is taking a 'holier than thou' attitude, wh[ich] may cause us infinite trouble. For if the 'whites' take an anti-S Africa line, how can we expect the Brown and Blacks to be more tolerant."[51]

Macmillan feared that Diefenbaker would take the lead, but Diefenbaker feared taking the lead. The next Commonwealth conference was scheduled for March of 1961, and Diefenbaker had embarked on a long voyage of avoidance. The British high commissioner, Sir Saville Garner, was the witness. Less than a month before the conference, one of his multiple meetings with Diefenbaker took place. The prime minister pointed to the strength of Canadian opposition to the South African regime, evident in newspaper editorials, and to his own reputation as a defender of the downtrodden. He aired his irritation that Macmillan and his colleagues had condemned apartheid in their Parliament while he had held his own House of Commons in check, making him look like a dinosaur. He was not a man to be trapped a second time. He was not going to be outdone in his opposition to South Africa's racial policies.[52]

Diefenbaker knew, however, where that expression of opposition could take him and the Commonwealth. He told Garner that the 1961 meeting should sidestep the problem because it would "place great strain on new members and could well lead to acute acrimony." Garner replied that the matter could not be postponed. Diefenbaker then spoke vaguely of an idea "which he thought might help," saying that he would telephone Macmillan "in a day or two," a promise that Garner had been hearing for almost three months. Garner pieced together the idea from his Canadian contacts. When South Africa came up at the conference, Diefenbaker was thinking, he would try his best to stay in the background. It was normal for him, as the prime minister of the oldest former colony, to talk at Commonwealth meetings immediately after the British prime minister. If he did, he would have to take a strong stand against apartheid. But if the newer members of the Commonwealth "could be induced to speak first and could indicate that they were ready to acquiesce in South Africa's continued membership, Mr. Diefenbaker and Canada would be 'off the hook.'"[53] The majority of the Diefenbaker cabinet counselled him not to run away from "the opportunity to give leadership," but that was his overriding motivation. He would not be held responsible for whatever might happen at the conference.[54]

Receiving accounts of Diefenbaker's unreliability and even rumours of his inclination not to support South Africa's continued participation in the Commonwealth, Macmillan was pessimistic as the conference neared.[55] Yet he learned from the Canadian after his arrival in London that, like the British, Diefenbaker aimed to keep South Africa in the club. If the order of speakers could be changed in the way Diefenbaker wished, Macmillan thought, that could be the conference's salvation, meaning that it could be his and South Africa's salvation.[56]

The talking arrangements did change, but not in a way that was helpful to Macmillan-Diefenbaker designs. Prime Minister Jawaharlal Nehru of India decided to take charge. He informed Diefenbaker, who thought that the initial mood of the conference favoured keeping things as they were, that India would "oppose the granting of consent by other members to South Africa continuing in the Commonwealth."[57] Nehru took Canada's place as the second to speak after Britain at the crucial sixth meeting of the conference. He expressed himself forcefully. Diefenbaker went next, still searching for even small concessions from South Africa. He argued to that end that the South African application to remain a Commonwealth member was premature, since republican status had not been declared, and that there was no need to deal with the matter right away. Diefenbaker, however, agreed with Nehru that the Commonwealth must declare itself against racial discrimination, and he went on to assert that "to accept South Africa's present request would be construed as approval of, or at least acquiescence in South Africa's racial policy."[58] "Not much disposition to face the issue," Basil Robinson, Diefenbaker's foreign policy assistant, had written of him on the eve of the conference.[59] But his prime minister had faced the issue – "as a champion of racial equality," in Robinson's later phrase, who had drawn himself away from his colleagues in the old Commonwealth.[60]

Led by Nehru and encouraged by Diefenbaker, representatives from Africa and Asia made declarations of their own. An unbending South Africa announced after two and a half acid days that it would withdraw from the association with which it had fought two world wars, placing the responsibility squarely at the feet of the "Canadian-African-Asian bloc."[61] The gathering momentum against South Africa and the logic of his case against apartheid had carried Diefenbaker into history as the sole leader of the old Commonwealth who stood with the new Commonwealth. Canada's role in the affair, soon exaggerated, became a badge of honour for the prime minister and for his country. It also put the Diefenbaker government on the other side of the Commonwealth from the UK and its leader, who lamented more division in a too-divided world.[62] Some in the UK began to wonder whether the Commonwealth was worth preserving if it had to be kept on a moralizing Canada's terms.[63]

Another rift had already opened up between Diefenbaker's Canada and Macmillan's United Kingdom, this time over Britain's intention to seek entry into the European Common Market. The issue raised memories of Britain's attempt to arrange a free trade area with the EEC and also of the Anglo-Canadian FTA debacle of 1957. Sir Saville (by then Lord) Garner admitted many years later that the proposal for Canada-UK free trade had "acutely" embarrassed the Canadians, "since in return for some immediate advantages ... they were asked to dismantle permanently the protection of their domestic industry against British goods." The antipathies generated then impaired confidence and might have found their way into the unbending stand that the Diefenbaker government took against Britain's application to join the EEC. The British meanwhile had resentments of their own. Hadn't Diefenbaker promised to help out with British exports?[64]

Macmillan visited Canada in April of 1961, at the tag end of a Washington trip, where he received an EEC endorsement from US president John F. Kennedy. Diefenbaker was unimpressed by arguments about what the EEC plus Britain would do to unite the forces of democracy and stabilize Europe. He was worried about the consequences for the Canadian economy. Macmillan responded that he "hoped it would be possible to secure some derogations in favour of Canadian trade."[65] Home in London with his cabinet, the British prime minister put the matter rather differently. Damage to the "economic interests" of Canada was almost inevitable.[66] Macmillan concluded that Diefenbaker was going to be "difficult" over Europe and he was right, just as the Canadian and his finance minister were right to worry about the impacts that might flow from a successful British application to join the EEC.[67]

Diefenbaker's capacity to be obstructive was reduced by his dwindling popularity, a Canadian public that leaned towards Britain's European aspirations, and his propensity to slide around an issue rather than to confront it. Canadian policy and policy-makers went off in many directions, as was common in the Diefenbaker government. Other chapters in this book demonstrate that much the same was happening in the rapidly deteriorating Canadian relationship with President Kennedy and the American administration. Diefenbaker was out to protect his western Canadian farmers, but his opposition to British membership in the EEC was at bottom instinctive. He believed that the United Kingdom was betraying its historic ties to Canada and the Commonwealth. Diefenbaker was aggrieved and mystified that Macmillan, the quintessential English gentleman, was willing to drive the United Kingdom into alien territory. In a final and cruel irony, Diefenbaker complained, the hated Kennedy was cooperating with Macmillan in the damaging of Commonwealth trade links and thus in the preparation of Canada for economic domination by the United States.[68]

Macmillan returned to Ottawa from Washington at the end of April 1962, during an election campaign that returned Diefenbaker to power, if barely. In advance of the visit, the British leader's sources reported that, at best, Diefenbaker's attitude to the EEC was "rather subjective" and that, at worst, he was losing his grip on reality.[69] Macmillan assured Diefenbaker that a decision about whether Britain's membership in the EEC was "in the best interests of the Commonwealth" was yet to come. It would be discussed at a prime ministers' meeting that the Canadian leader had been promoting.[70] Macmillan went on to a speech in Toronto, where he talked of Britain's double duty to the Commonwealth and to Europe. *Serious* people in Canada, he wrote in his diary, understood his priorities and did not share the views of the "extreme and demagogic Diefenbaker."[71]

Macmillan's claim of a double duty was doubtless sincere, but he was feeling his European duty more strongly. The attachment of British policy makers to the Commonwealth was vanishing, and Macmillan's commitment to Europe was of long standing. His Britain was determined to join the EEC, whatever the consequences for Canada.[72] The 1962 Commonwealth conference brought the British-Canadian relationship to the lowest point in its long history. Inside and outside the formal meetings, Diefenbaker hurled thunderbolts at Macmillan's European project. A "very false and vicious speech," Macmillan muttered of Diefenbaker's opening conference salvo, by "a very crooked man."[73] Some on the British side reciprocated by sneaking to the newspapers, smearing the character and questioning the mental balance of Diefenbaker, their most senior Commonwealth partner.[74] It was all for nothing. Judging Britain insufficiently "European," President Charles de Gaulle of France vetoed Britain's EEC application in early 1963.[75]

Macmillan's Europe policy had put his country's relationship with Canada at risk, amplifying already widespread suspicions that Britain could not be trusted and no longer cared about its dominions. The British prime minister had the damage without the rewards.

In the John Diefenbaker years, Canada and Britain took one another's path less often. The British Empire was falling fast, the Commonwealth divided as well as united, and the post-Second World War realignment of Anglo-Canadian destinies raced on unchecked. Lord Garner likened the two countries to a married couple in old age, relaxed and not indifferent, but missing intensity.[76] Publics interacted and officials cooperated, but against a background of government-to-government relationships that lacked substance and warmth. The media in the two countries were mutually neglectful. Canadians boasted that theirs was a nation on the march that had caught up to Britain, while the British resented pontificating from across the ocean and Canada's apparent unwillingness to help in times of need.[77] Popular though Queen Elizabeth was, the Canadian link to the monarchy was questioned as never before.[78] Ample emigration from Britain to Canada appeared to contradict the trend. Numbers dipped in the early 1960s, however, and throughout the decade Australia and New Zealand were much preferred destinations for British immigrants.[79]

Fault lines in leadership compounded, or at the least reinforced, the downward trajectory of Anglo-Canadian relations. There had been a spark of optimism in the Diefenbaker and Macmillan camps in 1957, but the Canadian leader was an exotic whose uncertain trumpet contrasted sharply with the steadiness of his Ottawa predecessors. He was derided and dismissed early on. Diefenbaker put the British on the spot at his first Commonwealth conference, and they returned the favour with a Canada-UK trade proposal that embarrassed the Ottawa government and generated bitterness that echoed down the years. Diefenbaker initially sided with the British over South African membership in the Commonwealth, but found himself very late in the day standing beside the African and Asian nations, a clumsily executed shift of position that magnified the damage to his relationship with Macmillan and Canada's reputation in the United Kingdom. During their EEC adventure, the two men were deeply suspicious of one another. Diefenbaker over-reacted to a reasonable British decision to move towards Europe and Macmillan was deceptive about what he could and would do to protect Canada's interests. The rich collaborations of the so recent past, real and imagined, were nowhere to be found.

NOTES

I thank Elizabeth Haines and Theresa LeBane for research assistance in London and Ottawa, and for their advice, Stephen Azzi, Robert Bothwell, Janice Cavell, Adam Chapnick, David Dilks, Hector Mackenzie, David McIntyre, Asa McKercher, Kevin Spooner, and Susan Whitney.

1 Quoted in Cara Spittal, "The Diefenbaker Moment" (PhD diss., University of Toronto, 2011), 244. Diefenbaker's reminiscences are full of bows to Canada's British heritage. See John Diefenbaker, *One Canada: Memoirs of the Rt. Honourable John G. Diefenbaker*, 3 vols. (Toronto: Macmillan of Canada, 1973–77).

2 Memorandum of CRO, "Political Background in Canada," August 1957, DO 35/5403, Records of the Commonwealth Relations Office (hereafter CRO), The National Archives of the United Kingdom (hereafter TNA).

3 Garner to Prime Minister Harold Macmillan, "Canada: Mr. Diefenbaker's Government," 26 September 1957, DO 35/5403, TNA.

4 John Diefenbaker, "Great Issues in the Anglo-Canadian-American Community," an address at Dartmouth College, 7 September 1957, Canada, Department of External Affairs, *Statements and Speeches*, No. 1957/30; Denis Smith, *Rogue Tory: The Life and Legend of John G. Diefenbaker* (Toronto: Macfarlane Walter and Ross, 1995), 251.

5 Michael D. Stevenson, ed., *Documents on Canadian External Relations*, vol. 24, *1957–1958*, pt. 1 (Ottawa: Department of Foreign Affairs and International Trade, 2003) (hereafter *DCER*, vol. 24), docs. 325–42 (quotations from 328 and 339, telegrams of the Canadian high commissioner in the UK to the secretary of state for external affairs [SSEA], 27 June and 5 July 1957). On the Diefenbaker election campaign of 1957, see Smith, *Rogue Tory*, 227–37.

6 *DCER*, vol. 24, doc. 342, memorandum of secretary to cabinet, 6 July 1957; H. Basil Robinson, *Diefenbaker's World: A Populist in Foreign Affairs* (Toronto: University of Toronto Press, 1989), 12.

7 *DCER*, vol. 24, doc. 341, report of the prime minister to cabinet, 6 July 1957. On Macmillan's Suez disappointment, see Peter Catterall, ed., *The Macmillan Diaries*, vol. 1, *The Cabinet Years, 1950–1957* (London: Macmillan, 2003), 588. Entry of 20 August 1956: "the Canadians are very wet."

8 Peter Catterall, ed., *The Macmillan Diaries*, vol. 2, *Prime Minister and After, 1957–1966* (London: Macmillan, 2011), 45–49. Entries for 24 and 28 June and 5 July 1957. The account in Macmillan's memoirs conveys a more guarded impression of Diefenbaker, doubtless reflecting the deterioration in their relationship after the 1957 Commonwealth conference. See Harold Macmillan, *Riding the Storm, 1956–1959* (London: Macmillan, 1971), 377.

9 Catterall, *Macmillan Diaries*, vol. 2, 48, entry for 5 July 1957. Macmillan was hopeful (ibid., 49) that Diefenbaker would tell Lord Beaverbrook, the influential Anglo-Canadian newspaper proprietor, that Canada had been well treated at the prime ministers' conference. As time went on, the strong links between the controversial Beaverbrook and Diefenbaker's attitudes and policies damaged the Canadian prime minister's standing with leading members of Britain's ruling Conservative Party.

10 Macmillan to Foreign Secretary, 18 October 1957, Prime Minister's Records (PREM) 11/2461, TNA.

11 Alistair Horne, *Macmillan*, vol. 2, *1957–1986* (London: Macmillan, 1989), 57 and 135. See also Robinson, *Diefenbaker's World*, 24–26.

12 David Dilks, in the introduction to his edited *Retreat from Power: Studies in Britain's Foreign Policy of the Twentieth Century*, vol. 2, *After 1939* (London: Macmillan Press, 1981), 32–33. For more on Commonwealth economics from the British point of view, see L.J. Butler, *Britain and Empire: Adjusting to a Post-Imperial World* (London: Tauris, 2002), 138.

13 Wolfram Kaiser, *Using Europe, Abusing the Europeans: Britain and European Integration, 1945–63* (London: Macmillan, 1996), 120–23.

14 Canadian High Commissioner in the UK to SSEA, 4 July 1957, *DCER*, vol. 24, doc. 338. See also memorandum of SSEA to cabinet, 23 June 1958, *DCER*, vol. 24, doc. 438.

15 Quoted in Tim Rooth, "Britain, Europe, and Diefenbaker's Trade Diversion Proposals, 1957–58," in *Canada and the End of Empire*, ed. Phillip Buckner (Vancouver: UBC Press, 2005), 124. See generally 124–25. France scotched Macmillan's FTA plan in 1958. A European free trade association (EFTA) was formed in 1960, consisting of the UK, Denmark, Norway, Austria, Switzerland, Portugal, and Sweden.

16 Quoted in J.L. Granatstein, *Canada, 1957–1967: The Years of Uncertainty and Innovation* (Toronto: McClelland and Stewart, 1986), 43–44.

17 Garner to Prime Minister Harold Macmillan, "Canada: Mr. Diefenbaker's Government," 26 September 1957, DO 35/5403, TNA.

18 Trevor Lloyd, *Canada in World Affairs, 1957–1959* (Toronto: Oxford University Press, 1968), 66.

19 Garner to Secretary of State for Commonwealth Relations, 18 October 1957, CRO Records, DO 35/8731, TNA.

20 Rooth, "Diefenbaker's Trade Diversion," 118; Granatstein, *Canada*, 44.

21 Donald R. Gordon, "The UK Trade Mission: What Did It Achieve?" *Saturday Night* 73 (18 January 1958), 31. The trade mission might have contributed to a temporary increase in British exports to Canada in the late 1950s. See *DCER*, vol. 24, doc. 434, Cabinet Conclusions, 3 December 1957; Rooth, "Diefenbaker's Trade Diversion," 121–22.

22 Garner to Secretary of State for Commonwealth Relations, 18 October 1957, CRO Records, DO 35/8731, TNA.

23 Granatstein, *Canada*, 45.

24 Garner to Secretary of State for Commonwealth Relations, 18 October 1957, CRO Records, DO 35/8731, TNA. See also Diefenbaker, *One Canada*, vol. 2, 72–73.

25 Garner to Prime Minister Harold Macmillan, "Canada: Mr. Diefenbaker's Government," 26 September 1957, CRO Records, DO 35/5403, TNA.

26 These impressions were gained from the author's long conversations with H. Basil Robinson, who worked by Diefenbaker's side from 1957 to 1962.

27 Garner to Secretary of State for Commonwealth Relations, 18 October 1957, CRO Records, DO 35/8731, TNA.

28 Catterall, *Macmillan Diaries*, vol. 2, 55, entry for 27 August 1957.

29 Rooth, "Diefenbaker's Trade Diversion," 118.

30 UK Treasury brief, 5 September 1957, CRO Records, DO 35/8731, TNA.

31 Garner to Secretary of State for Commonwealth Relations, 18 October 1957, CRO Records, DO 35/8731, TNA. For elaboration, see Rooth, "Diefenbaker's Trade Diversion," 118–21.

32 Garner to Sir Gilbert Laithwaite (CRO), 14 January 1959, PREM 11/3675, TNA. On Diefenbaker's "interminable cabinet meetings," see interview with Douglas Harkness, 1 November 1971, Peter Stursberg Papers, Library and Archives Canada (hereafter LAC), vol. 14, file 23, 6.

33 *DCER*, vol. 24, doc. 364, enclosure, "Commonwealth Trade and Economic Conference," 2 April 1958.

34 See his stultifying memoirs: *So Very Near: The Political Memoirs of the Honourable Donald M. Fleming*, vol. 1, *The Rising Years* (Toronto: McClelland and Stewart, 1985), chap. 46.

35 See, for example, John Hilliker and Greg Donaghy, "Canada's Relations with the United Kingdom at the End of Empire, 1956–73," in Buckner, *Canada and the End of Empire*, 32. Rooth, "Diefenbaker's Trade Diversion," 127–28, gives a short account of the Montreal conference.

36 Robinson, *Diefenbaker's World*, 57–58, chap. 8 and passim; David Webster, *Fire and the Full Moon: Canada and Indonesia in a Decolonizing World* (Vancouver: UBC Press, 2009), 67.

37 Robinson, *Diefenbaker's World*, 4, 13. See also Asa McKercher, "Sound and Fury: Diefenbaker, Human Rights, and Canadian Foreign Policy," *Canadian Historical Review* 92, 2 (2016): 171; and Francine McKenzie's chapter in this volume.

38 Quotations from Spittal, "Diefenbaker Moment," 284–85. On paternalism, see ibid., 291–95.

39 Minutes of meetings of Commonwealth prime ministers, 1962, first meeting, 10 September, Cabinet Office Records (hereafter CAB) 133/252, TNA.

40 Frank Heinlein, *British Government Policy and Decolonisation, 1945–1963: Scrutinizing the Official Mind* (London: Frank Cass, 2002), chaps. 4–5, quotation on 160.

41 Ibid., 246.

42 Address to South African Parliament, 3 February 1960, in Harold Macmillan, *Pointing the Way, 1959–1961* (London: Macmillan, 1971), 473–82.

43 McKercher, "Sound and Fury," 173.

44 Quoted in Smith, *Rogue Tory*, 356–57.

45 This and the next paragraph are based on Robinson, *Diefenbaker's World*, 81–82 and chap. 13; Macmillan, *Pointing the Way*, 170–77; Janice Cavell, ed., *Documents on Canadian External Relations*, vol. 27, *1960* (Ottawa: Foreign Affairs and International Trade Canada, 2007) (hereafter *DCER*, vol. 27), docs. 358, 362, 374, and 375, Cabinet Conclusions, 31 March, 20 April, 14 and 16 May 1960; *DCER*, vol. 27, doc. 366, Diefenbaker conversation with Louw of South Africa, 3 May 1960; *DCER*, vol. 27, doc. 369, Diefenbaker conversation with Nkrumah of Ghana, 7 May 1960.

46 *DCER*, vol. 27, doc. 366, Diefenbaker conversation with Louw of South Africa, 3 May 1960; *DCER*, vol. 27, doc. 375, Cabinet Conclusions, 16 May 1960.

47 Macmillan, *Pointing the Way*, 172, 174.

48 Catterall, *Macmillan Diaries*, vol. 2, 295, entry for 12 May 1960.

49 Interview with John Fisher, 3 July 1974, Stursberg Papers, LAC, vol. 14, file 6, 27; interview with Alvin Hamilton, 9 November 1972, Stursberg Papers, LAC, vol. 14, file 21, 13; and interview with William Hamilton, 3 February 1974, Stursberg Papers, LAC, vol. 14, file 22, 43. The quoted words belong to Alvin Hamilton.

50 Robinson, *Diefenbaker's World*, 174–76.

51 Catterall, *Macmillan Diaries*, vol. 2, 337, entry for 16 November 1960; Macmillan, *Pointing the Way*, 293.

52 Garner to Macmillan, 15 February 1961, CAB 21/4616, TNA.

53 Ibid.

54 See Janice Cavell, ed., *Documents on Canadian External Relations*, vol. 28, *1961* (Ottawa: Foreign Affairs and International Trade Canada, 2009) (hereafter *DCER*, vol. 28), doc. 470, memorandum of Diefenbaker, n.d. but February 1961; and *DCER*, vol. 28, doc. 472, Cabinet Conclusions, 2 March 1961; Robinson, *Diefenbaker's World*, 177.

55 British Ambassador to the US to Foreign Office, 21 February 1961, CAB 21/4404, TNA; P.F. de Zulueta (Prime Minister's Office) to Foreign Office, 26 February 1961, CAB 21/4404, TNA.

56 *DCER*, vol. 28, doc. 473, memorandum of Basil Robinson, 7 March 1961.

57 Ibid., docs. 474–5, Cabinet Conclusions, 9 March 1961 and memorandum of cabinet secretary, 12 March 1961.

58 Minutes of meetings of Commonwealth prime ministers, sixth meeting, 13 March 1961, CAB 133/251, TNA. For a summary of the sessions on South Africa, see Ronald Hyam, "The Parting of the Ways: Britain and South Africa's Departure from the Commonwealth, 1951–61," *Journal of Imperial and Commonwealth History* 26, 2 (1998): 166–72.

59 Quoted in Robinson, *Diefenbaker's World*, 182.

60 Ibid., 184.

61 Canadian High Commissioner in South Africa to SSEA, 17 March 1961, *DCER*, vol. 28, doc. 480; Minutes of Meetings of Commonwealth prime ministers, seventh to tenth meetings, 13–15 March, CAB 133/251, TNA. In Macmillan's immediate assessment of what (from his point of view) had gone wrong, Nehru figured heavily and Diefenbaker not at all. See Catterall, *Macmillan Diaries*, vol. 2, 366–67, entry for 24 March 1961. Kevin Spooner (Chapter 9, this volume) expertly balances contending interpretations of Diefenbaker's 1961 conference role. McKercher, "Sound and Fury," agrees with Spooner that Diefenbaker's stand was "important," while underlining that he was repeatedly "a far more reluctant, than eager, opponent of apartheid" (174–81). For the earlier scholarship, contrast Hyam, "Parting of the Ways," with Frank Hayes, "South Africa's Departure from the Commonwealth, 1960–1961," *International History Review* 2, 3 (1980): 471–84.

62 Macmillan, *Pointing the Way*, 300–1. On the conference as "a further stage in the decline" of the Diefenbaker-Macmillan relationship, see Robinson, *Diefenbaker's World*, 187.

63 Nigel Lawson, "Public Images and Perceptions," in *Britain and Canada: Survey of a Changing Relationship*, ed. Peter Lyon (London: Frank Cass, 1976), 179–80.

64 Lord Garner of Chiddingly, "Britain and Canada in the 1940s and 1950s," in Lyon, *Britain and Canada*, 100, 102. See also Blair Fraser, "What's Haunting Dief? The Ghost of Speeches Past," *Maclean's* 65 (6 October 1962), 2–4.

65 Record of Diefenbaker-Macmillan meeting, 10 April 1961, CAB 133/297, TNA.

66 UK Cabinet Conclusions, 20 April 1961, cited in Robert Bothwell, *Alliance and Illusion: Canada and the World, 1945–1984* (Vancouver: UBC Press, 2007), 144.

67 "Difficult" is from Horne, *Macmillan*, vol. 2, 261. On Finance Minister Fleming, see his carefully worded "Canada's Trade in a Changing World," Canadian Club of

Winnipeg, 19 January 1962, Department of External Affairs, *Statements and Speeches*, No. 1962/5. Canadian economists at the time differed on the consequences for Canada of British entry into the EEC. Note Roy A. Matthews, "Canada, Britain, and the Common Market," *World Today* 18, 2 (1962): 48–57, and a more optimistic article under the same title by H.I. MacDonald, *Canadian Forum* 41 (November 1961): 169–70.

68 Robinson, *Diefenbaker's World*, 210, 266, and, generally, chaps. 21 and 24–26. On the role of the Europe issue in the polluting of the American-Canadian and Kennedy-Diefenbaker relationships, see Asa McKercher, *Camelot and Canada: Canadian-American Relations in the Kennedy Era* (New York: Oxford University Press, 2016), chap. 4.

69 British High Commissioner in Ottawa (Lord Amory) to Garner (now head of CRO), 6 April 1962, CAB 21/5558, TNA; Edward Heath, *The Course of My Life: My Autobiography* (London: Hodder and Stoughton, 1998), 221–22.

70 Record of Diefenbaker-Macmillan meeting, 30 April 1962, CAB 133/300, TNA.

71 Catterall, *Macmillan Diaries*, vol. 2, 468–69, entry for 6 May 1962. The emphasis is Macmillan's.

72 Heinlein, *British Government Policy*, 273–78; Bothwell, *Alliance and Illusion*, 145–46. See also Harold Macmillan, *At the End of the Day, 1961–1963* (London: Macmillan, 1973), 136. On the basis of extensive research in government files, Heinlein, *British Government Policy*, 278, dates the weakening commitment of UK policymakers to the Commonwealth from 1961 on.

73 Catterall, *Macmillan Diaries*, vol. 2, 496, entry of 12 September 1962. The Diefenbaker speech is in minutes of meetings of Commonwealth prime ministers, 1962, fourth meeting, 11 September, CAB 133/252, TNA.

74 Janice Cavell, ed., *Documents on Canadian External Relations*, vol. 29, *1962–63* (Ottawa: Foreign Affairs, Trade and Development Canada, 2013), doc. 324, Cabinet Conclusions, 21 September 1962; Robinson, *Diefenbaker's World*, 279–81; Bothwell, *Alliance and Illusion*, 146. See also Diplomatic Staff, "Commonwealth's Longest Week," *Observer*, 16 September 1962; and Robert Duffy, "Commonwealth Meeting Releases Called Attempt to Blacken Diefenbaker," *Globe and Mail*, 21 September 1962.

75 Horne, *Macmillan*, vol. 2, 108–13, 444–51.

76 Garner, "Britain and Canada," 102.

77 Ibid., 98–103; John Holmes, "The Anglo-Canadian Neurosis: A Mood of Exasperation," *Round Table* 56, 223 (1966): 251–60; Donald Gordon, "The Ties with Britain Are Loosening," *Saturday Night* 76 (18 February 1961), 12–13.

78 Phillip Buckner, "The Last Great Royal Tour: Queen Elizabeth's 1959 Tour to Canada," in Buckner, *Canada and the End of Empire*, 84–90.

79 Freda Hawkins, "Migration as a Factor in Anglo-Canadian Relations," in Lyon, *Britain and Canada*, 152–54; Lawson, "Public Images and Perceptions," 178.

PART 2

Canadian-American Relations

3

The Spirit of '56
The Suez Crisis, Anti-Americanism, and Diefenbaker's 1957 and 1958 Election Victories

JANICE CAVELL

On New Year's Day 1957, a *Globe and Mail* editorial announced that Canada's first duty in the coming twelve months was to "reorient and reorganize" its foreign policy. As the *Globe*'s writer recounted, in the decade before 1956 the Canadian government had "marched closely in step with the foreign policy of the United States" and "unquestioningly accepted Washington's right and ability to guard, to guide, almost to govern, the Western Allies." But when US policy was put to the test by the Hungarian and Suez crises, "it collapsed like a pricked balloon." Canadians, not Americans, had solved the Suez dilemma. After such a triumph, the *Globe*'s writer opined, it was impossible to go back to following the American lead. Instead, "We are big enough now ... to have views of our own – and to make them felt in Washington no less than in London." Accordingly, the lesson of Suez was not that Canadians must cut the last ties binding them to the United Kingdom: the battle (if it could be called a battle) for political independence from London had already been won. But in the struggle for greater independence from Washington, Canada would need "new ideas, new approaches, new leaders."[1]

Many other writers took up the same theme in the early months of 1957. According to the *Halifax Chronicle-Herald*, Canada was "not a satellite of Britain, or of the United States"; instead, it was an independent nation with both the right and the duty to go its own way.[2] In *Saturday Night* Maxwell Cohen agreed that, after Canada's sudden "break-through to new levels of responsibility," its relations with its southern neighbour had "entered a new phase," and therefore "a national debate ... exceeding in depth and realism any similar discourse that has taken place for many years" was urgently needed.[3] A few writers wondered whether the ultimate outcome of such a debate would be positive or negative. Tom Kent, the editor of the *Winnipeg Free Press*, observed that, thanks to its close economic association with the United States, Canada was "incomparably better off, in material terms, than it could possibly be in any other way." But increasingly the question of "whether the country is thereby losing its soul, making a mockery of its political independence" lurked "undefined and incoherent ... in the back of Canadian minds." Kent foresaw the possibility of an "explosive" confrontation between economic reality and rising nationalist aspirations.[4] Clearly Suez, as Bruce Hutchison summed it up in the *Ottawa Citizen*, was "a pretty important date in the history of the Canadian mind."[5]

Throughout the political and journalistic debates sparked by Suez, Canada's relationship with the United States was the subject of far more negative comments than was its relationship with the United Kingdom. Many voices were raised in support of the "mother country," and even the nationalist *Canadian Forum* firmly denied that Canada's friendship for Britain had been seriously impaired.[6] Indeed, the range of opinion on Britain was remarkable. "Despite my pride in my British ancestry ... I am ashamed by [sic] the actions being taken by the British," declared one citizen in a letter to the press. "I am usually anti-British. In this particular case, however, I stand with Britain," explained another.[7] But when it came to the United States, resentment was unmistakably the dominant note.[8]

Both in the press and on the street there was a strong tendency to blame the United States for the very existence of a crisis and to cast US secretary of state John Foster Dulles as the villain.[9] Even amid the euphoria caused by Lester Pearson's successful diplomacy, the accusation by Conservative MP Howard Green that Canada was acting as Washington's "chore boy" cut deep. A Toronto letter-writer agreed with Green and referred to Louis St. Laurent's Liberal "regime" as "a puppet Government." Another citizen lamented: "Russia has her satellites but we are fast becoming a satellite of Washington ... we say, yes yes and act ... just like a sort of lap dog."[10] On Suez, Canada's initiative was accepted by the Americans. But what if the foreign policies of the two nations were to clash in the future? Would the Liberals maintain Canada's new stature? St. Laurent and Pearson might have achieved a diplomatic triumph, but some wondered whether their policies would strengthen or weaken Canada in the long term.

The only detailed scholarly examination of the Suez Crisis in relation to Anglo-Canadian nationalism is contained in José Igartua's *The Other Quiet Revolution: National Identities in English Canada, 1945–71*. According to Igartua, the events of 1956 "constituted a significant juncture in the dissolution of English-speaking Canada's self-representation as a British nation."[11] But by choosing to focus exclusively on opinions about Britain, he ignores the very question that most preoccupied English Canadians at the time. Indeed, it could be argued that the transition to a new type of English-Canadian nationalism described by Igartua stemmed less from a rejection of Britain's fast-waning power than from the growing fear of American influence. As former diplomat John Holmes shrewdly observed, the distaste many Canadians showed for the "relics of British suzerainty" during the 1960s gained much of its intensity from the need to compensate for "impotence against the realities of American domination."[12]

This chapter traces the expression of anti-American nationalist sentiment from the weeks before the crisis through the election campaigns of 1957 and 1958.[13] Because so many Anglo-Canadians strongly supported Britain in 1956, political scientists and historians have long wondered whether Suez played a key role in John Diefenbaker's unexpected election win over St. Laurent in 1957, after twenty-two years of Liberal rule, and his subsequent landslide victory in 1958.[14] The crisis had only a relatively small – though occasionally dramatic – place in campaign oratory, and opinion polls taken at the time seemed to show that Suez was not a major issue for voters. However, perhaps the question has been framed in the wrong way. Even Canadians who opposed or were uncertain about British actions in the Middle East could still worry that, in turning against London, St. Laurent's government might have brought Canada one step closer to being Washington's satellite. In a poll taken soon after the 1957 election, only 5.1 percent of former Liberal voters who switched to the Conservatives named the Suez Crisis itself as their reason for doing so. However, a large number (30 percent) said that they believed it was "time for a change"[15] – a response that echoed the *Globe*'s rhetoric and that could accommodate many shades of feeling.

The anti-American strain in Canadian nationalism increased markedly after Suez,[16] and Diefenbaker was often described as the leader who would most strongly maintain Canada's independence against American encroachment. The *Globe and Mail*'s call for "new ideas, new approaches, new leaders" in January 1957 pointed unequivocally to Diefenbaker. An underlying surge in deeply felt, but sometimes barely articulated, anti-American sentiment drove political debates in 1957 and 1958. As Maxwell Cohen observed in 1958, the election campaign was "filled with [the] yet uncrystallized feelings of many Canadians" about American domination.[17] Diefenbaker's famous Northern Vision offered what seemed to be a concrete, workable plan for the creation of a stronger and more independent Canada. But the vision failed, and resentment continued to rise. Anti-American arguments would soon be more systematically developed in books such as James Minifie's *Peacemaker or Powder-Monkey*, published in 1960. In the same year a Liberal Party study, based on two hundred in-depth interviews, identified Canadian-American relations as one of the four key issues that preoccupied voters. The interviews revealed "much anxiety and unhappiness" over Canada's political, economic, and cultural subordination to the US.[18]

Between 1958 and 1963, these feelings found an outlet in the controversy over nuclear weapons. The passionate debates on this subject have received extensive analysis,[19] while the period from 1956 to 1958 has not yet been given the attention it deserves. Foreign policy issues may not have provoked many dramatic episodes or memorable speeches during either of Diefenbaker's first two election campaigns as Conservative leader, but the journalism of the time demonstrates that the Suez Crisis was indeed, as Hutchison claimed, "a pretty important date in the history of the Canadian mind." The years immediately after Suez were a key period of development that set the stage for the ideological and political clashes of the early 1960s. This chapter accordingly shows how questions about Canada-US relations underlay Diefenbaker's initial appeal to voters. His electoral strategies were shaped by the ongoing shift in public opinion, and his campaign rhetoric reinforced the general trend.

As early as 1951, Lester Pearson had apprehensively observed "how easy it would be to work up a strong anti-American feeling in this country." Though he felt certain that the overwhelming majority of Canadians were firmly on the American side in the Cold War, he knew that "our feeling of dependence on the United States ... and frustration over the fact that we can't escape this no matter how hard we might try" was a "deep-seated, though often unconsciously felt" source of resentment.[20] However, until 1956 there were few if any occasions on which Canadians seriously believed that they should take a different line from the United States. But just how uncomfortable some nationalists felt about American influence, even before Suez, is demonstrated by a cartoon that appeared in the September 1956 issue of *Canadian Forum*. Young Mr. Canada, smitten by love, runs after a beautiful young woman named Nationalism, while in the background Uncle Sam stands next to a dowdy bride. "But son," the American cries, "the marriage is all arranged!" The caption notes that Mr. Canada "keeps forgetting the dowry."[21] The American bride, therefore, represents the material advantages of close association with the United States. However, Nationalism has more compelling attractions. She is alluringly curvaceous but also clearly an intelligent and up-to-date young woman. She wears a smartly tailored, business-like skirt and jacket, carries a portfolio and a furled umbrella, and strides confidently into the future. In the long term, might not equal prosperity, as well as greater satisfaction, be gained by following her?

To the *Forum*'s target audience of well-educated, left-leaning national-ists, the answer was apparently yes (or at least maybe). For those who shared such opinions, the developing crisis in the Middle East provided a conve-nient opportunity to criticize American foreign policy. In June 1956, Brit-ain withdrew its last troops from the Suez Canal Zone, in accordance with an agreement reached two years earlier. At the time of the withdrawal, the Egyptian government was attempting to negotiate loans for the construc-tion of the Aswan High Dam from the United States, Britain, and the World Bank. In the hope of improving the conditions attached to the Western loans, President Gamal Abdel Nasser let it be known that he was consider-ing an offer of aid from the Soviet Union. In the end, he had to accept the Western conditions, but Dulles then declared that the US would not provide funds on any terms. One Canadian cabinet minister privately observed that, in his opinion, this decision was "the greatest mistake a government of the Western world had made since the war."[22] Nasser quickly nationalized the canal so that he could use the revenues from it to finance the dam.

As the major shareholder in the Compagnie universelle du canal mari-time de Suez (which had built the canal in the 1860s), the British government was of course deeply concerned by this move. Most of the other sharehold-ers were French. Britain and France refused to rule out the use of force to restore the status quo. In the view of British prime minister Anthony Eden, a strong stand was necessary to curb both Nasser's ambitions and the growth of Soviet influence in the Middle East. Politicians in Washington and Ottawa, however, were convinced that aggression would only inflame anti-Western feelings throughout the developing world. Britain and France had been sorely provoked, but the use of force would have too many nega-tive consequences.

A letter to the *Globe and Mail* on 16 October blamed Dulles in particular and "Yankee imperialism" in general for this volatile situation. The writer, Kenneth Ingram, argued that American imperialism had roused far more resentment throughout the developing world than British or French imperialism had ever done. "Returning to the local and specific, he would be a rash and optimistic person to say that Canada in actual fact is anything more than a colony of the U.S., or rapidly becoming so," Ingram concluded. It was hardly a perceptive analysis, but it demonstrates how ready many Canadians were to blame the United States and how closely such criticisms were linked to the fear of becoming an American satellite. Another letter on the same date suggested that the Americans were attempting to cast themselves as champions of the "so-called oppressed nations." But in the writer's view, by failing to support other members of the Western alliance, Dulles was undermining NATO unity; because of his foolishness, the Soviets "must be having a good laugh."[23]

On 29 October, Israel attacked Egypt with the secret knowledge and encouragement of Eden and French premier Guy Mollet. In accordance with a plan arranged beforehand, London and Paris then issued an ultimatum to both sides, threatening to send in their own troops to protect the canal if the fighting did not stop. On 31 October, the British and French air forces began bombing Egypt; an invasion followed on 5 November. It seemed possible that, if the Soviet Union were to actively intervene on Egypt's side, the conflict might widen into a third world war.

These events came as a complete surprise to both the American and the Canadian governments. Washington was determined not to countenance the invasion and seemed indifferent to the humiliation this attitude would cause for Britain and France. In response to a request for Canadian "understanding" and "support" from Eden,[24] Prime Minister St. Laurent wrote bluntly that "without more information, and information different from that which we now have, about the action of Israel, we cannot come to the conclusion that the penetration of its troops into Egypt was justified or that the probable resistance of the Egyptians necessitated the decision of the U.K. and France."[25] The letter was not released to the press, but journalists were aware of its tenor and tone. Accordingly, Ottawa's stiff reply to the British appeal was the subject of extensive press commentary on 1 November.

The most extreme responses came from the Liberal *Toronto Star* and the Conservative *Calgary Herald*. In the *Star*, Peter Stursberg recounted that the British failure to consult or even inform Ottawa had roused a great deal of anger in the Canadian capital, and he speculated that severe damage was being done to the Commonwealth.[26] A letter to the editor sombrely noted: "In a matter of hours a great chasm has formed."[27] The *Herald*, in contrast, posed a series of angry, accusing questions: "What degradation is this? ... what sickening talk is this that Canada is 'hacking out a stand of her own'? Is it not more accurate to say that Washington has nibbled out, not hacked out, a place for us to stand among its puppets?" Here, Canada's Suez policy was seen as part of a deliberate plan. The Liberals had been "carefully preparing the way for years, discarding the ties of ancestry and Commonwealth one by one, selling out our natural resources and our industry ... And now we have the ultimate sell-out. They have sold out our decency and our honor."[28]

However, the great majority of newspapers took a moderate and judicious editorial stance, combining some degree of sympathy for Britain with an awareness that, at least on this issue, Canadian interests would not be best served by supporting Eden. The *Windsor Star* observed sensibly: "If the United Kingdom is to make unilateral decisions on affairs of concern to Canada and other Commonwealth countries, she cannot expect multilateral support from them."[29] According to the *Winnipeg Free Press*, it was no time for facile moralizing; instead, the country's leaders must "earnestly ... seek ways of halting the consequences of [Britain's] error."[30] Yet a lack of enthusiasm for the Eisenhower administration's blunt refusal to support Britain and France was often evident. In the *Ottawa Citizen*, Norman Campbell called the crisis "a heart-breaking situation" for Canadians. A choice, he wrote, had to be made – the choice "between a North American foreign policy which could hardly be born any place except Washington and a foreign policy born in London. ... We are being driven inexorably to Washington."[31] While Campbell could not approve of what Britain had done, he clearly saw the "inexorabl[e]" movement towards the US as an uninviting prospect.

When Pearson presented his plan for an international peacekeeping force to the United Nations on 4 November, this evidence of constructive Canadian policy was warmly welcomed. Not only would the peacekeepers avert the possibility of a wider conflict, but their presence would allow the British and French to retreat with some semblance of dignity. "There's Hope in the Pearson Plan," declared a headline in the *Montreal Gazette*.[32] The *Halifax Chronicle-Herald* observed: "members of the Canadian Government have chosen a course which all Canadians will agree is the right course – the course through the United Nations."[33] The *Ottawa Citizen* enthusiastically agreed that it was Pearson's hour: "Instead of mouthing regrets and talking in generalities, Mr. Pearson ... came forward with a definite proposal."[34]

Many Canadians were eager for their troops to be part of the new force.[35] Such emotions were reinforced when a Canadian, General E.L.M. Burns, was appointed to command the peacekeepers and the *Manchester Guardian* hailed Canada as the new moral leader of the Commonwealth.[36] "Canada's stature in world affairs has grown enormously," the *Montreal Gazette* wrote with pride.[37] The government responded to the popular mood by quickly arranging for a battalion of the Calgary-based Queen's Own Rifles to depart for the Middle East. The announcement was made on 7 November and, amid intense publicity, the battalion then travelled to Halifax, where it was supposed to embark in HMCS *Magnificent.*[38]

However, the excitement and approval soon evaporated. Nasser considered Canadian troops unacceptable because of Canada's ties to Britain. When he was informed of this attitude by the Egyptian representative to the United Nations on 11 November, the normally calm Pearson "blew up," knowing that he had been put "in a very difficult, indeed an impossible position."[39] Canada's new pride in its international role was about to receive a severe blow. After an embarrassing delay while the Queen's Own waited in Halifax, the government was forced to announce that initially the Canadian contingent would carry out only administrative duties. The Queen's Own would not be required until an unspecified later time – which, as it turned out, never came. The battalion returned to Calgary in December. General Burns had formally requested administrative personnel, and Pearson always insisted that Egyptian demands had nothing to do with the change. However, the story was generally viewed as a convenient fiction.[40]

Journalists and readers alike expressed their outrage and dismay. "Are we ... going to take off our hat and bow low before Mr. Nasser[?] ... If some of our leaders had a hundredth part as much steel in their back bones, as they have the gift of gab in their tongues, we would stuff Nasser's 'conditions' right down his throat," raged the author of a letter to the *Toronto Star.*[41] The *Saskatoon Star-Phoenix* thought it was an "absurdity" for Canada and the UN to let Egypt "act as if it were the conqueror dictating terms."[42] As the members of the cabinet ruefully admitted when they met on 20 November, there was a growing view that the British had been right about Nasser and that Canada's refusal to support them had inadvertently contributed to maintaining an unreasonable dictator in power.[43] *Saturday Night* initially dismissed the furor over the Queen's Own as "a petulant expression of childish pride," but a few weeks later the same journal observed with regret that the much-heralded international peacekeeping force might turn out to be "nothing more than a shabby symbol of UN impotence."[44]

A special session of Parliament was required to approve the funds for Canada's contingent, thus providing an opportunity for the Conservatives to express their views. When the session opened on 26 November the atmosphere was tense. The ensuing Conservative attack might not have been particularly effective if St. Laurent had not quickly lost his temper when the Opposition raised questions about the role of US policy in causing the crisis, about his government's apparent condemnation of Britain, and about the delay in sending the Queen's Own. Throughout the crisis, the prime minister had been testy and sardonic when speaking with the press.[45] Now he exploded in an angry diatribe, referring to Britain and France as the "supermen of Europe" who thought they could dominate the world but whose time had passed.[46] One shocked journalist described his remarks as "by turns self-righteous, superior and vicious."[47] Another thought that St. Laurent's ill-timed departure from his usual restrained manner was "painful" to watch.[48]

Pearson did a much better job of explaining the government's policy and its belief that UN intervention was the best way to help Britain and France out of an untenable position. However, he, too, lost his temper during a speech by Conservative MP Howard Green. Green predicted that, as the ultimate outcome of Suez, the US would replace Britain as the dominant power in the Middle East (which indeed proved to be the case),[49] and he suggested that the Americans were deliberately manoeuvring to produce such an outcome. Green then accused the government of "being the United States chore boy" in this endeavour.[50] Red-faced with anger, St. Laurent had already interrupted several times; Green responded by "flapping his arms and making furious punching motions, mocking the Prime Minister."[51] Pearson replied to the "chore boy" remark, but his words were no better chosen than his leader's. "It is bad to be a chore boy of the United States," he said heatedly. "It is equally bad to be a colonial chore boy running around shouting, 'Ready, aye, ready.'"[52] The outbursts by St. Laurent and Pearson made a strong impression on the public, leading many to believe that the government had indeed acted out of subservience to American interests.

"Has the public mind in Canada ... ever been more confused than during these past four weeks?" wondered Maxwell Cohen in the *Montreal Gazette*.[53] After the first few days of the special session, newspaper support for the Liberals declined noticeably, though it remained strong in such papers as the *Toronto Star* and the *Winnipeg Free Press*. Diefenbaker performed extremely well in the debates, eschewing violent attacks on the government and instead framing his criticism in terms of the damage done to the Western alliance. Soviet ambitions in the Middle East, he argued, made the situation there "too dangerous to permit of our placing ourselves in the position of being judges of the action taken by Britain, France and Israel." With regard to St. Laurent's "supermen" comment, Diefenbaker observed with careful restraint that such "condemnation of those nations which have stood for freedom for generations should not have fallen from the lips of a man who enjoys the respect the Prime Minister does."[54] His tone throughout was that of one who spoke more in deep and heartfelt sorrow than in anger.

Diefenbaker's well-received speech made his victory in the Conservative leadership race seem like a certainty, and he was indeed triumphant at the party convention, held on 15 December. He was acclaimed not only by Conservative papers but by such publications as the *Halifax Chronicle-Herald*, which had been steadfast in its admiration for Pearson throughout the crisis itself. In contrast to St. Laurent and Pearson, with their reputed close ties to Washington, Diefenbaker appeared as a determined, yet calm and reasonable, nationalist who could be counted on to defend Canada's independence.

Meanwhile, the views of Liberal supporters were neatly summed up in a Les Callan cartoon that appeared in the *Toronto Star* on 28 November with the title "The Right Road is Straight Ahead."[55] The members of St. Laurent's government arrive at a crossroads and unhesitatingly proceed forward on "Nationhood Avenue," ignoring the two side roads labelled "Chore Boy for U.K." and "Chore Boy for U.S.A." Such assurances that Canada was on the way to true independence were reinforced by articles describing the status enjoyed by Pearson at the UN. "Canada is almost a magic word here," reported Grant Dexter from New York.[56] But for many, even Pearson's new worldwide renown was not enough. The *Globe and Mail* complained that the United States had "encouraged the UN to accept terms from Egypt which destroyed both the strength and the freedom of the UN police force to do the job assigned to it." According to the *Globe*, "Not since the early years of the First World War has the United States been in such low esteem among the people of Canada." Whether Ottawa liked it or not, the newspaper argued, there had to be a reassessment of Canada-United States relations.[57]

Pearson's response to this widespread questioning of the Liberals' closeness to Washington was not well calculated to increase his popularity. When the new parliamentary session opened in January, he remarked that "to formulate ... foreign policies which do not take into account the closeness of all the ties which link us – and must do so – to the United States, would surely be nothing but unrealistic and unprofitable jingoism."[58] Later, in an interview given a few weeks before the 1957 election and printed a month after it, Pearson was even more blunt. "We have to readjust ourselves to this new situation in which the United States is even more dominant in the free world than it ever was before," he admitted.[59]

Such frank realism was unappealing to some journalists. As one tartly observed in the *Globe and Mail*: "One would think that as we grew stronger, wealthier, and more highly regarded in the world, we would find it easier to disagree with the U.S., if we so desired ... But Mr. Pearson puts it just the opposite way. We are now, he tells us, in a situation which makes any such disagreement virtually impossible."[60] In the *Winnipeg Free Press*, Tom Kent mused on the possibility of what he called "a third way." In Kent's view, the solution did not lie in a purely negative rejection of American influence; instead, both the politicians and the people must work to develop Canada's economy and its distinctive culture.[61] Since Britain could no longer serve as a counterweight to the US, Canada must either become stronger in itself or lose its independence.

The question, then, was whether the Liberals could provide the necessary vision and leadership or whether they were too set in a continentalist pattern. If they could not or would not keep Canada out of the satellite role, Diefenbaker appeared to be Canada's best hope of finding the right road. The new Conservative leader did not indulge in excessive amounts of anti-American rhetoric during the election campaign, which began in April 1957; instead, he held out to voters the prospect of some as yet undefined third way that would lead to greater national maturity and independence. He could thus appeal both to citizens whose anti-American feelings were intense and to those who simply wanted Canada to be bound neither to London nor to Washington.

Diefenbaker always maintained that the Conservatives were pro-Canadian rather than anti-American.[62] Despite occasional hits at Washington in his campaign speeches, he preferred broad statements that he was "fighting ... to preserve Canada for Canadians."[63] The *Chronicle-Herald* accordingly praised his "spirit of true Canadianism" and his "keen sense of changing needs for his country." Diefenbaker's goal, the paper informed its readers, was "a stronger, more united Canada with its bountiful resources put to work for the good of all and with its voice speaking out clearly and courageously and with wisdom in world affairs."[64] And, even though Suez in itself was never a major campaign issue, Conservative papers like the *Calgary Herald* frequently reminded readers that St. Laurent and Pearson were "always in a hurry to echo U.S. policies ... The Liberal government is willing to cringe in the shadow of its big brother, a new colonialism but colonialism nevertheless."[65]

The Liberals ran a lacklustre campaign. "The administration appears as it really is – tired, unimaginative and relying on hidden prompters," commented the *Winnipeg Tribune*.[66] The *Free Press* complained about St. Laurent's "pedestrian" performance and his "ghost-written speeches, woodenly worded and mechanically read." Pearson provided a welcome respite from this dullness when he energetically defended his Suez policy during a speech in Victoria, but overall he was not an exciting performer on the hustings.[67] The Liberals were further hampered by lingering public resentment about their use of closure in the May–June 1956 pipeline debate. Despite the lack of a single compelling campaign issue around which they could rally, the Conservatives had the advantage of appearing dynamic and favourable to new approaches, while the Liberals seemed merely to offer a continuation of the rather stultifying status quo.[68] On 10 June 1957 the Conservatives were victorious, but they did not obtain a majority.

Only eight months later, in February 1958, another election campaign began. This time, the lines were much more clearly drawn. Each party put forward a distinctive platform, with firm promises of change that would increase national prestige and pride.[69] St. Laurent had retired after the 1957 defeat, and Pearson, the new Liberal leader (who had been awarded the Nobel Peace Prize in December 1957), tried to play to his strengths by emphasizing Canada's potential role as a peacemaker on the international scene. Only an experienced statesman, the Liberals claimed, could guide Canada to new eminence. The slogan "Pearson for Peace" was prominently displayed at Liberal meetings, and Pearson himself introduced the issue at every opportunity.[70]

On the Conservative side, US economic dominance was mentioned often and unfavourably enough to remind some journalists of Robert Borden's "no truck nor trade with the Yankees" crusade against Sir Wilfrid Laurier's Liberals and their proposed reciprocity agreement with the US during the 1911 election.[71] However, there was little open or aggressive anti-Americanism; instead, Diefenbaker's Northern Vision stood front and centre, beginning with the prime minister's first campaign speech in Winnipeg on 12 February. Both then and later, the response was rapturous.

Through the Northern Vision, Diefenbaker promised innovation on both the domestic and the international levels. According to the Conservatives, developing northern resources would provide much-needed jobs (on domestic matters, unemployment was the main Liberal point of attack), but it would do far more than that. It would give Canadians the prosperity they needed to take control of their own destiny. Like the development of western resources under Sir John A. Macdonald's National Policy, it would revitalize the life of the nation. "I want to see Canadians given a transcending sense of national purpose," Diefenbaker declared. "This party has become the party of national destiny."[72] "The Northern Vision" was simply a more inspiring name for the third way, and northern development seemed to offer the possibility of a sound economic basis for a politically and culturally independent Canada.

In response, Pearson offered a detailed plan for world peace, calling for a speedy end to nuclear weapons tests. The *Winnipeg Free Press* loyally suggested that, under Pearson, Canada could take the lead in rebuilding and revitalizing the North Atlantic alliance. According to the *Free Press*, it was "only within such a community that this country can realize the peace and progress, the growth and greatness that we all want for Canada. This is the real Canadian vision."[73] Liberal candidate Jean Lesage further argued that, if the Conservatives had been in power at the time of Suez, Canada might have gone to war at Britain's side.[74] However, such claims were easily brushed aside by the observation that all parties in Canada were in favour of peace. The Liberal proposals could not compete with the Northern Vision. "To vote for the Conservative Government is ... to vote, at one time, both for a secure future and for an adventurous one, both for enjoyed stability and for enjoyable progress," enthused the *Globe and Mail*.[75] "Mr. Diefenbaker has touched something in the innermost hearts of millions of Canadians ... They want their country to grow mighty, and they want their Canadian identity not only preserved but burnished to an even greater brilliance," agreed the *Calgary Herald*.[76]

To add to the Liberals' woes, anti-American feelings were given a boost near the end of the campaign when the United Auto Workers union revealed that Washington had imposed its foreign assets control regulations on Ford of Canada, blocking the sale of Canadian-made vehicles to the People's Republic of China.[77] "Parent company executives in the U.S. are threatened with imprisonment and fines if their Canadian plants export automobiles to Mainland China. Submission by Canada to this pressure would involve more than the loss of some trade. A substantial and vital part of our sovereignty also would be lost," fumed the *Globe and Mail*.[78] A letter to the editor called it "an edict equal in arrogance to any that Russia has issued to a satellite state." According to the writer, "Canada's task during the next decade is to regain her independence ... and undoubtedly John Diefenbaker is the man who would best do the job."[79]

On 31 March 1958, the Conservatives won the largest majority in Canadian history up to that time. Amid all the rhetoric surrounding the Northern Vision, the disputes over Suez had faded into the past, yet the crisis and its aftermath clearly played a part in both the 1957 and the 1958 victories. It was Suez that made the Canadian public acutely aware of just how dominant the

US had become in the postwar world. Without this realization, the appeal of Diefenbaker's northern development policy would not have been so intense. Most Canadians, including Diefenbaker himself, conceived of the national- ist "right road," or "third way," as positive and constructive – the building of a stronger Canada, rather than the mere rejection of US influence. Diefen- baker was more than willing to work with the United States, and, as Greg Donaghy demonstrates in the next chapter, he put considerable effort into developing a good relationship with President Dwight D. Eisenhower. Yet an element of anti-Americanism remained latent in his thinking, and it would have major consequences in the years after 1960.

NOTES

I would like to thank Greg Donaghy and Norman Hillmer for their comments on this chapter. The views expressed are my own and do not represent the views of Global Affairs Canada.

1 "Ring in the New," *Globe and Mail*, 1 January 1957. It should be noted that the author of this piece seriously downplayed the role of US diplomats at the United Nations during the Suez Crisis.
2 "This Independence," *Halifax Chronicle-Herald*, 21 January 1957.
3 Maxwell Cohen, "A New Responsibility in Foreign Policy," *Saturday Night*, 19 Janu- ary 1957, 5–6, 28.
4 Tom Kent, "The American Boom in Canada (6): Nationalism Collides with the Boom," *Winnipeg Free Press*, 22 January 1957. On the origins of nationalist concerns about American investment, see Stephen Azzi, "Foreign Investment and the Paradox of Economic Nationalism," in *Canadas of the Mind: The Making and Unmaking of Can- adian Nationalisms in the Twentieth Century*, ed. Norman Hillmer and Adam Chap- nick (Montreal and Kingston: McGill-Queen's University Press, 2007), 63–88, on 69–70.
5 Bruce Hutchison, "Taking Pen in Hand," *Ottawa Citizen*, 24 January 1957. Despite the important role of the Suez Crisis as a catalyst for the expression of the ideas de- scribed in this paragraph, there had been earlier calls to rethink Canada's foreign policy. For example, see J.H. Stewart Reid, "Canada: Divided Nation without a Policy," *Saturday Night*, 10 November 1956, 7–8. This article, although published in the early stages of the crisis, was likely written just before it.
6 "Suez: An Assessment," *Canadian Forum* 36 (December 1956): 193.
7 Letter from Murray M. Philpott, *Toronto Star*, 6 November 1956; letter from Linda K. Randal, *Montreal Gazette*, 21 December 1956.
8 According to R.A. Farquharson, the information officer at the Canadian embassy in Washington, Canadian correspondents who wrote reports favourable to the United States were strongly criticized by their editors, and in many cases the stories were not printed. See Greg Donaghy, ed., *Documents on Canadian External Relations*, vol. 22, *1956–57*, pt. 1 (Ottawa: Department of Foreign Affairs and International Trade, 2001) (hereafter *DCER*, vol. 22), doc. 206, enclosure 2.

9   See James Eayrs, "Canadian Policy and Opinion during the Suez Crisis," *International Journal* 12, 2 (1957): 102, 107; and J.H. Aitchison, "Canadian Foreign Policy in the House and on the Hustings," *International Journal* 12, 4 (1957): 274. For a sampling of hostile press commentary on Dulles in the aftermath of the crisis, see "Dulles in the Doghouse," *Ottawa Citizen*, 2 February 1957; and "Mr. Dulles Has Certainly Changed All That," *Calgary Herald*, 29 April 1957. Dulles's role in the crisis and his anti-British reputation are assessed in Wm. Roger Louis, "An American Volcano in the Middle East: John Foster Dulles and the Suez Crisis," in *Ends of British Imperialism: The Scramble for Empire, Suez and Decolonization*, 639–64 (London and New York: I.B. Tauris, 2006).

10 Letter from W.D. Hamer, *Globe and Mail*, 1 December 1956; letter from Hugh M. Scott, *Montreal Gazette*, 4 December 1956.

11 José E. Igartua, *The Other Quiet Revolution: National Identities in English Canada, 1945–71* (Vancouver: UBC Press, 2006), 115. Like Igartua, most Canadian historians have seen the changes in English-Canadian nationalism after Suez primarily as a rejection of Britain. Christian Champion also overlooks the anti-Americanism factor in the response to Suez. See Christian P. Champion, *The Strange Demise of British Canada: The Liberals and Canadian Nationalism, 1964–68* (Montreal and Kingston: McGill-Queen's University Press, 2010), 23, 132, 199–200. Cara Spittal mentions anti-Americanism briefly but does not develop the theme. See Cara Spittal, "The Diefenbaker Moment" (PhD diss., University of Toronto, 2011), 260–61.

The major Canadian studies dealing with the crisis itself are Donald Creighton, *The Forked Road: Canada 1939–1957* (Toronto: McClelland and Stewart, 1976); Robert Bothwell, Ian Drummond, and John English, *Canada since 1945: Power, Politics, and Provincialism* (Toronto: University of Toronto Press, 1981); John W. Holmes, *The Shaping of Peace: Canada and the Search for World Order, 1943–1957*, vol. 2 (Toronto: University of Toronto Press, 1982); John English, *The Worldly Years: The Life of Lester Pearson*, vol. 2 (Toronto: Knopf Canada, 1992); Geoffrey Pearson, *Seize the Day: Lester B. Pearson and Crisis Diplomacy* (Ottawa: Carleton University Press, 1993); Norman Hillmer and J.L. Granatstein, *Empire to Umpire: Canada and the World to the 1990s*, 1st ed. (Toronto: Copp Clark Longman, 1994), rev. ed. (Toronto: Nelson, 2008); John Hilliker and Donald Barry, *Canada's Department of External Affairs*, vol. 2 (Ottawa: Institute of Public Administration of Canada/McGill-Queen's University Press, 1995); John Hilliker and Greg Donaghy, "Canadian Relations with the United Kingdom at the End of Empire, 1956–73," in *Canada and the End of Empire*, ed. Phillip Buckner, 25–46 (Vancouver: UBC Press, 2004); Michael Carroll, *Pearson's Peacekeepers: Canada and the United Nations Emergency Force, 1956–67* (Vancouver: UBC Press, 2009); Anthony Anderson, *The Diplomat: Lester Pearson and the Suez Crisis* (Fredericton: Goose Lane, 2015).

The standard international works on the crisis are Elizabeth Monroe, *Britain's Moment in the Middle East, 1914–1971*, 2nd ed. (London: Chatto and Windus, 1981); Wm. Roger Louis and Roger Owen, eds., *Suez 1956: The Crisis and Its Consequences* (Oxford: Clarendon, 1989); Keith Kyle, *Suez: Britain's End of Empire in the Middle East* (London and New York: I.B. Tauris, 2001); Robert McNamara, *Britain, Nasser and the Balance of Power in the Middle East, 1952–1967* (London and

Portland: Frank Cass, 2003); D.K. Fieldhouse, *Western Imperialism in the Middle East, 1914–1958* (Oxford and New York: Oxford University Press, 2006).

12 John W. Holmes, *The Better Part of Valour: Essays on Canadian Diplomacy* (Toronto: McClelland and Stewart, 1970), 40.

13 On the definition of "anti-Americanism," see Peter J. Katzenstein and Robert O. Keohane, "Varieties of Anti-Americanism: A Framework for Analysis," in *Anti-Americanisms in World Politics,* ed. Katzenstein and Keohane (Ithaca, NY: Cornell University Press, 2007), 9–38.

14 For example, see Aitchison, "Canadian Foreign Policy," 285–87; John Meisel, *The Canadian General Election of 1957* (Toronto: University of Toronto Press, 1962), 55–59; and James Eayrs, *The Commonwealth and Suez: A Documentary Survey* (London and New York: Oxford University Press, 1964), 383–85.

15 Dale C. Thomson, *Louis St. Laurent, Canadian* (Toronto: Macmillan, 1967), 519. Despite such polls, Liberal cabinet minister Jack Pickersgill thought that Suez "was perhaps the deepest emotional issue and may well have lost more seats than any other single cause." See J.W. Pickersgill, *My Years with Louis St. Laurent: A Political Memoir* (Toronto: University of Toronto Press, 1975), 322.

16 On the concept of anti-Americanism and its complicated relationship with Canadian nationalism, see Norman Hillmer, "Are Canadians Anti-Americans?" *Policy Options* 27, 6 (2006), at http://irpp.org/po; and Greg Donaghy, *Tolerant Allies: Canada and the United States, 1963–1968* (Montreal and Kingston: McGill-Queen's University Press, 2002). Hillmer and Donaghy point out that popular anti-Americanism during the 1960s had little effect on either the close political relationship between Ottawa and Washington or the growing cultural similarities between the two countries. However, the government had to come to terms with the public's need to believe in Canada's independence and cultural uniqueness. In response, it produced the potent new national symbols described by Igartua.

17 Maxwell Cohen, "National Politics and Foreign Affairs," *Saturday Night,* 29 March 1958, 38.

18 "A Motivational Research Study on the Issues of Paramount Interest to Canadian Voters," October 1960, Library and Archives Canada (hereafter LAC), Lester B. Pearson Papers, MG 26 N-1, vol. 106.

19 See especially Jocelyn Maynard Ghent, "Canadian-American Relations and the Nuclear Weapons Controversy, 1958–1963" (PhD diss., University of Illinois at Urbana-Champaign, 1976); J.L. Granatstein, *Canada 1957–1967: The Years of Uncertainty and Innovation* (Toronto: McClelland and Stewart, 1986); Erika Simpson, *NATO and the Bomb: Canadian Defenders Confront Critics* (Montreal and Kingston: McGill-Queen's University Press, 2001); and Patricia McMahon, *Essence of Indecision: Diefenbaker's Nuclear Policy, 1957–1963* (Montreal and Kingston: McGill-Queen's University Press, 2009).

20 Pearson to Hume Wrong, 16 April 1951, LAC, Pearson Papers, MG 26 N-1, vol. 17.

21 *Canadian Forum,* vol. 36 (September 1956): 125.

22 Pickersgill, *My Years,* 313.

23 Letters from Kenneth Ingram and Alan K. Bethune, *Globe and Mail,* 16 October 1956.

24 Eden to St. Laurent, 30 October 1956, *DCER,* vol. 22, doc. 110.

25 St. Laurent to Eden, 31 October 1956, *DCER*, vol. 22, doc. 113.

26 *Toronto Star*, 1 November 1956.

27 Letter from E.J. Taber, *Toronto Star*, 1 November 1956.

28 "The Shameful Day That Canada Ran Out," *Calgary Herald*, 1 November 1956.

29 Reprinted in *Toronto Star*, 3 November 1956.

30 "Be Fair to Britain," *Winnipeg Free Press*, 1 November 1956.

31 Norman Campbell, "Which Way Canada?" *Ottawa Citizen*, 2 November 1956.

32 *Montreal Gazette*, 5 November 1956.

33 "Canada's Lead," *Halifax Chronicle-Herald*, 5 November 1956.

34 "Mr. Pearson's Achievement," *Ottawa Citizen*, 7 November 1956.

35 For example, see letter from P. Rhodes, *Winnipeg Free Press*, 7 November 1956.

36 "Suez and Commonwealth," *Manchester Guardian*, 7 November 1956.

37 "The Canadian Who Will Command," *Montreal Gazette*, 9 November 1956.

38 On the initial publicity and excitement over the Queen's Own, see the comments by the interim Conservative leader, Earl Rowe. Canada, House of Commons, *Debates*, Special Session, 1956–57, 15–16.

39 John A. Munro and Alex I. Inglis, eds., *Mike: The Memoirs of the Right Honourable Lester B. Pearson*, vol. 2, *1948–1957* (Toronto: University of Toronto Press, 1973), 262.

40 For example, see "Canada's UNEF Contribution," *Ottawa Citizen*, 12 December 1956; and "The Troops That Never Sailed," *Montreal Gazette*, 14 December 1956.

41 Letter from V.B.R., *Toronto Star*, 21 November 1956.

42 Reprinted in *Globe and Mail*, 24 November 1956. There are similar comments from many other papers in this survey of press opinion.

43 Cabinet Conclusions, 20 November 1956, *DCER*, vol. 22, doc. 170.

44 "Misdirected Anger," *Saturday Night*, 8 December 1956, 6; "Police Force," *Saturday Night*, 22 December 1956, 5.

45 See George Bain, "Minding Your Business," *Globe and Mail*, 2 November 1956.

46 Canada, House of Commons, *Debates*, Special Session, 1956–57, 20.

47 George Bain, "Minding Your Business," *Globe and Mail*, 28 November 1956.

48 "Painful Departure," *Montreal Gazette*, 28 November 1958.

49 See Tore T. Petersen, *The Middle East between the Great Powers: Anglo-American Conflict and Cooperation, 1952–7* (Basingstoke: Macmillan, 2000); and Wm. Roger Louis, "American Anti-Colonialism, Suez, and the Special Relationship," in Louis, *Ends of British Imperialism*, 589–608.

50 Canada, House of Commons, *Debates*, Special Session, 1956–57, 51.

51 Bain, "Minding," 28 November.

52 Canada, House of Commons, *Debates*, Special Session, 1956–57, 51.

53 Maxwell Cohen, "The Burdens of Morality," *Montreal Gazette*, 3 December 1956.

54 Canada, House of Commons, *Debates*, Special Session, 1956–57, 140, 149.

55 *Toronto Star*, 28 November 1956.

56 Grant Dexter, "Why Canada Stands High: Mr. Pearson's Objective Achieved," *Winnipeg Free Press*, 26 November 1956.

57 "The Retreat from Suez," *Globe and Mail*, 30 November 1956. See also Audrey M. Ashley, "Colony or Nation?" *Ottawa Citizen*, 1 December 1956.

58 Canada, House of Commons, *Debates*, 1957, vol. 1, 179.

59 "Where Canada Stands in the World Crisis," *Maclean's*, 6 July 1957, 14.

60 "The Canadian Policy," *Globe and Mail*, 16 January 1957.

61 Tom Kent, "The American Boom in Canada (7): The Way to Stay Canadian," *Winnipeg Free Press*, 23 January 1957.

62 For example, see Diefenbaker, "Great Issues in the Anglo-Canadian-American Community," an address at Dartmouth College, 7 September 1957, Canada, Department of External Affairs, *Statements and Speeches*, No. 1957/30; John Diefenbaker, *One Canada: Memoirs of the Right Honourable John G. Diefenbaker – The Years of Achievement, 1957–1962* (Toronto: Macmillan, 1976), 73.

63 For example, see Clark Davey, "Diefenbaker Receives His Greatest Acclaim in Vancouver Overflow," *Globe and Mail*, 24 May 1957.

64 "A Great Challenge," *Halifax Chronicle-Herald*, 15 December 1956.

65 "Mr. St. Laurent and the Straw Men," *Calgary Herald*, 6 June 1957; "Unity?" *Calgary Herald*, 1 May 1957.

66 Reprinted in *Ottawa Citizen*, 18 May 1957.

67 "Victoria Off Its Feet: Mr. Pearson Takes Fire," *Winnipeg Free Press*, 21 May 1957. For an overview of other occasions on which Suez was mentioned, see Eayrs, *Commonwealth and Suez*, 383–85.

68 For the Liberals' exceptionally meagre platform, see D. Owen Carrigan, *Canadian Party Platforms, 1867–1968* (Toronto: Copp Clark, 1968), 224.

69 Carrigan, *Party Platforms*, 242–55.

70 "Not a Party Issue," *Globe and Mail*, 12 March 1958.

71 "Canada's Election and the U.S.," *Ottawa Citizen*, 26 February 1958.

72 Diefenbaker, "A New Vision," at www.canadahistory.com/sections/documents/Primeministers/diefenbaker. Diefenbaker had put forward similar proposals in 1957, but they received relatively little attention at that time. On the origins of the Northern Vision platform, see Diefenbaker, *One Canada*, 10–13; and Denis Smith, *Rogue Tory: The Life and Legend of John G. Diefenbaker* (Toronto: Macfarlane Walter and Ross, 1995), 224–27.

73 "A Plan for Peace," *Winnipeg Free Press*, 19 March 1958. See also "Mr. Pearson's Peace Plan," *Ottawa Citizen*, 20 March 1958.

74 "The Old, Sour Song," *Globe and Mail*, 20 March 1958.

75 "Only One Issue," *Globe and Mail*, 25 March 1958.

76 "The Decision," *Calgary Herald*, 29 March 1958.

77 Though this was not the first incident of its kind, it was the most important because of the timing. Later in 1958, Washington agreed that Canadian subsidiaries of US companies could export their goods to communist countries, provided that the sale was approved by Ottawa. See LAC, RG 25, vol. 7589, file 11045-H-40.

78 "Intolerable, Inexcusable," *Globe and Mail*, 24 March 1958.

79 Letter from H.M. Tandy, *Globe and Mail*, 28 March 1958.

4

When the Chips Are Down
Eisenhower, Diefenbaker, and the Lebanon Crisis, 1958

GREG DONAGHY

John Diefenbaker remains a polarizing figure in Canadian history. At an event in 2014 celebrating Diefenbaker's legacy, Conservative foreign minister John Baird enthusiastically praised him as "a leader whom I've long admired." He was, said Baird, a politician who "spoke with clarity and conviction," and who "was never on the side of wrong."[1] Carleton professor Andrew Cohen immediately shot back. "History has dismissed and discarded Diefenbaker," he raged. Cohen, like most of the prime minister's critics, fingered his inept handling of Canada's all-important ties with Washington as his besetting sin. "Anti-American in instinct," he wrote, Diefenbaker "declined to support the US during the Cuban Missile Crisis and refused to honour Canada's commitment to NORAD ... John F. Kennedy, who loathed him, called him a liar and blackmailer."[2]

Diefenbaker's poor relations with Kennedy have cast a shadow backwards, obscuring his US diplomacy during the first three years of his tenure from 1957 to 1960, when President Dwight Eisenhower sat in the White House and bilateral exchanges ran more smoothly. Historians have tended to treat the period as a prelude to the real history to come, while emphasizing Eisenhower's skill at taming the cranky Canadian. H.B. Robinson's account of Diefenbaker's foreign policy, for instance, credits the harmonious partnership with Washington to Eisenhower's "conciliatory genius."[3] Journalist Knowlton Nash echoes that judgment. "Diefenbaker," he writes, "succumbed readily to the combination of Eisenhower's charm, flattery, and considerateness, and to his own hero-worship."[4] Historian Robert Bothwell is even more dismissive, insisting that Diefenbaker was simply "mesmerized" by the American.[5] Asa McKercher's recent study of Canada-US relations in 1958 reflects this dominant narrative in its title, "Dealing with Diefenbaker."[6]

There is certainly much to commend this view. As Canada-US relations soured in the mid-1950s, marred by trade disputes and bitter recriminations over internal security, Diefenbaker rode into office on a wave of nationalist resentment. Prosperous, strong, and confident, perhaps even a little innocent in its expectations, the US responded tolerantly. "Canada of necessity has been on the tail of the kite," US Ambassador to Canada Douglas Stuart wrote his boss, Secretary of State John Foster Dulles, in May 1956. "We as a nation have been inclined to take Canada for granted. This I think is a mistake."[7] By the spring of 1958, Congress, the State Department, and the National Security Council were searching for ways to "improve our political and economic relations with Canada."[8]

By far the most important influence on US policy, however, was the president himself. Eisenhower was justifiably proud of his successful role as an Allied commander during the Second World War and of his capacity to manage the often outsized egos of generals and his political superiors, including de Gaulle, Churchill, and Roosevelt. The experience left him with one cardinal rule: "Don't pick fights with members of your own team."[9] Postwar exposure to American financial and economic heavyweights in New York sharpened his economic judgments. He refined his political skills further with a stint as NATO supreme commander at the height of the Cold War.

Eisenhower worked hard to win Diefenbaker's confidence, often handling the small details himself. There were warm birthday wishes and Christmas greetings, and personal notes written by hand. When the president wrote to allied leaders before his 1959 European tour, he held Diefenbaker's letter back, revising it himself to make it "a little more personal."[10] Similarly, he tracked Diefenbaker to a remote prairie hamlet in April 1958 to invite him to Washington, and when the Canadian demurred, Eisenhower readily agreed to go north. And after hearing that relations with Canada were fraying a little in April 1960, the president was soon on the phone, arranging a visit and "a little more of the red carpet treatment."[11]

There was substance behind the flattery. Canada caught Eisenhower's eye. He queried the State Department, for instance, about an editorial in the *New York Times* on Canadian concerns about US extra-territoriality, and he scolded defence officials for simply assuming Canadian assent to a decision on North American missile placements. "Have you ever asked them?" he demanded. He also resisted the State Department's inclination to exclude Canada from Anglo-American consultations. "We have a partnership over here," Eisenhower reminded acting secretary Christian Herter in March 1959.[12]

Eisenhower was not immune to the frustrations encountered by many who dealt with Diefenbaker. "When he sees him they agree," the president told British prime minister Harold Macmillan, "but when Mr. Diefenbaker speaks in public he blames America for all Canada's troubles."[13] Eisenhower found Diefenbaker's hesitations over nuclear weapons "disturbing,"[14] and he wondered why the prime minister did not simply use his "terrific majority" to "jam the hard realities down the throats of his people."[15] In the spring of 1960, Eisenhower confided, he "was distressed ... that a Liberal government in Canada seems more desirable ... than a Conservative government."[16]

Most of the time, however, the level-headed president rolled with the punches. He was untouched by panicked State Department warnings about "radical nationalism" in Canada, dismissing concerns over Diefenbaker's plan to divert Canadian trade to England. "Trade is conducted by the businessman," he shrugged, and a businessman "makes the deal where best he can."[17] "The whole [nationalist] issue was largely politics," he told the National Security Council a year later.[18] Indeed, when preparing to leave office, Eisenhower judiciously summed up his two-sided experience with the Canadian prime minister. "Diefenbaker was not difficult to deal with if he were kept informed in advance," he told his advisors, "even though he was inclined to make impetuous statements and then to refuse to modify them if they turned out to be wrong."[19]

The attention paid to Diefenbaker and Canada by the US and Eisenhower paid dividends. "The many evidences of your friendship to me will always be amongst the happiest of my memories," the Canadian fondly wrote in 1961. "I felt that we were friends – and as friends could speak with frankness regarding the problems of our two countries."[20] One of those problems was the Cold War crisis in Lebanon, which dominated the global agenda through the summer of 1958. The documentation clearly illustrates an entirely different dimension of Canada-US relations during the Eisenhower era. A temporary UN Security Council member when the crisis erupted, Ottawa was drawn into the search for solutions and forced to take sides. As the prospect of US military intervention increased, the search pitted

Diefenbaker's desire for good relations with Eisenhower against Canadian calculations of the broader strategic interest, which favoured a UN solution that limited Western exposure to the dangerous currents of the postcolonial Middle East. Harmoniously reconciling those demands required a nimble and sometimes courageous diplomacy not often associated with John Diefenbaker.

A former Ottoman and French imperial outpost, Lebanon emerged from French rule as an independent republic in 1943. Propped on the eastern edge of the Mediterranean, its postcolonial survival rested on a careful political compromise that preserved the country's fragile confessional balance, where Christians outnumbered Muslims by a ratio of six to five. Under its constitution, the president was a Christian, the prime minister was a Sunni Muslim, and the parliamentary speaker a Shi'ite Muslim.

Democratic and capitalist, moderate on Israeli-Palestine issues and fiercely anti-communist, Lebanon became an important US Cold War ally in the 1950s under President Camille Chamoun and his Harvard-educated foreign minister, Charles Malik.[21] Indeed, Lebanon was the only Arab state to embrace the "Eisenhower doctrine," which promised military and financial help to any Middle East country threatened by communist aggression. Many Arabs viewed the president's January 1957 declaration as an effort to bolster Western influence in the region and contain Egyptian president Gamal Nasser's popular pan-Arab nationalism.

As opposition to his pro-Western and anti-Nasser policies grew, Chamoun won the June 1957 parliamentary election with the help of bags of CIA cash. He was soon pressing for a constitutional amendment to allow him a second term as president, denouncing his outraged Muslim and Christian opponents as communists. When Egypt and Syria merged in early 1958 with loose Soviet backing to form the United Arab Republic (UAR), Chamoun linked Syrian and Egyptian nationalists with Soviet subversion. Spurred on by anti-Chamoun broadcasts from Cairo and Damascus, protesters took to the streets, and, by May, fighting had erupted in Tripoli and Beirut. The Lebanese president urged Washington to begin "forward planning" for military intervention.[22]

There were doubts in Washington. "Gun boat policy," Dulles and Eisenhower agreed, "no longer represented an acceptable practice."[23] Intervention would inflame anti-Western feeling, jeopardizing access to the Suez Canal and Middle East pipelines. However, with communist insurgents subverting pro-Western governments in South America and Asia, American credibility was clearly at stake. "If we did nothing," Dulles summed up, "we would have to accept heavy losses not only in Lebanon but elsewhere."[24] On 13 May, the US promised to send in the Marines under three conditions: Chamoun must seek UN help to resolve the crisis; he must obtain support from at least one other Arab state; and he must renounce his campaign for a second term.

Canada, five months into a two-year term on the UN Security Council and its president for May, watched with mounting concern. A range of considerations underpinned Canadian policy. Most important, Canadian policy-makers were unhappily conscious that they were "out of line" with their American and British counterparts over Western policy in the Middle East.[25] Since 1955, some of the best minds in External Affairs, including Norman Robertson, John Holmes, Jules Léger, and Robert Ford, had questioned the Anglo-American effort to keep the Soviet Union out of the Middle East with sweetheart arms deals and economic aid. The failure of Western diplomacy to either curb Arab-Israeli conflict or prevent Soviet meddling, argued Holmes, demanded "urgently desperate remedies."[26] This difference in view persisted in alliance discussions about including the Middle East in East-West summit talks. Ottawa thought it "absurd" to deny the USSR's "substantive interest" in the Middle East when Moscow "might be willing to negotiate.[27] "Perhaps," Léger even speculated, "our main goal should be to attempt to remove the whole area from Great Power contest, and insofar as possible, bring it under the aegis of the United Nations."[28] It was a view shared by Diefenbaker and his secretary of state for external affairs, Sidney Smith.

External Affairs was also concerned that murky Middle East politics were breeding suspicion and mistrust between its two closest allies, the US and the UK, raising memories of the recent Suez Crisis. "UK policy towards popular Arab movements tends to be rigid and inflexible," warned Ross Campbell, head of the department's Middle East Division, "whereas it is in the US interest to conciliate popular Arab nationalism."[29] This fear was reinforced by doubts about British and US transparency. When External Affairs carefully tracked Chamoun's campaign for UN Security Council support through US cables supplied to Ottawa, it became obvious that someone had misled Canada's Beirut representative, Paul Beaulieu, about the course of events.[30] "What is disturbing is the resentment which has grown up between us and the British over the Middle East – echoes of Suez involved," Canada's UN ambassador, Charles Ritchie, reflected in June. "They proceed by indirection, pretend to scruples, perhaps even feel them, but they do not count the full cost in the Middle East."[31]

Top officials in External Affairs also harboured doubts about knee-jerk Anglo-American opposition to pan-Arab nationalism. They thought that Washington and London undervalued Arab nationalism, which Ottawa accepted as a legitimate response to postwar decolonization.[32] These doubts extended to the crisis in Lebanon. The government and its advisors were sceptical of Chamoun's claims of external aggression. Despite hysterical reports from Whitehall, there was little hard evidence of subversion from the UAR. Veteran Canadian ambassadors in Cairo and Moscow R.M. Macdonnell and David Johnson, respectively, accepted Nasser's assurances that he would keep his "hands off Lebanon."[33] Nasser was not "under the thumb of the USSR," added Léger. Diefenbaker himself saw a crisis as the "likely outcome" of Chamoun's efforts to retain power.[34]

Diefenbaker, Smith, and their foreign policy advisors were united: Anglo-American intervention would be hard to support.[35] With only an indirect stake in the region as a contributor to the UN Emergency Force (UNEF) in Sinai, Canada looked to the UN to contain the crisis, which entered its second phase on 23 May, when Lebanon formally charged the UAR with aggression. Ritchie, who arrived in New York in January 1958, directed Canada's UN diplomacy. One of the country's most seasoned diplomats, Ritchie was known for his cultured intelligence, light touch, and retiring manner. An experienced UN hand, he was a conservative realist, who thought the UN provided a modest "framework for the resolution of problems or at least the papering-over of cracks and the averting of explosions."[36] In this case, his caution about the UN's capacity was reinforced by his unfamiliarity with the subject matter. "My ignorance of the Middle East makes it difficult for me to gauge Arab reactions," he complained.[37] As security council president, Ritchie slipped into the background to preserve "a certain flexibility of position."[38]

The Security Council met on 6 June and 10 June to debate the Lebanese complaint. Malik, a popular UN regular, presented Lebanon's case skilfully, marshalling an array of dates, names, and places to link the UAR with Lebanon's recent internal disturbances. The UAR's foreign minister, Omar Loufti, categorically denied the charges. Both the US and the UK made strong statements in support of Lebanon, pressing Canada for support.[39]

But Ritchie remained close-mouthed. According to Geoffrey Murray, his deputy, the delegation was conscious of being watched "to see whether we would play our usual independent and conciliatory role or whether we would obediently fall into line. Our performance on this case could not help but have some consequences for our relations with and reputation

amongst the uncommitted countries."[40] Equally important, Ritchie was playing nursemaid to Swedish efforts to frame a resolution for UN "observation"
machinery, a resolution that emerged over the course of 10 June. Stressing the UN's obligation to find "effective and practicable solutions," Canada enthusiastically backed the new UN Observation Group in Lebanon
(UNOGIL) as "wise and statesmanlike."[41] By the time the resolution passed
on 11 June (with the Soviet Union abstaining), UN secretary-general
Dag Hammarskjöld had a team in place, headed by Norwegian general
Odd Bull.[42]

The creation of UNOGIL sharpened Canadian policy, though it hardly
eased the government's anxieties. Ottawa immediately approved a UN request to redeploy Canadian army major G.D. Mitchell from the UN Truce
Supervision Organization in Palestine to Beirut. On 16 June, cabinet sent
another ten officers to help the UN ensure that no personnel or supplies
crossed the border between Syria and Lebanon.[43] At the same time, Smith
asked Macdonnell to press Cairo to restrain its radio broadcasts.[44]

As the week unfolded without political progress in Lebanon, Canadian
fears rose on a wave of renewed talk of US-UK military intervention. En
route home from Washington, British prime minister Harold Macmillan stopped in Ottawa to tell Diefenbaker that the "Anglo-American
guarantee ... stands."[45] There was also bad news from New York. Neither the
US nor the UK was being frank with the secretary-general, who was planning to travel to the Middle East, and the two delegations differed on how
an Anglo-American intervention might be cloaked under a UN umbrella.
The British especially underestimated the likely strain on the world body,
whose communist and non-aligned members would surely balk at recognizing an Anglo-American force as a UN agent. "We have reason to believe," Ritchie warned, "that some of our NATO partners, particularly the
Scandinavians, would not be able to support the USA and UK in the UN if
they intervened ... Such intervention would probably make their continued
participation in UNEF impossible and might even jeopardize their NATO
membership."[46]

"Irresponsible" talk of military intervention in Beirut was even more
alarming, reported Beaulieu. Military intervention into Lebanon's political
crisis, even at Chamoun's request, would be a "tragic error." Anglo-American
intervention would compromise what was left of Western influence and
shatter the UN's prestige in the Middle East.[47] Beaulieu urged Smith to
press his counterparts in Washington and London, as well as Canada's other
NATO allies, to let Hammarskjöld and the UN machinery do their work.

The minister, who saw the crisis as a crucial test of the UN's peacemaking ability, agreed.[48]

By the time Smith's instructions arrived in Washington and London, Canadian diplomats were pushing on open doors. Hammarskjöld's progress in resolving the conflict would clearly mean another round of Security Council talks, Dulles secretly told Chamoun.[49] Senior US officials cheerfully assured Robertson that they "agreed with every word" of Smith's statement.[50] In London, the Foreign Office's deputy undersecretary, Sir William Hayter, confidently estimated the odds of intervention at "a hundred to one against."[51] British foreign secretary Selwyn Lloyd, citing US communications with Chamoun, personally reassured Diefenbaker that "whatever we decide to do must now, therefore, clearly be presented in the UN framework."[52]

Yet there were still grounds for unease. British officials in Ottawa were anxious to know how Canada would react if UNOGIL could not meet the crisis and Chamoun presented London and Washington with an urgent demand for help. Neither Lloyd nor Dulles was pleased with the response. Ottawa would support a UNEF-like force for Lebanon provided it enjoyed support from two-thirds of UN member states. But, added Léger, Canada would not support Anglo-American intervention outside a UN framework.[53] Moreover, Diefenbaker, who approved this policy, wanted to defer a Security Council meeting indefinitely, making it clear that he would be guided by the secretary-general's views. When the prime minister later asked for the text of Dulles's letter to Chamoun, he set alarms ringing in Washington. "I have always sensed that the Canadian attitude in this matter was not very understanding and seemed to minimize the gravity of the consequences of 'letting Nasser smoothly acquire another province,'" Dulles wrote Lloyd. "Perhaps when I am in Ottawa with the President next week, I may have a chance to talk to Diefenbaker and Smith about this."[54]

Lebanon was far from the top of the agenda when the Americans arrived in Ottawa. In part, this reflected Hammarskjöld's success in defusing tensions during his mission to Lebanon, when he convinced Nasser to refrain from interfering and persuaded Chamoun to begin serious political talks. More important, it was a function of the visit's North American focus. A "social visit" intended primarily to "establish the same mutual confidence and close working relationship" that the White House had enjoyed with the previous Liberal government, the three days were heavy with photo-ops and light on substance.[55]

The two leaders had met twice before: in Washington during the October 1957 Royal Visit and at the NATO ministerial meetings in December 1957. There were grounds for an easy rapport between them. Progressive conservatives in outlook, they were of the same First World War and Depression generation, and shared a modest rural prairie upbringing, German ethnicity, and a love of fishing. "Eisenhower is a great man," Diefenbaker once declared, repeating the American's 1952 election slogan, "I like Ike."[56]

They continued to get along well in Ottawa, but there would be no speedy breakthrough in their relations. Trade with China, US import restrictions on lead and zinc, and continental defence dominated the short business sessions. Nonetheless, there was time for Lebanon. Eisenhower was briefed on Canadian hesitations, and in his opening *tour d'horizon* with Diefenbaker, he led off with Lebanon, pointing out the Soviet Union's "obvious intent" to make trouble in the Middle East.[57] Though Lebanon seemed "superficially" better, the US stood ready to fulfill its pledge to repel aggression. The prime minister offered "no divergence."[58]

The American tutorial helped stiffen Canadian backs just as the Middle East crisis entered its most dangerous phase in mid-July. On 14 July, left-wing nationalist officers deposed Iraq's pro-Western government, throwing the region into turmoil and prompting Chamoun to call for Anglo-American military support. Almost immediately, King Hussein of Jordan, in a loose federation with Iraq, demanded similar British support. Pro-Western leaders in Turkey, Iran, and Pakistan endorsed intervention. If the US and UK failed to respond, insisted Riyadh, "they are finished as powers in the Middle East."[59]

The US response was swift. Eisenhower had already decided to send in US forces, a decision reviewed by his senior foreign policy advisors in the morning and cleared with a bipartisan group of senators and congressman. By late afternoon, Eisenhower was on an open line with Macmillan coordinating their interventions. The British prime minister suggested a call to Diefenbaker.

At about 7:00 p.m., Eisenhower called Diefenbaker "to ask for help in [the] UN Security Council," which the US planned to summon in the morning to approve its intervention and to establish a UN force to protect Lebanon, allowing American forces to withdraw.[60] Diefenbaker backed the American president, and by the time they hung up the phone five minutes later, the two were "Ike" and "John," astounding the president's personal staff.[61] It remains unclear how strongly Diefenbaker expressed his support.

When US ambassador Livingston Merchant arrived at 24 Sussex Drive an hour later with a secret presidential message outlining US invasion plans and the Security Council proposal, he found Diefenbaker closeted with Smith and Léger. The latter two predicted that the US proposal would not win sufficient UN support either in the Security Council or in the General Assembly, stranding the American intervention outside a UN framework. They feared, too, for the safety of Canadian troops already in Lebanon and with the UNEF.

According to Merchant, Diefenbaker "impatiently brushed [them] aside," insisting that he had promised Eisenhower to support the US proposal. Later, Diefenbaker seemed to go even further. "I told the Prime Minister (and he confirmed)," recorded Merchant, "that I would report Prime Minister said Canada will support US action in Lebanon and intended proposal in SC."[62]

Diefenbaker was more circumspect the next morning. As the Security Council gathered in New York, his cabinet considered instructions for the Canadian representative. The prime minister told his colleagues that he had only promised to support the US in bringing the matter to the UN, to support further UN action, and to "show no opposition to US actions." As the US proposal was likely to be vetoed in the Security Council by the USSR and subsequently to fail to win General Assembly support, Smith explained that US intervention would be judged "a bilateral move," leaving Washington isolated. To avoid a Western defeat in Lebanon and the Middle East it was important to support the US proposal, while enlarging or maximizing its UN content. Canada could do this, the cabinet concluded, "by reconciling current UN action in the Lebanon with measures that might now be taken by the US and UK."[63] Canada's statement at the Security Council, which emphasized the "complementarity" of UN and US objectives, tried to do just that.[64] Certainly, it was enough for Eisenhower. "I cannot tell you," he wrote Diefenbaker that evening, "how deeply appreciative I am of your prompt and decisive action."[65]

The unhappy UN debate dragged out over the following week. It began badly when American ambassador Lodge introduced the US resolution on 16 July without consulting his Western colleagues. The Canadians were unamused, and they took a grim pleasure in watching Soviet ambassador Arkady Sobolev skilfully oppose the US motion.[66] Overnight, the Canadians went to work on the US draft, eventually finding language to indicate that the American action was "complementary – or perhaps even subordinate" to UNOGIL's, opening the way for the substitution of UN forces.[67]

And by the time it was clear that every resolution would be vetoed, Canada had joined Japan in crafting a motion to invite the UN secretary-general to strengthen UNOGIL "as a means to allow the US to withdraw." Should this, too, fail, Smith instructed the delegation, Canada should back a "consensus procedure" that would give Hammarskjöld the authority to act without UN approval. As anticipated, when the Japanese resolution was finally vetoed by the USSR on 22 July, the only hopeful sign was Hammarskjöld's indication that he would act on the sense of the debate and reinforce UNOGIL on his own.

While Ritchie fought to get the US out and to keep the UN in, Canadian fears that the crisis might spiral out of control built. Washington was feverish. "The situation was more serious than at any time since the end of World War II," Dulles told Smith, who rushed to the US capital for consultations on 18 July.[68] As US marines advanced into Beirut, Washington placed Canadian and American forces assigned to the North American Air Defence Command on "alert" status without the promised consultations with Ottawa, stoking Diefenbaker's fears about abandoning civilian control to the military.[69]

Nor was Moscow idle. On 17 July, the Soviet Union announced military exercises along its borders with Turkey and Iran. Top NATO strategists dismissed the move as routine, but it sent a spasm of fear through some of the alliance's smaller members, including Canada. "The question mark is," worried Johnson in Moscow, "what the USSR would do if negotiations in the UN or elsewhere for the withdrawal of US and UK troops break down. It would, I think, be dangerous to count on continued Soviet inaction."[70]

Already upset by London's failure to consult and surprised by its "very poor intelligence" on Iraq, Diefenbaker told cabinet that "the situation was very explosive."[71] Convinced that the views of the "smaller powers" and "world opinion" ought to be heard, Diefenbaker stirred into action when Soviet premier Nikita Khrushchev offered to attend a Security Council summit on Middle East issues. The British were keen, the French undecided, and the Americans sceptical. The DEA, however, judged the proposal attractive. The offer dropped Moscow's long-standing demands for parity at the table and for a regional arms embargo, and it conceded UN and non-aligned representation.[72] Here was a chance not to be missed, and Diefenbaker resolved to give Washington a push. He unilaterally endorsed Moscow's summit in letters to Eisenhower, Macmillan, and Khrushchev. The object, Ottawa wired Canadian missions, "is to maintain the status quo while proceeding in the UN towards a solution of the Lebanese and Jordanian crises and at the same time opening the door to high level talks ... to reach some broader settlement of remaining Middle East problem."[73]

Washington was uncomfortably aware of its looming differences with Ottawa. Herter and Dulles urged Diefenbaker to avoid discussing the possibility of East-West conflict as likely to undercut American insistence on the West's peaceful intentions. But Khrushchev's initiative had generated a chorus of voices within NATO urging Washington to pursue more forthcoming policies. In late July, a frustrated Merchant upbraided Léger for the alliance's "sad state." The normally mild-mannered undersecretary bristled: "Consultation on the Middle East during the last two or three years had *followed* decisions by the Great Powers but had not *preceded* them ... If ... the Alliance was 'in a sad state' on this particular issue ... the Great Powers had to bear the main responsibility."[74]

Washington and Moscow bickered over a summit for another week before agreeing to convene a special session of the UN General Assembly to handle the Middle East crisis. The organization's third special session opened on 8 August, but then adjourned until 13 August, when it got down to work.

This was Smith's moment to shine. A prominent Progressive Conservative, Smith was president of the University of Toronto when Diefenbaker named him secretary of state for external affairs on 9 September 1957. Though smart, energetic, urbane, and charming, he was a political rookie. Fair-minded but lacking international experience, Smith's balanced efforts invited the Liberal Opposition to mock him for nailing "his colours firmly to both sides of the fence." He was hurt, too, by the lack of a close and trusting relationship with the prime minister.[75] However, he did well at the spring 1958 NATO ministerial meetings, and the Americans welcomed his "friendly" willingness to pursue "intelligent and positive" solutions.[76]

Smith arrived in New York primed for action. Before leaving Ottawa, he had been in touch with Norway's foreign minister, Halvard Lange. Fearful that the UN meeting might degenerate into a nasty East-West confrontation, they agreed to canvass ideas to convert "a sterile propaganda battle" into "a constructive negotiation."[77] Smith refused to endorse Eisenhower's opening statement calling for an Arab development bank and a stand-by UN peacekeeping force. It focused "too often, too obviously" on the Arab role in regional conflict, rendering Canadian support "premature and unwise."[78] Instead, Smith toyed with resolutions to restrain the Mid-East arms trade and to "freeze" the region's status quo in order to force "a necessary minimum of cooperation between the Great Powers."[79] However, when the

Soviet Union announced its support for an amended version of the Japanese resolution vetoed three weeks earlier, British foreign secretary Selwyn Lloyd tempted Smith with much bigger fish: the prospect of "the major middle power initiative of the current Assembly."[80]

By mid-week, Smith, Hammarskjöld, and Norwegian deputy foreign minister Hans Engen had come up with a motion to defuse the Lebanon Crisis. Based on a US draft, the Norwegian-Canadian resolution asked the secretary-general to make arrangements enabling the UN to guarantee the "integrity and political independence" of Lebanon and Jordan and to make possible the withdrawal of Anglo-American forces.[81] Smith and Engen were unhappy with the US refusal to include a terminal date for withdrawal but practical enough to acknowledge that a viable motion required American support.[82] Soviet foreign minister Andrei Gromyko was dismissive, while India and the Afro-Asian bloc refused to participate. Still, Smith pressed ahead with his anemic seven-power resolution, issuing an "all-out plea for Great Power and small power support."[83]

Though support was tepid, the Norwegian-Canadian initiative had one happy result, spurring the Arab states to act alone. Overnight, they crafted their own resolution. Its preamble drew heavily on the language of the non-aligned movement to provide a framework for inter-Arab peace. Its operative paragraphs borrowed from the seven-power resolution but further strengthened the secretary-general's role and directed him to facilitate the US withdrawal.[84] It was, Smith rightly claimed, an "eminently satisfactory outcome" and the "evolution and fulfillment of the Norwegian-Canadian resolution."[85] It provided a concordat for peaceful Arab relations and a formula to oversee the US withdrawal. Most important, it preserved the UN's regional role. Others shared his assessment. He won a vote of thanks from Dulles and a celebratory dinner with Lloyd. "I am not ashamed of Canada's contribution," the minister told his boss, who was monitoring Smith from Ottawa.[86]

Historians often like to think of Diefenbaker as different.[87] Yet the storyline in this chapter is not unlike the narrative in other case studies of Canadian Cold War diplomacy in distant, ex-colonial quarters: a wary eye cocked for US reaction as Ottawa manoeuvred to limit Cold War confrontation by reinforcing UN authority and shifting peacemaking responsibility to regional powers with more at stake.

Far from being mesmerized by Eisenhower, Diefenbaker pursued an independent crisis diplomacy that at least partly attained its strategic objective of getting the US out and keeping the UN in. It certainly did not hurt

Canada's standing in New York. As the 1958 General Assembly ended, the Swedish ambassador hosted a dinner for Arab and non-aligned representatives to re-hash the crisis: Canadian John Holmes was the only Western diplomat present. "It is useful for us to maintain in the UN a position which leads to our participation in gatherings of what, in some circles, would be considered dubious characters," he later reflected. "The position, however, is not one which we can maintain unless we continue to earn it."[88]

Remarkably, Diefenbaker earned it. At the heart of the crisis, as American forces landed in Lebanon, John sided with Ike. And that mattered. In a later conversation with the prime minister, Eisenhower emphasized that he "had much experience in working with Allies" and that "[t]he essential ingredient was to have faith in each other. The spirit of nationalism sometimes got out of bounds and would be used to attack St Peter himself, but it was the maintenance of good faith which counted."[89] Eisenhower would never lose his belief in Diefenbaker's good faith. In late October 1962, as the aftermath of the Cuban Missile Crisis roiled bilateral relations, the retired president wrote to thank the prime minister for a recent note, acknowledging what both these men already knew: "that when the chips are down, there is no question that your country and ours stand firmly together."[90]

NOTES

I would like to thank Patrick Belanger, Michael Carroll, Norman Hillmer, Joel Kropf, Michael Stevenson, and Alex Wieland for their help. I am grateful to the Eisenhower Foundation for assisting with my research expenses. The views expressed are my own and do not represent the views of the Government of Canada.

1 John Baird, "Canadian Diplomacy for the 21st Century," 27 March 2014, at http://www.international.gc.ca/media/aff/speeches-discours/2014/03/27a.aspx?lang=eng.
2 Cited in Michael Stevenson, "'Tossing a Match into Dry Hay': Nuclear Weapons and the Crisis in US-Canadian Relations, 1962–1963," *Journal of Cold War Studies* 16, 4 (2014): 5.
3 Harold Basil Robinson, *Diefenbaker's World: A Populist in World Affairs* (Toronto: University of Toronto Press, 1989), 17.
4 Knowlton Nash, *Kennedy and Diefenbaker: Fear and Loathing across the Undefended Border* (Toronto: McClelland and Stewart, 1990), 56.
5 Robert Bothwell, *Alliance and Illusion: Canada and the World, 1945–1984* (Vancouver: UBC Press, 2007), 176.
6 Asa McKercher, "Dealing with Diefenbaker: Canada-US relations in 1958," *International Journal* 66, 4 (2011): 1043–60.
7 Stuart to Dulles, J.F. Dulles Papers, General Correspondence and Memoranda Series, box 3, file: Strictly Confidential-Q-S (4), Dwight David Eisenhower Library (hereafter DDEL).

8 By June 1958, an ad hoc NSC committee State Department, the ODM, the Defense Department, and the Joint Chiefs of Staff, were working on Canada.

9 Jean Edward Smith, *Eisenhower in War and Peace* (New York: Random House, 2013), 527.

10 White House Confidential Files (hereafter WHCF), Christian Herter Papers, telephone conversation with the president, 30 November 1959, box 10: Presidential Telephone Calls 1959 (2), DDEL.

11 WHCF, Christian Herter Papers, memorandum of telephone conversation with the president, 8 April 1960, box 10: Presidential Telephone Calls 1–6/60 (2), DDEL.

12 WHCF, Christian Herter Papers, telephone conversation with the president, 2 March 1959, box 10: Presidential Telephone Calls 1959 (2), DDEL.

13 Note by the prime minister, Canada, 22 March 1959, FO 371/1052/4, TNA.

14 Discussion at the 440th meeting of the National Security Council, 7 April 1960, DDE Presidential Papers, NSC Series, box 10, DDEL.

15 John Eisenhower, memorandum of conference with the president, 10 May 1960, WHCF, Herter Papers, box 10, Canada 20, DDEL.

16 A.J. Goodpaster, memorandum of conference with the president, 3 June 1960, WHO, Office of the Staff Secretary, State Department Subseries, box 4, file June–July 1960 (1), DDEL.

17 Pre-press conference briefing, 17 July 1957, Eisenhower Presidential Papers, DDE Diary series, box 25 July 1957, Misc., DDEL.

18 Discussion at the 376th meeting of the National Security Council, 15 August 1958, DDE Presidential Papers, NSC Series, box 10, DDEL.

19 Discussion at the 446th meeting of the National Security Council, 31 May 1960, DDE Presidential Papers, NSC Series, box 12, DDEL.

20 Diefenbaker to Eisenhower, 26 February 1961, DDE Presidential Papers, International Series, box 6, file 1, DDEL.

21 This discussion of Lebanese politics is drawn from Douglas Little, "His Finest Hour? Eisenhower, Lebanon, and the 1958 Middle East Crisis," *Diplomatic History* 20, 1 (1996): 27–54; and Salim Yacqub, *Containing Arab Nationalism: The Eisenhower Doctrine and the Middle East* (Chapel Hill: University of North Carolina Press, 2004): 205–36.

22 Cited in Little, "His Finest Hour," 39.

23 Memorandum of a conversation, White House, Washington, 13 May 1958, 5:50 p.m., in *Foreign Relations of the United States, 1958–1960*, vol. 11, *Lebanon and Jordon*, ed. Louis J. Smith (Washington: US Government Printing Office, 1992), 45–48 (hereafter *FRUS*).

24 Ibid., 48.

25 Washington to Ottawa, tel 727, 1 April 1958, Library and Archives Canada (hereafter LAC), RG 25, vol. 5823, file 50131–40.

26 J.W. Holmes, memorandum for the USSEA, 8 March 1956, in Greg Donaghy, ed., *Documents on Canadian External Relations* (hereafter *DCER*), vol. 22, *1956–57*, pt. 1 (Ottawa: Department of Foreign Affairs and International Trade, 2001), 5–12.

27 Secretary of State for External Affairs (hereafter SSEA) to heads of post, Circular Document A2/58, 10 January 1958; and Ottawa to Washington, tel ME-73, 27 March 1958. Both in LAC, RG 25, vol. 5823, file 50131–40.

28 Jules Léger's marginal note on sixth meeting on the Summit Conference, 21 February 1958, LAC, RG 25, vol. 5823, file 50131–40.

29 Campbell to USSEA, 5 June 1958, LAC, RG 25, vol. 5823, file 30131–40.

30 Middle East Division to USSEA, 22 May 1958, LAC, RG 25, vol. 5870, file 50162-A-40.

31 Charles Ritchie, *Diplomatic Passport: More Undiplomatic Diaries, 1946–62* (Toronto: Macmillan, 1981), 147–48. On other aspects of Canada's response to British and American policies in the Middle East during this period, see Janice Cavell, "Suez and After: Canada and British Policy in the Middle East, 1956–1960," *Journal of the Canadian Historical Association* 18, 1 (2007): 157–78.

32 Watkins (via Léger) to Smith, 27 May 1958, LAC, RG 25, vol. 5823, file 50162-A-40.

33 Cairo to Ottawa, tel 116, 17 May 1958, LAC, RG 25, vol. 5870, file 50162-A-40; and Léger, memorandum to the minister, 2 June 1958, LAC, RG 25, vol. 5823, file 50131–40.

34 Smith to Prime Minister, 16 May 1958, LAC, RG 25, vol. 5823, file 50162-A-40.

35 Smith, memorandum for the prime minister, 16 May 1958, in Michael Stevenson, ed., *Documents on Canadian External Relations*, vol. 25, *1957–58* (Ottawa: Department of Foreign Affairs and International Trade, 2004) (hereafter *DCER*, vol. 25), 674.

36 Ritchie, *Diplomatic Passport*, 134.

37 Ibid., 146.

38 New York to Ottawa, tel 803, 27 May 1958, *DCER*, vol. 25, 682–84.

39 New York to Ottawa, tel 869, 7 June 1958, *DCER*, vol. 25, 689; and Livingston Merchant, aide-memoire, 9 June 1958, LAC, RG 25, vol. 5870, file 50162-A-40.

40 Campbell, memorandum for the USSEA, 10 June 1958, LAC, RG 25, vol. 5870, file 50162-A-40.

41 New York to Ottawa, tel 886, 11 June 1958, LAC, RG 25, vol. 5870, file 50162-A-40.

42 Salim Yaqub, *Containing Arab Nationalism: The Eisenhower Doctrine and the Middle East* (Chapel Hill: University of North Carolina Press, 2004), 214.

43 Smith, memorandum for cabinet, *DCER*, vol. 25, 694–95.

44 Ottawa to Cairo, tel ME-138, 14 June 1958, LAC, RG 25, vol. 5870, file 50162-A-40.

45 "Talks with Mr. Macmillan, 12 June 1958," LAC, RG 25, vol. 5870, file 50162-A-40.

46 New York to Ottawa, tel 934, 17 June 1958, LAC, RG 25, vol. 5870, file 50162-A-40.

47 Beirut to Ottawa, tel 85, 18 June 1958, *DCER*, vol. 25, 700.

48 Ottawa to London and Washington, tel ME-144, *DCER*, vol. 25, 701–2.

49 State to Embassy in Beirut, 19 June 1958, *FRUS, 1958–1960*, vol. 11, *Lebanon and Jordan*, 158–60.

50 Washington to Ottawa, tel 1409, 19 June 1958, LAC, RG 25, vol. 5870, file 50162-A-40.

51 London to Ottawa, tel 2194, 20 June 1958, LAC, RG 25, vol. 5870, file 50162-A-40.

52 Lloyd to Diefenbaker, 20 June 1958, LAC, RG 25, vol. 5870, file 50162-A-40.

53 Léger, memorandum for the prime minister, 20 June 1958, *DCER*, vol. 25, 705–6; High Commissioner in Canada to Commonwealth Relations Office, tel 654, 20 June 1958, FO 371/134124, TNA.

54 Dulles to Lloyd, 2 July 1958, J.F. Dulles Papers, Chron Series, July 1958 (4), DDEL.

55 Dulles, memorandum for the president, 3 July 1958, DDE Papers, International Series, box 6, file Canada 7, DDEL.

56 Nash, *Kennedy and Diefenbaker*, 55.

57 Memorandum of conversation, 8 July 1958, DDE Papers, International Series, box 6, file Canada 7, DDEL.

58 Memorandum of conversation, 10 July 1958, DDE Papers, International Series, box 6, file Canada 7, DDEL.

59 Cited in Little, "His Finest Hour," 44.

60 Note, 14 July 1958, DDE Papers, International Series, box 6, file Canada 6, DDEL.

61 Ann Whitman, memorandum for Phyllis Bernau, 15 July 1958, DDE Papers, Dulles-Herter Series, box 10, DDEL.

62 Ottawa to State Department, tel 56, Midnight, 15 July 1958, DDE Papers, International Series, Box 6, File Canada 6, DDEL.

63 Cabinet Conclusions, 15 July 1958, *DCER*, vol. 25, 717–18.

64 In Ritchie's absence, John Holmes represented Canada.

65 Eisenhower to Diefenbaker, State Department to Ottawa, tel 50, 7:59 p.m., 15 July 1958, DDE Papers, International Series, box 6, file Canada 6, DDEL.

66 New York to Ottawa, tel 1085, 16 July 1958, *DCER*, vol. 25, 722–24.

67 The quote reflects Ottawa's instructions to New York, tel ME-181, 16 July 1958, *DCER*, vol. 25, 721–22.

68 Memorandum of a conversation between Messrs. Dulles, Lloyd and Smith, Washington, DC, 18 July 1959, LAC, RG 25, vol. 5823, file 50162-A-40.

69 Record of a conversation between the secretary of state and Mr. Diefenbaker on 4 November 1958, PREM 11/2606, TNA.

70 Moscow to Ottawa, tel 303, 21 July 1958, LAC, RG 25, vol. 5823, file 50131–40.

71 Cabinet Conclusions, 22 July 1958, LAC.

72 Ottawa to Nato, tel ME-200, 21 July 1958, LAC, RG 25, vol. 5823, file 50131–40.

73 Ottawa to Nato, tel ME-194, 20 July 1958, LAC, RG 25, vol. 5823, file 50131–40.

74 Ottawa (Léger) to Washington, tel G-163, 1 August 1958, LAC, RG 25, vol. 5823, file 50131–40.

75 John Hilliker and Donald Barry, *Canada's Department of External Affairs*, vol. 2, *Coming of Age, 1946–1968* (Montreal and Kingston: McGill-Queen's University Press, 1995), 143–46.

76 Briefing Note, Smith, Sidney Earle, DDE Papers, International Meeting Series, box 3, bile Canada 3, DDEL.

77 Ottawa to Oslo, tel ME-246, 6 August 1958, LAC, RG 25, vol. 5823, file 50131–40.

78 New York to Ottawa, tel 1227, 13 August 1958, LAC, RG 25, vol. 5823, file 50131–40. The dinner with Lloyd is covered in New York (Smith) to Ottawa (for Prime Minister), tel 1221, 13 August 1958, LAC, RG 25, vol. 5823, file 50131-40.

79 New York to Ottawa, tel 1237, 14 August 1958, *DCER*, vol. 25, 773–74.

80 New York to Ottawa, tel 1237, 14 August 1958, *DCER*, vol. 25, 773–74.

81 New York to Ottawa, tel 1235, 14 August 1958, *DCER*, vol. 25, 772–73.

82 Howard Greer, "Canada-backed Motion Treated with Contempt Will 'Invite' Amendment," *Toronto Star*, 19 August 1958.

83 E.R. Rettie, memorandum for file, 19 August 1958, *DCER*, vol. 25, 776–77.

84 E.R. Rettie, memorandum for file, 20 August 1958, *DCER*, vol. 25, 779–80.

85 New York to Ottawa (for Prime Minister), tel 1282, 21 August 1958, *DCER*, vol. 25, 782–83.

86 New York to Ottawa, tel 1282, 21 August 1958, LAC, RG 25, vol. 5823, file 50131–40.

87 For an exception to this general trend, see Daniel Macfarlane, "Courting War over a Rubber Stamp: Canada and the 1961 Berlin Wall Crisis," *International Journal*, 63, 3 (2008): 751–68.

88 Holmes, memorandum for the USSEA, 16 December 1958, LAC, RG 25, vol. 5823, file 50131–40.

89 Memorandum of conversation, 27 September 1960, Eisenhower Presidential Papers, International Relations Series, box 6, file 1, DDEL.

90 Eisenhower to Diefenbaker, 9 November 1962, Diefenbaker Papers, MG 01/XII/D/76 Eisenhower, Diefenbaker Centre.

5

The Problem Child
Diefenbaker and Canada in the Language of the Kennedy Administration

STEPHEN AZZI

Walt Butterworth was fed up. As US ambassador in Ottawa he had supported his government's "patient tolerance of [an] unrealistic Canadian view of [the] external world." But Canadian officials had exhausted that patience, and in early 1963 Butterworth urged that the State Department challenge Prime Minister John Diefenbaker's deceptive statements about Canada's defence commitments and the state of Canada-US relations. Butterworth was pleased when Washington issued a press release that directly contradicted the prime minister. It was, as he told Secretary of State Dean Rusk, a "sudden dose of cold water" that resulted in "traditional psychopathic accusations of unwarranted US interference in domestic Canadian affairs." For Butterworth, the difficulty was not that Canada had different views or interests; rather, it was a "psychological problem" that afflicted Canadians, particularly the prime minster, who seemed "determined to carry on in [a] dream world."[1]

In the extensive literature on the Canada-US relationship in the early 1960s, most of the blame for the strains between the two countries has been assigned to Diefenbaker, who has been portrayed as overly sensitive, even paranoid.[2] Certainly, the prime minister had trouble working with others, not just US president John F. Kennedy. Diefenbaker alienated fellow world leaders, his own cabinet, and, eventually, his own party. But, by the same token, US relations with several other allies also suffered during the Kennedy years. Tensions developed between the US and France, the US and West

Germany, and the US and the Netherlands, despite the president's personal popularity in those countries.

For many years, the Americans tended both to conduct foreign policy without consulting their allies and to trivialize any concerns that other governments might raise. From the beginning of the Cold War, Washington dismissed any disagreements as the product of irrationality rather than of often-legitimate policy differences. In their private communications, US officials used emotive language to portray allies as neurotic and emasculated.[3] This tendency became more pronounced in the Kennedy years, exacerbated by the administration's distinctive mores, particularly the enormous confidence of Kennedy and his people in their own abilities and their strident anti-communism. This culture impeded US relations with the government of John Diefenbaker, preventing several key US officials from grasping that Canada might reasonably want to diverge slightly from the American position. A thorough review of the Kennedy administration's records and of later testimony from officials – a review that pays particular attention to the use of language – shows that Kennedy's people seldom appreciated the Canadian position. Instead, they often portrayed Canada as a child or as a neurotic.

Most of the senior figures in the Kennedy administration shared the president's background and worldview. They were young, fit, white, male, and financially secure. Kennedy was the youngest person ever elected to the US presidency, and he led the youngest cabinet of the twentieth century, with an average age of forty-seven – that is, eighteen years younger than John Diefenbaker.[4] The Kennedy entourage placed, as journalist David Halberstam noted, "great emphasis on style."[5] They were good looking and well dressed, and the media depicted them as glamorous and dashing.

Kennedy's people were cultured, well educated, and well read. About one-third of the senior posts in the administration went to Harvard alumni, while Yale graduates filled many others.[6] Secretary of State Dean Rusk, Deputy National Security Advisor Walt Rostow, and Ambassador to Canada Walton Butterworth were all Rhodes Scholars. At least four members of the administration had written books, two of which had won the Pulitzer Prize: Kennedy's *Profiles in Courage* and Arthur Schlesinger's *Age of Jackson*.[7] The Kennedy people saw themselves as reasonable – in fact, they often considered themselves uniquely reasonable, in the sense that they viewed anyone who disagreed with them as unreasonable. "To the Americans, the irrationality of their allies and their own rationality is an absolute assumption," Canadian ambassador Charles Ritchie wrote in his diary in July 1963.[8]

There were exceptions to these generalizations. The most prominent was Secretary of State Dean Rusk, who never fit in. He came from poverty, attended North Carolina's Davidson College, and was modest in demeanour. When Rusk was with the Kennedy crowd, he looked like the bartender – or so he once said.[9] Kennedy never addressed Rusk by his first name, as he did all his other cabinet secretaries. The president's brother and attorney general, Robert Kennedy, was visibly hostile towards Rusk. To paraphrase A.J.P. Taylor, it becomes wearisome to add "except Dean Rusk" to every generalization. Henceforth, it may be assumed.

Kennedy could be engaging, witty, and graceful, but he also had a sense of entitlement that could manifest itself as rudeness or roughness. "That young man, he never says please, he never says thank you, he never asks for things, he demands them," grumbled Kennedy's onetime rival, Adlai Stevenson.[10] Ambassador Ritchie described the president as "an Irish street fighter with a layer of sophistication on top."[11] Exacerbating these traits was Kennedy's sardonic wit and love of teasing, a tendency that was not universally appreciated. His extreme sense of competitiveness further sharpened his edge. "That's the only thing Jack really gets emotional about – when he loses," noted the president's sister, Eunice.[12] At the same time, Kennedy was "the most thin-skinned of presidents," according to Charles Roberts, the White House correspondent for *Newsweek*. Kennedy and his staff "were extremely intolerant of anything critical." As White House aide Kenny O'Donnell once said, "You are either for us or against us."[13] When Kennedy took power, there was a new tone in the American capital and, in the words of Arnold Heeney, Ritchie's predecessor as Canadian ambassador, "a new asperity in the relations between Ottawa and Washington."[14]

From the start, Kennedy and his people were insensitive, sometimes even rude, to Diefenbaker. The historiography focuses on Diefenbaker's overreaction to several minor incidents, but, overreaction or not, Kennedy's behaviour was inappropriate. When Kennedy came to office, Diefenbaker had been prime minister for almost four years, but the president had no idea how to pronounce his name. Neither did Dean Rusk, the secretary of state. Rusk asked Foy Kohler, assistant secretary of state for European affairs (whose bureau was responsible for Canada), but Kohler did not know either. He assumed that it would have a German pronunciation and did not think it worth checking. Knowlton Nash has recounted that Kennedy called the prime minister "John G. Diefenbawker" at a press conference shortly after taking office.[15] In fact, the recording at the Kennedy Library shows a second mistake. Kennedy called the prime minister "John F. Diefenbawker."[16] Presumably, the prime minister's middle name was Fitzgerald.

When the two were together, the president frequently offended the prime minister. In their first meeting in Washington, Kennedy teased Diefenbaker. In a discussion about fishing, the prime minister mentioned that he had caught a 140-pound marlin in Jamaica. "You didn't catch it!" Kennedy scoffed.[17] Upon his arrival in Ottawa, Kennedy publicly mocked Diefenbaker's poor French, provoking laughter in the audience. In a private conversation with Diefenbaker, Kennedy urged Canada to join the Organization of American States (OAS). Despite receiving a negative response, Kennedy proceeded to raise the issue in his address to Parliament. Canada's ambassador in Washington, Arnold Heeney, had said that the Canadian government would not object if the president mentioned the OAS in his speech, but circumstances changed after Diefenbaker rejected the idea. As US ambassador Livingston Merchant admitted, the passage should have been excised from the speech.[18] Later, at a dinner party at the ambassador's residence, Kennedy clearly exhibited his preference for opposition leader Lester Pearson over Diefenbaker. This was not simply a case of Diefenbaker's legendary paranoia. Even American officials commented on it. "We all saw it," US diplomat Willis Armstrong remembered. "It was absolutely discourteous."[19]

Perhaps the best illustration of Kennedy's insensitivity is the decision to dispatch Butterworth to Ottawa as US ambassador when the relationship between the two countries was delicate. A career diplomat, Butterworth had been close to the Kennedy family after working for the president's father, Joe Kennedy, when he was US ambassador in London from 1938 to 1940.[20] As a Princeton graduate and Rhodes Scholar, Butterworth fit in well with the president's associates, and he shared their over-confidence. Charles Ritchie found his American counterpart a "very overbearing and arrogant man."[21] Butterworth's American colleagues agreed. "In some ways, he was a pompous ass," remembered Rufus Smith, the US embassy's political counsellor. "He ... had supreme confidence in his own abilities."[22] Willis Armstrong thought that Butterworth was "not the best choice because he was so overbearing in style."[23] But there was a logic to the appointment. Butterworth was "just the s.o.b. the Canadians deserve," in the words of his predecessor, Livingston Merchant.[24] The new ambassador was perfect for conducting diplomacy in the rough style of the Kennedy White House.

All US administrations reflect the personality and approach of the president – none more so than Kennedy's. Decisions were made in the Oval Office after consulting only a few people representing a limited number of viewpoints. In part, this was because Kennedy and his coterie focused on the immediate situation, disdaining those who engaged in long-range planning. As a result, much of Kennedy's foreign policy was by crisis management. The Kennedy people often neglected the long-term implications of their actions, ignoring what would happen if others did not see things the way they did. This had important consequences in the Bay of Pigs, in Vietnam, and, to a much lesser extent, in Canada.

Kennedy and his closest advisors had a low tolerance for tedium. According to Gloria Emerson, a journalist and friend of the first lady, Kennedy became weary "when people ... made their case at too great length."[25] The president and his national security advisor, McGeorge Bundy, thought that boring others was "almost the worst offense a man could commit," according to Halberstam.[26] Kennedy's friend, journalist Charles Bartlett, agreed: "You could kick him. You could rob him. But you must never bore him."[27] After his trip to Ottawa in May 1961, Kennedy told people that Diefenbaker was "boring," a clear sign the relationship was heading for trouble.[28]

The Kennedy people were men of conviction who were sure of themselves, sure of their own rectitude, and sure that they knew the difference between right and wrong, particularly in international affairs. But this certainty made it difficult for them to understand anyone who did not share their background and outlook. The president and his officials saw the world through an American lens: they thought of American values, American needs, American interests, American goals. They had trouble placing themselves in other people's shoes, whether those other people were Chinese, Cuban, or Canadian. They found it particularly difficult to understand Diefenbaker and his external affairs minister, Howard Green. "To most of the American officials concerned with foreign and defence policy, the firm of Diefenbaker and Green was a gigantic enigma with which they found it impossible to come to terms," according to Diefenbaker's foreign policy aide, Basil Robinson, who had moved to Washington in the summer of 1962 to take up a post in the Canadian embassy.[29] In a rare moment of retrospective clarity, McGeorge Bundy recognized that the US should not have pushed so hard for Canada to support American policies in Latin America. "It is still annoying to others when Americans assume that what is good for them has to be good for everyone else on the continent."[30]

Part of the problem was inexperience. When Vice-President Lyndon Johnson remarked on the intellect of the Kennedy people, House Speaker Sam Rayburn responded, "Well, Lyndon, you may be right ... but I'd feel a whole lot better about them if just one of them had run for sheriff once."[31] The lack of experience was particularly glaring in international affairs. For John Kenneth Galbraith, the Harvard professor who served as Kennedy's

ambassador in New Delhi, the Kennedy people had no foreign policy expertise: "they were men who had not travelled around the world and knew
nothing of this country and the world" – other than "the difference between
a Communist and an anti-Communist."[32]

Southeast Asia provides the perfect illustration of this tendency. Canadians tried to help extricate the United States from its growing entanglement in
Vietnam, but for US officials, there was nothing rational about the Canadian
position. Instead, Ambassador Butterworth engaged in pop psychology:
Canada did not fully support the US position because "the Canadians
didn't want to be the running dog of the Americans. It hurt their pride,
it hurt their feelings, and also it gives them a chance to satisfy the kind of
thing little brothers like to engage in."[33]

Since they were so sure of themselves, Kennedy's people were not inclined to consult with others. As historian Frank Costigliola has written,
the Kennedy administration viewed American allies "not as fit partners but
as emotional or obtuse clients to be manipulated into accepting America's
wiser judgement."[34] US officials were "totally impervious to any idea or suggestion which did not originate in Washington," according to Ambassador
Ritchie. "The United States version of consultation with their allies meant
listening patiently to their views and then informing them of American decisions."[35] To give one example, the US promised to sell Britain the Skybolt missile in exchange for permission to base submarines in Scotland, but
Kennedy decided to cancel the development of the missile on 23 November 1962. More than two weeks later, Defense Secretary Robert McNamara
met the British, ostensibly to seek their input on a decision that had already
been made.[36] This lack of consultation was a problem for American allies,
particularly Canada. The close integration of the Canadian and American
economies and military meant that Canada could only protect its interests if
there were constant discussion and negotiation between the two countries.

The Kennedy administration's attitude towards consultation could be
seen clearly during the Cuban Missile Crisis. US officials feared that the Soviets were building a missile base in Cuba, but the Americans did not tell allied governments. Even when photographs confirmed their suspicions, the
Americans waited one week before sharing the information. At no point did
the Kennedy administration seek the advice of other countries on how to respond. A nuclear war between the Soviet Union and the United States could
have destroyed large parts of North America, but communication between
American and Canadian leaders was limited, provided at the last moment,
and handled in an amateurish fashion. Not wanting to talk to Diefenbaker,

Kennedy called External Affairs Minister Green. Unable to connect with Green, the president called National Defence Minister Douglas Harkness, who was not available. The president instead talked to Pierre Sévigny, who held the minor post of associate minister of national defence.[37] On the telephone, Kennedy would only say that Ambassador Merchant would deliver a message on his behalf. Merchant and Diefenbaker met at 5:15 p.m. on 22 October 1962, less than two hours before Kennedy was to make a public statement on the crisis. The ambassador briefed the prime minister and presented the text of the speech Kennedy was about to make. When Basil Robinson complained to Merchant about the lack of discussion, the US ambassador responded, "I didn't think Canada had earned, by its actions and by certain non-actions, the right to the extreme intimacy of relations which had existed in years past," most likely a reference to Diefenbaker's delay over accepting nuclear weapons for the Canadian military.[38] After Kennedy's speech, US officials issued a statement that mentioned Canada's support for the US position – support that Diefenbaker had not offered.[39]

Diefenbaker's response to the Cuban Missile Crisis may have been petulant, but the Dutch, West Germans, Italians, Belgians, and Turks all resented the secretive way the White House handled the crisis.[40] When former secretary of state Dean Acheson briefed Charles de Gaulle, the French president began the meeting by drawing attention to the failure to seek his input: "In order to get our roles clear, do I understand that you have come from the president to inform me of some decision taken by your president – or have you come to consult me about a decision which he should take?"[41] The allies generally supported Kennedy's actions in public, while privately decrying the absence of consultation. The Turks, in particular, were upset that they were not consulted before the US removed Jupiter missiles that had just come under the control of the Turkish army. Throughout the crisis, it was Rusk, the outsider in the Kennedy inner circle, who urged dialogue, reminding his colleagues of his country's treaty commitments to its allies.[42]

Perhaps the most distinctive element in the ethos of the Kennedy administration was the high value placed on toughness and masculinity. In the 1950s, Republicans had successfully portrayed the Democrats as weak, even effeminate. Adlai Stevenson, twice the Democratic nominee for president, was depicted as soft and irresolute; his opponents questioned his sexuality and called him Adelaide. Determined never to be seen as feminine, Kennedy and his entourage overcompensated, always seeking to portray themselves as bold, virile, and masculine.[43] As his closest advisors, the president chose hawks. Toughness became the "most highly prized virtue" in the White House, the Pentagon, the CIA, and the State Department, according to State Department official Richard J. Barnet. The national security managers called it the "hairy chest syndrome."[44] The Kennedy people were unrelenting in their opposition to communism and deeply sceptical about negotiation, which they equated with weakness. As a result, the Kennedy White House was ineffective in the give-and-take of politics, whether on Capitol Hill, where Kennedy's legislative program stalled, or in foreign capitals, where tensions developed between the US and several other countries. The administration's distrust of compromise led to disdain both for the State Department and the practice of diplomacy. "They're not queer at State," Kennedy told a friend, "but ... well, they're sort of like Adlai."[45] The admiration of strength and power was also linked to a private contempt for moralism. For the Kennedy people, the worst thing you could do, according to journalist David Halberstam, "was confess openly to high idealism."[46] This attitude had important implications for Canada–US relations, as Kennedy's entourage would encounter few people as idealistic as Howard Green, the diligent, righteous man who served as Canada's external affairs minister and the leader of Canada's international disarmament efforts.

Over the last two decades, several historians have examined the role of gender in the making of US foreign policy – not the role of women in history but, to use Thomas Zeiler's words, gender as an "ideological building block" in the discourse of American foreign policy.[47] Kristin Hoganson has shown that gender politics helped provoke the Spanish-American and Philippine-American Wars, Robert Dean has demonstrated how the ideology of masculinity shaped US Cold War foreign policy, Kyle Cuordileone has linked US Cold War politics to a crisis in American masculinity, and Mary Ann Heiss has argued that the US helped overthrow Iranian prime minister Mohammed Mossadeq, in part, because American policy-makers viewed him as effeminate.[48] Together, these works reveal US paternalistic attitudes towards others and a tendency to feminize weaker countries and dismiss their concerns as the product of softness. At the same time, American policy-makers portrayed the Soviet Union in an exaggerated masculine manner. The US had to stand up to the Soviets for fear of being seen as weak.

As with previous US administrations, the Kennedy people tended to portray the country's allies as feminine. But they did not do so with Diefenbaker. One of Kennedy's favourite words – one he often equated with masculinity – was "vigor."[49] Repeatedly, US officials described Diefenbaker as vigorous.[50] On a few occasions the president described the Canadian prime minister as a "prick," and, in one heated moment, Kennedy ranted about Diefenbaker and talked about "cutting his balls off."[51] Diefenbaker's masculinity, at least in the Kennedy White House, appeared unquestioned. This put Canada in the same category as the Soviet Union and Castro's Cuba – countries depicted as masculine because they did not defer to the United States.

Instead of effeminacy, the Kennedy administration produced two images of Diefenbaker and Canadian officials. The first was of an immature adult who continued to behave like a child, requiring a mixture of patience and firmness from the parent – in this case, the United States. Diefenbaker was said to be "querulously questioning" when talking to Kennedy's chief of protocol Angier Biddle Duke during the prime minister's first visit to Washington, a description that suggested sulking or whining.[52] After the president met with two senior Canadian cabinet ministers, George Hees and Donald Fleming, US undersecretary of state George Ball reported that the Canadians "promised to be good boys so far as Cuba was concerned."[53] Shortly after Kennedy took office, US ambassador Livingston Merchant explained the Canadian viewpoint to Dean Rusk: "Their criticism of us for policies in Asia, Africa or Latin America is often levelled from [the] position of bystander and not of [a] responsible participant." It was useful to remind Canadians that "whimpering and whining are out of place."[54] When Diefenbaker complained about the president's private conversation with opposition leader Lester Pearson in the White House before a dinner for Nobel Prize winners, US ambassador Merchant told the prime minister that he was being "childish."[55]

The other dominant image was that of mental illness. Canada was portrayed in terms that ranged from mildly neurotic to psychopathic. Diefenbaker himself was frequently described as volatile and unbalanced. The prime minister, noted the US embassy's Willis Armstrong, was "never noted for his emotional stability."[56] Duke said that he had never seen a man so nervous as Diefenbaker was before meeting Kennedy the first time.[57] In May 1962, Merchant wrote that Diefenbaker was "excited to a degree disturbing in a leader of an important country" and was close to "hysteria."[58]

Kennedy's officials frequently implied that the Canadian point of view was not rational and not deserving of serious consideration. A briefing note to prepare Kennedy for his first meeting with Diefenbaker illustrates this tendency:

The primary problem the United States faces in its bilateral relations with Canada lies in an evolving Canadian attitude of introspection and nationalism. The magnitude of neighboring U.S. wealth and power has long engendered a Canadian inferiority complex which is reflected in a sensitivity to any real or fancied slight to Canadian sovereignty. Thus the essential element in problems involving Canada tends to be psychological.[59]

The same ideas were repeated in the briefing note for Kennedy's May 1961 trip to Ottawa, often verbatim. This time, the author added the observation that "anti-American sentiment in Canada comes and goes, often without any identifiable connection with what the United States in fact does. Therefore it is impossible completely to rectify the situation psychologically by any list of specific government actions."[60]

The tensions between the Kennedy administration and Diefenbaker government culminated with the conflict over nuclear arms. Canada had agreed to accept weapons systems with nuclear arms but then delayed negotiations to acquire them.[61] On 3 August 1961, Kennedy sent a letter to Diefenbaker expressing concern over the lack of progress towards obtaining the weapons for the Canadian armed forces. He suggested that the two countries renew their negotiations "with vigor."[62] Eight days later, the prime minister sent a positive response.[63] In private, he was clear about his position, telling foreign policy aide Basil Robinson that he could not understand those Canadians who wanted to reject nuclear arms.[64] He was equally clear in public, saying that Canada would accept nuclear weapons for its NATO forces in Europe, once appropriate arrangements could be made.[65] The US embassy's Willis Armstrong reported to Washington that Diefenbaker and Harkness were "obviously engaged in [a] well-organized and Cabinet-approved public campaign, in and out of Parliament, which foreshadows [a] decision to adopt weapons." Opposition politicians believed that the government had already made its decision, and Armstrong expected action within the "next week or two."[66]

But the White House did not think it enough to prod Diefenbaker in private. Officials in Washington had to brag that they had pushed the prime minister. *Newsweek* reported on a "behind-the-scenes row between the U.S. and Canada." The president had sent the prime minister "a straight-from-the-shoulder letter" that would "resolve the impasse."[67] The piece caused a stir in Ottawa: Diefenbaker was asked about it in the House of Commons and was, in private, "unusually agitated," according to Basil Robinson.[68] The White House acknowledged to a Canadian Press reporter that the president had written to Diefenbaker about nuclear weapons, and other US officials confirmed the contents of the letter, suggesting that the leak was intentional and was authorized by someone at a high level.[69] In fact, the source might well have been Kennedy himself, as one of *Newsweek's* senior editors was Ben Bradlee, a close friend of the president.[70]

Armstrong lamented this turn of events. The situation was sensitive, and he feared that "this totally unnecessary publicity" could lead Diefenbaker, who had trouble making decisions in the best of times, to delay action on the nuclear issue.[71] Diefenbaker and his ministers were anxious about the public reaction to Canada's acquisition of nuclear weapons, and with good reason. Throughout the Kennedy presidency, Diefenbaker's Conservatives were behind the Liberals in public opinion polls.[72] It might well hurt the government if it appeared that Kennedy had forced nuclear weapons on Canada. Merchant reported that the Canadian government became "virtually paralyzed on this question" after the *Newsweek* story and appeared "determined not [to] face [the] issue until after [the] next general elections."[73] The president should have been able to understand the situation. After all, he had been reluctant to proceed on several domestic issues – such as civil rights – because of a lack of support in Congress and a fear of damaging his popularity. Yet Diefenbaker's position baffled Kennedy. According to Merchant, Kennedy "expressed himself as being completely unable to understand Prime Minister Diefenbaker's reasoning."[74]

Tired of Diefenbaker's delaying tactics and misleading reports on the state of negotiations between Canada and the US over nuclear weapons, the Kennedy administration decided to intervene in Canadian politics. In January 1963, the State Department issued a press release contradicting several statements Diefenbaker had made in the Commons. This was not diplomacy, it was a battering ram: the Kennedy administration had called the prime minister a liar. Butterworth supported this new approach. "We have reached a point where our relations must be based on something more solid than accommodation to [the] neurotic Canadian view of us and [the] world," he wrote to Rusk. "We should be less the accoucheur of Canada's illusions."[75] Later, Butterworth expressed disdain for the State Department's "old ways of treating Canada like a problem child for whom there was always at the ready a cheek for the turning."[76] Soon after the press release, Defence Minister Harkness resigned from cabinet, the government was defeated in the House of Commons, and the country was thrust into an election campaign.

US officials had not thought out the long-term implications of their actions. According to Harkness, the press release was "a piece of complete stupidity" that turned Diefenbaker's position from delaying to opposing the acquisition of nuclear weapons.[77] "I'm not going to let the State Department tell me what to do," the prime minister insisted.[78] The release also provided Diefenbaker with buckshot to use during the election, allowing him to fire at the bullying Americans in the defence of Canadian sovereignty. Pearson's aide Richard O'Hagan thought the release was "a gift to the Conservatives," and Pearson later told Kennedy that it probably cost the Liberals fifty seats.[79] This was an exaggeration, but even a judicious observer could conclude that the White House had deprived the Liberals of at least five seats, robbing Pearson of a majority.

The White House was more prudent during the election campaign. Kennedy had been warned not to harm Liberal prospects by trying to help, and he seemed to understand. National Security Advisor Bundy sent a memorandum to Rusk and Defense Secretary McNamara instructing State and Defense to stay out of the Canadian election: "The President wishes to avoid any appearance of interference, even by responding to what may appear to be untruthful, distorted, or unethical statements or actions."[80] But Kennedy could barely help himself. "One of our chief problems was keeping Mr. Kennedy out of the Canadian election," remembered Armstrong, "because he just wanted to get in there and campaign for Pearson." Armstrong understood that Kennedy's involvement would have been counterproductive, "but the White House was very impatient, very impatient indeed."[81] Kennedy wanted to connect by telephone with Pearson even though Diefenbaker could have portrayed such a conversation as proof that Pearson was taking instructions from Washington. The president "could have been a terrible embarrassment to Pearson," observed Armstrong, "but when Kennedy wanted something, he charged."[82] At one point, Kennedy slipped and publicly referred to Pearson as "my friend." "Tell the silly bastard to keep his mouth shut!" Pearson's campaign chair, Walter Gordon, told Lou Harris, pollster for both Kennedy and Pearson.[83]

Even after Diefenbaker's defeat, the Kennedy administration continued to view Canada as childish and needing psychological help. "We must remember [that the] Liberals are none the less Canadians and their relative sophistication does not mean they do not suffer from familiar national compulsion to demonstrate to themselves and others that they are not Americans," Butterworth warned Rusk one week after the Liberal victory in the April 1963 election.[84] "What the Canadians need is a psychoanalyst's couch," commented one US official after the new finance minister, Walter Gordon, presented the Pearson government's first budget, one that sought to limit foreign investment in Canada.[85]

Analyzing the language of US policy-makers illuminates the ways they thought and the reasons they acted as they did. The tropes of childhood and mental illness reflected US perceptions of Canada, and these perceptions, in turn, shaped US policy and actions. US officials created dichotomies between the adult United States and the adolescent Canada, between the rational US and the irrational Canada, between the mentally sound US and the neurotic (or even psychotic) Canada. For US officials, the Canadian position was incomprehensible, based on folly. This practice of viewing Canadian policy and policy-makers as immature or mentally unbalanced had the effect of trivializing the Canadian position and denying legitimate Canadian concerns.

The Diefenbaker government had good reason to be concerned about the fragile state of world peace and to try to moderate US policies. It was perfectly reasonable for Canada to try to extricate the US from Vietnam, just as it made sense for Green to work against the proliferation of nuclear weapons and for the Canadian cabinet to take time to deliberate before expanding the nuclear club. After all, a nuclear war might well mean the end of humanity. Canadian officials had every right to worry about their degree of control over nuclear weapons stationed on Canadian soil and to hesitate before obtaining expensive weapon systems that might soon be obsolete. Yet US officials could see little logic in any of these positions.

Portraying Canada as a child meant that US officials did not need to try to understand the Canadian point of view. They knew best where Canada's real interests lay. To the Kennedy administration, Canada was a young man living in his parents' basement, suffering from some form of mental illness. He needed to grow up, take responsibility, and pull his own weight. In the meantime, the parent could make key decisions for the child. In the view of the Kennedy people, the January 1963 press release was not an ill-conceived interference in Canadian politics: it was a stern measure motivated by a genuine desire to help Canadians protect their own interests.

NOTES

The author is grateful to Norman Hillmer, Denis Smith, Janice Cavell, and Ryan Touhey for their helpful comments on the manuscript; to Kurt Montgomery and Jennifer Levin Bonder for assistance with the research; and to Robert Dean for advice on how to situate gender in the discourse of US foreign policy.

1 Butterworth to Rusk, telegram no. 990, 3 February 1963, John F. Kennedy Presidential Library, Papers of John F. Kennedy, Presidential Papers, National Security Files (hereafter JFKNSF), vol. 18, file 13, in *Foreign Relations of the United States, 1961–1963*, vol. 13, *Western Europe and Canada*, ed. Charles S. Simpson and James E. Miller (Washington: US Government Printing Office, 1994) (hereafter *FRUS*), doc. 445, pp. 1196–99.

2 See, for example, Peter C. Newman, *Renegade in Power: The Diefenbaker Years* (Toronto: McClelland and Stewart, 1963); Peyton V. Lyon, *Canada in World Affairs, 1961–1963* (Toronto: Oxford University Press, 1968); J.L. Granatstein, *Canada, 1957–1967: The Years of Uncertainty and Innovation* (Toronto: McClelland and Stewart, 1986); J.L. Granatstein, "When Push Came to Shove: Canada and the United States," in *Kennedy's Quest for Victory: American Foreign Policy, 1961–1963*, ed. Thomas G. Paterson (New York: Oxford University Press, 1989), 86–104. Robert Bothwell, *Alliance and Illusion: Canada and the World, 1945–1984* (Vancouver: UBC Press, 2007).

3 For examples, see Frank Costigliola, "The Nuclear Family: Tropes of Gender and Pathology in the Western Alliance," *Diplomatic History* 21, 2 (1997): 163–83, esp. 174–75; Frank Costigliola, "Reading for Meaning: Theory, Language, and Metaphor," in *Explaining the History of American Foreign Relations*, 2nd ed., ed. Michael J. Hogan and Thomas G. Paterson, chap. 17 (Cambridge: Cambridge University Press, 2004), 301; Shane J. Maddock, *Nuclear Apartheid: The Quest for American Atomic Supremacy from World War II* (Chapel Hill: University of North Carolina Press, 2010), 186; Frank Costigliola, "The Pursuit of Atlantic Community: Nuclear Arms, Dollars, and Berlin," in *Kennedy's Quest for Victory: American Foreign Policy, 1961–1963*, ed. Thomas G. Paterson, chap. 1 (New York: Oxford University Press, 1989), 37.

4 John D. Morris, "Kennedy Cabinet Sets Precedents," *New York Times*, 18 December 1960.

5 David Halberstam, *The Best and the Brightest* (New York: Random House, 1972), 21.

6 For the estimate that one-third of the senior appointments went to Harvard alumni, see G. Scott Thomas, *A New World to Be Won: John Kennedy, Richard Nixon, and the Tumultuous Year of 1960* (Santa Barbara: Praeger, 2011), 269. The Harvard graduates included the president himself; Robert Kennedy, the president's brother and attorney general; McGeorge Bundy, national security advisor; Robert McNamara, secretary of defense; Douglas Dillon, treasury secretary; J. Edward Day, postmaster general; Willard Wirtz, secretary of labor; Paul Nitze, assistant secretary of defense for international security affairs; and Kenny O'Donnell, appointments secretary. The Yale alumni in Kennedy's circle included McGeorge Bundy; Walt Rostow, deputy national security advisor; William Bundy, deputy assistant secretary of defense for international security affairs; Chester Bowles, undersecretary of state; and Averell Harriman, ambassador at large and then undersecretary of state for political affairs.

7 John F. Kennedy, *Why England Slept* (London: Hutchinson, 1940); John F. Kennedy, *Profiles in Courage* (New York: Harper, 1956); W.W. Rostow, *British Economy of the Nineteenth Century* (Oxford: Clarendon Press, 1948); W.W. Rostow, *The Process of Economic Growth* (New York: Norton, 1952); W.W. Rostow with Alfred Levin, *The Dynamics of Soviet Society* (Cambridge: Centre for International Studies, Massachusetts Institute of Technology, 1952); W.W. Rostow with Richard W. Hatch, Frank A. Kierman, Jr., and Alexander Eckstein, *The Prospects for Chinese Communist Society* (Cambridge: Center for International Studies, Massachusetts Institute of Technology, 1954); W.W. Rostow with Richard W. Hatch, *An American Policy in Asia* (New York: John Wiley and Sons, 1955); Max F. Millikan and W.W. Rostow, *A Proposal: Key to an Effective Foreign Policy* (New York: Harper, 1957); W.W. Rostow, *The United*

States in the World Arena: An Essay in Recent History (New York: Harper, 1960); Arthur M. Schlesinger, Jr., *Orestes A. Brownson: A Pilgrim's Progress* (Boston, Little Brown, 1939); Arthur M. Schlesinger, Jr., *The Age of Jackson* (Boston: Little Brown, 1945); Arthur M. Schlesinger, Jr., *The Vital Center: The Politics of Freedom* (Boston: Houghton Mifflin, 1949); Richard H. Rovere and Arthur M. Schlesinger, Jr., *The General and the President, and the Future of American Foreign Policy* (New York: Farrar, Straus and Young, 1951); Arthur M. Schlesinger Jr., *The Age of Roosevelt*, 3 vols. (Boston: Houghton Mifflin, 1957, 1958, 1960); Max Taylor, *The Uncertain Trumpet* (New York: Harper, 1960). The authorship of Kennedy's books is disputed. Journalist Arthur Krock rewrote *Why England Slept*. The ideas in *Profiles in Courage* might have been Kennedy's, but most of the words were those of his aide and speechwriter, Theodore Sorensen.

8   Diary entry, 5 July 1963, Thomas Fisher Rare Book Library, University of Toronto, Ms. Coll. 00626, Charles Ritchie Diaries, box 3, published in Charles Ritchie, *Storm Signals: More Undiplomatic Diaries, 1962–1971* (Toronto: Macmillan, 1983), 52.
9   Halberstam, *Best and the Brightest*, 36.
10 Ibid., 27.
11 Knowlton Nash, *Kennedy and Diefenbaker: Fear and Loathing across the Undefended Border* (Toronto: McClelland and Stewart, 1990), 254.
12 Nancy Gager Clinch, *The Kennedy Neurosis* (New York: Grosset and Dunlap, 1973), 98.
13 "Image and Reality," interview with Charles Roberts, in *The Kennedy Presidency: Seventeen Intimate Perspectives of John F. Kennedy*, ed. Kenneth W. Thompson (Lanham, MD: University Press of America, 1985), 181.
14 Arnold Heeney, *The Things That Are Caesar's: Memoirs of a Canadian Public Servant*, ed. Brian D. Heeney (Toronto: University of Toronto Press, 1972), 177.
15 Nash, *Kennedy and Diefenbaker*, 63. Basil Robinson claimed that Kennedy mispronounced the prime minister's name at the Uplands airport after arriving in Ottawa. A recording at the JFK Library shows that the president pronounced the name correctly. Robinson was likely confusing the two incidents. H. Basil Robinson, *Diefenbaker's World: A Populist in Foreign Affairs* (Toronto: University of Toronto Press, 1989), 198; and "Remarks Upon Arrival at the Royal Canadian Air Force Uplands Airport in Ottawa," 16 May 1961, John F. Kennedy Presidential Library, White House Audio Collection, ser. 1, vol. 30, https://www.jfklibrary.org/Asset-Viewer/Archives/JFKWHA-030-003.aspx.
16 Audio recording of press conference, 8 February 1961, John F. Kennedy Presidential Library, White House Audio Collection, ser. 1, vol. 9, https://www.jfklibrary.org/Asset-Viewer/Archives/JFKWHA-009.aspx.
17 Nash, *Kennedy and Diefenbaker*, 97.
18 Heeney, *Things That Are Caesar's*, 175.
19 Nash, *Kennedy and Diefenbaker*, 128.
20 Extract of an interview with Charles Ritchie, quoted in Peter Stursberg, *Lester Pearson and the American Dilemma* (Toronto: Doubleday, 1980), 188; David E. Koskoff, *Joseph P. Kennedy: A Life and Times* (Englewood Cliffs, NJ: Prentice-Hall, 1974), 558n198.
21 Nash, *Kennedy and Diefenbaker*, 174.
22 Ibid., 173.

23 Willis C. Armstrong, transcript of interview conducted by Charles Stuart Kennedy, 29 November 1988, Association for Diplomatic Studies and Training, Foreign Affairs Oral History Project, lcweb2.loc.gov/service/mss/mfdip/2004/2004arm03/2004arm03.pdf.

24 Bruce Muirhead, *Against the Odds: The Public Life and Times of Louis Rasminsky* (Toronto: University of Toronto Press, 1999), 345n70.

25 Seymour M. Hersh, *The Dark Side of Camelot* (Boston: Little Brown, 1997), 31.

26 Halberstam, *Best and the Brightest*, 59.

27 Nash, *Kennedy and Diefenbaker*, 99.

28 Ibid., 131. See also Nash, *Kennedy and Diefenbaker*, 12 and 99; and Willis C. Armstrong, transcript of interview conducted by Charles Stuart Kennedy, 29 November 1988, Association for Diplomatic Studies and Training, Foreign Affairs Oral History Project, lcweb2.loc.gov/service/mss/mfdip/2004/2004arm03/2004arm03.pdf.

29 Robinson, *Diefenbaker's World*, 277.

30 McGeorge Bundy, "Canada, the Exceptionally Favored: An American Perspective," in *Friends So Different: Essays on Canada and the United States in the 1980s*, ed. Lansing Lamont and J. Duncan Edmonds (Ottawa: University of Ottawa Press, 1989), 236.

31 Halberstam, *Best and the Brightest*, 41.

32 Ibid., 60.

33 W. Walton Butterworth, transcript of interview conducted by Dennis J. O'Brien, 28 May 1970, in Princeton, New Jersey, John F. Kennedy Presidential Library, John F. Kennedy Oral History Collection (hereafter JFKOH), https://www.jfklibrary.org/Asset-Viewer/Archives/JFKOH-WIWB-01.aspx.

34 Frank Costigliola, "Kennedy, the European Allies, and the Failure to Consult," *Political Science Quarterly* 110, 1 (1995): 115. See also Frank Costigliola, "Kennedy, De Gaulle, and the Challenge of Consultation," in *De Gaulle and the United States: A Centennial Reappraisal*, ed. Robert O. Paxton and Nicholas Wahl (Oxford: Berg, 1994), 169–94.

35 Ritchie, *Storm Signals*, 3.

36 Costigliola, "Kennedy, the European Allies, and the Failure to Consult," 119.

37 Nash, *Kennedy and Diefenbaker*, 183.

38 Merchant to Rusk, [December 1962?], JFKNSF, vol. 18, file 4, in *FRUS, 1961–1963*, vol. 13, *Western Europe and Canada*, doc. 441, pp. 1190–91.

39 Nash, *Kennedy and Diefenbaker*, 189–90.

40 Cees Wiebes and Bert Zeeman, "'I Don't Need Your Handkerchiefs': Holland's Experience of Crisis Consultation in NATO," *International Affairs* 66, 1 (1990): 91–113, esp. 96–101.

41 Dean Acheson, transcript of interview with Lucius D. Battle, 27 April 1964, JFKOH, https://www.jfklibrary.org/Asset-Viewer/Archives/JFKOH-DGA-01.aspx.

42 Sheldon M. Stern, *The Cuban Missile Crisis in American Memory: Myths Versus Reality* (Stanford: Stanford University Press, 2012), 71.

43 See K.A. Cuordileone, "'Politics in an Age of Anxiety': Cold War Political Culture and the Crisis in American Masculinity, 1949–1960," *Journal of American History* 87, 2 (2000): esp. 544–45.

44 Richard J. Barnet, *The Roots of War: The Men and the Institution behind US Foreign Policy* (Baltimore: Penguin, 1973), 109.

45 Richard Reeves, *President Kennedy: Profile of Power* (New York: Simon and Schuster, 1993), 72.

46 Halberstam, *Best and the Brightest*, 21. As Kyle Cuordileone notes perceptively, idealism was "reserved for public political speeches." See K.A. Cuordileone, *Manhood and American Political Culture in the Cold War* (New York: Routledge, 2005), 218.

47 Thomas W. Zeiler, "The Diplomatic History Bandwagon: A State of the Field," *Journal of American History* 95, 4 (2009): 1067.

48 Kristin L. Hoganson, *Fighting for American Manhood: How Gender Politics Provoked the Spanish-American and Philippine-American Wars* (New Haven: Yale University Press, 1998); Mary Ann Heiss, "Real Men Don't Wear Pajamas: Anglo-American Cultural Perceptions of Mohammed Mossadeq and the Iranian Oil Nationalization Dispute," in *Empire and Revolution: The United States and the Third World since 1945*, ed. Peter L. Hahn and Mary Ann Heiss (Columbus: Ohio State University Press, 2001), 178–94; Mary Ann Heiss, *Empire and Nationhood: The United States, Great Britain, and Iranian Oil, 1950–1954* (New York: Columbia University Press, 1997); Robert D. Dean, "Masculinity as Ideology: John F. Kennedy and the Domestic Politics of Foreign Policy," *Diplomatic History* 22, 1 (1998): 29–62; Robert D. Dean, *Imperial Brotherhood: Gender and the Making of Cold War Foreign Policy* (Amherst: University of Massachusetts Press, 2001); Cuordileone, "Politics in an Age of Anxiety," 515–45; Cuordileone, *Manhood and American Political Culture.*

49 See, for example, an article for *Sports Illustrated* in which Kennedy used the words "vigor" or "vigorous" nine times (including in the title). John F. Kennedy, "The Vigor We Need," *Sports Illustrated*, 16 July 1962.

50 Livingston Merchant to Dean Rusk, 12 April 1961, telegram no. 780, JFKNSF, vol. 018, file 002.

51 Benjamin C. Bradlee, *Conversations with Kennedy* (New York: W.W. Norton, 1975), 183; Nash, *Kennedy and Diefenbaker*, 160, 288.

52 Angier Biddle Duke, transcript of interview with Frank Sieverts, 7 April 1964, JFKOH, https://www.jfklibrary.org/Asset-Viewer/Archives/JFKOH-ABD-01.aspx.

53 Record of telephone conversation between George Ball and Douglas Dillon, 26 April 1961, John F. Kennedy Presidential Library, George Ball Personal Papers, vol. 2, file 5.

54 Merchant to Rusk, 12 April 1961, telegram no. 780, JFKNSF, vol. 18, file 2.

55 Merchant to George Ball, 5 May 1962, JFKNSF, vol. 18, file 4, in *FRUS, 1961–1963*, vol. 13, *Western Europe and Canada*, doc. 433, pp. 1172–1177.

56 Willis Armstrong to Rusk, telegram no. 138, 30 July 1962, JFKNSF, vol. 18, file 11.

57 Angier Biddle Duke, transcript of interview with Frank Sieverts, 7 April 1964, JFKOH, https://www.jfklibrary.org/Asset-Viewer/Archives/JFKOH-ABD-01.aspx..

58 Merchant to George Ball, 5 May 1962, JFKNSF, vol. 18, file 4, in *FRUS, 1961–1963*, vol. 13, *Western Europe and Canada*, doc. 433, pp. 1172–77.

59 Memorandum for meeting with Prime Minister Diefenbaker [February 1961?], John F. Kennedy Presidential Library, Papers of John F. Kennedy, Presidential Papers, President's Office Files (hereafter JFKPOF), vol. 113, file 4.

60 "President's Trip to Ottawa, 16–18 May 1961, Scope Paper," 2 May 1961, JFKPOF, vol. 113, file 9.

61 The systems were the Bomarc B missile, the CF104 Starfighter fighter/bomber, the Honest John rocket, and the CF-101 Voodoo interceptor aircraft.

62 Rusk to Merchant, 3 August 1961, JFKNSF, vol. 20, file 1, in *FRUS, 1961–63*, vol. 13, *Western Europe and Canada*, doc. 426, pp. 1162–63.

63 Armstrong to Rusk, telegram no. 138, 15 August 1961, JFKNSF, vol. 20, file 1.

64 Robinson, *Diefenbaker's World*, 229.

65 Langevin Côté, "Diefenbaker Calls on All NATO Nations to Bring Forces to Full Strength," *Globe and Mail*, 16 August 1961.

66 Armstrong to Rusk, telegram no. 290, 14 September 1961, JFKNSF, vol. 20, file 1.

67 "The Periscope," *Newsweek*, 25 September 1961, 19. The issue was dated 25 September but was published several days earlier. Diefenbaker was asked about the story in the Commons on 19 September.

68 Robinson, *Diefenbaker's World*, 230.

69 Harold Morrison, "JFK Presses Canada on Nuclear Warheads," *Montreal Gazette*, 20 September 1961.

70 Kennedy leaked secret information about Canada-US relations to Bradlee on at least one occasion. See Bradlee, *Conversations with Kennedy*, 183. Bradlee describes his friendship with the president in *A Good Life: Newspapering and Other Adventures* (New York: Simon and Schuster, 1995).

71 Armstrong to Rusk, telegram no. 317, 20 September 1961, JFKNSF, vol. 20, file 1. For more on how the press leak delayed progress on the nuclear issue, see Merchant to Rusk, telegram 807, 26 February 1962, JFKNSF, vol. 20, file 1.

72 Canadian Institute of Public Opinion, "Liberals 45 p.c., Tories 38 p.c. Survey Reveals," *Toronto Star*, 9 May 1962; Canadian Institute of Public Opinion, "Popularity of Liberals Holds at 47 Per Cent," *Toronto Star*, 11 January 1963; Canadian Institute of Public Opinion, "Gallup Poll: 41 Per Cent for Liberals, 32 Per Cent PCs," *Toronto Star*, 6 April 1963.

73 Merchant to Rusk, telegram 807, 26 February 1962, JFKNSF, vol. 20, file 1.

74 "Recent Developments in Canada," 10 November 1961, JFKNSF, vol. 18, file 7.

75 Butterworth to Rusk, telegram no. 990, 3 February 1963, JFKNSF, vol. 18, file 13.

76 Butterworth to Rusk, telegram no. 1327, 15 April 1963, JFKNSF, vol. 18a, file 1, in *FRUS, 1961–1963*, vol. 13, *Western Europe and Canada*, doc. 447, p. 1200.

77 Interview with Douglas Harkness, 22 July 1974, cited in Jocelyn Maynard Ghent, "Did He Fall or Was He Pushed? The Kennedy Administration and the Collapse of the Diefenbaker Government," *International History Review* 1, 2 (1979): 26.

78 Nash, *Kennedy and Diefenbaker*, 266.

79 Ibid., 307.

80 McGeorge Bundy to Rusk and McNamara, 1 April 1963, in *FRUS*, vol. 13, doc. 446, pp. 1199–1200.

81 Willis C. Armstrong, transcript of interview conducted by Charles Stuart Kennedy, 29 November 1988, Association for Diplomatic Studies and Training, Foreign Affairs Oral History Project, lcweb2.loc.gov/service/mss/mfdip/2004/2004arm03/2004arm03.pdf.

82 Nash, *Kennedy and Diefenbaker*, 281.

83 Ibid., 279.

84 Butterworth to Rusk, telegram no. 1328, 15 April 1963, JFKNSF, vol. 018a, file 1.

85 Diary entry, 5 July 1963, Ritchie diaries, box 3. Ritchie slightly altered the quotation in the published version of his diary. See Ritchie, *Storm Signals*, 52.

PART 3

Nuclear Weapons

6 The Defence Dilemma, 1957–63
Reconsidering the Strategic, Technological, and Operational Contexts

ISABEL CAMPBELL

On 24 May 1957, the North Atlantic Council[1] approved an American-led strategy of massive retaliation through "the greatest intensity of nuclear exchange" at the outset of a war.[2] The decision put pressure on NATO forces to acquire tactical weapon systems armed with American atomic warheads and created controversy within the alliance over the control of those warheads.[3] The massive retaliation strategy, known as MC 14/2, highlighted American dominance, exacerbating national angst and divisions within NATO. Then the next decade exploded with a rapid series of strategic, technological, and operational transitions that turned defence planning into a political minefield. Faced with insufficient conventional forces and limited defence budgets, NATO militaries developed unrealistic nuclear battle plans and used arguments about equality for their forces to gain access to tactical nuclear weapons systems that had questionable strategic value and, in many cases, substantive performance limitations.

John Diefenbaker took office on 21 June 1957, just as these events began to unfold. Canada's contributions to North American and European defence and to United Nations peacekeeping missions stretched its modest resources; at first, tactical nuclear weapons appeared to offer cheaper, more effective options for the first two areas. The Diefenbaker government approved the acquisition of several tactical nuclear systems and the Departments of External Affairs and National Defence began to negotiate with the Americans for access to the warheads.

Early input from the Department of External Affairs focused on ensuring Canadian or joint control over the release of the warheads,[4] but by 1960 Howard Green, the secretary of state for external affairs, and his undersecretary, Norman Robertson, had become concerned about the rapid growth in nuclear weapons and the problem of fallout, and they therefore promoted arms control.[5] External's negotiating tactics now seemed designed to prevent agreement in order to allow disarmament discussions to proceed. The prolonged negotiations coincided with a new American strategy of flexible response, which promoted a "conventional pause" (i.e., the use of conventional weapons only) at the outbreak of war, followed by the possible gradual use of tactical nuclear weapons and increasing to strategic nuclear retaliation only if aggression was not halted. Nevertheless, senior Royal Canadian Air Force (RCAF) leaders clung to the massive retaliation strategy, ignoring subordinates who urged consideration of the conventional pause doctrine.

Faced with the growing split between External Affairs and National Defence, Diefenbaker appeared to waver, unable to make up his mind. Canada might have reconsidered its nuclear commitments before the weapons systems were actually in place, but Diefenbaker took no initiative in that direction until almost the end of his time in office. To some observers he seemed incompetent and unable to manage the government, resulting in the eventual resignation of Defence Minister Douglas Harkness, the loss of a confidence vote in Parliament, and an election win for Lester B. Pearson's Liberals in April 1963.

By January 1963, Diefenbaker had recognized the strategic potential of the submarine-mounted Polaris missile, which could lurk undetected under ocean water layers, providing a second-strike capability that effectively ruled out a pre-emptive Soviet attack. However, by then it was too late. Diefenbaker's attempt to justify his delays by stating that the December 1962 Nassau agreement regarding Polaris missiles changed the requirement for Canada's nuclear commitments was given short shrift – but he was right. Canadian historians and others have belittled Diefenbaker's words,[6] but Polaris had changed the strategic picture. While it did not directly impact Canada's forces, it added enormously to deterrent capabilities, rendering the small Canadian nuclear commitments almost irrelevant. In retrospect, the Diefenbaker government's investments in conventional capabilities such as communications and signals systems, tanker-supply ships, and destroyers armed with helicopters delivered a better long-term value for Canada's defence dollar.[7] This chapter provides new information and a reassessment of the value of the Diefenbaker government's defence policies.

Cooperative North American defence planning dated back to 1940, when the American and Canadian militaries drew up joint plans treating the defence of North America as a single problem and used their forces in cooperation under separate commands. Canada's ambivalence about nuclear deterrence and disarmament can be traced to early 1946 when, under Prime Minister W.L.M. King, Defence Minister Douglas Abbott called for American nuclear deterrence to bolster Canadian conventional forces, even as Canadian diplomats unsuccessfully pursued United Nations control of nuclear weapons.[8] In practical terms, the paradox mattered little during the late 1940s and early 1950s: Canada carried on futile disarmament discussions while exporting uranium for American weapons development and relying upon those weapons for deterrence. Together the Americans and Canadians constructed early warning systems in North America;[9] Canada also sent a brigade group and an air division to Europe to deter a Soviet attack.

By 1955, both governments became alarmed in the wake of the crucial American Killian report, which examined the possibility of a surprise first-strike attack on North America, warning that as few as two hundred nuclear bombs might result in a Soviet victory.[10] As a result of the report's recommendations, the United States invested in powerful intercontinental ballistic missiles (ICBMs), downgrading the future role of bombers and interceptor aircraft.[11] The US updated procedures for overflying Canadian airspace with atomic weapons and negotiated the North American Air Defence Command agreement,[12] placing American and Canadian forces under a single command.

In 1957 the Soviets successfully tested their first ICBM, a year before the Americans, and launched the Sputnik satellite. These developments exacerbated European fears of American abandonment in the event of a Soviet attack and fuelled an urgent demand for NATO tactical nuclear arms,[13] in accordance with the new MC 14/2 strategy. Canada's military leaders balked at NATO's 1957 request to assume a nuclear strike and reconnaissance role, fearing that resources were insufficient for both this new role and the traditional air defence. They also panned an alliance request to acquire the dual-capable (nuclear and conventional) Honest John missile, which seemed exorbitantly priced and inappropriate for brigade support in Europe.[14] After Defence Minister George Pearkes and Lieutenant-General Charles Foulkes, the Chairman, Chiefs of Staff (CCOS), negotiated to replace the Honest John with the cheaper Lacrosse system on 1 October 1958, cabinet approved this acquisition.[15]

Meanwhile, with the appearance of unidentified submarines off their coast, Canadians became more concerned about the defence of their own territory.[16] As a result of American pressure and gaps in the protection of Ontario and Quebec, in the summer of 1958 Pearkes initiated requests for the American Bomarc-B missile to be located at sites in these provinces.[17] Diefenbaker announced the decision to acquire the Bomarc-B on 23 September 1958. At the same time, he revealed that the future of Canada's technically advanced but expensive Avro Arrow interceptor was in question.[18] Some considered that ICBMs would render interceptors obsolete, and Canada had been unable to obtain orders for the Arrow from the United States or other allies.

The Bomarc-B was controlled by a complex computer system (SAGE), which was vulnerable to jamming and likely to be overwhelmed in an attack; however, without better alternatives, cabinet and the military sought merely to limit the expenditure.[19] Lacking a full appreciation of the drawbacks of tactical nuclear weapons, Pearkes asked his colleagues to consider "whether Canadian forces should be as well-equipped as U.S. forces alongside them and performing the same tasks."[20] The implication was that conventional forces were always inferior to nuclear-armed ones. This perception led air force leaders and Pearkes to ignore the uncomfortable fact that tactical nuclear warfare was suicidal: military planners anticipated staggering death rates. Nuclear weapons were useful for deterrence rather than for fighting actual battles.[21] But because military projections were highly classified, the equality argument gained ground and seemed to have a common-sense appeal.[22]

Given the dismal progress in disarmament talks,[23] officials at External Affairs initially accepted the nuclear proposals, arguing that a nuclear-armed Canada might hold the United States back from "any rash or hasty decision."[24] While an American pre-emptive strike against the Soviet Union seemed improbable, American plans included this option. Diefenbaker's cabinet agreed with external's arguments: the ministers "wished ... to ensure the proper use of these [nuclear] weapons."[25]

By early 1959, the chiefs of staff and Pearkes had over-ruled air leaders who fought hard to protect the Arrow. On 20 February, Diefenbaker rose in Parliament and revealed the Arrow's demise. In one stroke, the government put nearly thirty thousand people out of work, damaged national pride, and made it necessary to find compensatory programs to assist Canada's aircraft industry.[26] The shock of the Arrow decision overshadowed Diefenbaker's next words about impending negotiations for nuclear warheads to arm the Bomarc and Lacrosse systems. The two systems were still under development; Diefenbaker stressed Canada's obligation to pursue disarmament while waiting for them to become available. The leader of the Opposition, Lester Pearson, spoke immediately after the prime minister. Like Diefenbaker, the cabinet, and the bureaucrats, Pearson saw no contradiction in acquiring nuclear weapons systems while at the same time promoting disarmament.[27]

In Europe, General Lauris Norstad, the Supreme Allied Commander,[28] lacked sufficient conventional forces and therefore pushed NATO members hard to fulfill the tactical nuclear requirements. In May 1959, Norstad visited Ottawa to once again ask the government to approve the strike role. His offer was attractive: the strike role would replace the conventional air defence role, reducing the number of aircraft per squadron, while airframes and engines could be produced under licence in Canada, softening the blow of the Avro cancellation and possibly allowing Canada to market aircraft parts to other NATO nations.[29] A few defence insiders pointed out that airfields in Europe were vulnerable to Soviet missiles, while others argued that RCAF resources might be better used in defending Canada itself, but the chiefs of staff committee did not explore these topics in any depth.[30]

External Affairs and the cabinet recognized the urgency of the matter, but some ministers probably failed to appreciate the operational challenges of the new role. Pearkes informed his cabinet colleagues that the role was one of "counter-attack," leaving out the information that if the Soviets struck first with nuclear missiles, they would undoubtedly wipe out the few Canadian air bases. After extended discussion, cabinet approved the selection of the American Lockheed F104 (Starfighter).[31]

Shortly before this decision was made, Howard Green took over as secretary of state for external affairs. He was briefed on the issue by Norman Robertson, who had served as undersecretary since October 1958. Although Robertson had previously expressed to Diefenbaker his personal misgivings about the arms race, he warned Green that if Canada did not re-equip its air division it might start "a chain reaction" among the "lukewarm members of NATO" and that any delay on this matter "would undoubtedly result in some considerable weakening of our influence within the alliance." Robertson was well aware that the NATO request involved a change from "the essentially defensive task of intercepting enemy bombers" to "attacking with tactical nuclear bombs special targets in Eastern Europe." He briefly fretted that the change was "not too clear to the Canadian public"; nevertheless, Robertson was convinced that Canada should do as Norstad asked.[32]

At this stage, Robertson and Green believed that Canada's acceptance of the strike role would strengthen its voice in NATO Council, and Robertson argued that NATO reassessment might well have an impact on disarmament talks.[33] During 1959, this foreign policy justification for the nuclear role, along with the advantages associated with possible West German and other European aircraft orders, dominated government discussions.[34] Cabinet ministers readily agreed that Canada's "military contribution should be geared to make our political voice as effective as possible."[35] Green did not object to the nuclear strike role or to the decision to acquire the F104s at any of the first three cabinet meetings he attended after his new appointment.[36]

Like Canada, most NATO members purchased American systems to avoid the astronomical development costs,[37] creating not only an irksome sense of dependence but also resentment when systems failed, were cancelled, or had to be replaced by other systems. For example, in 1960, after the Lacrosse performed poorly, Canada replaced it with the Honest John, which was now cheaper, though its battlefield performance was doubtful.[38] NATO decision makers overlooked such issues because these systems contributed to deterrence, and, by helping to offset American defence expenditures in Europe, they seemed essential to financing the American presence there.[39]

Most performance reports were classified, but enough information came out during Congressional hearings in Washington to cause public speculation about system failures. In July 1959, Pearson used this information to challenge the government's approach. Abandoning his earlier agreement with Diefenbaker, Pearson now argued that Canadian acceptance of American nuclear warheads would increase American dominance and that NATO planners might adopt a flexible response to minor attacks. While he accepted the immediate demand for tactical nuclear weapons, Pearson hoped it would soon be possible for Canada to renegotiate its nuclear commitments.[40]

Diefenbaker held to his original insistence that Canada would both negotiate for access to the warheads and pursue disarmament. However, Green was strongly influenced by new scientific evidence about fallout, and, by early 1960, his support for nuclear weapons unravelled.[41] As Michael Stevenson describes in Chapter 12 (this volume), Green's dogged efforts clashed with US and NATO strategies and the defence procurement decisions, creating anxiety for military leaders and allies alike. General E.L.M. Burns, Canada's disarmament advisor, considered Green's stand too inflexible,[42] but his own concerns were serious enough to override this consideration.

Together Green, Robertson, and Burns mounted a vigorous campaign to halt the spread of nuclear weapons.

At the same time, US general Maxwell Taylor, who had resigned because of his disagreement with the massive retaliation strategy, began to promote flexible response. In early 1960 he published a book, *Uncertain Trumpet*. It privately influenced presidential candidate John F. Kennedy, but President Dwight D. Eisenhower and senior officers of the United States Air Force (USAF) rejected Taylor's arguments.[43] Like their USAF counterparts, Canada's military chiefs adhered to massive deterrence. While such strategic dogmatism did not impair most of Canada's growing flexible conventional capabilities, it seriously affected key RCAF decisions.

The 1959 Cabinet Defence Committee submission for the F104 had specified the "capability of delivering [both] conventional and nuclear warheads."[44] Nevertheless, on 1 February 1960, Air Marshal Hugh Campbell – who firmly opposed nuclear disarmament and conventional options[45] – ordered air staff to delete the conventional requirement from the CF104 program. Later Air Council minutes incorrectly stated that the F104 was incompatible with conventional weapons.[46] As a result, Canada became the only NATO member with the F104 lacking conventional strike capability, just as NATO planners began to contemplate flexible response.

Norstad's decision to rely on tactical nuclear weapons was made more difficult when news about fallout created public opposition to their acquisition.[47] With tensions rising over Berlin, Norstad and French general Jean Valluy recommended that NATO build up its conventional forces to allow for a flexible response in the event of a limited Soviet attack.[48] In April 1960, West German general Adolph Heusinger explained that both he and Defence Minister Franz Josef Strauss believed "NATO forces should be ... able to offer effective resistance for at least a few days using conventional weapons only" if the enemy was not using atomic weapons. Because it might "take a considerable time before NATO Council authorized use of nuclear weapons," they insisted upon a dual conventional-nuclear capability in the F104.[49] Campbell was aware of these views, but in late 1960 he ruled out conventional capability in the Canadian version due to the alleged "great cost" and his belief that it might invite attack.[50]

Canada's other military chiefs did not challenge Campbell's decision. Even as NATO leaders and strategic critics called for more conventional forces, most member governments, except for West Germany, actually reduced their numbers in Europe. Canada's all-volunteer forces were particularly expensive; the chiefs believed its nuclear commitments helped to compensate for limited numbers. Pearkes took a severe battering in the press during the spring of 1960 over the Bomarc's poor performance in tests, but he refused to reconsider his 1958 recommendation even when the Americans wanted to cancel the program. Diefenbaker backed him up and personally intervened with President Eisenhower, ensuring that the controversial missile program would continue.[51]

In the meantime, Foulkes became alarmed by the growing divergence within the government, and perhaps also by the press stories ridiculing the Bomarc's failures. In May 1960, Foulkes asked Brigadier D.A.G. Waldock, chief of the Joint Ballistic Missile Defence Staff (JBMDS) to prepare a report on defence disarmament views. Foulkes proposed to meet with Robert Bryce (the secretary to cabinet) and Robertson to reach an agreement in principle to create a more integrated government approach, followed by a detailed briefing of the Cabinet Defence Committee (CDC).[52] In the early Diefenbaker years, the CDC rarely met because Pearkes, a former army general, resented discussing military matters with Green and others who disagreed with him.[53]

The CDC and the Chiefs of Staff Committee were designed to produce well-integrated foreign and defence policies, but both bodies failed to perform this function. According to their terms of reference, the chiefs were to invite the secretary to cabinet and the undersecretary of state for external affairs to their meetings whenever "major policy items" or items outside of a "purely military concern" were raised.[54] However, Foulkes had let this essential procedure slip by 1960. His belated attempt to recover foreign and defence policy coordination was dashed when the deputy minister of national defence, Frank Miller (a former RCAF officer), disagreed with the need for a special meeting.[55] After Miller replaced Foulkes as CCOS in June, he continued to ignore the requirement to discuss major policy decisions with the top bureaucrats.[56]

Miller also dismissed written input from External Affairs. For example, shortly after the Americans first tested the Polaris missile in July 1960, Robertson observed to Miller that the new weapon gave a "strategic striking capability far beyond the requirements currently envisaged for the NATO shield forces" and wondered if NATO strategy and Canada's nuclear commitments might change as a result of these new capabilities.[57] Miller insisted that Polaris would "not affect Canada's present military commitments to NATO," focusing on the immediate tactical picture, which remained the same.[58] Polaris certainly could not fill the CF104's tactical role, which called for greater precision than the Polaris could provide. Yet, as an easily concealed, powerful second-strike weapon, Polaris almost eliminated the chance of a Soviet first strike, adding to the massive growth in strategic and tactical missile capability that rendered Canada's nuclear commitments almost superfluous.

Pearkes, Miller, and other Canadian leaders were hampered in their assessment of defence requirements because they lacked accurate knowledge of American nuclear capabilities and targets. In August 1960, Eisenhower ordered the American forces to coordinate their nuclear targeting; the resulting report, which exposed shocking facts on nuclear "overkill,"[59] was not shared with allies. Later on, Canadians learned that targets "were covered as many as three, four, or five times by different missiles or bombers."[60] Knowledge of this redundancy might have led to a Canadian reassessment, but, without a complete picture of American capabilities, Canada's air leaders did not question existing commitments.

On 12 October 1960, Douglas Harkness, a "tough, abrasive, and courageous" decorated veteran, took over the defence portfolio after Pearkes's resignation.[61] When Harkness asked for a brief on nuclear weapons, Miller shut down the military officers who attempted to examine alternatives to the nuclear-only tactical imperative. On 15 November 1960, Brigadier Waldock prepared a draft brief for the new minister, proposing that the RCAF develop "an effective non-nuclear capability in addition to their proposed nuclear capability" with respect to its strike role.[62] Waldock argued that a failure to address the need for limited warfare with conventional weapons "could result in the ground disappearing under existing Canadian defence policy" because "an exclusively nuclear NATO defence posture is becoming less viable both politically and militarily."[63] Apparently Waldock (who was an army officer) was unaware that cabinet had actually approved a dual-capable aircraft, but Miller certainly knew it. Regardless of their personal opinions, the chiefs should have examined the costs involved and invited Robertson and Bryce to objectively weigh all the pros and cons of the dual-role case, but Miller unilaterally rejected it.[64]

Two days later, the JBMDS prepared a substitute brief that assured Harkness that a conventionally armed CF104 "would be an impotent weapon in a theatre committed to a nuclear strategy."[65] The new brief focused on short-term operational plans, failing to mention possible future implementation of the conventional pause doctrine. Nor did it consider the likely delays in NATO's authorization for the use of nuclear weapons, the obvious vulnerability of nuclear-armed aircraft, or the utility of conventional forces for deterrence of minor Soviet incursions into allied territory. Worse, it stated that tactical nuclear weapons were "essential" for the battlefield, failing to mention the dangers they posed. The paper discounted second-strike strategic nuclear weapons such as Polaris. Because Harkness received only this one-sided brief, Diefenbaker now had two strong ministers who took starkly opposing views on nuclear issues.

In contrast, Burns provided Green with a better, long-term analysis, correctly stating that Canadian forces would become targets as soon as the Soviets knew they were nuclear-armed. Their short-range delivery systems, Burns pointed out, would leave them vulnerable to longer-range Russian nuclear rockets.[66] Emphasizing NATO's need for conventional strength, Burns advised Canada to reconsider the decision to acquire nuclear warheads in favour of offering moderate increases in land and air forces equipped with modern conventional weapons. The Chiefs of Staff Committee failed in its duty to engage Bryce and Robertson in debates about such future options. The winter of 1960–61 thus marked a missed opportunity for coordinating foreign and defence policy and developing alternatives for the government to consider.

When cabinet discussed a disarmament resolution put forward at the United Nations by Ireland in December 1960, members realized if Canada voted in its favour, negotiations for nuclear warheads would likely be delayed. With the CF104s and Bomarcs expected to be ready for service at the end of 1961, the Department of National Defence worried about embarrassment over "having very expensive, virtually useless equipment" on its hands. Deprived of Waldock's analysis, Harkness was poorly informed about likely changes in NATO doctrine. He therefore insisted upon the nuclear-only option; he also inaccurately informed his colleagues that the CF104 would require extensive redesign to take conventional warheads.[67]

In January 1961, Bryce, a trusted advisor, recommended that Diefenbaker complete negotiations for the nuclear warheads, concluding that they were currently needed, even if IBCMs would render Canadian commitments less important in a few years. Bryce's opinion about an immediate requirement might have been different had he realized the extent of American nuclear overkill. But even if he had known this, it was still true that, as he pointed out to Diefenbaker, there would be "serious trouble here and in Europe in cancelling or frustrating the huge F104 programme."[68] In other words, commitments that involved defence production arrangements, with their economic benefit to Canada, could not easily be changed.

In Washington, the newly elected John F. Kennedy took office and learned about plans for over eighteen thousand American strategic and tactical nuclear warheads to be used in a single strike, with few options for any other response to even a minor attack.[69] Kennedy and his secretary of defence, Robert McNamara, pushed for increased European conventional forces, announcing new ideas and strategies without any consultation with allies.[70] At the same time, the USAF's Air Defense Command objected to over-reliance on the Bomarc.[71] These developments might have provided an opportunity to explore new options for Canada's defence contributions, trading its small nuclear obligations for conventional increases. However, nothing of the sort occurred. Ottawa had no alternative plans ready, and perhaps the new president would not have been interested in any case. From the beginning of his term in office, Kennedy was focused on getting Canada to move forward with the existing arrangements.

In February 1961, during the two leaders' first meeting, Diefenbaker told Kennedy that "so long as serious disarmament negotiations continued, Canada did not propose to determine whether or not to accept" the warheads: there would be no agreement on acquisition until Canada considered that nuclear weapons were actually needed.[72] Kennedy suggested a "two key" system if and when arrangements were made, and he believed that Diefenbaker had agreed to this, while Diefenbaker probably did not consider that his vague response had constituted a firm agreement.[73]

When Kennedy visited Ottawa and addressed Parliament in May 1961, he stressed that "we must strengthen the conventional capability of our Alliance as a matter of the highest priority."[74] Yet, in his private conversations with Diefenbaker, he again asked for action on nuclear weapons. To sweeten the arrangements, the president offered a "swap deal" whereby Canada would get dual-capable F101 (Voodoo) interceptors for continental defence, take over the cost of Pinetree radar stations, and build F104 aircraft for NATO partners. Diefenbaker declined to accept delivery of the F101s with nuclear warheads, and Kennedy acquiesced. It seemed to be a coup for Diefenbaker, benefiting the domestic aircraft industry while he again reserved his right to decide about nuclear weapons.[75] However, the Americans clearly informed him that they considered their own defence would degrade if the Canadian F101s were not nuclear-armed,[76] and they therefore believed that Diefenbaker would soon equip the new planes (which arrived in Canada in July 1961) with nuclear warheads.

Kennedy's expectations were crystal clear when he wrote to Diefenbaker on 3 August, stressing the need to renew nuclear negotiations as a way to signal allied resolve in view of rising tensions in Berlin.[77] As Stephen Azzi recounts in Chapter 5 (this volume), the prime minister replied favourably, but a White House press leak upset him, delaying matters again. The F101s remained equipped with conventional warheads only, and when the first Bomarc missiles arrived later in 1961, they had no warheads at all. However, Diefenbaker did answer Kennedy's call for additional conventional forces.

In September 1961, Diefenbaker increased the Canadian brigade in Europe by 1106 members, the air division by 250, and the RCN by 1,749; he also augmented army reinforcements in Canada.[78] But the government got little political credit for this increase because Harkness chose this moment to push the nuclear weapons agenda. The Soviets had just resumed atomic testing; with tensions over Berlin high and weapons systems coming on stream, Harkness wanted the nuclear agreements signed as much as Kennedy did. However, when Harkness raised the matter in Parliament, Paul Hellyer, the Liberal defence critic, immediately accused him of being out of touch with flexible response strategy.[79]

By January 1962, Diefenbaker seemed to be reconsidering Canada's nuclear commitments, but with understandable trepidation.[80] Not only was he hesitant to alter programs providing employment, but NATO had not yet advanced its discussions about key issues that might impact future commitments,[81] and so any definite decision seemed premature.[82] External Affairs considered a scheme to store warheads in the United States and bring them into Canada only during an alert, a proposal similar to one put forward by Norway and Denmark.[83] Robertson also quietly investigated dual and conventional options for Canada's nuclear-only systems, encountering solid resistance from Miller.[84]

Canada's proposals irritated American defence representatives, who complained that if the Canadian Bomarcs and F101s had been stationed south of the border, they would be nuclear-armed and contributing to defence. Canada, they argued, had taken these systems and now had an obligation to fully equip them for the joint task.[85] In August 1962, Harkness informed Diefenbaker that the idea of stockpiling warheads for Canadian use in the United States was unworkable because the early warning lines provided only two hours' warning, and at least fifteen hours would be required for the transfer.[86]

In Europe, the CF104s would soon be in the same situation as the Bomarcs. It was clear that a "full scale defence crisis" was looming.[87] Then the Cuban Missile Crisis of October 1962 brought American-Canadian difficulties to a head, putting Diefenbaker under extraordinary pressure to resolve the nuclear issue. In November, he and his cabinet agreed to pursue a "missing parts" proposal, reasoning that parts could be transferred in a much shorter time than the warheads themselves.[88] American officials considered and then rejected the Canadian suggestion, perhaps concerned that other allies might follow this example or make other unwelcome demands.[89]

In December 1962, Kennedy met with British prime minister Harold Macmillan to broker the Nassau Agreement. The agreement compensated the British for the unilateral American cancellation of the Skybolt missile, which the British had relied upon to arm their bomber force.[90] Diefenbaker joined the two leaders for lunch near the end of these negotiations, reporting that Macmillan was delighted with Kennedy's promise to supply British submarines with Polaris missiles – a much better strategic solution than the cancelled Skybolt. According to Diefenbaker, Macmillan emphasized his freedom to meet Soviet threats with these weapons, "regardless of the attitude of each or any of the other NATO partners."[91] With the powerful Polaris now available to the British, the situation had indeed changed.

Washington's attempt to market the Nassau arrangement as part of a NATO multilateral nuclear force fell apart when Macmillan provoked European outrage by bragging about his bilateral triumph.[92] Observing that it was too soon to understand the implications for Canada, Robertson told Diefenbaker that, at the December NATO meeting, Norstad had complained of "insufficient nuclear strike forces," while McNamara insisted that there was "sufficient capability to cover all significant military targets in Eastern Europe."[93] (Unbeknownst to Canadians, McNamara had quietly fired Norstad the previous summer, and Norstad had voiced thinly veiled criticisms of Kennedy's policies ever since.[94]) These American disputes further fed Diefenbaker's doubts about the need for Canadian forces to have the warheads.

The alliance was still in an uproar when Norstad visited Canada on a farewell tour on 3 January 1963 and held a press conference organized by the RCAF's public relations office.[95] In response to a reporter's question, Norstad agreed that, unless Canada negotiated for access to nuclear warheads, it was not fulfilling its NATO commitments.[96] Norstad hedged when pressed about a written Canadian commitment to take nuclear warheads (there was none), but his words were quickly interpreted in the press to imply that Diefenbaker had failed to honour explicit promises. Norstad's declaration, along with the absurdity of having weapon systems without any armaments whatever, likely influenced Pearson's 12 January 1963 statement that, if elected, he would "equip our forces with nuclear weapons under joint control with the US and afterwards discuss with our allies" a more realistic defence role without these weapons.[97]

Diefenbaker countered Pearson's new policy in Parliament on 25 January, arguing that the strike-reconnaissance role had been placed under doubt by the Nassau deal and suggesting a re-evaluation of allied defence plans at the forthcoming NATO meeting in May. He also made reference to the recent classified nuclear discussions with Washington.[98] Outraged by these indiscretions (and apparently forgetting Washington's own indiscretion in 1961), the State Department issued a press release, stating that Diefenbaker was wrong about Nassau.[99] Pearson also belittled Diefenbaker's interpretation,[100] while Harkness, fed up with the delays, resigned. Shortly afterwards, Diefenbaker lost a vote of confidence and was forced to call an election. Diefenbaker's public assessment of the Nassau agreement contributed to his political downfall, but his statement had merit, even though the agreement itself was not directly related to Canadian commitments.[101]

The strategic, technological, and operational shifts from 1957 to 1963 created a chaotic defence planning environment. Harkness and Canada's top air leaders believed that Canada would be weak without nuclear arms, insisting that conventional weapons were not sufficient. Initially, Green and officials at External Affairs seemed convinced that acceptance of nuclear arms would increase Canada's influence on the world stage. Yet the massive growth in American and Soviet nuclear weapons eclipsed Canadian and other allied contributions: by comparison, nuclear-armed or not, they seemed mere tokens. Arguably, Canada's conventional readiness during the Berlin and Cuban crises contributed to deterrence without dramatic nuclear brinkmanship. The focus on Diefenbaker's nuclear wavering has inadvertently caused most historians to overlook the value of Canada's conventional contributions during these two crises.[102] Ironically then, Canada's small but effective conventional forces supplied exactly the flexible options Kennedy seemed to want. Yet he relied on nuclear threats, insisting that Canada acquire tactical nuclear warheads despite his knowledge of American overkill capacity.

Despite the lack of strategic logic in Kennedy's position and the misinformation provided to cabinet by the Department of National Defence, Diefenbaker was far from blameless. He could have actively explored the full foreign policy and defence implications of changing Canada's nuclear policies in 1960, soon after Green began to object to them. Such a discussion might have yielded a compromise solution or at least produced a better understanding of the future defence alternatives. Instead, Diefenbaker intervened to halt the cancellation of the Bomarc in 1960 and accepted the F101s in 1961, exacerbating American frustrations when he did not follow through on what seemed to be renewed nuclear commitments. He showed poor political acumen by leaving systems without warheads after they were in place. While his argument about the Nassau agreement was perceptive, by 1963 his call for a reassessment was long overdue, and it proved to be not only futile but also politically disastrous.

NOTES

While this chapter draws upon research performed for official history, it represents the author's personal opinions and not the views of the Department of National Defence. The author thanks her National Defence colleagues for comments and hopes to publish further on various aspects of nuclear decision making.

1 The North Atlantic Council included representatives of Belgium, Canada, Denmark, France, the Federal Republic of Germany, Iceland, Italy, Luxembourg, the Netherlands, Norway, Portugal, Turkey, the United Kingdom, and the United States.

2 Greg Pedlow, ed., *NATO Strategy Documents, 1949–1969* (Brussels: NATO, 1997), xx, 290.

3 Strategic nuclear weapons were designed to destroy missile and military bases, industrial and populated centres. Tactical nuclear weapons were designed for battlefield use.

4 See Michael Stevenson, ed., *Documents on Canadian External Relations*, vol. 25, *1957–58*, pt. 2 (Ottawa: Department of Foreign Affairs and International Trade, 2004) (hereafter *DCER*, vol. 25), docs. 74, 87.

5 Daniel Heidt, "'I Think That Would Be the End of Canada': Howard Green, the Nuclear Test Ban, and Interest-Based Foreign Policy, 1946–1963," *American Review of Canadian Studies* 42, 3 (2012): 343–69.

6 Andrew Richter, *Avoiding Armageddon: Canadian Military Strategy and Nuclear Weapons, 1950–63* (Vancouver: UBC Press, 2002), 100–1; Patricia McMahon, *Essence of Indecision: Diefenbaker's Nuclear Policy, 1957–1963* (Montreal and Kingston: McGill-Queen's University Press, 2009), 164–67.

7 The Canadian Army increased its armoured and reconnaissance capabilities, while the RCAF and Royal Canadian Navy (RCN) improved anti-submarine warfare capabilities, including sonar and weaponry. All three services improved radar communications and signals. The RCN never acquired a nuclear capability and the Canadian Army had only the Honest John rocket.

8 Douglas Abbott, "Atomic Energy and National Defence," ca. February 1946, Douglas Abbott Fonds, Library and Archives Canada (hereafter LAC), MG 32, B 6, vol. 15, file 2; Albert Legault and Michel Fortmann, *The Diplomacy of Hope: Canada and Disarmament, 1945–1988* (Montreal and Kingston: McGill-Queen's University Press, 1992), 56–60.

9 New studies are beginning to evaluate the impact of Cold War defence initiatives on Aboriginals and others living in remote areas of Canada.

10 Report by the Technological Capabilities Panel of the Science Advisory Committee, 14 February 1955, *Foreign Relations of the United States, 1955–1957*, vol. 19 (Washington, DC: Government Printing Office, 1990), doc. 9.

11 Ibid.

12 Howard Green to Arnold Heeney, 5 November 1960, Janice Cavell, ed., *Documents on Canadian External Relations*, vol. 27, *1960* (Ottawa: Foreign Affairs and International Trade Canada, 2007) (hereafter *DCER*, vol. 27), doc. 286.

13 John Baylis and Kristen Stoddard, *The British Nuclear Experience: The Role of Beliefs, Culture, and Identity* (Oxford: Oxford University Press, 2015), 82.

14 Ray Stouffer, *Swords, Clunks and Widowmakers: The Tumultuous Life of the RCAF's Original 1 Canadian Air Division* (Ottawa: Department of National Defence, 2015), chap. 6; Isabel Campbell, *Unlikely Diplomats* (Vancouver: UBC Press, 2013), 165. Given the Honest John system's limited range, a nuclear warhead was as dangerous to the troops using it as it was to the enemy.

15 Cabinet Conclusions, 1 October 1958, LAC, RG 2, http://www.bac-lac.gc.ca/eng/discover/politics-government/cabinet-conclusions/Pages/cabinet-conclusions.aspx (hereafter online version).

16 Isabel Campbell, "Brave New World, 1945–1960," in *The Naval Service of Canada, 1910–1920*, ed. Richard Gimblett (Toronto: Dundurn, 2010), 134–36.

17 Early versions of the Bomarc were dual-capable, but the Bomarc-B took only a nuclear warhead. Pearkes did not emphasize the nuclear-only factor to his cabinet colleagues; however, officials at External Affairs were well aware of the facts from the beginning. See *DCER*, vol. 25, docs. 7, 72, 74, 87. Press stories immediately after Diefenbaker's announcement hinted that Canada would now ask the US for nuclear warheads. See *Toronto Star*, 24 September 1958; *Globe and Mail*, 24 September 1958.

Had Canada been willing to pay for a conventional warhead, no doubt Boeing would have developed one, though it would have been even more ineffective than the nuclear version. See Jon McLin, *Canada's Changing Defence Policy, 1957–1963* (Baltimore: Johns Hopkins University Press, 1967), 86. In 1961, Douglas Harkness informed his colleagues that a conventional warhead could be produced within six months, but ordering one never seems to have been seriously considered. Cabinet Conclusions, 21 November 1961, in Janice Cavell, ed., *Documents on Canadian External Relations*, vol. 28, *1961* (Ottawa: Foreign Affairs and International Trade Canada, 2009) (hereafter *DCER*, vol. 28), doc. 362.

18 McLin, *Canada's Changing Defence Policy*, 225–28.

19 John Clearwater, *Canadian Nuclear Weapons: The Untold Story of Canada's Cold War Arsenal* (Toronto: Dundurn, 1998), 55–58; McMahon, *Essence of Indecision*, 37–41; Cabinet Conclusions, 19 June 1959 (online version).

20 Cabinet Conclusions, 9 December 1958 (online version).

21 For British criticisms of these weapons, see David French, *Army, Empire and Cold War: The British Army and Military Policy, 1945–1971* (Oxford: Oxford University Press, 2011). On casualty projections, see Campbell, *Unlikely Diplomats*, 167–70, 179–87. On the deterrence value of the Bomarc, see Sean Maloney, "Secrets of the Bomarc: Re-examining Canada's Misunderstood Missile," pts. 1 and 2, *Royal Canadian Air Force Journal*, Volumes 3 and 4 (2014): 33–43, 65–78.

22 Secrecy impeded knowledge within the American services and political control of the military. See David Alan Rosenberg, "The Origins of Overkill: Nuclear Weapons and American Strategy, 1945–1960," *International Security* 7, 4 (1983): 16–39.

23 Legault and Fortmann, *Diplomacy of Hope,* 151.

24 Douglas LePan to the Minister, 15 October 1958, DHH, 2004/79, file 38.

25 Cabinet Conclusions, 15 October 1958 (online version).

26 Russell Isinger, "The Avro Canada CF 100 Arrow Programme" (MA thesis, University of Saskatchewan, 1997); Palmiro Campagna, *Storms of Controversy: The Secret Avro Arrow Files Revealed* (Toronto: Stoddart, 1998), 110–12; Statement of George Pearkes, DHH, 79/469, file 19.

27 Canada, House of Commons, *Debates,* 20 February 1959. On Pearson and nuclear weapons, see Isabel Campbell, "Pearson's Promises and the NATO Nuclear Dilemma," in *Mike's World: Lester B. Pearson and Canadian External Affairs,* ed. Asa McKercher and Galen Roger Perras (Vancouver: UBC Press, 2017), 275–96.

28 Supreme Allied Commander Europe (SACEUR) was an American-held NATO post responsible for the defence of Western Europe.

29 Memorandum to Cabinet Defence Committee, 5 June 1959, DHH, 2002/17, file 91.9.

30 Chiefs of Staff Committee, minutes, 12, 23 March 1959, DHH, 73/1223, file 1314. For objections to the strike role, see various documents, January to June 1959, DHH, 2002/17, file 91.9. For RCAF discussions, see Stouffer, *Swords, Clunks and Widowmakers,* chap. 6.

31 Chiefs of Staff Committee Minutes, 30 June 1959, DHH, 72/1223, file 1310; Cabinet Conclusions, 19, 30 June and 2 July 1959 (online version). The chiefs preferred the McDonnell F4H but quickly approved the F104 to obtain profitable West German orders. On the risks, see Bob McIntyre, *CF-104 Starfighter: Canadian Profile* (Ottawa: Sabre Publishing, 1984), 6. Declassified defence analysis supports McIntyre's conclusions.

32 Robertson to Green, undated [June 1959], DHH, 2004/79, file 38.

33 Robertson to Green, 12 June 1959 and Robertson to Green, 12 November 1959, in Janice Cavell, Kevin Spooner, and Michael Stevenson, eds., *Documents on Canadian External Relations,* vol. 26, *1959* (Ottawa: Foreign Affairs and International Trade Canada, 2006) (hereafter *DCER,* vol. 26), docs. 95, 13.

34 West Germany and other NATO allies did make purchases that offset Canadian defence expenditures in Europe. See Chiefs of Staff Committee, minutes, 23 September 1959, DHH, 73/1223, file 1314; David L. Bashow, *Starfighter: A Loving Retrospective of the CF-104 Era in Canadian Fighter Aviation, 1961–1986* (Stoney Creek, ON: Fortress Publications, 1990); Raymond F. Toliver and Trevor J. Constable, *Holt Hartmann von Himmel!* (Stuttgart: Motorbuch Verlag, 1985).

35 Cabinet Conclusions, 19 June 1959 (online version).

36 Cabinet Conclusions, 19 and 30 June, 2 July 1959 (online version).

37 Alan G. Draper, *European Defence Equipment Collaboration: British Involvement, 1957–1987* (New York: St. Martin's Press, 1990), 17–18.

38 Clearwater, *Canadian Nuclear Weapons,* chap. 5.

39 Hubert Zimmermann, *Money and Security: Troops, Monetary Policy and West German Relations with the United States and Britain, 1950–1971* (Cambridge: Cambridge University Press, 2002), 194–96; Stephen A. Kocs, *The Franco-German Relationship and Europe's Strategic Choices, 1955–1995* (Westport, CT: Praeger, 1995), 83.

40 Canada, House of Commons, *Debates*, 2, 3, 4 July 1959, 5358–59, 5414–15, 5470–75.

41 Heidt, "I Think That Would Be the End," 350–52.

42 Ibid., 329.

43 Maxwell Taylor, *Uncertain Trumpet* (New York: Harper, 1960). On responses to the book, see Rosenberg, "Origins of Overkill," 64–68. During this era, conventional air capabilities deteriorated: for example, USAF general Nathan Twining refused requests for lightweight jet fighters for conventional battlefield support, insisting that all tactical fighters and bombers be nuclear-capable. See Elliott E. Converse III, *Rearming for the Cold War, 1945–1960* (Washington, DC: Office of the Secretary of Defense, 2012), 460.

44 Appendix to Cabinet Defence Committee submission, 8 June 1959, DHH, 2002/17, file 91.9.

45 Hugh Campbell, speech to Training Command Conference, 24 November 1960, DHH, 181.009 (D2638).

46 Air Council Minutes, 1 February 1960, DHH, 73/1223, file 1836. See also Air Council Minutes, 13 July 1960, DHH, 73/1223, file 1836, when Air Council agreed to study the performance of both nuclear and conventional weapon systems. However, the same minutes then oddly recorded that the CF104 and conventional weapons were incompatible and that only nuclear weapons would be planned for. Campbell thus made his decision without comparing performance differences or actual costs.

47 Paul Schulte, "Tactical Nuclear Weapons in NATO and Beyond: A Historical and Thematic Overview," in *Tactical Nuclear Weapons in NATO*, ed. Tom Nichols, Douglas Stuart, and Jeffrey D. McCausland (Carlisle: United States Army War College, 2012), 38–40.

48 Donald A Carter, *Forging the Shield: The US Army in Europe, 1951–1962* (Washington, DC: Center for Military History, 2015), 297–98.

49 Escott Reid, 20 April 1960, DHH, 73/1223, file 491.

50 Campbell, speech to Training Command Conference, 24 November 1960, DHH, 181.009 (D2638).

51 McLin, *Canada's Changing Defence Policy*, 94–99; Clearwater, *Canadian Nuclear Weapons*, 55–58; McMahon, *Essence of Indecision*, 37–41; Cabinet Conclusions, 19 June 1959 (online version); Memorandum of conversation, 3 June 1960, *FRUS*, vol. 7, pt. 1 (Washington, DC: Government Printing Office, 1993), doc. 320.

52 Chiefs of Staff Committee, minutes, 6 May 1960, DHH, 73/1223, file 1314.

53 Reginald Roy, *For Most Conspicuous Bravery: A Biography of Major-General George R. Pearkes, VC, through Two World Wars* (Vancouver: UBC Press, 1977), 340–41.

54 Canadian Chiefs of Staff Organization, 14 June 1957, DHH, 73/1223, file 3412.

55 Chiefs of Staff Committee, minutes, 6 May 1960, DHH, 73/1223, File 1310A.

56 Robertson and Bryce attended key meetings during 1959, but they were not invited after Miller became CCOS.

57 Robertson to Miller, 29 July 1960, *DCER*, vol. 27, doc.191.

58 Miller to Robertson, 2 September 1960, *DCER*, vol. 27, doc. 193.

59 Rosenberg, "Origins of Overkill," 66.

60 Paul Hellyer, *Damn the Torpedoes* (Toronto: McClelland and Stewart, 1990), 117.

61 The description is from Donald Fleming, *So Very Near: The Political Memoirs of the Honourable Donald M. Fleming* (Toronto: McClelland and Stewart, 1985), 238.

62 Waldock to Miller, 15 November 1960, DHH, 73/1223, file 301. For another dissent-ing view by an RCAF officer, see John Gellner, "Some Thoughts on the Relationship of National Policies and Armed Force," *RCAF Staff College and Air Force College Journal* 4 (1959): 53–58.

63 Waldock to Miller, 15 November 1960, DHH, 73/1223, file 301.

64 Chief of Staff Committee, minutes, November and December 1960, DHH, 73/1223, file 1314.

65 Brief, 17 November 1960, DHH, 73/1223, file 301.

66 Burns to Green, 5 December 1960, *DCER*, vol. 27, doc. 218.

67 Cabinet Conclusions, 6 December 1960 (online version). The F104, designed as a high-level interceptor, required extensive alteration for the low-level strike role but only minor changes were needed for it to take conventional warheads.

68 Bryce to Diefenbaker, 8 January 1961, in Janice Cavell, ed., *Documents on Canadian External Relations*, vol. 28, *1961* (Ottawa: Foreign Affairs and International Trade Canada, 2009) (hereafter *DCER*, vol. 28), doc. 325.

69 Rosenberg, "Origins of Overkill," 68–69.

70 Thomas Alan Schwartz, "The United States and Western Europe," in *The Diplomacy of the Crucial Decade: American Foreign Relations during the 1960s*, ed. Diane Kunz (New York: Columbia University Press, 1994), 128; Ivo Dalder, *The Nature and Prac-tice of Flexible Response: NATO Strategy and Theatre Nuclear Forces since 1967* (New York: Columbia University Press, 1991), 30. Later in the year, McNamara would formally incorporate the idea of a second strike force into American strategy. See Rosenberg, "Origins of Overkill," 70–71.

71 Barry Leonard, ed., *History of Strategic Air and Ballistic Missile Defense*, vol. 2, *1956–1972* (Darby, PA: Diane Publishing, 2011), 151–53.

72 W.H. Barton to Robertson, 10 March 1961, *DCER*, vol. 28, doc. 336; Memorandum of conversation, 20 February 20, *Foreign Relations of the United States, 1961–1963*, vol. 13 (Washington, DC: Government Printing Office, 1994) (hereafter *FRUS*, vol. 13), doc. 418.

73 Cabinet Conclusions, 21 February 1961, *DCER*, vol. 28, doc. 333; Memorandum of conversation, 20 February 1961, *FRUS*, vol. 13, doc. 418.

74 Kennedy, speech to Canadian Parliament, 17 May 1961, *Public Papers of the Pres-idents of the United States: John F. Kennedy, 1961* (Washington, DC: Government Printing Office, 1962), doc. 192.

75 Michael Stevenson, "A Very Careful Balance: The 1961 Triangular Agreement and the Conduct of Canadian-American Relations," *Diplomacy and Statecraft* 24 (Spring 2013): 91–311; Cabinet Conclusions, 12 June 1961 (online version).

76 Memorandum of conversation, 17 May 1961, *FRUS*, vol. 13, doc. 425.

77 Kennedy to Diefenbaker, 3 August 1961, *FRUS*, vol. 13, doc. 426.

78 Canada, House of Commons, *Debates*, 7 September 1961, 8053.

79 Canada, House of Commons, *Debates*, 12 September 1961, 8225. Confusion arose over whether flexible response involved only a conventional pause or whether it also involved the escalating use of tactical nuclear weapons before massive retaliation – a strategic question not yet resolved.

80 H.B. Robinson to Robertson, 10 January 1962, in Janice Cavell, ed., *Documents on Canadian External Relations*, vol. 29, *1962–63* (Ottawa: Foreign Affairs, Trade and

Development Canada, 2013) (hereafter *DCER*, vol. 29), doc. 21; Robinson to Diefenbaker, 19 January 1962, DHH, 2004/79, file 41.

81 Green to Léger, 2 April 1962, *DCER*, vol. 29, doc. 120.

82 Robertson to Green, 2 February 1962, *DCER*, vol. 29, doc. 130.

83 L.A.D. Stephens to Robertson, 19 January 1962, *DCER*, vol. 29, doc. 212.

84 Ignatieff to Robertson, 12 September 1962, LAC, MG 31, E 44, vol. 2.

85 Chairman, Canadian Section, Permanent Joint Board on Defence, to Bryce, 11 May
1962, *DCER*, vol. 29, doc. 316. Knowlton Nash, *Kennedy and Diefenbaker: Fear and
Loathing across the Undefended Border* (Toronto: McClelland and Stewart, 1990),
144–45, 191–212, states that, beginning in early 1962, the US ambassador and William Lee, an RCAF public relations officer, orchestrated a media campaign to force
Diefenbaker to accept nuclear warheads.

86 Harkness to Diefenbaker, 17 August 1962, *DCER*, vol. 29, doc. 220.

87 R.P. Cameron, memorandum, 29 August 1962, 1 October 1962, *DCER*, vol. 29, doc.
222; Ross Campbell memo to Cameron, 1 October 1962, *DCER*, vol. 29, doc. 224.

88 Michael Stevenson, "'Tossing a Match into Dry Hay': Nuclear Weapons and the
Crisis in US-Canadian Relations, 1962–1963," *Journal of Cold War Studies*, 26, 4
(2014): 5–34.

89 "NATO and Nuclear Weapons," 3 December 1962, DHH, 2004/79, file 30 (memorandum, possibly by Bryce for Diefenbaker).

90 Donette Murray, *Kennedy, Macmillan, and Nuclear Weapons* (New York: St. Martin's Press, 1999), chap. 4.

91 "Conversations with Prime Minister Macmillan," 21 December 1962, *DCER*, vol. 29,
doc. 431; Memorandum by J.H. Warren and Marcel Cadieux, 23 December 1962,
DCER, vol. 29, doc. 437.

92 Andrew Priest, *Kennedy, Johnson and NATO: Britain, America and the Dynamic of
Alliance* (London: Routledge, 2006).

93 Robertson to Diefenbaker, 2 January 1963, *DCER*, vol. 29, doc. 160.

94 Robert S. Jordan, *Norstad: Cold War NATO Supreme Commander, Airman, Strat-
egist, Diplomat* (New York: St. Martin's Press, 2000), 3–11, 208–11.

95 Nash, *Kennedy and Diefenbaker*, 222–25.

96 Peyton V. Lyon, *Canada in World Affairs, 1961–1963* (Toronto: Oxford University
Press, 1968), 130–37.

97 Address to the York-Scarborough Liberal Association, Toronto, 12 January 1963,
LAC, MG 26, N6, vol. 32, file Defence-Liberal Policy Statements 1959–63.

98 Canada, House of Commons, *Debates*, 25 January 1963, 3125–37. After Pearson's reversal, the Kennedy administration refused further concessions on a missing parts solution
that Canada had proposed. See Stevenson, "Tossing a Dry Match," 20–23.

99 Stevenson, "Tossing a Dry Match," 24–26.

100 Canada, House of Commons, *Debates*, 31 January 1963, 3303.

101 On the strategic significance of the deal and the "masterly ambiguity" with which it
was presented, see Murray, *Kennedy, Macmillan, and Nuclear Weapons*, 101.

102 For exceptions, see Daniel Macfarlane, "Courting War over a Rubber Stamp: Canada
and the 1961 Berlin Crisis," *International Journal* 62, 3 (2008): 751–68; Peter Hay-
don, "Canadian Involvement in the Cuban Missile Crisis Re-reconsidered," *Northern
Mariner* 17, 2 (2007): 39–65.

7

"I Would Rather Be Right"
Diefenbaker and Canadian Disarmament Movements

NICOLE MARION

"One can only thank heaven that, in this time of crisis, Canada has at its helm a man of the stature and vision of John Diefenbaker," proclaimed a letter to the editor of the *Toronto Daily Star* in February 1963, praising Prime Minister John G. Diefenbaker's willingness to reconsider the acquisition of nuclear weapons for Canada.[1] Such a positive assessment seems incongruous next to characterizations of Diefenbaker's approach to nuclear weapons as being marked by insecurity and indecision.[2] Diefenbaker's nuclear policy has often been criticized for disastrous dithering, but anti-nuclear activists celebrated his hesitation as a sane response to an insane world.

Yet Diefenbaker was no real friend to Canadian disarmament movements. He was sometimes congenial with activists, but at other times he ignored them or spoke of them with derision. However, he often referred to public opposition to nuclear arms when justifying delays in negotiations with the US government regarding the conditions for the acquisition and storage of nuclear weapons in Canada. An examination of Diefenbaker's disingenuous relationship with disarmament movements and his behaviour regarding negotiations with the Americans demonstrates that the prime minister opportunistically used anti-nuclear sentiment as a tool in a larger tactic of purposeful lingering, while he attempted to forge an agreement that would have the greatest public appeal.

Diefenbaker was a committed Cold Warrior, who believed that Canada should contribute to Western deterrence power. But in early 1960, he became concerned that the acquisition of American nuclear weapons might compromise Canadian sovereignty. In order to postpone decision making in hopes of securing the best deal possible, Diefenbaker encouraged disarmament efforts, while cautiously engaging in nuclear negotiations with the United States. The prime minister's discomfort with the state of nuclear talks was then exacerbated by what he perceived to be American interference in Canadian affairs. By the time his government fell in 1963, Diefenbaker had positioned himself as an ally of nuclear disarmament movements. He did so not out of sympathy for their cause, or fear of their potential political strength, but because he had decided that resistance to American pressure to accept nuclear warheads was what would most appeal to voters.

Contemporary observers and historians have made numerous attempts to understand why Diefenbaker held so firmly to what would become a fatal strategy for his government. Diefenbaker's papers reveal little about his rationale.[3] Moreover, his memoirs represent a combination of "selective recollection" and "inattentiveness to factual detail."[4] Thus, left to conjecture, there is no consensus among scholars seeking to explain Diefenbaker's dallying.

Many, following journalist Peter Newman, have argued that the hesitation was caused by the prime minister's flawed character, particularly his indecisiveness and paranoia.[5] Political scientists Brian Bow and Erika Simpson and historian Sean Maloney emphasize the influence of pro-disarmament elements in the Department of External Affairs.[6] Journalist Patrick Nicholson and historian Patricia McMahon contend that growing anti-nuclear movements caused Diefenbaker to dither on decision making because he was worried about potential domestic political fallout.[7] Political scientist Andrew Richter suggests that negotiations were mired by a combination of factors, including the prime minister's political style, domestic opposition to nuclear arms, animosity between Diefenbaker and US president John F. Kennedy, the political threat posed by Liberal leader Lester B. Pearson, and the influence of the anti-nuclear cohort in the Department of External Affairs.[8] All these explanations imply that there was no driving force in Diefenbaker's approach to nuclear arms for Canada but that the prime minister was struggling throughout to make up his own mind on the matter, leaving him susceptible to his anxieties or to outside influences.

In contrast, another body of thought assumes that there was an underlying strategy to Diefenbaker's drawn-out nuclear deliberations. John Hilliker and Donald Barry have proposed that Diefenbaker tailored his approach to nuclear weapons based on his understanding of Canadian public opinion.

They have contended that Diefenbaker sought to appear to support both sides of the nuclear debate, purposefully keeping "everybody off-base."[9]

Such an understanding is supported by the assessment of H. Basil Robinson, who worked as Diefenbaker's external affairs liaison officer. Diefenbaker, according to Robinson, carefully weighed the political consequences of any decision and had a tendency to proceed cautiously with potentially controversial decisions.[10] Diefenbaker had also, as Cara Spittal has demonstrated, achieved the largest majority government in Canadian history in 1958 on the basis of his ability to "play up to the whims of the strategically calculated mass audience."[11] Observers and historians have argued that Diefenbaker was particularly concerned with Canadian public opinion related to Canadian-American relations as he often referred to anti-American sentiment found in his mailbag.[12] Canadian ambassador to the United States Arnold Heeney intimated in his memoirs that Diefenbaker had shrewdly positioned himself as a staunch nationalist in response to growing anti-Americanism in Canada.[13] Diefenbaker's approach to nuclear weapons for Canada followed a pattern of careful accommodation of public opinion – until the prime minister's paranoia and concern for his personal popularity began to influence him in the spring of 1962.[14]

Popular sentiment towards nuclear arms was precarious from 1957 to 1963. Polls consistently showed greater approval for Canadian acquisition of nuclear arms than opposition but, at the same time, implied increasing public support for disarmament and a nuclear test ban.[15] In this context, Diefenbaker sought to bide his time as he waited to see which decision on nuclear weapons would publicly be "considered right."[16]

In the late 1950s, there were few signs that the demands of anti-nuclear activists would find friendly ears within the Diefenbaker government. Following the Conservative victory in the June 1957 election, Diefenbaker promptly accepted the idea of the North American Air Defence Command agreement. This early action, taken without significant consultation with either cabinet or the Department of External Affairs, demonstrated the prime minister's support for American deterrence policy. Later developments on the same issue, however, illustrated his perennial concern for the protection of Canadian sovereignty. NORAD was not formally approved until June 1958 due to Diefenbaker's insistence on the inclusion of a guarantee that Canada would be consulted before NORAD forces could be put on alert, a position that he used to squash opposition criticism of his initial hasty move.[17] Furthermore, in 1958 and 1959 Canada ordered Bomarc-B missiles, accepted a strike-reconnaissance role for armed forces in Europe, and

purchased CF104 fighter-bomber aircraft with very little resistance from
Canadians who were growing fearful of nuclear arms.[18]

When Diefenbaker announced on 20 February 1959 that Canada would
acquire nuclear-armed Bomarc and Lacrosse missiles, he emphasized that
defensive nuclear weapons were necessary given the improbability of the
United Nations developing a successful disarmament agreement. With this,
Diefenbaker revealed that the Canadian government was beginning to explore with the American government the conditions for Canada's acquisition of nuclear warheads.[19]

As would become his pattern, Diefenbaker cushioned his announcement,
emphasizing that Canada would "continue to support effective measures
for disarmament" and that the Bomarc decision was taken only after "much
soul-searching."[20] Cloaking what was largely a pro-nuclear statement with support for disarmament, Diefenbaker revealed his desire to come to a decision
that, "in the light of the expectations of the future, will be considered right."[21]
When it came to nuclear arms, Diefenbaker wanted to make the most publicly favoured choice. This speech, which Diefenbaker would quote repeatedly
when asked to clarify his position on nuclear weapons, set the stage for his
approach to the issue for the remainder of his time as prime minister.[22]

Despite his careful wording, Diefenbaker's announcement catalyzed
growing Canadian anti-nuclear movements. His speech coincided with
rising international concerns over radioactive fallout, a situation that revi-
talized the decade-old Canadian Peace Congress (CPC) and instigated the
formation of two organizations that would quickly develop national support. In April 1959, Mary Van Stolk started the Canadian Committee for
the Control of Radiation Hazards (CCCRH) in Edmonton. A collective of
Montreal university students formed the Combined Universities Campaign
for Nuclear Disarmament (CUCND) in November, leading the first student
demonstration since the end of the Second World War when they marched
through Ottawa on Christmas Day 1959.[23]

Disarmament activists had reason to expect Diefenbaker would be sympathetic. In May 1959, the CPC-affiliated Toronto Association for Peace
expressed confidence that, because of his assurances that he was troubled
by nuclear fallout, the prime minister would act to stop nuclear weapons
testing.[24] Politicians generally reserved no more than forty-five minutes
for anti-nuclear lobby groups, but in December 1959 the prime minister
spent an exceptional hour and a half with a delegation from the University
of Toronto, during which he assured the group that disarmament was his
main diplomatic priority.[25]

In January 1960, Diefenbaker acknowledged that Canadian disarmament movements "could not be ignored" when he introduced demands for "joint control" into nuclear talks with the United States, which had been intermittently under way since the December 1957 NATO summit meeting.[26] At a 12 January 1960 cabinet meeting, Diefenbaker advised his ministers that no acquisition agreement should be signed until it was made clear that "there would be no use of these weapons without the consent of the Canadian government."[27] He pushed the issue further in cabinet three days later when he argued that he "had to be able to say that, in so far as defensive weapons for Canada's forces were concerned, the government had the right of joint custody and the ultimate decision as to their use."[28] This position was a reversal of Diefenbaker's previous acquiescence to legal requirements that nuclear arms remain under American control.[29]

While Diefenbaker had, in part, offered up "joint custody" as a means of appeasing disarmament movements, there was much more to this requirement than merely answering to the demands of a group whose efforts he dismissed as having never "led to the prevention of war."[30] The prime minister and the public had concerns about American nuclear policy, which was defined by the principles of nuclear overkill and preventive attack.[31] In his discussion of "joint control," Diefenbaker advised cabinet that Canadians were opposed to the presence of offensive nuclear weapons on Canadian soil for fear that "the U.S. might launch a war from Canadian bases."[32] This emphasis on "joint custody" was based on a legitimate desire to ensure that no pre-emptive nuclear attack on the Soviet Union could be initiated by the United States from Canadian soil without the permission of the Canadian government.

The insistence on "joint custody" created an immediate issue for negotiations with the United States. Very shortly after the idea was brought up in cabinet, Secretary of State for External Affairs Howard Green and Diefenbaker received warnings from the Americans that Canada's proposal for "joint responsibility" needed to be kept secret until negotiations were finalized.[33] The language of "joint control" or "joint custody" was problematic for the Americans as, at the time, American nuclear weapons deployed in Turkey and Italy were under American "control." Furthermore, the Canadian definition of joint control demanded Canadian approval for any launch, removal, or transportation of nuclear warheads. This definition went beyond the "two-key" agreement reached with the British, which required joint Anglo-American consent only for the use of nuclear weapons.[34] As a contentious issue for the Americans, the question of joint custody highlighted

Diefenbaker's reasonable alarm over allowing such powerful weapons on Canadian soil under the control of a foreign government.

On 14 July 1960, Diefenbaker advised his cabinet that holding out for a full package was more advantageous than completing individual nuclear weapons agreements. At this time Canadian-American nuclear talks involved four separate issues: the acquisition of nuclear warheads for Canadian forces in Canada; the acquisition of nuclear warheads for Canadian forces in Europe; the storage of anti-submarine weapons for American and Canadian forces at Argentia, Newfoundland; and the storage of nuclear arms for American forces at Goose Bay, Labrador, and Harmon Air Force Base, Newfoundland.[35] The fourth issue was close to being settled. However, Diefenbaker told his cabinet that to conclude these storage negotiations would cost the government "some bargaining power over warheads for Canada's forces."[36] Diefenbaker was confident that, by holding the storage question hostage, he could gain the best deal possible when it came to nuclear warheads for Canadian forces.

Meanwhile, his reception of anti-nuclear organizers in the summer of 1960 left activists optimistic. Leaders of the women's peace organization the Voice of Women (VOW) found Diefenbaker to be supportive of their efforts in their first meeting with him in June 1960.[37] Even though his wife, Olive, declined the VOW's invitation to sponsor the group, VOW leaders were convinced that Olive, like her husband, was "in sympathy" with the purposes of their organization.[38] Members of the Edmonton branch of VOW later claimed that the group had "the official backing of the Conservative Government."[39] Diefenbaker also conceded in a July letter to Rabbi Abraham Feinberg, leader of the Toronto Committee for Disarmament, that he found the interest shown by this collective of "serious-minded Canadians" on the important question of disarmament to be "greatly encouraging."[40]

The confidence of these activists was further sustained by the work of Canadian representatives at the United Nations. Green and the undersecretary of state for external affairs, Norman Robertson, encouraged the delegation to function under the principle that "Canada continues to regard disarmament as the most important issue facing the world."[41] Many contemporary observers noted a dramatic shift in the Canadian government's approach to nuclear weapons after Diefenbaker selected Green as secretary of state for external affairs in June 1959, following the death of Sidney Smith.[42] While Smith had been convinced that Canada's contribution to American deterrence power was necessary to combat the Soviet threat, Green was a sincere advocate of disarmament and an opponent of nuclear weapons testing.[43] Prominent officials within External Affairs were also growing uncomfortable with nuclear arms. Robertson, his assistant undersecretary George Ignatieff, and Green were all "on the same wavelength" when it came to the desperate need to put an end to the arms race.[44]

In his memoirs, Ignatieff revealed that he, Green, and Robertson had introduced the principle of "joint control" as a deliberate "holding action" to prevent the Canadian acquisition of nuclear weapons.[45] This admission led Sean Maloney to accuse the trio of dangerous recklessness.[46] Such an assessment is unfairly critical as it fails to acknowledge that, despite complicating negotiations, demands for joint control did not unduly delay Canada's acquisition of nuclear arms until after the weapons systems were actually ready.[47] Joint control, depending on its definition, was also a reasonable expectation, especially given the Anglo-American arrangement and the fact that the United States had faced similar demands in nearly every negotiation of conditions for the deployment of American nuclear weapons on foreign soil. American officials themselves had suggested as early as January 1960 that "joint responsibility" would be acceptable.[48]

As Michael Stevenson argues in Chapter 12 (this volume), Green was in command of Canadian foreign policy as secretary of state for external affairs. He also held a certain influence over Diefenbaker – they were old friends, and Green had greater access to Diefenbaker than any other minister.[49] Nevertheless, the prime minister maintained an independent interest in nuclear weapons.[50] He had insisted to cabinet that all announcements regarding nuclear arms were to be made by him or should use his words.[51] Green and proponents of disarmament in External Affairs did not impose the condition of joint control on Diefenbaker; rather, it was a condition that the prime minister believed was a necessary component of any agreement for Canada's acquisition of nuclear arms.

Diefenbaker had great respect for Green and therefore hoped to avoid any action that might embarrass Canada's United Nations representatives.[52] He was willing to support nuclear disarmament efforts but realized that, without verification procedures, which the Soviets refused, such efforts were doomed.[53] Recognizing this in December 1960, Diefenbaker dismissed the efforts of "long-hairs talking in favour of there being no nuclear defences."[54] While he considered disarmament to be "a laudable purpose," he was reluctant to see the Conservatives "dubbed the disarmament party."[55] In the context of failing disarmament talks, Diefenbaker and many of his advisors, Minister of National Defence Douglas Harkness in particular, were certain that no positions should be adopted at the United Nations that would interfere with Canada's ability to be "as strongly and most effectively armed and equipped as possible."[56]

Despite Diefenbaker's initial concern that the world was "closer to war" than ever, with the narrow victory of the aggressively anti-communist Kennedy in the November 1960 American election, his first meeting with the new president on 20 February 1961 was cordial.[57] However, no progress was made on the nuclear question. Diefenbaker declined to discuss the storage of American nuclear weapons on Canadian soil and informed Kennedy that Canada would not make a decision on nuclear weapons while disarmament negotiations were making progress.[58] In this meeting, Diefenbaker followed through on his assurances to Green and Harkness that he saw "nothing inconsistent with maintaining Canada's defence while at the same time pressing forward for disarmament."[59] In early 1961, Diefenbaker continued to follow these two positions on nuclear arms, though this balancing act (which, as Isabel Campbell points out in Chapter 6 [this volume], had been a traditional one among Canadian politicians since 1946) became precarious as the Americans pushed harder for an agreement.[60]

The prime minister had also advised Kennedy in May 1961 that the storage of nuclear arms in Canada was politically impossible because his mail was "running very heavy in letters" that were representative of "very widespread public opinion against" the Bomb.[61] Nevertheless, Diefenbaker continued to prefer Canadian participation in deterrence. Diefenbaker and his cabinet responded favourably to a telegram from Kennedy on 3 August 1961 calling for nuclear talks to be "renew[ed] with vigor," after formal negotiations had been suspended since the spring of 1960 for the presidential election.[62] Kennedy's request came in the midst of intensifying tension in Europe as Soviet premier Nikita Khrushchev renewed threats to cut off Western access to West Berlin in the spring and to erect the Berlin Wall in the summer. The Berlin crisis led the Kennedy administration to consider the need to strengthen conventional NATO forces, an appraisal that Diefenbaker supported by sending an additional 1,106 soldiers to the brigade in Germany.[63] But this reassessment of NATO strategy did not undermine the assumption of Canada's need for nuclear weapons. In the summer of 1961, cabinet focused on national surveys that suggested a majority of Canadians were in favour of nuclear warheads, and Robinson was certain that Diefenbaker was considering "a generally more tolerant stance towards nuclear weapons."[64]

Furthermore, Diefenbaker's behaviour towards disarmament movements at this time did not reflect apprehensiveness about anti-nuclear opinion. On

25 September 1961, a delegation of nearly one hundred VOW members, many accompanied by their children, presented a brief to the prime minister. Diefenbaker's memorandum regarding his reception of the leaders of the delegation indicated indifference towards their requests and focused instead on their displeasure with his revelation that Russian women were now using the VOW name.[65] Moreover, Diefenbaker ignored the larger group of women and children who stood waiting in the corridor hoping to meet him.[66] A little over a week before the meeting with VOW representatives, Diefenbaker had written to his brother Elmer that opposition to nuclear defence was an opinion held by the uninformed and that was "most beneficial to the Communists."[67]

Diefenbaker had implicitly used the VOW as his excuse for delay when he advised Kennedy in May 1961 that a "woman's committee" was stirring up hostility to nuclear arms in Canada.[68] Yet the prime minister's lukewarm reception of the VOW in September and his dismissal of disarmament efforts as pro-communist suggest that disarmament activists had not convinced him of the validity of their cause. Diefenbaker's expressions of concern over Canadian public opinion were used to defend his cautious approach to nuclear negotiations. In fact, Diefenbaker might have anticipated some understanding from Kennedy, who was himself facing significant public resistance to the dissemination and testing of nuclear arms.[69]

Historians have identified the fall of 1961 as the point at which Diefenbaker began to lean more towards disarmament.[70] First, on 26 September 1961, Kennedy made a statement to the United Nations General Assembly, during which he proclaimed the need for success in disarmament negotiations and implied that the transfer of control over nuclear weapons needed to be blocked in order for disarmament to become reality.[71] As was part of a larger pattern of the Kennedy administration, the pronouncement was made with little consideration for the impact it would have on American allies.[72] The Canadian press and politicians interpreted Kennedy's address as preventing any possibility for joint control, thus having "killed nuclear weapons in Canada" in the prime minister's mind.[73]

Then, on Thanksgiving weekend in October, the CCCRH presented the prime minister with 141,000 signatures against nuclear arms for Canada. The petition, which eventually accumulated 200,000 signatures, was the most widely publicized and successful action by nuclear disarmament movements in Canada.[74] It was representative of a growing discomfort towards nuclear arms. Canadians had become increasingly concerned with the dangers of nuclear fallout since it had become public in 1954 that American thermonuclear weapons tests at Bikini Atoll had resulted in serious illnesses.[75] Notably, disarmament organizations were multiplying and steadily expanding; the Saskatchewan and British Columbia legislatures had passed unanimous resolutions in opposition to the production and testing of nuclear weapons; and a Gallup poll from the summer of 1961 hinted that 80 percent of Canadians supported a nuclear test ban.[76] Lawrence Wittner, Bruce Douville, and Patricia McMahon have all suggested that the petition caused nuclear negotiations to stall almost as soon as they had been revived in the fall of 1961.[77] According to this understanding, the petition stood as conclusive evidence for Diefenbaker that there would "be a violent reaction in Canada against the Government" if nuclear weapons were acquired.[78]

In fact, even though Diefenbaker had told Kennedy that anti-nuclear sentiment in Canada needed to be taken seriously, his actual response to the petition suggests a continued lack of interest in the arguments of disarmament activists. In the press, the CCCRH focused on Diefenbaker's promise that there would be no nuclear weapons in Canada during peacetime.[79] Yet, in their private report on the event, CCCRH leaders revealed that the prime minister "hardly expressed sympathy with our point of view."[80]

A month later, Diefenbaker advised American ambassador Livingston Merchant that cabinet would shortly be reviewing the nuclear question. He also explained that Canadian-American nuclear talks had become "paralyzed" in the fall because a White House official had leaked word of the president's 3 August personal telegram to Diefenbaker to *Newsweek* in September.[81] Diefenbaker informed Merchant that any suggestion that Canada was "acting under pressure from Washington" made progress on negotiations impossible.[82] Following the leak, personal communications had ceased between Kennedy and Diefenbaker, which Kennedy attributed to the embarrassment it had caused Diefenbaker.[83] Kennedy's intervention in the nuclear debate had influenced Diefenbaker's thinking on nuclear arms for Canada to a greater extent than had considerations of public opposition to the Bomb.

In the summer of 1962, Diefenbaker's government faced a financial crisis and rising unemployment.[84] Because weapons systems requiring nuclear warheads would soon be available to Canadian forces, his continued delays and other leadership failures eroded confidence in his government. Diefenbaker recognized that the Liberals and the press were battering his party over the question of why they could not "be more decisive."[85] Though the nuclear issue played only a minor role in the election of June 1962, the loss of ninety-two Conservative seats, and thus his historic parliamentary majority, undermined Diefenbaker's ability to continue his ambiguous approach.[86]

To add to this new domestic stressor, Diefenbaker's relationship with Kennedy was becoming increasingly tense. In addition to the press leak of September 1961, an older grievance was revived. Diefenbaker had grown agitated over a memo left behind during Kennedy's May 1961 visit to Ottawa by Walt Rostow, one of the president's advisors. The memo, according to Diefenbaker's interpretation of it, implied that the Americans intended to "push" Canada to accept nuclear weapons.[87] In the spring of 1962, Diefenbaker became distressed by a conversation between Pearson and Kennedy at a White House dinner for Nobel Prize winners. As he discussed the dinner with Merchant, Diefenbaker presented the Pearson-Kennedy conversation as evidence of a conspiracy against him and threatened to publicize the Rostow memo, which he had kept to himself until then. Merchant reported that Diefenbaker had become "excited to a degree disturbing in a leader of an important country, and closer to hysteria than I have seen him."[88] Diefenbaker's threat to release the memo was perceived to be in such bad taste and so potentially harmful to Canadian-American relations that Kennedy expressed "no intention or desire" to meet with Diefenbaker in the near future.[89] By the fall of 1962, what had previously been a reasonable, though opportunistic, strategy to ensure the best possible nuclear deal for Canadian interests was starting to become unravelled by Diefenbaker's sometimes valid and sometimes exaggerated worries over American interventions in Canadian affairs and his determination retain political power.

In October 1962, the thirteen-day confrontation between the United States and the Soviet Union over the deployment of Soviet ballistic missiles in Cuba heightened Canadian fears of a nuclear war.[90] During the Cuban Missile Crisis Diefenbaker's dithering and the division in his cabinet were revealed when it took the prime minister three days to clearly declare his support for the American military blockade of Cuba, which had been established to prevent the delivery of additional weapons.[91] For Harkness and other pro-nuclear ministers, the shock of the Cuban emergency was evidence that the acquisition of nuclear warheads could no longer be delayed. For Diefenbaker, on the other hand, the insult of Kennedy's decision to wait a week before notifying the prime minister of the brewing Cuban crisis and the complete lack of consultation with Canada, which contravened the 1958 NORAD agreement, justified continued deferment of any decision making on the matter.[92]

As he defended his response to the crisis, Diefenbaker referred again to his mailbag overflowing with anti-nuclear letters.[93] However, for the time being public opinion was largely against disarmament.[94] Diefenbaker's response to the crisis not only exhausted the public's patience with the Conservative government's obscurity on the nuclear question but also further frustrated relations with the United States.[95]

Perhaps in recognition of this precarious position, Diefenbaker agreed to revive nuclear negotiations in November. Interested in avoiding a deadlock, Diefenbaker selected the more detached Gordon Churchill, minister of Veterans Affairs, as the tiebreaker to join Harkness and Green on the negotiating team.[96] Progress was made on an agreement for the provision of nuclear arms for Canada's forces in Europe. But no workable solution was reached on the Canadian proposal that a "missing piece" of the weapons be stored out of the country until an emergency so that it could still be claimed that there were "no operational nuclear weapons on Canadian soil."[97] While negotiations struggled to move past the "missing piece" issue, the December Anglo-American meeting in Nassau prompted Diefenbaker to shelve a decision until the May 1963 NATO ministerial meeting.[98] As Isabel Campbell explains in Chapter 6 (this volume), Diefenbaker interpreted the discussions in Nassau as demanding a re-evaluation of the need for Canada's acquisition of nuclear warheads.

In January 1963, two external interventions finally forced Diefenbaker to abandon his strategy of purposeful ambiguity. General Lauris Norstad, the retiring NATO Supreme Allied Commander, Europe, publicly revealed in Ottawa on 3 January 1963 that Canada had to accept nuclear weapons if it was to fulfill its NATO commitments, as Hugh Segal elaborates in Chapter 13 (this volume). Diefenbaker was humiliated and interpreted Norstad's visit as part of a Kennedy-orchestrated plot to undermine his government.[99] While there certainly was disdain in the Kennedy administration for Diefenbaker, Norstad's comments cannot be attributed to the American government as his retirement had been forced upon him by Kennedy, who had grown intolerant of the general's strong stance on expanding European access to nuclear weapons.[100]

Then, on 12 January, Pearson announced that a Liberal government would accept nuclear arms in Canada.[101] Harkness saw this shift in Liberal policy as an opportunity to finally settle the nuclear question and complete negotiations free of criticism, but Diefenbaker would not "follow" Pearson.[102] With the combined embarrassment of Norstad's and Pearson's statements, Diefenbaker's emotions pushed him closer to an anti-nuclear position.

A week following Pearson's announcement, Diefenbaker intervened to prevent the Progressive Conservative Association of Canada from adopting a resolution supporting nuclear weapons for Canada at its annual general meeting.[103] In the House of Commons on 25 January, Diefenbaker emphasized that Canada would "not be a pawn or be pushed around by other nations" but, instead, would be "a useful and ever-ready agent for peace."[104] Repeating the sentiment of his Bomarc announcement, Diefenbaker revealed that, when it came to nuclear weapons and the question of Canada's sovereignty, "I would rather be right" in the long run than act "on the impulse of the moment."[105]

The speech was interpreted as a rejection of nuclear warheads for Canada, to the shock and disappointment of Harkness, after cabinet – including Green – had agreed that Canada had made the commitments to which Norstad had referred.[106] The statement led the Department of State to issue a press release challenging the veracity of Diefenbaker's claims that Canada was not obligated to accept nuclear weapons.[107] The Americans had no appreciation for Diefenbaker's cautious deliberations and had finally had enough of what they considered to be his "neurotic Canadian view of [the] world." With the press release, its architect, W. Walton Butterworth, the American ambassador to Canada, consciously destabilized Diefenbaker's minority government, leaving the fate of nuclear negotiations in the hands of the Canadian people.[108]

While the 1963 election did involve economic issues, it was "one of the few Canadian foreign policy elections par excellence" in which Canada's nuclear policy was a central concern.[109] From the day his government fell, Diefenbaker moved closer to a non-nuclear stance as he attempted to use anti-American sentiment to appeal to voters.[110] Correspondence from disarmament activists characterized Diefenbaker as "the only Canadian Prime Minister since Sir John A. with any guts."[111] In a demonstration of support for Diefenbaker, the CPC took out an ad in the *Globe and Mail*, calling for Canadians to demand "no nuclear arms for Canada."[112] British and Australian anti-nuclear groups commended Diefenbaker's resistance to "tremendous U.S. pressure to accept U.S. Nuclear weapons in Canada."[113] Letters to Pearson assured him that the Liberal Party's position on nuclear weapons was sending former supporters to the Conservatives.[114] During the 1963 election, disarmament activists were convinced that Diefenbaker could be trusted to put "Canadian interests first" by keeping the nation free of nuclear arms.[115]

As the election campaign drew to a close, Diefenbaker's hesitation was validated by the publication of American secretary of defence Robert McNamara's claim that the "Bomarc is no good" because the weapon was costly and vulnerable to enemy attack.[116] McNamara's revelation raised

Diefenbaker's spirits immensely. The remainder of his campaign rested on the argument that nuclear arms on Canadian soil would only make the country a "decoy duck."[117]

The extent to which the election results were based on the nuclear question is unclear. Anti-nuclear activists read the election of a minority government for Pearson as a vote against nuclear arms for Canada and, thus, as a moral victory for the Conservatives who "fought very hard for disarmament."[118] Green, who had been celebrated by disarmament movements, lost his seat, while Harkness, who had split with Diefenbaker over nuclear weapons, was re-elected.[119] Harkness claimed that the Conservatives could have won a majority if Diefenbaker had clearly supported nuclear warheads for Canada.[120] Yet Tom Kent, advisor to and speechwriter for Pearson, theorized that the Liberals would have attained a majority had Pearson not changed the party's defence policy.[121] Pearson's turnaround cost him the support of a growing left-leaning francophone element in the Liberal Party, many anglophone academics, and many voters in the province of Quebec.[122] Nevertheless, Segal argues in Chapter 13 (this volume) that the close outcome of the election is best attributed to Diefenbaker's spirited campaigning techniques and public apprehension about Pearson and the Liberal Party.

Years later, Diefenbaker used his memoirs to argue that the "elimination of nuclear weapons" was one of the major goals of his government.[123] Published in the mid-1970s, when Canadian public opinion had largely turned against nuclear weapons, the memoirs suggested that Green, a "sincere and distinguished man of peace," should have been awarded a Nobel Peace Prize.[124] However, perhaps because of the immediately recognized flaws in his account, Diefenbaker was unable to erase the memory of his nuclear policy as a blunder.[125]

In an attempt to come to a nuclear agreement that would be most acceptable to the Canadian public, Diefenbaker, though himself a proponent of nuclear deterrence, intentionally delayed a decision on nuclear arms for Canada. His plan to encourage both disarmament activists and nuclear proponents was not formulated out of fear of Canadian disarmament movements. His strategy did not change when anti-nuclear organizations made their greatest demonstration of strength in the fall of 1961. Instead, his hampering of negotiations was tied to concerns for Canadian sovereignty. It was only in January 1963, when Norstad's press conference caused public embarrassment for Diefenbaker and when Pearson took a pro-nuclear stance, that his approach finally shifted. Driven by both ego and legitimate discomfort with American nuclear policy, Diefenbaker moved towards a reassessment of the requirement for nuclear weapons. Disarmament movements did not pose a real political threat to Diefenbaker, but they did serve as a useful excuse, as he waited – too long – to reach a decision that would be remembered as being "right."

NOTES

I wish to thank Janice Cavell, Ryan Touhey, Isabel Campbell, Norman Hillmer, Susan Whitney, and Casey Hurrell for their comments on this chapter, and the Social Sciences and Humanities Research Council of Canada for funding the research.

1 Edward Andrew, "Voice of the People: Taste of Irony," *Toronto Daily Star,* 5 February 1963.

2 Denis Smith, *Rogue Tory: The Life and Legend of John G. Diefenbaker* (Toronto: Macfarlane Walter and Ross, 1995), 328, 578; Robert Bothwell, "The Canadian Isolationist Tradition," *International Journal* 54, 1 (1998–99): 84; Patrick Nicholson, *Vision and Indecision* (Don Mills, ON: Longmans Canada, 1968), 169, 176; "An End to Indecision," *Toronto Daily Star,* 4 February 1963.

3 Daniel Macfarlane, "Courting War over a Rubber Stamp: Canada and the 1961 Berlin Wall Crisis," *International Journal* 63, 3 (2008): 752.

4 Donald C. Story, Review of *One Canada: Memoirs of the Right Honourable John G. Diefenbaker: The Crusading Years, 1875–1956,* ed. John H. Archer and John A. Munro, *Canadian Journal of Political Science/Revue canadienne de science politique* 1, 1 (1977): 181.

5 Peter C. Newman, *Renegade in Power: The Diefenbaker Years* (Toronto: McClelland and Stewart, 1973), xx–xxi, xxiii, 333, 341; Robert Bothwell, *The Big Chill: Canada and the Cold War* (Toronto: Canadian Institute of International Affairs, 1998), 65; J.L. Granatstein, *A Man of Influence: Norman A. Robertson and Canadian Statecraft, 1929–68* (Ottawa: Deneau, 1981), 356; Smith, *Rogue Tory,* 328, 553, 578; Paul H. Robinson, Jr., interview by Willis Armstrong, 1989, "Frontline Diplomacy," 7, Library of Congress, http://lcweb2.loc.gov/service/mss/mfdip/2004/2004rob03/2004rob03.pdf.

6 Brian Bow, "Parties and Partisanship in Canadian Defence Policy," *International Journal* 64, 1 (2008–09): 81; Sean M. Maloney, *Learning to Love the Bomb: Canada's Nuclear Weapons during the Cold War* (Washington, DC: Potomac Books, 2007), 226–27, 230, 259–60; Erika Simpson, "New Ways of Thinking about Nuclear Weapons and Canada's Defence Policy," in *The Diefenbaker Legacy: Canadian Politics, Law and Society since 1957,* ed. Donald C. Story and R. Bruce Shepard (Regina: Canadian Plains Research Centre, 1998), 40.

7 Patricia McMahon, *Essence of Indecision: Diefenbaker's Nuclear Policy, 1957–1963* (Montreal and Kingston: McGill-Queen's University Press, 2009), x–xii; Nicholson, *Vision and Indecision,* 207–8.

8 Andrew Richter, *Avoiding Armageddon: Canadian Military Strategy and Nuclear Weapons, 1950–63* (Vancouver: UBC Press, 2002), 87.

9 John F. Hilliker and Donald Barry, "The PM and the SSEA in Canada's Foreign Policy: Sharing the Territory, 1946–1968," *International Journal* 50, 1 (1994–95): 179; John F.

Hilliker, "The Politician and the 'Pearsonalities': The Diefenbaker Government and the Conduct of Canadian External Relations," *Historical Papers/Communications historiques* 19, 1 (1984): 166.

10 H. Basil Robinson, *Diefenbaker's World: A Populist in Foreign Affairs* (Toronto: University of Toronto Press, 1989), 319.

11 Cara Spittal, "The Diefenbaker Moment" (PhD diss., University of Toronto, 2011), 142–43.

12 Ivan B. White, memorandum of conversation, 17 May 1961, *Foreign Relations of the United States, 1961–1963*, vol. 13 (Washington, DC: United States Government Printing Office, 1994) (hereafter *FRUS*, vol. 13), doc. 423; Ivan B. White, memorandum of conversation, 17 May 1961, *FRUS*, vol. 13, doc. 425; "Telegram from the Embassy in Canada to the Department of State," 27 November 1961, *FRUS*, vol. 13, doc. 427; "Supplying of Nuclear Arms to the Canadian Forces," 4 February 1963, *Executive Sessions of the Senate Foreign Relations Committee*, vol. 25 (1963), https://babel. hathitrust.org/cgi/pt?id=mdp.39015039034460;view%3D1up;seq%3D1, 131; Andrew Richter, Review of *Essence of Indecision: Diefenbaker's Nuclear Policy, 1957–1963*, by Patricia McMahon, *International Journal* 65, 4 (2010): 1065; Nicholson, *Vision and Indecision*, 159; Simpson, "New Ways," 38; Newman, *Renegade*, xxi; Granatstein, *Man of Influence*, 356; McMahon, *Essence of Indecision*, 175; Arnold Heeney, *The Things That Are Caesar's: Memoirs of a Canadian Public Servant*, ed. Brian D. Heeney (Toronto: University of Toronto Press, 1972), 164.

13 Heeney, *Things That Are Caesar's*, 171. See also A.D.P. Heeney, memorandum of conversations with the prime minister in Ottawa, Janice Cavell, *Documents on Canadian External Relations*, vol. 27, *1960* (Ottawa: Foreign Affairs and International Trade Canada, 2007) (hereafter *DCER*, vol. 27), doc. 228; Asa McKercher, "Diefenbaker's World: *One Canada* and the History of Canadian-American Relations, 1961–63," *Historian* 75, 1 (2013): 94; Janice Cavell, "Like Any Good Wife: Gender and Perceptions of Canadian Foreign Policy, 1945–75," *International Journal* 21, 1 (2008): 396.

14 Newman, *Renegade*, xx–xxi; Smith, *Rogue Tory*, 553.

15 "Increase among those who say 'Ban the Bomb,'" in *Gallup Report 1960–61* (Toronto: Canadian Institute of Public Opinion, 1961) (hereafter *Gallup Report 1960–61*), 2; "Majority Say Army Should Be Given Nuclear Weapons," in *Gallup Report 1960–61*, 2; "Belief in Disarmament Has Risen Sharply in Six Years," in *Gallup Report 1962* (Toronto: Canadian Institute of Public Opinion, 1962) (hereafter *Gallup Report 1962*), 1; "Majority Say Our Forces Should Have Nuclear Arms," in *Gallup Report 1962*, 2.

16 Canada, House of Commons, *Debates*, vol. 3, 1962, 3137.

17 McMahon, *Essence of Indecision*, 12–13, 14; Maloney, *Learning to Love the Bomb*, 102, 122, 129–30; Robinson, *Diefenbaker's World*, 19, 21.

18 Greg Donaghy, *Tolerant Allies: Canada and the United States, 1963–1968* (Montreal and Kingston: McGill-Queen's University Press, 2002), 6; Howard H. Lentner, "Foreign Policy Decision Making: The Case of Canada and Nuclear Weapons," *World Politics* 29, 1 (1976): 43.

19 Canada, House of Commons, *Debates*, vol. 2, 1959, 1223.

20 Ibid.

21 Ibid., 1224.
22 "Extract from Cabinet Conclusions," 4 July 1960, *DCER*, vol. 27, doc. 272; Canada, House of Commons, *Debates*, vol. 1, 1960, 73; "Extract from Cabinet Conclusions," 14 February 1961, in Janice Cavell, ed., *DCER*, vol. 28, *1961* (Ottawa: Foreign Affairs and International Trade Canada, 2009) (hereafter *DCER*, vol. 28), doc. 331; Canada, House of Commons, *Debates*, vol. 1, 1963, 124.
23 Tarah Brookfield, *Cold War Comforts: Canadian Women, Child Safety, and Global Insecurity, 1945–1975* (Waterloo: Wilfrid Laurier University Press, 2012), 72; Lawrence Wittner, *The Struggle Against the Bomb*, vol. 2 (Stanford: Stanford University Press, 1997), 2, 31, 78; Jacqueline Dineen to Louise Harvey, 8 December 1959, Library and Archives Canada (hereafter LAC), James G. Endicott and Family (Endicott) Fonds, MG30-C130, vol. 7, file 123, 1; McMahon, *Essence of Indecision*, 66; "Bomb Ban Petition Grows," *Globe and Mail*, 19 December 1959; Bryan Palmer, *Canada's 1960s: The Ironies of Identity in a Rebellious Era* (Toronto: University of Toronto Press, 2009), 257.
24 Toronto Association for Peace, "Submission to the Right Honourable John Diefenbaker," 4 May 1959, LAC, Endicott Fonds, MG30-C130, vol. 7, file 124, 2, 3.
25 Wittner, *Struggle*, 348; Douglas Kay Campbell, *A History of the Ban-the-Bomb Movement, Toronto 1959–1961*, pt. 1 (Toronto, 1961), William Ready Division of Archives and Research Collections, McMaster University Library (MUL), CUCND-SUPA Fonds, box 1, file: CUCND Toronto Office 1960–61, 5; "Canada and Disarmament," *Globe and Mail*, 16 December 1959.
26 "Extract from Cabinet Conclusions," 15 January 1960, *DCER*, vol. 27, doc. 262.
27 "Extract from Cabinet Conclusions," 12 January 1960, *DCER*, vol. 27, doc. 257.
28 "Extract from Cabinet Conclusions," 15 January 1960, *DCER*, vol. 27, doc. 262.
29 Canada, House of Commons, *Debates*, vol. 2, 1959, 1224; "Aide-Mémoire by Embassy of the United States," 17 January 1960, *DCER*, vol. 27, doc. 265.
30 "Extract from Cabinet Conclusions," 15 January 1960, *DCER*, vol. 27, doc. 262.
31 David McDonough, "Nuclear Superiority or Mutually Assured Deterrence: The Development of the US Nuclear Deterrent," *International Journal* 60, 3 (2005): 814; David Alan Rosenberg, "The Origins of Overkill: Nuclear Weapons and American Strategy, 1945–1960," *International Security* 7, 4 (1983): 6, 66.
32 "Extract from Cabinet Conclusions," 15 January 1960, *DCER*, vol. 27, doc. 262. See also Heeney, *Things That Are Caesar's*, 164–65.
33 Ambassador in United States, "Acquisition of Nuclear Weapons," 16 January 1960, *DCER*, vol. 27, doc. 264; "Aide-Mémoire by Embassy of the United States," 17 January 1960, *DCER*, vol. 27, doc. 265.
34 Howard Green, "Acquisition of Nuclear Weapons," 16 January 1960, *DCER*, vol. 27, doc. 263; Ambassador in United States, "Acquisition of Nuclear Weapons," 16 January 1960, *DCER*, vol. 27, doc. 264; John Baylis and Kristan Stoddart, *The British Nuclear Experience: The Role of Beliefs, Culture, and Identity* (Oxford: Oxford University Press, 2015), 79; S. J. Ball, "Military Nuclear Relations between the United States and Great Britain under the Terms of the McMahon Act, 1946–1958," *Historical Journal* 38, 2 (1995): 449.
35 Robinson, *Diefenbaker's World*, 107; Erika Simpson, *NATO and the Bomb: Canadian Defenders Confront Critics* (Montreal and Kingston: McGill-Queen's University

Press, 2001), 106; Don Munton, "Going Fission: Tales and Truths about Canada's Nuclear Weapons," *International Journal* 51, 3 (1996): 520.

36 "Extract from Cabinet Conclusions," 14 July 1960, *DCER*, vol. 27, doc. 303; Richter, *Avoiding Armageddon*, 98.

37 Mrs. F. Davis to John Diefenbaker, 22 June 1960, LAC, Voice of Women (VOW) Fonds, MG28-I218, vol. 1, file: Correspondence – Members of Parliament (re formation), 1.

38 Olive Diefenbaker to VOW, 8 August 1960, LAC, VOW Fonds, MG28-I218, vol. 1, file: Correspondence – Members of Parliament (re formation), 1; Mrs. F. Davis to Mrs. John Diefenbaker, 3 September 1960, LAC, VOW Fonds, MG28-I218, vol. 1, file: Correspondence – Members of Parliament (re formation), 1.

39 Cst. W.A. Woods, "Re: Communist Party of Canada, Provincial Executive Committee, Alberta," 9 March 1961, LAC, CSIS files, RG 146, vol. 2843, pt. 3 (obtained under access to information), 4.

40 John Diefenbaker to Rabbi Feinberg, 29 July 1960, LAC, Abraham Feinberg Fonds, MG31-F9, vol. 3, file: Toronto Committee for Disarmament, 17 May–1 September 1960, 1–2.

41 Secretary of State for External Affairs, "Instructions for the Canadian Delegation to the Fifteenth Session of the General Assembly of the United Nations," 16 September 1960, *DCER*, vol. 27, doc. 96.

42 Hilliker and Barry, "The PM," 179; Bow, "Parties and Partisanship," 81; Maloney, *Learning to Love the Bomb*, 226–27, 230, 259–60; Robinson, *Diefenbaker's World*, 97; Simpson, "New Ways," 29, 40; Douglas S. Harkness, "Tense Days Led to a Showdown," *Calgary Herald*, 19 October 1977; Memorandum from secretary to cabinet to prime minister, 8 January 1961, *DCER*, vol. 28, doc. 325.

43 Robinson, *Diefenbaker's World*, 133, 97; Bothwell, *Big Chill*, 65.

44 George Ignatieff, with Sonja Sinclair, *The Making of a Peacemonger* (Toronto: University of Toronto Press, 1985), 198.

45 Ibid., 189–90.

46 Maloney, *Learning to Love the Bomb*, 230.

47 "Extract from Cabinet Conclusions," 4 July 1960, *DCER*, vol. 27, doc. 272; Richter, *Avoiding Armageddon*, 92; John Clearwater, *Canadian Nuclear Weapons: The Untold Story of Canada's Cold War Arsenal* (Toronto: Dundurn Press, 1998), 20.

48 A.E. Ritchie, memorandum by assistant undersecretary of state for external affairs, 17 July 1962, Janice Cavell, ed., *DCER*, vol. 29, *1962–63* (Ottawa: Foreign Affairs, Trade and Development Canada, 2013) (hereafter *DCER*, vol. 29), doc. 219; Ralph Dietl, "In Defence of the West: General Lauris Norstad, NATO Nuclear Forces and Transatlantic Relations, 1956–1963," *Diplomacy and Statecraft* 17 (2006): 381; "Extract from Cabinet Conclusions," 12 January 1960, *DCER*, vol. 27, doc. 257.

49 Robinson, *Diefenbaker's World*, 98; Heeney, *Things That Are Caesar's*, 180.

50 R.B. Bryce, "Suggested Points for Discussion with President Kennedy," 15 May 1961, *DCER*, vol. 28, doc. 348; Hilliker and Barry, "The PM," 175.

51 Extract from Cabinet Conclusions, 6 December 1960, *DCER*, vol. 27, doc. 111; "Extract from Cabinet Conclusions," 14 February 1961, *DCER*, vol. 28, doc. 331.

52 Canada, House of Commons, *Debates*, vol. 3, 1962, 3125; J.G. Diefenbaker, "Disarmament," 3 December 1960, *DCER*, vol. 27, doc. 110; Harkness, "Tense Days."

53 Albert Legault and Michel Fortmann, *A Diplomacy of Hope: Canada and Disarmament, 1945–1988* (Montreal and Kingston: McGill-Queen's University Press, 1992), 171, 178, 185.

54 Diefenbaker, "Disarmament," 3 December 1960, *DCER*, vol. 27, doc. 110.

55 "Extract from Cabinet Conclusions," 6 December 1960, *DCER*, vol. 27, doc. 111.

56 Ibid.; Maloney, *Learning to Love the Bomb*, 259; Simpson, *NATO*, 111.

57 H. Robinson, "Result of US Elections," 9 November 1960, *DCER*, vol. 27, doc. 239; McKercher, "Diefenbaker's World," 100.

58 Extract from Cabinet Conclusions, 21 February 1961, *DCER*, vol. 28, doc. 333; R.B. Bryce, memorandum from secretary to cabinet to prime minister, 15 February 1961, *DCER*, vol. 28, doc. 332; Memorandum of conversation, 20 February 1961, *FRUS*, vol. 13, doc. 418.

59 J.G. Diefenbaker, memorandum from prime minister to secretary of state for external affairs and minister of national defence, 13 February 1961, *DCER*, vol. 28, doc. 330.

60 Legault and Fortmann, *Diplomacy,* 17–18.

61 White, memorandum, *FRUS*, vol. 13, doc. 423; White, "Memorandum," *FRUS*, vol. 13, doc. 425.

62 Telegram from the Department of State to the embassy in Canada, 3 August 1961, *FRUS*, vol. 13, doc. 426; Extract from Cabinet Conclusions, 22 August 1961, *DCER*, vol. 28, doc. 354.

63 Isabel Campbell, *Unlikely Diplomats: The Canadian Brigade in Germany, 1951–64* (Vancouver: UBC Press, 2013), 173–74.

64 Extract from Cabinet Conclusions, 23 August 1961, *DCER*, vol. 28, doc. 355; Robinson, *Diefenbaker's World*, 229.

65 John Diefenbaker, memorandum re. meeting with Voice of Women delegation 25 September 1961, 27 September 1961, University of Saskatchewan University Archives and Special Collections (USUASC), John G. Diefenbaker (Diefenbaker) Fonds, MG-01/XII/C/445, Diefenbaker Centre, row 9, vol. 78, 1.

66 J. Fisher, memo to the prime minister, 25 September 1961, USUASC, Diefenbaker Fonds, MG-01/XII/C/445, Diefenbaker Centre, row 9, vol. 78, 1.

67 John Diefenbaker to Elmer, 14 September 1961, in *Personal Letters of a Public Man: The Family Letters of John G. Diefenbaker,* ed. Thad McIlroy (Toronto: Doubleday Canada, 1985), 107.

68 White, memorandum, *FRUS*, vol. 13, doc. 425.

69 Dario Fazzi, "The Blame and the Shame: Kennedy's Choice to Resume Nuclear Tests in 1962," *Peace and Change* 39, 1 (2014): 3, 13.

70 Wittner, *Struggle*, 348, 389; McMahon, *Essence of Indecision*, 175; Robinson, *Diefenbaker's World*, 231–32.

71 "Text of President Kennedy's Address to the United Nations General Assembly," *Globe and Mail,* 26 September 1961.

72 Frank Costigliola, "The Pursuit of Atlantic Community: Nuclear Arms, Dollars, and Berlin," in *Kennedy's Quest for Victory: American Foreign Policy, 1961–1963,* ed. Thomas G. Paterson (Oxford: Oxford University Press, 1989), 24–25, 28, 51.

73 Walter Gray, "Government Policy Unchanged: Ottawa in the Eye of a Nuclear Hurricane," *Globe and Mail,* 3 October 1961; H.B. Robinson, "Nuclear Weapons Policy," 6 October 1961, *DCER*, vol. 28, doc. 359.

74 Research section, Ottawa, "National Committee for the Control of Radiation Hazards – January 1962," 23 July 1977, LAC, CSIS files, RG 146, vol. 2844, pt. 13 (obtained under access to information), 14, 19; Wittner, *Struggle*, 197.

75 Brookfield, *Cold War Comforts*, 72; Wittner, *Struggle*, 2, 31, 78.

76 F.C. Hunnius to James Thomson, 22 September 1961, MUL, CCND Fonds, box 3, file 9, 1; Federal Secretariat CUCND, inter-branch memo, 15 September 1961, MUL, CUCND-SUPA Fonds, box 1, file: CUCND Toronto Office 1960–61, 2; Christine Ball, "The History of the Voice of Women/La Voix des Femmes: The Early Years, 1960–1963" (PhD diss., University of Toronto, 1994), 135, 436; "Report of the Proceedings of the National Council of the Canadian Peace Congress," 3–4 December 1960, LAC, Endicott Fonds, MG30-C130, vol. 8, file 134, 7; "Submission of the Saskatchewan Peace Council to the members of the Saskatchewan Legislature," 13 March 1959, LAC, Endicott Fonds, MG30-C130, vol. 7, file 119; Hugh Keenleyside to J.G. Diefenbaker, 30 March 1961, MUL, CCND Fonds, box 2, file 13, 1; "The Vast Majority Want Nuclear Tests Stopped," in *Gallup Report 1960–61*, 1.

77 Wittner, *Struggle*, 348, 389; Bruce Douville, "Project La Macaza: A Study of Two Canadian Peace Protests in the 1960s," in *Worth Fighting For: Canada's Tradition of War Resistance from 1812 to the War on Terror*, ed. Lara Campbell, Michael Dawson, and Catherine Gidney (Toronto: Between the Lines, 2015), Kindle ed., loc. 3064; McMahon, *Essence of Indecision*, 175.

78 H. Keenleyside to Howard Green, 4 November 1960, LAC, Lester B. Pearson (Pearson) Fonds, MG26-N2, vol. 49, file 806, 2.

79 Walter Gray, "Cleric Says PM Vows No A-Arms in Peace," *Globe and Mail*, 7 October 1961.

80 Minutes of the meeting of the Third Annual Conference of the Canadian Committee for the Control of Radiation Hazards, 26–27 February 1962, MUL, CCND Fonds, box 18, file 1, 6.

81 McKercher, "Diefenbaker's World," 105–6; Robinson, *Diefenbaker's World*, 230.

82 "Telegram from the Embassy in Canada to the Department of State," 27 November 1961, *FRUS*, vol. 13, doc. 427; "Just What Was Said," *Globe and Mail*, 20 September 1961.

83 A.D.P. Heeney, "Ambassador in United States to Prime Minister," 3 November 1961, *DCER*, vol. 28, doc. 317.

84 McMahon, *Essence of Indecision*, 138.

85 H.B. Robinson, memorandum from special assistant to prime minister to under-secretary of state for external affairs, 10 January 1962, *DCER*, vol. 29, doc. 211.

86 Simpson, *NATO*, 177; Newman, *Renegade*, 323, 333.

87 Letter from the Ambassador to Canada (Merchant) to Acting Secretary of State Ball, 5 May 1962, *FRUS*, vol. 13, doc. 433.

88 Ibid.

89 George Ball, telegram from the Department of State to the embassy in Canada, 8 May 1962, *FRUS*, vol. 13, doc. 434.

90 See, for example, Howard Green's statements on his reaction to the crisis on 24 January 1963 in Canada, House of Commons, *Debates*, vol. 2, 1962, 3068.

91 Diefenbaker had been informed by Green that the legality of the blockade, which Kennedy referred to as a "quarantine," was "by no means clear," justifying Diefen-

baker's delayed response. See H.C. Green, "United States Quarantine Against Cuba," 23 October 1962, *DCER*, vol. 29, doc. 660. See also John Bird, "Dief Indecisive on Canada's Role in Crisis," *Toronto Daily Star*, 25 October 1962; "Canada's Stand on Cuba Criticized by Truman," *Globe and Mail*, 26 October 1962; "Ottawa Wishy-Washy, Young PCs Charge," *Globe and Mail*, 26 October 1962.

92 Jocelyn Ghent, "Canada, the United States and the Cuban Missile Crisis," *Pacific Historical Review* 48, 2 (1979): 172–73, 183; Smith, *Rogue Tory*, 452, 462; Lentner, "Foreign Policy," 32; McMahon, *Essence of Indecision*, 147–48.

93 Nicholson, *Vision and Indecision*, 159; Newman, *Renegade*, 342.

94 "Majority Say Our Forces Should Have Nuclear Arms," in *Gallup Report 1962*, 22; Jacqueline Dineen to Mel Doig, 15 November 1962, LAC, Endicott Fonds, MG30-C130, vol. 8, file 148, 1; Kay Macpherson, *When in Doubt, Do Both: The Times of My Life* (Toronto: University of Toronto Press, 1994), 98.

95 Newman, *Renegade*, 333; Jocelyn Ghent, "Did He Fall or Was He Pushed? The Kennedy Administration and the Collapse of the Diefenbaker Government," *International History Review* 1, 2 (1979): 247.

96 Extract from Cabinet Conclusions, 30 October 1962, *DCER*, vol. 29, doc. 231; Harkness, "Tense Days."

97 Michael D. Stevenson, "'Tossing a Match into Dry Hay': Nuclear Weapons and the Crisis in US-Canadian Relations, 1962–1963," *Journal of Cold War Studies* 16, 4 (2014): 13; US Senate, Committee on Foreign Relations, Subcommittee on Canadian Affairs, "Supplying of Nuclear Arms," 131.

98 Stevenson, "Tossing a Match," 18.

99 "Norstad View Finds Ottawa Off Guard," *Globe and Mail*, 5 January 1963; "General Norstad's Reminder," *Globe and Mail*, 5 January 1963; Harkness, "Tense Days"; John G. Diefenbaker, *One Canada: Memoirs of the Right Honourable John G. Diefenbaker – The Tumultuous Years, 1962–1967* (Toronto: Macmillan of Canada, 1977), 2, 16.

100 Campbell, *Unlikely Diplomats*, 175; Dietl, "In Defence," 376.

101 "Text of an address by the Honourable Lester B. Pearson," 12 January 1963, LAC, Pearson Fonds, MG26-N2, vol. 50, file 806.2 pt. 3, 7.

102 Harkness, "Tense Days"; Robinson, *Diefenbaker's World*, 318–19.

103 Harkness, "Tense Days"; Progressive Conservative Association of Canada, "Draft Report of the Resolutions Committee Annual General Meeting," 17–19 January 1963, LAC, Progressive Conservative Party of Canada Fonds, MG28IV-2, vol. 292, file: Kits – Annual Meeting 1963, 11.

104 Canada, House of Commons, *Debates*, vol. 3, 1962, 3126.

105 Ibid., 3137.

106 "Nuclear Policy Muddied by Dief: Harkness Upset," *Ottawa Citizen*, 24 October 1977; "Under Pearson Fire, Diefenbaker Denies Nuclear Reneging," *Globe and Mail*, 26 January 1963; McMahon, *Essence of Indecision*, 164.

107 Memorandum from the assistant secretary of state for European affairs to the under-secretary of state, 29 January 1963, *FRUS*, vol. 13, doc. 443; Department of State Press Release No. 59, 30 January 1963, *FRUS*, vol. 13, doc. 444.

108 Telegram from the Embassy in Canada to the Department of State, 3 February 1963, *FRUS*, vol. 13, doc. 445; Douglas S. Harkness, "Resignation Delayed under Cabinet Pressure," *Calgary Herald*, 20 October 1977; Ghent, "Did He Fall," 268–69.

109 Bothwell, *Big Chill*, 66; CPC, "No Nuclear Arms for Canada," ca. 1963, LAC, Endicott Fonds, MG30-C130, vol. 9, file 164, 1.

110 Canada, House of Commons, *Debates*, vol. 3, 1963, 3440.

111 Marie Moreau to Mrs. Diefenbaker, 6 February 1963, USUASC, Diefenbaker Fonds, MG-01/V/F/483, Diefenbaker Centre, row 1, vol. 77, 1.

112 Jacqueline Dineen, "Annual Report," 25 March 1964, LAC, Endicott Fonds, MG30-C130, vol. 10, file 178, 1; "Display ad 14: 'No Nuclear Arms for Canada,'" *Globe and Mail*, 16 January 1963.

113 Campaign for Nuclear Disarmament Sydney, "The Fall of the Diefenbaker Government in Canada," *CND Newsletter* 3 (February 1963), MUL, CCND Fonds, box 11, file 13, 2; Mike Warwood, 22 March 1963, MUL, CCND Fonds, box 12, file 4, 1.

114 Charlotte McEwen to Lester Pearson, 28 January 1963, LAC, Pearson Fonds, MG26-N2, vol. 50, file 806.2 pt. 3, 1.

115 Fred M. Swaine to Lester Pearson, 1 February 1963, LAC, Pearson Fonds, MG26-N2, vol. 50, file 806.2 pt. 4, 1.

116 "McNamara Cites Missile's Defects," *Globe and Mail*, 30 March 1963.

117 William MacEachern, "PM Claims He's 'Vindicated' on Bomarc," *Toronto Daily Star*, 1 April 1963; Bruce Macdonald, "Liberal Defense Policy PM's Chief Target," *Globe and Mail*, 1 April 1963; Sam Lubell, "Missile Debate Helps Tories But Not Enough," *Toronto Daily Star*, 4 April 1963.

118 Sheila Young to Gertrude Worker, 13 April 1964, University of British Columbia Rare Books and Special Collections, Women's International League for Peace and Freedom Fonds, RBSC-ARC-1626, box 3, fol. 9, 1; CPC, memorandum to the North Atlantic Treaty Organization Council Meeting, May 1963, LAC, Endicott Fonds, MG30-C130, vol. 9, file 166, 2.

119 McMahon, *Essence of Indecision*, 169.

120 "PCs Viewed as Winner If A-Arms Backed," *Globe and Mail*, 10 April 1963.

121 Tom Kent, *A Public Purpose* (Montreal and Kingston: McGill-Queen's University Press, 1988), 193, 195.

122 John English, *The Life of Lester Pearson*, vol. 2 (Toronto: Lester and Orpen Dennys, 1992), 263; Gérard Rancourt to Lester B. Pearson, 7 May 1963, LAC, Pearson Fonds, MG26-N3, vol. 31, file 109.11 pt. 2, 1.

123 John G. Diefenbaker, *One Canada: Memoirs of the Right Honourable John G. Diefenbaker – The Years of Achievement, 1957–1962* (Toronto: Macmillan of Canada, 1976), 122–23.

124 Michel Fortmann and Martin Larose, "An Emerging Strategic Counterculture? Pierre Elliott Trudeau, Canadian Intellectuals and the Revision of Liberal Defence Policy Concerning NATO (1968–1969)," *International Journal* 59, 3 (2004): 547–48; Clearwater, *Canadian*, 21, 87, 152; Diefenbaker, *One Canada, Tumultuous Years*, 75.

125 Story, Review of *One Canada*, 181; Peyton V. Lyon, Review of *One Canada: Memoirs of the Right Honourable John G. Diefenbaker – The Tumultuous Years, 1962–1967*, by John Diefenbaker, *International Journal* 33, 2 (1978): 462–63; Smith, *Rogue Tory*, 328, 578; Bothwell, "Canadian Isolationist," 84.

PART 4

The Developing World

8

A Limited Engagement
Diefenbaker, Canada, and Latin America's Cold War, 1957–63

ASA McKERCHER

In May 1958, Richard Nixon got stoned. Not stoned like the students who would protest his presidency just over a decade later. Rather, on a goodwill trip through Latin America, then vice-president Nixon's motorcade was attacked by angry Venezuelan protestors pelting rocks. Commenting on the incident from neighbouring Colombia, Canadian ambassador Robert Ford chalked the incident up to "an expression of pent-up emotions" stemming from "resentment" of US economic policies, anger at US "political neglect or in some cases support of unpopular regimes," and a "psychological reaction" to American wealth and power.[1] No doubt as a Canadian Ford could well appreciate how such factors led to anti-US sentiment. In any case, his analysis deftly captured the ferment in Latin America.

In the mid- to late 1950s, the region had seen the collapse of a raft of authoritarian governments, notably in Argentina, Brazil, Colombia, and Venezuela. As a result, fragile democracies looked to expand their economies and meet mounting demands for social and economic reform. The impetus for change became acute following the success of the Cuban revolution in 1959 – itself initially an anti-dictatorial revolt – and the radical changes wrought by Fidel Castro's revolutionaries, who challenged US economic and political hegemony. In turn, many Latin American leaders hoped that Washington would take steps to assist their economic development and combat the poverty that seemed to be the wellspring of revolutionary discontent.

For US officials, the potential for Cuban-style revolutions and the attendant fear of communist expansion meant that Latin America was, as President John F. Kennedy told Canadian prime minister John Diefenbaker, "more dangerous than any other place we are facing in the world."[2] Kennedy's signature initiative to combat communist subversion in the hemisphere was the Alliance for Progress, which called for development projects and the construction of schools, hospitals, and infrastructure to promote Latin American social and economic advancement; Latin American and US authorities also sought to stem the communist tide, real or imagined, through more nefarious means. Indeed, Latin America became one of the regions where the Cold War was frequently bloody.[3] What these developments all meant from a Canadian perspective was that the years of Diefenbaker's premiership coincided with a period of great upheaval in Latin America. This turbulence conditioned Canada's engagement with the region.

Although Canada is physically a part of the western hemisphere, rarely have Canadians acknowledged this fact. Rather, Canadian foreign policy-makers and other elites have typically viewed their country in terms of the North Atlantic. Only during the Second World War did Ottawa begin establishing diplomatic relations with states in the hemisphere, mainly because of the loss of markets in German-occupied Europe. Yet, due to wariness of being drawn into disputes between Washington and Latin American governments, Canadians showed little political interest in their southern neighbours. As Diefenbaker complained in 1960: "To a greater or lesser extent Canadians seldom look beyond the United States. They act as though their vision was limited by the United States."[4] Joined by his two foreign ministers, Sidney Smith and Howard Green, Diefenbaker pursued a policy of engagement with Latin America.[5] However, as this chapter emphasizes, there were strong limits to his approach. For although he became the first Canadian prime minister to travel south of the Rio Grande and, in relative terms, devoted considerable attention to Latin America through an expanded diplomatic and trade presence, in actuality Diefenbaker displayed caution, the result of the regional Cold War dynamic.

Latin America's Cold War constrained Canadian policy even as it meant that Latin Americans and the US government looked to Canada – wealthy and secure – for political and economic support.[6] As several historians of the Cold War have recently stressed, the overarching bipolar struggle was shaped by various regional conflicts. For Canada, the Cold War was important largely in terms of Europe and, to a lesser extent, East Asia; as this chapter makes clear, Diefenbaker, despite his reputation as a fierce Cold Warrior, had little desire to be drawn into Latin America's Cold War.[7]

Overall, I judge that Diefenbaker proved deft in his handling of Latin America, with his actions reflecting a shrewd calculation of Canadian interests and abilities, if an uninspiring conceptualization of Canada's role in the world. In Latin America, Canadian internationalism had its limits. Still, as a "populist in foreign affairs," the prime minister was mindful that the Canadian public was wary about political or economic commitments to Latin America and that the region was a grey area on Canadians' mental maps.[8] Moreover, in terms of the themes of this collection, it is evident that Diefenbaker's Latin American policy, with its avoidance of involvement in that region's Cold War, was largely supported by Canadian diplomats, though there is an important nuance in that Howard Green sought far deeper involvement in hemispheric affairs than the prime minister was willing to countenance. Diefenbaker's approach to Latin America should force some revisions to the typical characterization of him as a foreign policy ingénue for, with the western hemisphere emerging as a Cold War battleground, he charted a prudent course.

Although in Opposition John Diefenbaker had paid little attention to Latin America, Prime Minister Louis St. Laurent's Liberals had hardly been vigorous champions of hemispheric engagement. Rather, the Liberal focus had been commercial, with the signal event of the so-called "Golden Decade" in Canadian foreign policy being a month-long goodwill visit in 1953 led not by diplomat Lester Pearson but by Trade and Commerce Minister C.D. Howe. Thus, Latin America was an area where Diefenbaker could put his own stamp on foreign policy. However, early in his prime ministership he told his cabinet that he viewed the region largely through economic lenses; certainly, he did not want to be drawn into diplomatic disputes via entry into the Organization of American States.[9] Whatever Latin America's potential as an economic counterweight to the United States, Diefenbaker's initial focus was on Europe and the Commonwealth, the destinations of his 1958 world tour. Indeed, he would never rate Latin America as a priority issue – as the chapters in this volume attest, his plate was full – especially once it was clear that the Cold War was seeping into the region. Moreover, he looked down upon Latin America, doubtless reflecting a North American sense of superiority over the region and its people. To the British, for instance, he complained "about the tendency of Americans to treat Canada like Mexico or Brazil," a comment indicating indignation that US officials might put Canadians on the same plane as Latin Americans. Years later he characterized his treatment at the hands of the Kennedy administration as a sign that, to Americans, "Canada was to be pushed around as though it was an insignificant Banana Republic."[10] Thus, it was left to Sidney Smith to take the initial plunge.

Canadian diplomats in Latin America urged a ministerial visit. In early 1958, Robert Ford counselled that Smith, not the minister of trade and commerce, should tour several countries. "Although our interests in Latin America are as much commercial as political," he explained, "the Latin Americans do not particularly like being reminded of this."[11] Smith agreed with this suggestion and so, in late 1958, he became the first Canadian foreign minister to travel to Latin America, visiting Brazil and Mexico. In an indication of how the visit expanded his own mental map, Smith told the House of Commons Standing Committee on External Affairs: "I learned, not only some geography but also some psychology ... It just seems to be inherent that they do not think of the American hemisphere as being divided into two continents," and hence Latin Americans "would like to get help from us in their difficulties."[12]

Smith's visit to Mexico was largely perfunctory: he attended the inauguration of President Adolfo López Mateos. Meanwhile, in Brazil he marvelled at the country's economic development, including the construction of a new capital city, and he remarked to Brazilian president Juscelino Kubitschek "that the vast continental size of Brazil and of Canada raised comparable problems, and that Canadians were interested in Brazilian solutions."[13] Although dazzled by Brazilian development, when Brazil's foreign minister raised Kubitschek's plan for a hemispheric social and economic development program, called Operation Pan America, Smith referred to Canada's small population, high per capita contributions to aid programs, and "astronomical" sums devoted to defence, adding lamely that, since "we were 'in the same boat,'" Canadian money spent on aid to the Commonwealth benefitted Latin America indirectly. He allowed, though, that his trip showed a "deeper realization of Canada's hemispheric responsibilities."[14] Here, Smith had his first taste of Latin Americans' desire to see Canada become more involved in hemispheric affairs. Reporting to the prime minister on his visit, he emphasized that "the whole area is fast increasing in importance" and that Ottawa should ensure close links with Brazil and Mexico, two countries poised to become major economic players. In regard to this emphasis on trade prospects, he added: "The need to study our relations with Latin America and to take some practical steps was becoming more urgent due to the fact that we may be in danger of losing our relative share in the trade with this area."[15]

Soon afterwards, Fidel Castro and his leftist revolutionaries took power in Havana, replacing Fulgencio Batista, a vicious and corrupt dictator who had been backed by the United States. Castro had yet to either declare himself a Marxist-Leninist or move Cuba into the Soviet orbit. "As there are Canadian investments in Cuba," Diefenbaker was advised, "it is highly desirable that Canada should not lag in the recognition of the new government."[16] Ottawa indeed gave quick recognition, but there were reservations about Castro's actions during his first months in power, notably summary executions of Batista-era secret policemen. When a new Canadian ambassador, Allan Anderson, arrived in Havana that autumn, he was told to display patience towards the revolutionary government while being mindful that Castro's "ambitious" reforms had "already begun to produce serious reactions at home and abroad."[17] Concerned by such reactions, Anderson's immediate predecessor, Hector Allard, had warned in his valedictory despatch that events in the hemisphere were moving quickly and precariously. He urged the Department of External Affairs (DEA) "to consider our Latin American posts as an important part of our diplomatic activities" because even modest improvements to the efficiency of Canadian missions in the region would benefit Canada's position.[18]

From his vantage point in Havana, Allard had witnessed not only the first months of Castro's revolution but also its initial impact abroad. Castro's victory increased internal pressure on dictatorial regimes in the Caribbean basin and ratcheted up international tensions between, but also among, anti-dictatorial governments in Cuba, Venezuela, and Costa Rica and reactionary regimes in the Dominican Republic, Haiti, and Nicaragua. With the threat of war in early 1959 between Cuba and the Dominican Republic, Ottawa barred the sale of twelve aging de Havilland Vampire fighter jets to the Dominican, while Castro-supported expeditions against Rafael Trujillo's regime in the Dominican and Anastasio Somoza's regime in Nicaragua in the spring of 1959 led Ottawa to suspend exports of strategic goods to Caribbean countries starting that July.[19] These developments highlighted the regional tensions between revolutionary and reactionary forces, which were only about to worsen.

Smith's successor, Howard Green, championed a Canadian role in hemispheric affairs. In October 1959, Green and Diefenbaker hosted Mexico's president López Mateos and foreign minister Manuel Tello Baurraud. The talks were friendly if inconsequential, with the Mexicans indicating their desire to see Canada enter the OAS, as did Venezuela's foreign minister, who also came to the Canadian capital that autumn.[20] In March 1960, Brazil's foreign minister, Horácio Lafer, visited Ottawa. The Brazilian millionaire, Green noted, was "a firm believer in free enterprise who had occasionally expressed warm admiration for Canada and a desire for closer collaboration between the two countries." But Lafer also came prepared to press Canada on participation in Operation Pan America, and Canadian diplomats cautioned Green about this "vague and rather grandiose" program.[21] Green and his fellow ministers did their best to steer Lafer away from development and towards the ample opportunities for Canadian exporters, especially in machinery and wheat. The Brazilian also met with Diefenbaker, whom he pressed on OAS membership.[22] The prime minister, too, avoided a commitment, preferring to focus on trade and investment.

Diefenbaker's emphasis on economics was typical of Canada's long-time approach to Latin America. Still, he visited Mexico City in April 1960, a trip that Arthur Irwin, Canada's ambassador in Mexico, judged to be a success from a public relations standpoint and "a significant milestone" in Canadian-Mexican relations, if not in Canada's relations with Latin America.[23] Indeed, it was the first time that a Canadian prime minister had travelled to the region. The only hiccup came when the prime minister spoke publicly in Spanish. As Diefenbaker later joked, López Mateos had then turned to him and quipped: "That was a very good speech, but we don't speak Portuguese."[24] For the prime minister, the trip was important in terms of trade for, as he recalled in his memoirs: "Whenever I travelled or received official visitors, I tried to advance Canadian commercial interests."[25] In his meetings with López Mateos, Diefenbaker reviewed trade matters as well as issues at the United Nations. The Mexican president expressed appreciation for a small technical aid project, through which the Polymer Company of Canada would provide planning for the construction of a synthetic rubber plant by Mexico's state oil company, and he appealed both for similar projects and for increased Canadian investment. Diefenbaker welcomed this economic focus, but he could not escape the matter of political engagement. As Manuel Tello emphasized, Canada would be welcomed into the OAS and the organization would undoubtedly benefit from both Canadian economic wisdom and political stability.[26] Again, both politically and economically, Canada was in demand.

Diefenbaker sensed the importance being placed upon Canada. Latin America, he told Green upon his return from Mexico, offered the promise of a vast export market, while the OAS "symbolizes to the Latin nations a new world and emphasizes the need of American solidarity." In order to capture this market, he hinted at the need for OAS membership, adding:

"I am more and more convinced that the political future of the Americas will depend on the OAS. We are losing ground." He then bemoaned Latin America's limited place within the DEA, where Canada's hemispheric affairs were managed by the American Division, which was primarily concerned with Canada-US relations.[27] Enamoured with his Mexican fiesta, at this point Diefenbaker expressed his most explicit interest in OAS membership, mainly as a key to trade. Yet as he had noted, there was a Latin American emphasis on solidarity, both political and financial.

Green soon made his own trip south. In May and June, visiting Argentina, Chile, and Peru, and landing in Mexico briefly on his return voyage, he encountered regional authorities who wanted increased Canadian involvement in their affairs. For instance, Argentine president Arturo Frondizi urged Canada to join the OAS, a point raised by Chilean ministers, by Manuel Tello, and by the Peruvian president, who stressed Canada's potential for alleviating regional poverty and for counteracting the threat of communism.[28] Like Diefenbaker, Green returned home with thoughts of expanding Canada's regional presence. Latin Americans, he told the House of Commons in a report on his trip, were upset that "Canadians do not seem to realize that Canada is a very important member of the western hemisphere family." To address this shortcoming, he announced the creation of a Latin American Division as a full-fledged unit within the DEA devoted to hemispheric affairs.[29] This step signalled both greater involvement in the region and increased attention to its importance. Building on the suggestion that Diefenbaker had made after his return from Mexico, it also reflected Green's sense, as he had told a Latin American Heads of Post meeting in Buenos Aires, that Canadian trade with the region was unsatisfactory and, more important, that "Latin American countries had shown that they possessed an independent outlook and deserved to be consulted and cultivated. In the interests of an independent and influential Canadian foreign policy, Canada must not overlook an area which commanded 20 votes in the United Nations."[30] Green, who hoped to spearhead international disarmament initiatives, had an evident interest in deepening Canada's hemispheric relations.

As further evidence of his concern with the region, Green pressed for the expansion of Canadian representation in Central America through the establishment of a diplomatic mission in Costa Rica. He took this step against the advice of his advisors, who sought posts exclusively in newly decolonized countries in Asia and Africa (1960 alone saw a dozen new states gain independence).[31] Announcing this move in July 1960, Green declared that it reflected a realization that "we cannot get away from the effect of many of the events which take place on this side of the Atlantic."[32] Indeed, at that very moment, officials in Ottawa were confronted with the realities of the Latin American Cold War.

In July 1960, Cuban-US relations reached their latest nadir when Cuba nationalized US-owned petroleum refineries on the island; Washington responded by barring imports of Cuban sugar. Worried by the worsening situation, López Mateos sought support for a joint mediation effort from Diefenbaker and Brazil's Kubitschek.[33] Seizing on the Mexican proposal, an eager Green advised the prime minister that a tripartite overture to Havana and Washington "*might* get results." Diefenbaker agreed that preliminary soundings be made.[34] However, he also informed Green of his reluctance to do anything that "would be regarded by the United States as unjust, unfair, if not completely undiplomatic," adding, significantly: "I regard the establishment of a Communist bridge-head in North America as fraught with terrible consequences." Therefore, he directed Green to notify US authorities of the Mexican plan. Green did so, telling American officials that Canada would not participate in the mediation effort unless the White House approved.[35] With Washington opposed to mediation, when the ultimately fruitless initiative went forward in early August, active and formal Canadian participation was lacking. Instead, Canada merely associated itself with the Brazilian and Mexican initiative, a diplomatic distinction that distanced Ottawa from the overture.[36] There were clear limits, then, to Diefenbaker's commitment to inter-American affairs, especially on an issue of importance to the United States. Subsequently, the momentum he had voiced about OAS membership in April dissipated. Moreover, Diefenbaker had made clear his distaste for the Castro government, its leftward tilt, and the deepening ties between Moscow and Havana, though evidently he thought the best course was to leave the situation to Washington.

By steering clear of involvement in the Mexican-Brazilian mediation effort Diefenbaker sought to avoid entanglement in Latin America's Cold War, which meant evading commitments to any side. Thus, Canada consistently shunned US entreaties to participate in American efforts to contain Cuba. American cabinet secretaries had pressed the point with their Canadian counterparts at a summit at Montebello in July 1960, just as López Mateos was reaching out to Diefenbaker with his mediation offer. Green resisted the Americans' appeal for help, instead warning them that they "might be very disappointed" by Latin American reactions to US policy towards Castro. Ottawa's cool attitude at Montebello left US president Dwight Eisenhower "somewhat surprised" at the Diefenbaker government's "disinterest" in containing Cuba.[37] But what Canadian officials were trying to do was to sidestep the worsening situation. On this score, Green's warning to the Americans proved prescient: an OAS foreign ministers' conference in San José in August 1960 exposed divisions between the United States and Latin American governments, with the latter refusing to back a US resolution sanctioning Cuba. Instead, Washington was forced to support an OAS resolution condemning the Trujillo regime, which had sponsored an assassination attempt on Venezuelan president Romulo Betancourt that June. With sanctions against the Dominican going into effect, Norman Robertson, the undersecretary of state for external affairs, counselled Green that Canada was "not a party to the quarrel" and that to side with the OAS "would create a precedent which might place this country in an embarrassing position."[38] So just as Ottawa ducked the US embargo of Castro's Cuba, so, too, did it avoid involvement with sanctioning Trujillo's Dominican Republic.

The censuring of the Dominican Republic, but especially the Cuba-US confrontation, cast dark shadows over inter-American affairs in the latter half of 1960. Furthermore, Cuba became an irritant in Canada's relations with the United States. In October, Washington imposed a partial export ban. Ottawa refused to follow suit. As Green told the cabinet, he and the DEA saw Canadian-Cuban relations as "normal."[39] Furthermore, Ottawa viewed economic embargoes as an imprudent strategy – hence its similar opposition to sanctions against apartheid South Africa. However, Diefenbaker had his own reservations about Cuba, and, despite his nationalist bluster, he was concerned about an American backlash against attempts by Canadian firms either to expand their market share or to assist US firms in smuggling goods into Cuba. In December, he offered public assurances on these points.[40] Beyond this implicit support for the US embargo, early the next month, with the breaking of US-Cuban diplomatic relations, Ottawa agreed to gather intelligence for the Americans through Canada's Havana embassy.[41]

Despite the Cuban fracas, Green remained convinced of the need for a greater presence in Latin America. On 20 January 1961, he announced to the House of Commons the formal establishment of diplomatic relations with the countries of Central America through the new embassy in Costa Rica and an exchange of ambassadors with Ecuador.[42] Two weeks later, the cabinet approved a proposal to extend diplomatic representation to Paraguay and Bolivia, the only remaining Latin American countries in which Canada was not represented.[43] These steps were important, but they were a far cry from a deep regional commitment. Despite Green's hopes, in 1961

Diefenbaker took a firm stance against further involvement in the hemisphere, the result, largely, of the US-Cuba dispute and the issues surrounding it.

In April, an American-sponsored invasion of Cuba foundered at the Bay of Pigs. Reacting to the invasion privately, Diefenbaker confided that he was "concerned about Cuba and determined to say publicly that we were disturbed about Communism there," while, publicly, he condemned the Cubans in a speech to the House of Commons.[44] Nevertheless, he was adamant that "he did not wish the United States Government to be left with the impression that they could count on Canadian support for anything foolish they might do with regard to Cuba," adding that Canada "would not be 'tied up in' any OAS moves in respect of Cuba."[45] With Latin America now very much a Cold War battleground, Diefenbaker had no desire to tie Canada too closely to the United States. After all, he valued the region for its economic potential, not as a place to work as a mediator.

Because of the ill-advised Cuban invasion, Diefenbaker ruled out OAS membership and involvement in Kennedy's Alliance for Progress. During his May 1961 visit to Ottawa – covered in more detail by Stephen Azzi (Chapter 5, this volume) – Kennedy raised both issues with Diefenbaker. The prime minister's advisors counselled that Canada should keep away from the Alliance for Progress – just as it avoided Operation Pan America – both because of Canada's other aid commitments and because of the unlikelihood that vested Latin American political and economic elites would make the requisite reforms at the heart of the program.[46] Diefenbaker agreed with this judgment and rejected the president's appeals for Canadian help. Commenting soon afterwards about his stance on OAS membership, Diefenbaker cited both opposition from Canadians and "unsettling events" in the region, a combination of factors that led him away from being drawn into inter-American squabbles.[47] Years later, he gloated in his memoirs: "Kennedy's mission to Ottawa was a failure."[48] Rebuffing the US president might have soothed Canadian nationalist sentiments, but it obscures the fact that Kennedy, like various Latin American leaders, saw a role for Canada – stable and wealthy – in the hemisphere. Yet, for the prime minister, regional initiatives were risky both politically and strategically.

Green, however, retained hopes of a greater role for Canada. Like Diefenbaker, he had been concerned by the Bay of Pigs, warning US secretary of state Dean Rusk several weeks after the invasion that "drastic action ... might serve only to force the Castro regime deeper into the Communist camp and jeopardize the possibilities of common action on an inter-American basis."

He had added a hope that the Americans had not ruled out talks with the Cubans, noting that "Canada being further removed might take a more objective view of the situation. It was our desire to be helpful if we could."[49] Green's hint at mediating the Havana-Washington dispute was ill received by US officials, but it stood as an indication of the secretary of state for external affairs' hankering for a greater Canadian role in hemispheric affairs. It also spawned a series of correspondence among Canada's ambassadors in Latin America over whether the US-Cuba confrontation could be salved. As these reports attest, there was considerable pessimism over the state of inter-American relations for it seemed that the heart of the issue was a "conflict of ideologies in the Americas" complicated by the history of US hegemony in the region, which was not only being challenged by the Cubans but was also "a complicating factor in any idea that some friend of the United States such as Canada could mediate in this quarrel with Cuba." As Ottawa's man in Havana concluded, "we wonder whether Canada will not have to learn to live with acute tension in the Caribbean."[50] For Canadian diplomats, the Latin American Cold War was reason enough to steer clear of further political or economic commitments.

Despite his officials' grim views, in advance of an August 1961 inter-American summit at which US officials were set to reveal the details of the Alliance for Progress, Green pressed his cabinet colleagues to approve a minor Canadian technical assistance program for Latin America. His appeal was rejected.[51] At the summit, meanwhile, Pierre Sévigny, the head of Canada's observer mission, was inundated with invitations for Canada to join the OAS. Returning to Ottawa, Sévigny stressed publicly that Latin America was at a "crossroads" between "democratic free enterprise" and communism and that Canada had a role to play in directing these countries along the right path. Privately, he urged cabinet approval of OAS membership.[52] In the House of Commons, meanwhile, Paul Martin, the Liberal external affairs critic and a long-time advocate of closer Canada-Latin America relations, attacked Diefenbaker's avoidance of "responsibilities to our own sister American continents."[53] But beyond these voices there was little zeal in Canada for a greater hemispheric role, especially one linked to Washington's anti-communist agenda. Diefenbaker remained unmoved since neither editorial nor public opinion – tracked by the prime minister – advocated a change in course.[54] Even so, he continued supporting regional engagement, agreeing to host Argentine president Frondizi and Brazilian president Jânio Quadros on separate visits to Ottawa in late 1961 and early 1962. Although Quadros's trip was cancelled following his resignation, Diefenbaker had approved the visit on the grounds of "furthering good relations between Canada and our Western Hemisphere neighbours."[55]

Diefenbaker's opposition to OAS membership proved fortuitous. At an inter-American summit in January 1962, the organization suspended Cuba's membership, increasing Cuba's isolation from the hemisphere. Luckily, Canada was not faced with the dilemma of whether or not to support this measure. The prime minister publicly defended Canada's stance on Cuba – thrown into stark relief by the result of the OAS summit and criticized by several Kennedy administration officials – averring that, although Canada naturally preferred to cooperate with friendly governments, the country's course on Cuba would be made "on the basis of policies which we believe are appropriate to Canada."[56] Still, Diefenbaker was worried. Reflecting in May on the US-Cuba rift, he told British prime minister Harold Macmillan that Castro's influence was spreading and "that there were at least five countries in Latin America seriously vulnerable to Castro's influence."[57] Green had similar concerns, telling an aide that "the Cuban régime had been getting progressively more communist-oriented," and he was cognizant of Cuban subversion in countries such as Argentina and Peru. The issue, Green said, was "a hemispheric problem, for the containment of which we had to share responsibility." He recommended, and won cabinet approval of, greater restrictions on Canadian exports of strategic goods to Cuba.[58]

Diefenbaker's policy appears timid, but it was based on a shrewd calculation of Canadian interests as well as of Canada's ability to affect events in a region dominated by the United States and ravaged by revolution and counter-revolution. In his memoirs, he wrote: "Castroism was at worst a symptom and the most radical manifestation of the social and economic tensions existing in Latin America. One treats an illness by getting rid of its causes, not by erasing its symptoms ... I was prepared to wait and see whether Kennedy's much vaunted Alliance for Progress would effect a single fundamental change."[59] In short, Diefenbaker recognized the root of regional problems but was leaving the search for a solution to the Americans.

Canadian diplomats in the region shared this judgment of the situation, but, recognizing its seriousness, they urged more involvement. In early 1962, in response to an American *démarche* pushing for allied help on Cuba, Canada's ambassadors in Latin America reviewed Ottawa's Cuban policy. Castro had openly declared himself a communist in December 1961 and, with the ever-deepening Cuba-USSR tie, some urged a tougher line. "It is not in our interest or that of the West," wrote Canada's chargé d'affaires in Ecuador, "to have this additional constant threat to political stability hanging over Latin America." Richard Bower, writing from Buenos Aires, counselled that Canada had to make a "gesture" indicating concern over Cuba's drift into the communist bloc. Along similar lines, Ted Newton, ambassador in Colombia, noted the "value in a statement reiterating, as did all nations in Americas ... our strong opposition to Communism as exemplified in Cuba." Some, like Paul Tremblay in Santiago, even urged that "to be consistent with our assessment that social and economic development in Latin American countries is ultimately the only effective antidote to Cuban threat, Canada might offer to commit itself to objectives of the Alliance for Progress."[60] Ultimately, this advice was ignored by Diefenbaker, who, by 1962, had to cope with many domestic and foreign policy problems and who had no time to embark on potentially controversial initiatives in a second-tier region. Even so, the sentiments expressed in these reports indicate Canadian diplomats' acute sense of the sorry state of inter-American affairs. Indeed, in early 1963, Arthur Irwin warned: "The one certainty is that, Castro or no Castro, turbulence is, and will be, epidemic in the Latin America of the 'sixties.'"[61]

There was evidence of a new trend in regional tension in March 1962, when Argentine military officers overthrew Arturo Frondizi's government. Friendly towards Canada, Frondizi had met with Green in 1960 and with Diefenbaker in 1961. As he had explained on his 1961 trip to Canada, Latin Americans believed that they and Canadians shared "many common problems."[62] But Ottawa wanted no part in the region's political squabbles. Canada quickly and quietly recognized Argentina's new government, doing the same in response to a series of coups across Latin America that proceeded, between 1962 and 1964, to remove democratic governments in Peru, Guatemala, Ecuador, Honduras, and Brazil.[63] Prudently, if ungallantly, Canada opted to steer clear of the tumult.

Under Diefenbaker, diplomatic relations with remaining Latin American governments were extended, a Latin American division was formed, and trade increased – all signs of engagement.[64] However, just as Canadian policy avoided involvement in either the US campaign against Cuba or the Latin American drive against the Dominican Republic, it also stopped short of the type of engagement sought by Latin American governments, by Washington, and by certain Canadians. Beyond disquiet surrounding Latin America's Cold War, Diefenbaker was concerned about the level of commitment that would be required of Canada. He saw engagement with the region and membership in the OAS as means to open doors for Canadian exporters. However, both financially and politically, Latin Americans and the United States sought Canada's involvement in their problems, especially in terms of staving off

Cuban-style revolutions. Diefenbaker abjured such a role, while Green harboured an interest in it. Indeed, Green saw a place for Canada not only within the OAS but in acting to solve regional disputes, including the US-Cuba dispute, and in extending technical assistance. Yet such a policy would have marked a significant alteration of Canada's approach to the hemisphere.

While the Americans attempted to inoculate Latin America against revolutionary upheaval, such a role was foreign to Canada, which lacked the resources and will of a great power. Furthermore, many Canadians simply had little interest in Latin America, which was simply too far away in spatial and political terms. As Norman Robertson acknowledged in early 1961: "Canadians ... are not on the whole attracted to the concept of hemispheric solidarity."[65] The Cuban revolution and the political turbulence of the 1960s and 1970s brought Latin America into increasing focus for leftists and human rights activists.[66] But because the region's Cold War was frequently hot, Diefenbaker's decision against involvement was sensible if uninspiring. Ultimately, his policy differed little from that of his Liberal predecessors and successors, all of whom saw the region primarily through economic lenses.[67] Diefenbaker's approach to Latin America was typical of Canada's shallow involvement in inter-American affairs and shows that, despite the cogent argument put forward by Francine McKenzie (Chapter 1, this volume) that he was more of a liberal internationalist than he has been given credit for, there are limits to such a characterization. The comparison with the Commonwealth is striking. As McKenzie notes, under Diefenbaker the Commonwealth received considerable Canadian aid and attention. Such a policy was a product of historical ties (real and imagined) and of the prime minister's deep sense of the Commonwealth's importance to Canada and to world affairs. In Latin America, Diefenbaker similarly pursued a policy of engagement. However, this policy had firm limits: avoiding multilateral commitments, it was based around a shrewdly conceived sense of Canadian interests and capabilities in a region that was riven by local and Cold War tensions and that had long been long dominated by the United States. As has so often been the case for Canada, Latin America proved to be too far distant.

NOTES

For their very helpful suggestions, comments, and criticisms, I thank the anonymous reviewers and especially the editors.

1 Bogotá to DEA, tel. 32, 14 May 1958, LAC, RG 25, vol. 6880, file 4901–40-pt. 11.2. On Nixon's tour, see Alan McPherson, *Yankee No! Anti-Americanism in US-Latin American Relations* (Cambridge, MA: Harvard University Press, 2003), 9–37.

2	Kennedy quoted in John Diefenbaker, *One Canada: Memoirs of the Right Honourable John G. Diefenbaker – The Years of Achievement, 1957–1962* (Toronto: Macmillan, 1976), 171. And see Stephen Rabe, *The Most Dangerous Area of the World: John F. Kennedy Confronts Communist Revolution in Latin America* (Chapel Hill: University of North Carolina Press, 1999).

3	Stephen Rabe, *The Killing Zone: The United States Wages Cold War in Latin America* (New York: Oxford University Press, 2011); Hal Brands, *Latin America's Cold War* (Cambridge, MA: Harvard University Press, 2010); Gilbert Joseph and Daniela Spenser, eds., *In From the Cold: Latin America's Encounter with the Cold War* (Durham, NC: Duke University Press, 2008); Greg Grandin, *The Last Colonial Massacre: Latin America in the Cold War* (Chicago: University of Chicago Press, 2004). Latin America's Cold War was a long one, extending from the Mexican Revolution of 1910. See Greg Grandin and Gilbert Joseph, eds., *A Century of Revolution: Insurgent and Counterinsurgent Violence during Latin America's Long Cold War* (Durham, NC: Duke University Press, 2010).

4	Memorandum from the prime minister to SSEA, 24 April 1960, Janice Cavell, ed., *Documents on Canadian External Relations*, vol. 27, *1960* (Ottawa: Foreign Affairs and International Trade Canada, 2007) (hereafter *DCER*, vol. 27), 1238.

5	J.C.M. Ogelsby, *Gringos of the Far North* (Toronto: Macmillan, 1976); D.R. Murray, "Canada's First Diplomatic Missions in Latin America," *Journal of Interamerican Studies and World Affairs* 16 (1974): 153–72; James Rochlin, *Discovering the Americas: The Evolution of Canadian Foreign Policy towards Latin America* (Vancouver: UBC Press, 1994), 11–48; Peter McKenna, *Canada and the OAS* (Ottawa: Carleton University Press, 1995), 75–84; John Hilliker and Donald Barry, *Canada's Department of External Affairs*, vol. 2, *Coming of Age, 1946–1968* (Montreal and Kingston: McGill-Queen's University Press, 1995), 174–75.

6	This chapter partly synthesizes information from: Asa McKercher, "Southern Exposure: Diefenbaker, Latin America, and the Organization of American States," *Canadian Historical Review* 93 (2012): 57–80; Asa McKercher, "A Helpful Fixer in a Hard Place: Canadian Mediation in the US Confrontation with Cuba," *Journal of Cold War Studies* 17 (2015): 4–35; and Asa McKercher, "'The Most Serious Problem'? Canada-US Relations and Cuba, 1962," *Cold War History* 12 (2012): 69–88.

7	On Diefenbaker as a Cold Warrior, see Jamie Glazov, *Canadian Policy toward Khrushchev's Soviet Union* (Montreal and Kingston: McGill-Queen's University Press, 2002). On the regional nature of the Cold War, see Lorenz Lüthi, *The Regional Cold Wars in Europe, East Asia, and the Middle East* (Palo Alto: Stanford University Press, 2015); Robert J. McMahon, *The Cold War in the Third World* (Oxford: Oxford University Press, 2013); Tsuyoshi Hasegawa, *The Cold War in East Asia, 1945–1991* (Palo Alto: Stanford University Press, 2011); Nigel J. Ashton, *The Cold War in the Middle East: Regional Conflict and the Superpowers, 1967–73* (Abingdon: Routledge, 2007).

8	H. Basil Robinson, *Diefenbaker's World: A Populist in Foreign Affairs* (Toronto: University of Toronto Press, 1989). On mental maps, see David Webster, *Fire and the Full Moon: Canada and Indonesia in a Decolonizing World* (Vancouver: UBC Press, 2009). While English-speaking Canadians have long displayed ignorance of Latin America, Québécois have been far more involved in forging social and cultural links with the region. See Maurice Demers, "Promoting a Different Type of North-South Interactions: Québécois Cultural and Religious Paradiplomacy with Latin America," *American Review of Canadian Studies* 46 (2016): 196–216; and Maurice Demers, *Connected Struggles: Catholics, Nationalists, and Transnational Relations between Mexico and Quebec, 1917–1945* (Montreal and Kingston: McGill-Queen's University Press, 2014). In a DEA-commissioned analysis of Canadian public interest in Latin America from 1957 to 1967, analyst J.C.M. Ogelsby found little difference between English- and French-Canadian opinion on hemispheric issues. "But the point," he wrote, "has been made that almost everyone, English or French, *thinks* there is this affinity, and it is ever regarded thus." See "Appendix: The Extent, Focus, and Changes of Canadian Public Interest in Latin America, 1957–67," in Ogelsby, *Gringos*, 328. And see Daniel Gay, *Les élites québécoises et l'Amérique latine* (Montréal: Nouvelle optique, 1983).

9   Cabinet Conclusions, 20 August 1957, LAC, RG 2, vol. 1893.

10 Macmillan to Home, 30 June 1957, The National Archives, UK, PREM 11/2133; John Diefenbaker, "Across the Border," in *The Star-Spangled Beaver*, ed. John H. Redekop (Toronto: Peter Martin Associates, 1971), 44. On American attitudes towards Latin America, see Lars Schoultz, *Beneath the United States: A History of US Policy toward Latin America* (Cambridge, MA: Harvard University Press, 1998).

11 Bogotá to DEA, D-180, 30 April 1958, LAC, RG 25, vol. 6375, file 4035–40-pt. 4.2.

12 Canada, House of Commons, *Standing Committee on External Affairs* (5 March 1959), 8–9.

13 Memorandum of conversation, 19 November 1958, LAC, RG 25, vol. 7603, file 11253-J-40-pt. 1.

14 Minister's calls on Brazilian foreign minister, n.d., LAC, RG 25, vol. 7603, file 11253-J-40-pt. 1.

15 Smith to Diefenbaker, 5 December 1958, LAC, RG 25, vol. 7603, file 11253-J-40-pt. 1.

16 Smith, minute, on Smith to Diefenbaker, "Recognition of New Cuban Government," 8 January 1959, LAC, John Diefenbaker Papers, MG 01/VIII/840/C962, File Canada and Foreign Countries, General, Cuba, 1958–63.

17 Secretary of State for External Affairs to Ambassador in Cuba, 25 September 1959, in Janice Cavell, ed., *Documents on Canadian External Relations*, vol. 26, *1959*, (Ottawa: Department of Foreign Affairs and International Trade, 2006) (hereafter *DCER*, vol. 26), 961–65. See John Kirk and Peter McKenna, *Canada-Cuba Relations: The Other Good Neighbor Policy* (Gainesville: University Press of Florida, 1997); and Robert Wright, *Three Nights in Havana: Pierre Trudeau, Fidel Castro and the Cold War World* (Toronto: HarperCollins, 2007).

18 Havana to DEA, D-304, 20 June 1959, LAC, RG 25, vol. 7603, file 11253-J-40-pt. FP.2a.

19 Ambassador in Cuba to SSEA, 30 January 1959, *DCER*, vol. 26, *1959*, 971; Cabinet Conclusions, 30 July 1959, LAC, RG 2, vol. 2745–6.

20 Hardy to Campbell, 22 October 1959, and attached memo, "Conversation between our Minister and Mexican Foreign Minister, 16 October 1959," 19 October 1959, LAC, RG 25, vol. 2646, file 3136–40-pt. 1; Caracas to DEA, tel. 1, 5 February 1960,

Robertson to Green, "Canadian-Venezuelan Relations," 11 February 1960, LAC, RG 25, vol. 6812, file 2226–40-pt. 10.1.

21 Green to Diefenbaker, 15 October 1959, LAC, RG 25, vol. 7848, file 12850-B-8-1-40-pt. 1.1; Ritchie to Green, "Visit of Brazilian Foreign Minister," 16 March 1960, LAC, RG 25, vol. 6812, file 2226–60-pt. 10.

22 Ritchie, memorandum for file, 17 March 1960, and Ritchie, memorandum for file, 18 March 1960, LAC, RG 25, vol. 7848, file 12850-B-8-1-40-pt. 1.2; DEA to Rio de Janeiro, X-103, 22 March 1960, LAC, RG 25, vol. 7848, file 12850-B-8-1-40-pt. 12; Rio to DEA, tel. 74, 26 April 1960, LAC, RG 25, vol. 5465, file 11563–20–40-pt. 1.

23 Ambassador in Mexico to SSEA, 7 May 1960, *DCER*, vol. 27, 1238–42.

24 "Diefenbaker Criticizes Pacifism: Freedom Being Eroded 'Bit by Bit,'" *Globe and Mail*, 27 January 1976.

25 Diefenbaker, *One Canada*, 116.

26 Memorandum from USSEA to SSEA, 25 April 1960, and attached memos, *DCER*, vol. 27, 1233–7.

27 Memoranda from PM to SSEA, 24 April 1960, *DCER*, vol. 27, 1237–8.

28 Ambassador in Argentina to USSEA, 27 May 1960, *DCER*, vol. 27, 1250–1; Ambassador in Chile to SSEA, 4 June 1960, *DCER*, vol. 27, 1269–70; Ambassador in Peru to USSEA, 3 June and 1960 and Ambassador in Mexico to USSEA, 3 June 1960, *DCER*, vol. 27, 1262–4.

29 Canada, House of Commons, *Debates*, 30 May 1960, 4335–38.

30 Minutes of Meeting with SSEA, 22 May 1960, *DCER*, vol. 27, 1252–9.

31 Robertson to Green, "New Missions," 7 July 1959, Hardy to Ritchie, memo with attached minutes, 5 February 1960, LAC, vol. 7760, file 12426–40-pt. 1.1; Green minute on Robertson to Green, "Statement by Ex-President Jose Figueres," 26 April 1960, LAC, RG 25, vol. 7760, file 12426–40-pt. 2.

32 Canada, House of Commons, *Debates*, 14 July 1960, 6298.

33 Draft translation of a letter in Spanish addressed by Dr. Adolfo Mateos to John Diefenbaker, [July 1960], LAC, MG 31 E44, vol. 1.4; and Mexico City to DEA, 134, 15 July 1960, LAC, RG 25, vol. 5050, file 2444-A-40-pt. 1.

34 Green to Diefenbaker, 15 July 1960, LAC, MG 01/XII/C/120, file Cuba n.d., 1960–62.

35 Diefenbaker to Green, 17 July 1960, LAC, MG 01/VIII/845/C962, file Canada and Foreign Countries – International Situation – Cuba; Ottawa to State Department no. 63, 24 July 1960, US National Archives and Records Administration, RG 84, Classified General Records (CGR), box 62, fol. Cuba 1959–61.

36 Ottawa to State Department no. 80, 29 July 1960, NARA, RG 84, CGR, box 62, fol. Cuba 1959–61.

37 Memorandum by USSEA, 13 July 1960, *DCER*, vol. 27, 1154; Memorandum of meeting with the president, 19 July 1960, 5:30 p.m., DDEL, White House, Office of the NSA, Special Assistant Series, Presidential Subseries, box 5, fol. 1960 – Meetings with the President – vol. 2.

38 Caracas to DEA, D-340, 24 August 1960 and Robertson to Green, "San Jose Conference of the Organization of American States," 13 September 1960, RG 25, vol. 7055, file 7296-B-40-pt. 2.1. On the Canadian diplomatic life in Trujillo's Dominican

Republic, see John W. Graham, *Whose Man in Havana? Adventures from the Far Side of Diplomacy* (Calgary: University of Calgary Press, 2015).

39 Robinson to Robertson, "Cuba," 19 October 1960, and Robinson to file, "Cuba," 20 October 1960, LAC, MG 31 E83, vol. 3, file 10; Cabinet Conclusions, 20 October 1960, LAC, RG 2, vol. 2747.

40 Canada, House of Commons, *Debates,* 12 December 1960, 700–1.

41 Battle to Bundy, "Canadian Reporting from Havana," 1 December 1961, John F. Kennedy Presidential Library (JFKL), National Security Files (NSF), box 35, fol. Cuba, General, 6/61–12/61.

42 Canada, House of Commons, *Debates,* 20 January 1961, 1255.

43 Cabinet Conclusions, 31 January 1961, LAC, RG 2, vol. 6176. This policy was accomplished through double-accreditation, which proved controversial: Alfred Pick, Canada's ambassador in Peru, suddenly found himself representing Canada in Bolivia. But, as he complained, poor communications and the infrequency of travel over the Andes limited his effectiveness. See Pick to Beaulne, 11 August 1961, LAC, RG 25, vol. 6851, file 3881–40-pt. 3.2.

44 Basil Robinson Diary, 19 April 1961, LAC, MG 31 E83, vol. 35; Canada, House of Commons, *Debates,* 19 April 1961, 3795. As Robinson noted in this diary entry, Diefenbaker accused the DEA of being too soft on Cuban communism, hence his desire to publicly condemn Havana.

45 Robinson to Robertson, 27 April 1961, LAC, MG 31 E83, vol. 5, file 4.

46 Bryce to Diefenbaker, "Suggested points for discussion with President Kennedy," 15 May 1961, LAC, MG 31 E83, vol. 5, file 8.

47 Diefenbaker to file, "Heeney," 22 May 1961, LAC, MG 31 E44, vol. 2, file 9; Cabinet Conclusions, 23 May 1961, LAC, RG 2, vol. 6176.

48 Diefenbaker, *One Canada,* 184. And see memoranda of conversation between President Kennedy and Prime Minister Diefenbaker, 17 May 1961, JFKL, NSF, box 18, fol. Canada, General, Ottawa Trip 5/17/61, memoranda of conversation. Perhaps crucially, pushing for greater Canadian involvement in Latin America was one of the items on the infamous "Rostow Memorandum," the innocuous list of talking points left by Kennedy in Diefenbaker's office – see the introduction to this volume.

49 NATO Delegation to SSEA, 11 May 1961, Janice Cavell, ed., *Documents on Canadian External Relations,* vol. 28, *1961* (Ottawa: Foreign Affairs and International Trade Canada, 2009) (hereafter *DCER,* vol. 28), 1358–9.

50 Ambassador in Chile to SSEA, 16 May 1961, *DCER,* vol. 28, 1364–66; Ambassador in Peru to SSEA, 9 June 1961, *DCER* vol. 28, 1370–72; Embassy in Cuba to USSEA, 8 June 1961, *DCER,* vol. 28, 1369–70. Canadian ambassadors in the region were also canvassed on their views as to whether or not Canada should commit to OAS membership; opinion was divided but there was agreement that membership would need to be backed by a significant economic commitment coinciding with the Alliance for Progress. See McKercher, "Southern Exposure," 77–78.

51 Cabinet Conclusions, 15 July 1961, LAC, RG 2, vol. 6177.

52 "Latin Americans Will Go Red Unless Given Aid, Sévigny," *Globe and Mail,* 24 August 1961; Sévigny to Churchill, 11 September 1961, and attached memo, "Memorandum concerning my recent trip to South America," LAC, Gordon Churchill Fonds, MG 32 B9, vol. 57, file Trade, Economic Relations, Latin, South, and Central America.

53 Canada, House of Commons, *Debates*, 7 September 1961, 8081.
54 Robinson to Latin American Division, 8 July 1961, LAC, RG 25, vol. 5043, file 2226–40-pt. 12.
55 Robertson to Green, invitation to President Quadros of Brazil to visit Canada, 27 February 1961, and Diefenbaker minute, RG 25, vol. 5579, file 12850–89–9–40.
56 Canada, House of Commons, *Debates*, 2 February 1962, 479–80. And see "Green Scores Remarks by President's Adviser," *Ottawa Citizen*, 30 January 1962; "Rusk Hopeful Canada Will Join Boycott of Cuba," *Globe and Mail*, 2 February 1962.
57 Summary of conversation, 1 May 1962, LAC, RG 25, vol. 61551, file 50412–40-pt. 4.
58 Memorandum from special assistant, Office of SSEA, to USSEA, 23 February 1962, Janice Cavell, ed., *Documents on Canadian External Relations*, vol. 29, *1962–63* (Ottawa: Foreign Affairs, Trade and Development Canada, 2013) (hereafter *DCER*, vol. 29), 1066.
59 Diefenbaker, *One Canada*, 175.
60 Chargé d'affaires in Ecuador to SSEA, 2 March 1962, *DCER*, vol. 29, 1069–70; Ambassador in Argentina and Uruguay to SSEA, 2 March 1962, *DCER*, vol. 29, 1070–71; Ambassador in Colombia to SSEA, 5 March 1962, *DCER*, vol. 29, 1071–2; Ambassador in Chile to SSEA, 6 March 1962, *DCER*, vol. 29, 1074–76.
61 Mexico City to DEA, D-60, 9 February 1963, RG 25, vol. 8561, file 12797–40-pt. 3.
62 "Frondizi Sees Closer Contact with Canada," *Globe and Mail*, 28 November 1961.
63 Pick, "Relations with New Governments in Latin America," 8 June 1964, LAC, RG 25, vol. 5010, file 261–40-pt. 2.
64 See appendix in Rochlin, *Discovering the Americas*. Between 1960 and 1965 Latin America's portion of Canada's overall trade grew marginally from 3.5 to 3.7 percent. But exports to all countries except Brazil, Haiti, and Honduras grew exponentially, with total annual exports nearly doubling from $183 million to $314 million.
65 Robertson to Diefenbaker, "Canadian and United States Relations with Latin America," 16 February 1961, LAC, MG 31 E83, vol. 4, file February 1961; "The Brazilian Foreign Minister's Call on the President," 18 March 1960, *Foreign Relations of the United States, 1958–1960*, vol. 5 (Washington, DC: US Government Printing Office 1991), 769.
66 See David Sheinin, "Cuba's Long Shadow: The Progressive Church Movement and Canadian-Latin American Relations, 1970–1987," in *Our Place in the Sun: Canada and Cuba in the Castro Era*, ed. Robert Wright and Lana Wylie (Toronto: University of Toronto Press, 2009), 121–42; and, in the same volume, Cynthia Wright, "Between Nation and Empire: The Fair Play for Cuba Committees and the Making of Canada-Cuba Solidarity in the 1960s," 96–120.
67 Brian Stevenson, *Canada, Latin America, and the New Internationalism: A Foreign Policy Analysis, 1968–1999* (Montreal and Kingston: McGill-Queen's University Press, 2000); Peter McKenna, ed., *Canada Looks South: In Search of an Americas Policy* (Toronto: University of Toronto Press, 2012).

9

The Diefenbaker Government and Foreign Policy in Africa

KEVIN A. SPOONER

It is not surprising that Africa has rarely ranked high on the agenda of Canadian governments. In this respect, the government of John G. Diefenbaker in the late 1950s and early 1960s was no different. The intense drama of the Cuban Missile Crisis, controversies over trade with the United Kingdom, and divisions over nuclear policy far overshadowed almost any concern that arose in Africa during Diefenbaker's time in office. Even the world tour he undertook early in his majority government focused almost entirely on Europe and Asia: Africa did not even warrant a stopover.

That said, Africa could not be completely ignored either. Diefenbaker's years in government coincided with the beginning of a period of dramatic upheaval on the continent as colonies achieved independence and swelled the ranks of sovereign nation-states. In the now well-worn phrase of then British prime minister Harold Macmillan, the "wind of change" was indeed blowing. The fear that the Soviet Union would turn these upheavals to its own advantage gave an added Cold War urgency to the decolonization process. Consequently, the Diefenbaker government was confronted by the need to formulate responses to trends and events in Africa, leading to seminal developments in Canadian-African relations. In part, the formative nature of the period stemmed merely from the coincidence of timing. Yet Diefenbaker's personal convictions sometimes played their part in setting Canada on the path that his successors followed.

This chapter first reviews early Canadian-African relations, culminating in a discussion of the Diefenbaker government's approach to South African racial policies within the Commonwealth context. The wider implications of African decolonization are then addressed, as is the Diefenbaker government's response to one of the most critical episodes of the Cold War in Africa – the Congo Crisis.

The Development of Early Relations and South Africa's Place in the Commonwealth

Canadian engagement with Africa, in the late nineteenth and early twentieth centuries, was limited. Certainly, there were intermittent efforts in support of European colonialism on the continent: William Stairs, a Nova Scotian, aided colonial expeditions to Africa in the nineteenth century; Canadians served with the British effort to relieve the besieged colonial forces of Major-General Charles Gordon in Khartoum, Sudan, in the mid-1880s; and, most notably, Canada provided military forces to assist Britain in the South African War.[1] More systematic and consistent was the presence of Canadian missionaries. First arriving in the 1800s, they numbered close to twenty-five hundred by the end of the 1950s.[2] By that point in time, Canadian business was not entirely absent either. Canada's Aluminum Limited, for instance, sought out opportunities arising from the presence of bauxite deposits and the potential hydroelectric resources of major rivers such as the Volta and the Congo. But on the whole, Canadian-African economic relations were very limited. By the end of the 1950s, exports to the continent were a mere $72.2 million (less than 1.5 percent of total Canadian exports), and imports were even less impressive at $24.6 million (less than 0.5 percent of total Canadian imports). Trade with South Africa represented the lion's share of even this small exchange of goods.[3] All in all, Canada's showing in Africa was relatively meagre.

Though Africa was rarely considered in Canadian foreign policy before the 1950s, there were signs this was beginning to change. Well into the 1950s, Canada had limited representation on the continent, and few departmental resources at the Department of External Affairs were devoted exclusively to Africa. The Commonwealth Division was responsible for all of Africa south of the Sahara, and it was not until 1956 that a single desk officer in that division was appointed to cover African affairs. By 1959, though, three officers staffed an African section, and consideration was given to the establishment of a full-fledged African division. South Africa, early on the most important African nation for Canada, had not received a Canadian high commissioner to foster direct bilateral relations until the early 1940s. In the Diefenbaker years, however, the number of Canadian embassies and high commissions on the continent slowly increased as the government carefully considered which newly independent nations most warranted diplomatic represen-tation.[4] Yet another sign of the increased attention paid to Africa can be seen in the 1960 decision to extend foreign aid to Commonwealth countries there. While Canada already provided some aid to Africa through the UN, the Diefenbaker government committed $10.5 million over three years to the Special Commonwealth African Assistance Program.[5]

While efforts to address Canada's deficiencies in African affairs had started with Diefenbaker's Liberal predecessor, Louis St. Laurent, change was more evident with the Progressive Conservatives, particularly under the leadership of Howard Green, who took over the external affairs portfolio in June 1959. An experienced politician and cabinet minister, Green was well disposed to the idea that Canada could play a greater role in Africa. Consequently, such important administrative changes as the formation of an African and Middle Eastern division and increased diplomatic represen-tation on the continent occurred during his tenure.[6] In part, the minister advocated closer relations with new African nations because he recognized that they could be important allies for Canadian initiatives at the United Nations.[7] As a staunch advocate of disarmament, who used the UN as a primary venue for his initiatives in this field, it is not surprising that Green firmly placed Africa on Ottawa's diplomatic horizon.

In a contemporary analysis for the 1959–61 volume of *Canada in World Affairs*, Richard Preston was particularly struck by what he termed "The Discovery of Africa." Preston suggested that "the emergence of Africa" and the resulting increase in Canadian relations with these new, non-aligned na-tions was highly significant.[8] Ghana's independence in 1957 was recognized as a key turning point. Preston pointed out that this period of decoloniza-tion and transition opened the door for a greater Canadian role since many Africans believed "that Canada was rather different from the other white powers because she had no record of imperialism and because she herself had once been a colony."[9]

While Preston, and Canadians generally, may have recognized the signi-ficance of decolonization only in the late 1950s and early 1960s, it is worth noting how as early as the mid-1950s, under the St. Laurent government, External Affairs had considered the wider implications of Ghana's then impending independence for both the Commonwealth and Canadian for-eign policy generally. A memorandum titled "Canadian Relations with an

Awakening Africa" was drafted following intradepartmental consultations and discussion at the highest levels, involving Undersecretary Lester B. Pearson, assistant undersecretaries, and multiple heads of division.[10] In their view, the Commonwealth was on the cusp of "far-reaching change." The decolonization of some 50 million (mostly African) subjects was expected to cement earlier changes brought about by India's and Pakistan's independence, turning the association "from a predominantly pink to a predominantly brown Commonwealth."[11]

Just a few years later, under a new government, a departmental panel assessed the implications of sweeping African decolonization. Over twenty African states had achieved independence in the past five years and thereby "dramatically increased the impact of African issues and development." Although Canada had few direct interests in the continent, it could not escape the impact of these changes.[12] Clearly, the St. Laurent Liberals had anticipated important policy implications in Canadian-African foreign relations, but the timing of widespread independence meant the realities of African political developments had to be confronted more directly after Diefenbaker came to power.

The emerging significance of Africa was further affirmed in 1960, when the Canadian ambassador to France, Pierre Dupuy, toured the continent and returned a strong advocate for future Canadian engagement. His final report on the tour was replete with accounts of the effusive praise heaped upon Canada by countless African dignitaries. "Canada," he claimed, "enjoys in Africa a reputation – one could say a prestige – which few non-Africans, and even Canadians, are fully aware of." Canada's development as a French and British colony "grown into a modern nation, full of dynamism" was proffered as an "encouraging example for newly born states." Dupuy partly attributed this fine reputation to the fact that "the problem of racial discrimination has scarcely arisen with our people" and that Canada was not suspected of "expansionist ambitions."[13] Canadian economic interests in Africa were certainly limited, though aspirations in this regard were subtly on the rise. More pointedly, the nation's history was hardly free from the taint of racial discrimination. It might well be argued that Canada not only gained from African ignorance of Canadian history and aims but also profited greatly by not being one of the traditional imperial powers. Indeed, as Dupuy openly acknowledged, "We are benefiting from comparisons made with other Western countries, whose colonial past, racial prejudice or economic expansion have caused much criticism." He loftily concluded, "It is the conviction of many of the African leaders we have met, as it is our own, that African confidence in the soundness of Canadian political judgment is such as to make Canadians acceptable as advisers, guides and arbiters."[14] Dupuy's proposed agenda for Canada was truly ambitious.

As the ambassador toured the continent, a prime opportunity for Canada to assume the role of helpful conciliator ("arbiter" would be too strong a word) arose within the Commonwealth. In May 1960, at a meeting of the Commonwealth prime ministers, the issue of South African apartheid had reared its ugly head. In Chapter 2 (this volume), Norman Hillmer provides a detailed account of this episode, assessing its significance to Canadian-British relations. Still, it is worth highlighting here as well: South Africa's departure from the Commonwealth is one of the most notable developments of the Diefenbaker years, with clear implications for Canadian relations with the Commonwealth African states.

While the basic tenets of Canadian policy towards South African racial policies were in evidence at the United Nations from the late 1940s on, most notably in the yearly consideration of General Assembly resolutions condemning South Africa, the Commonwealth ultimately proved to be the venue where the issue played out most dramatically.[15] The precise role played by Diefenbaker in the Commonwealth's eventual split with South Africa remains a matter of historical debate.[16] In his memoirs, Diefenbaker claims he was "charged with driving South Africa out of the Commonwealth," but Hillmer's account of the impact of these events on Canadian-British relations reasonably argues this may well be an exaggeration of the role both Canada and Diefenbaker played.[17]

What is clear is that Diefenbaker felt conflicted by the dilemma South Africa's racial policies posed for the Commonwealth. The prime minister had strong and considered personal convictions with respect to human rights, a mindset well illustrated by Francine McKenzie in Chapter 1 (this volume), where she shows that Diefenbaker clearly recognized and expressed the importance of social justice and racial equality for the Commonwealth. To reconcile those sincere views with the South African system of apartheid would have been a tall order for him. Yet at first he was also clearly reluctant to be perceived as the leading force behind South Africa's departure from the community. Just months ahead of the May 1960 meeting of prime ministers, his reticence was notable in the Canadian government's muted response to the Sharpeville Massacre, when he rather meekly emphasized the importance of maintaining channels of communication within the Commonwealth.[18] At the May meeting, Diefenbaker ignored the advice of his clerk of the Privy Council, Robert B. Bryce, who advocated openly confronting South Africa at the conference table and pressing for a public statement emphasizing the principle of racial equality.[19] Instead of Diefenbaker, it was Tunku Abdul Rahman, the prime minister of Malaya, who took the lead in raising the issue at the 1960 meeting. When British prime minister Harold Macmillan intervened to urge the matter be raised in private conversations, and not at the conference table, Diefenbaker concurred.

Private meetings between Diefenbaker and the South African minister of external affairs, Eric Louw (who attended the meeting in place of Prime Minister Hendrik Verwoerd), were hardly reassuring for the prospects of compromise, and these meetings undoubtedly coloured the prime minister's opinion of his South African counterparts. Diefenbaker told Louw that, "unless there was some liberalization of the South African Government's racial policies, the Canadian Government would find it increasingly difficult to maintain [a] moderate line."[20] Diefenbaker later recalled how he had urged Louw to consider even token representation for black South Africans in their Parliament. When Louw rejected the idea, Diefenbaker tersely replied, "Your policies are not only wrong, but dangerous."[21] In fact, historian Ronald Hyam has written that Diefenbaker "felt personally resentful of the abusive treatment he had received from Louw."[22] He was not alone in feeling slighted. In the view of the British high commissioner to South Africa, Sir John Maud, Louw was "unfitted to the delicate task of retaining Commonwealth goodwill; he was embittered, spiteful, pedantic, self-righteous, vain, and dreary."[23]

Macmillan managed to skirt Louw's ill-advised request that the Commonwealth provide assurances South Africa could retain its membership if an impending referendum resulted in that country becoming a republic. Diefenbaker was certainly pleased that a showdown had been avoided.[24] He later reported to cabinet that the conference results were gratifying and would require South Africa "to take some action to modify its apartheid policy if it wished to remain within the Commonwealth."[25] Whatever his genuine misgivings concerning apartheid, Diefenbaker was fine with the postponement of a definite resolution to the South African dilemma.

Ahead of the next meeting of Commonwealth prime ministers, arranged for the following March, Diefenbaker initially seemed to stiffen in his resolve to address South African intransigence on the principle of racial equality, but then he wavered. He initially told Basil Robinson, his special assistant on external relations, that he "could not possibly afford to adopt at the next meeting an attitude as tolerant of South Africa as he had before and during the last meeting."[26] As Hillmer notes in Chapter 2 (this volume),

Diefenbaker alarmed Macmillan when the Canadian made known to the British prime minister his intention to forewarn the South Africans that he expected significant changes to their racial policies if and when they pressed for membership in the Commonwealth as a republic.[27] According to Macmillan's biographer Alistair Horne, the British prime minister recognized that Diefenbaker's position at the conference could be "decisive."[28] When Macmillan quickly issued an almost desperate plea to Diefenbaker not to pre-judge the situation, it appeared to have some effect. Early in 1961, Diefenbaker was suddenly telling Robinson about his positive emotional reaction to South Africa because of its wartime record and long-standing Commonwealth association. He once again expressed his reluctance "to be responsible for South Africa's expulsion."[29]

Bryce, however, remained a vocal and influential advocate for a firm stand against South African readmission; indeed, he argued for Canada to take the lead at the upcoming March meeting.[30] While Macmillan urged restraint and Bryce advocated action, cabinet repeatedly but inconclusively debated the South African issue. Some ministers were against Canada leading the charge to exclude South Africa, but others worried the Canadian public and media would see compromise with South Africa as inconsistent with Diefenbaker's reputation as a champion of equality and civil rights. Diefenbaker left for London without a definite position and with his cabinet advising him to use his own best judgment.

At the outset of the conference, Diefenbaker seemed ready to compromise. Other delegates appeared willing to see South Africa readmitted, so the prime minister contemplated "a less aggressive position." The cabinet, however, was particularly attuned to press coverage at home and urged Diefenbaker to condemn apartheid, firmly and clearly.[31] A meeting between Diefenbaker and R.K. Nehru, the Indian secretary-general for external affairs, also proved important. The Indian minister, dispatched by Prime Minister Jawaharlal Nehru to consult with the Canadians, made it clear India was not keen to see South Africa readmitted. If India's consent was definitely required, it did not intend to give it.

At this point, a course of action began to take shape. Diefenbaker suggested that discussion of South Africa's readmission should be delayed until its Parliament actually passed legislation to implement constitutional change. At the same time, the conference could issue a statement condemning apartheid. Diefenbaker expected that, if this were done, "South Africa would withdraw from the meeting and probably from the Commonwealth as well, without direct action having to be taken to exclude her."[32]

On 13 March, Prime Minister Nehru was first out of the gate with the proposition for a clear Commonwealth declaration against racial discrimination.[33] Diefenbaker spoke next, advising his fellow prime ministers that the Canadian government believed some "public recognition of the multi-racial character of the Commonwealth was necessary" and that all Commonwealth states should "subscribe to the principle of non-discrimination between human beings on the grounds of race or colour."[34] Over the next few days, Macmillan attempted to arrive at a draft communiqué acceptable to all, but any declaration that apartheid was inconsistent with Commonwealth ideals was too much for Verwoerd. Ultimately, he formally withdrew South Africa's request to remain a Commonwealth member state. Just as Diefenbaker predicted in his discussion with R.K. Nehru, South Africa had left the Commonwealth without any member nation having to explicitly withhold its consent for readmission.

How crucial was Diefenbaker to this outcome? As Hillmer suggests, the role played by Canada, through Diefenbaker, has likely been over-amplified. Hyam agrees, noting it is "unnecessary to invoke him [Diefenbaker] as the prime mover of events."[35] Diefenbaker's own actions, during both the 1960 and 1961 meetings, are consistent with this interpretation. He was undoubtedly reluctant to take the lead in an effort that would drive South Africa out of the Commonwealth to which it had belonged for so many years. But he was also a person with a strong sense of individual political rights. At home, the Canadian Bill of Rights had cemented his reputation in this regard; advice from cabinet and Bryce doubly served to remind him of this reputation. Looking past South African apartheid was not easy.

In the end, South Africa's departure had much more to do with Indian initiative and South African intransigence than with Diefenbaker's diplomacy. Yet some of Diefenbaker's prime ministerial colleagues were unforgiving in their assessments of him, suggesting his actions, if not truly decisive, were also not unimportant. Years later, Macmillan claimed, "Without him, we could have got through."[36] Australian prime minister Robert Menzies accused Diefenbaker of leading "the attack upon South Africa."[37] From Cape Town, Canadian diplomats reported that Verwoerd and Louw "made it quite clear to South Africans that in their view the Prime Minister of Canada supplied the push which led to the South African withdrawal from the Commonwealth."[38] On the charge of driving South Africa from the Commonwealth, Diefenbaker appears to have been found guilty by his white peers. Of course, this finding of guilt would be viewed quite differently from the perspective of his Asian and African counterparts. Similarly, as his cabinet colleagues had advised from home, domestic political opinion expected consistency from the prime minister on issues of human rights, especially given Diefenbaker's domestic rights agenda. This political constituency would not have been disappointed.

Decolonization

Though Canada was never a colonial power in Africa, the consequences of colonialism on that continent nonetheless had to be dealt with by Canadian governments of the 1950s and 1960s. Both Liberal and Progressive Conservative governments in these decades recognized the international significance of the widespread constitutional changes brought about by decolonization, not least of which was the emergence of a host of new nations. As just seen, the drama of South Africa's departure from the Commonwealth played out over two Commonwealth prime ministers' meetings at which newly decolonized nations outnumbered the old, white Commonwealth member states.

On the one hand, decolonization afforded a golden opportunity for a middle power to garner new allies, which was especially important for Howard Green, who wanted to attract supporters for his disarmament initiatives. And, as Pierre Dupuy had found on his African tour, new nations there seemed willing to give Canada, a Western power relatively free from the taint of imperialism, the benefit of the doubt. On the other hand, African nationalism leading to independence complicated matters when it conflicted with the interests, both political and economic, of metropolitan, European powers such as Britain, France, and Belgium. These states were allied to Canada through the North Atlantic Treaty Organization for the purpose of defending the West against the threat of communism. Canada was in a difficult position, sometimes wanting to demonstrate empathy for African aspirations to self-determination, yet fearful of offending European allies who were clearly the targets of anti-colonialism.

Equally troubling, the pace of change from colonial rule to independence was seen by some Canadian officials as too rapid and likely to result in varying degrees of political instability, creating conditions ripe for interference by the Soviet Union. Independence was a reasonable objective, but the containment of communism was starting to be recognized as important in Africa, following precedents in Asia. Here, then, we see the intersection of decolonization with the Cold War. Cold War concerns are evident in Canadian views on Ghana, the first sub-Saharan British colony since South Africa to achieve independence, and Algeria, a particularly challenging case given the intense political turmoil associated with this North African colony's separation from France.

Canada's diplomatic representation in sub-Saharan Africa doubled in 1957, with the opening of a high commission to Ghana soon after that country achieved independence. Newly appointed high commissioner Evan Gill held relatively favourable views of Prime Minister Kwame Nkrumah, and these views were maintained, even as reports began to circulate that the Ghanaian leader was developing certain authoritarian tendencies. Gill acknowledged Ghana as the "focal point of African nationalism" but suggested that the "multi-racial communities" were more likely to prove challenging to the Commonwealth. He emphasized the need to take into account "local conditions" as he outlined the difficulties Nkrumah faced: "What he has to work with is ... a population, the vast majority of which lives at a subsistence level, is illiterate, animistic and split by tribalism. This population has been given adult suffrage. Independence and the parliamentary system of government have little or no meaning for the illiterates."[39] Ultimately, Gill advanced an argument for adapting the Western world's conception of democracy to suit Africa.

In effect, Gill called for a "wait-and-see" attitude that accepted the need for a strong central government in Ghana, where conditions were "not yet propitious for multi-party parliament on the Westminster model."[40] The Cold War was an undeniable factor in the suggestion of such an approach. So long as Ghana was stable, even if not entirely democratic, it was less susceptible to communist influences. In the end, though, this policy was justified by references to social underdevelopment (e.g., illiteracy) and, more significantly, racialized perceptions of animism and tribalism. Gill tended to explain political and social development in Africa through a Eurocentric lens that then enabled Canadian policy to be justified on the basis of perceived racial shortcomings.

In Ottawa, the currency of Gill's perceptions was in evidence during a meeting between the head of the Commonwealth Division, George Glazebrook, and Sir Charles Arden-Clarke, the last governor of the Gold Coast and first governor-general of Ghana. Practically echoing Gill, Glazebrook outlined the departmental attitude towards Ghana:

... because of the cultural environment, the continuing influence of tribalism, and local mysticism, and the relative inexperience in operating British forms of government, we cannot reasonably expect Ghana to develop precisely along the lines of democracy as we know it, but rather we must make an effort to be patient and understanding and ready to give assistance and tactful advice when asked for it.[41]

The notion that Canada might find itself in a position to provide either assistance or advice was a recurring idea that Gill had encouraged in earlier dispatches to Ottawa, particularly in advance of Nkrumah's July 1958 visit to Canada. The high commissioner had suggested then that Ghana, in an effort not to appear too dependent on the United States, tended instead to "look first" to countries such as Canada for assistance. That said, in private meetings between Diefenbaker and Nkrumah during the Ghanaian leader's state visit, apparently no specific requests for additional assistance were made.[42] Still, Canada's Commonwealth connection and lack of colonial past had placed it in a relatively good position to establish positive relations with this important English-speaking African nation.

Just a year after his arrival in Accra, Gill witnessed the first of three meetings of the All-African Peoples' Conference – a gathering of notable delegates drawn together by the shared objectives of securing the formal independence of African colonies and working against neocolonialism. From the outset, Gill was suspicious of this early development in pan-African nationalism: "Since most of those attending the conference will be radicals and nationalists," he wrote to External Affairs, "the indications are that discussions and resolutions will lean to extreme denunciations of colonial powers. I do not expect that the conference will do anything to encourage a moderate and responsible approach." Chinese and Soviet observers were present, and the high commissioner immediately recognized the gathering's Cold War implications. He fully expected the event to furnish the communists with ample propaganda to damage Western interests and "further encourage irresponsible sections of black African opinion."[43]

Following the event, Gill's reports to Ottawa both confirmed and qualified his earlier assessment. He was particularly troubled by the views of African leaders from British multi-racial territories. In this regard, he reinforced the already embedded predilection at External Affairs to distinguish between Britain's African colonies in a manner that recognized and reinforced the racial privilege of white settlers when they constituted a significant minority. Gill found East African leaders to be uncompromising on the principle of securing "complete political control" and doing so "very soon." He opined: "They showed themselves as unrealistic and irrational in their cry of 'Africa for the Africans' and in their contention that the problems of this continent could be dealt with in isolation." In sum, Gill believed the conference had "ushered in a new phase in the African revolution" that would now be led, to a much greater extent than had earlier been the case, by the extremists.[44]

Yet Gill reported positively on Nkrumah's interventions at the conference. Nkrumah spoke against the use of force to achieve independence and had cautioned his colleagues to be aware "that imperialism might come in a different guise, not necessarily from Europe." On the Cold War front, Gill seemed satisfied that many Africans had recognized for themselves the dangers of communist penetration, but he continued to worry that they might still pursue independence by means that undermined "orderly" change and created conditions favourable "for the USSR to exploit."[45] Again, Gill's key message for Ottawa was that African nationalism and many of its proponents were evolving in increasingly extreme and irresponsible directions, though it is possible to recognize in Gill's approach a distinction between African nations such as Ghana and those such as Kenya; in the case of the latter, there were ensconced white settler groups whose social, economic, and political privileges were directly threatened by the project of independence.[46]

In French-speaking Africa, the situation was quite complex. Robin Gendron, in his definitive study of Canadian relations with French Africa during this period, has demonstrated that the Diefenbaker government did not generally attach much importance to French-speaking African nations. He credits the Progressive Conservatives with beginning "the slow process of expanding Canada's diplomatic, political, aid, and economic relations with these countries" but recognizes that Diefenbaker's government paid more attention to the Commonwealth.[47] The most that can be said, particularly in relation to French-speaking sub-Saharan Africa, is that the Diefenbaker government laid administrative and diplomatic groundwork that would enable his Liberal successor, Lester Pearson, to take up the issue of Canadian relations with French Africa in the mid- to late 1960s, when the significance of diplomacy with this part of the world had as much to do with Quebec and the domestic political situation at home as it did with ambitions to develop substantive bilateral and even multilateral relations with French-speaking African states.

The decolonization of North Africa, however, could not be so easily overlooked. Relations with Tunisia, and to a lesser degree Morocco, were advanced modestly during the Diefenbaker years, but the independence of Algeria was the most important issue related to French colonies to confront the Progressive Conservatives. From the mid-nineteenth century, Algeria had been administered by the French as an integral part of the nation – an important distinction when compared with colonial relationships France maintained with its sub-Saharan colonies and other colonies in North Africa. For decades, French settlers had taken up residence in Algeria, and their descendants vigorously resisted any efforts to achieve complete independence or self-determination. The resulting Algerian War began in earnest by the mid-1950s, during the St. Laurent government, but it reached its climax in the Diefenbaker years.

Routinely criticized by the Afro-Asian bloc at the annual sessions of the UN General Assembly for its political intransigence and military interventions, France was keenly sensitive to any wavering in support from its NATO allies on this issue. And there were moments when Canada did seem to waver. In 1958, for example, Undersecretary Jules Léger contemplated meeting with a delegation from the Conference of Independent African States, intent on lobbying Canada to support Algerian independence; the French embassy in Ottawa was nearly apoplectic, albeit for naught as the Africans ultimately cancelled the trip.[48]

Two years later, in an effort to appease Morocco and Tunisia, Green considered abstaining on an Afro-Asian sponsored resolution when the issue of Algeria was debated at the UN. Officials at External Affairs managed to convince him not to do so, fearing the degree to which France would be alienated.[49] Ultimately, Green was also influenced by the American position. The minister suggested there was "no reason why Canada should be more forthcoming than the United States in supporting France on this issue."[50] In the end, both the United States and Canada voted against the Afro-Asian resolution. The decision to do so was made easier by political developments in Algeria. President Charles de Gaulle was making significant moves to end the Algerian War, and it could be argued that Canada did not want to undermine these efforts. Still, negotiations with the National Liberation Front (FLN) over Algeria's future were not without their difficulties. In a June 1961 meeting between de Gaulle and Pierre Dupuy, the French president criticized FLN representatives as "petty agitators without any sense of reality, of government, of the future of Algeria."[51] Nonetheless, by early 1962 a formal ceasefire was in place and, following a referendum later that year, Algeria gained its independence.

Canada could rest a little easier knowing that one of the thorniest decolonization dilemmas routinely forcing Canada to choose between a NATO ally and Afro-Asian friends had finally been resolved. Francine McKenzie, in her assessment of Diefenbaker's 1958 Commonwealth tour, highlights the critical intersection between the Cold War and decolonization (see Chapter 1, this volume). As seen here, this intersection was very much in play with respect to Canadian relations with English- and French-speaking Africa. In the balancing act this intersection required, Canada mostly empathized with its NATO allies but not without a cautious and critical eye to the implications for its relations with newly independent African states.

Peacekeeping and the Congo Crisis

As had been the case in Algeria, decolonization and independence in the Belgian Congo proved especially complicated and messy. In fact, the Congo Crisis was the most dramatic African foreign policy issue to confront the Diefenbaker government. Occurring in July 1960, at a time of heightened Cold War tensions, this crisis in the heart of Africa threatened to further destabilize the already deteriorating relations between the United States and the Soviet Union.

The Congo gained independence in June 1960, after Belgian intransigence was dramatically transformed into hurried political reform, compelled by increased Congolese agitation and unrest. The mutiny of the Congolese combined military and police force, the Force Publique, ignited a political crisis soon after independence. The civil chaos that ensued was compounded by a constitutional crisis in September, when the president of the Congo, Joseph Kasavubu, and Prime Minister Patrice Lumumba each tried to dismiss the other from office. Before this interregnum, however, the two leaders had acted together to call upon the UN to intervene, an act of solidarity prompted by Belgium's decision to redeploy military forces from bases it had retained in the Congo. Summoned by Secretary-General Dag Hammarskjöld to consider this growing threat to international peace and security, the Security Council authorized the dispatch of peacekeepers not only to assist in the maintenance of law and order but also to supervise the withdrawal of Belgian forces.[52]

Just four years earlier, the Suez Crisis in the Middle East had led to the creation and deployment of the first major UN peacekeeping force, the United Nations Emergency Force (UNEF). Lester Pearson played a critical diplomatic role in New York, working with Secretary-General Hammarskjöld to establish UNEF. Canadian forces then provided important logistical support for the peacekeeping mission, and a Canadian, Lieutenant General E.L.M Burns, led the operation.[53] With the UN poised to deploy peacekeepers to the Congo, expectations were aroused: Was the UN now about to turn to Canada once again for soldiers to serve in what would become its largest Cold War peacekeeping operation, the Opération des Nations Unies au

Congo (ONUC)? Journalists and parliamentarians speculated on the likelihood that a standby battalion earmarked for UN service might be called
into action. Basil Robinson later recalled that, as rumours mounted, the
prime minister "shot out of his chair and told me to see that Hammarskjöld
was told right away not to proceed with the idea of troops from Canada."[54]
Concerns for the safety of potentially French-speaking, white peacekeepers
undoubtedly explained Diefenbaker's hesitant attitude, a view shared by his
respected undersecretary at External Affairs, Norman Robertson.

However, Charles Ritchie, Canada's representative at the United Nations, was in close communication with Hammarskjöld and knew full well
the secretary-general had no intention of requesting front-line infantry,
such as the standby battalion, from Canada – a NATO-aligned nation. In
the context of the Congo Crisis, this was politically unthinkable. Ambassador Ritchie's repeated cables reassuring Ottawa on this point were not
fully appreciated until a clear request from New York finally did arrive. As
with UNEF, the UN once again needed support troops and not infantry. In
particular, Canada was asked for bilingual communications personnel, air
transport, and a few officers to play important roles at ONUC headquarters. Following a debate in the House of Commons, cabinet approved an
order-in-council on 5 August that authorized up to five hundred officers
and men to serve in support of UN operations in the Congo.[55]

Canada had long tried to balance support for its Western allies against
the need to convince Africans that its membership in NATO did not detract
from support for the UN or "sympathy with the aspirations of African states
to pursue independent policies of their own."[56] The Congo Crisis, involving
as it did a former colony of a NATO ally, is another example of just how
difficult this balancing act was. For instance, while some historians have
emphasized the significance to Belgium and to NATO of Belgian military
bases in the Congo, notably at Kamina, Canada was reluctant to support
Belgian claims to these military bases. Doing so, External Affairs advised the
Canadian embassy in Belgium, would "give substance to charges of Western
aggression ... [and] would seem calculated to create the worst possible impression among African and anti-colonial powers generally."[57]

Moreover, the Belgian ambassador in Ottawa did not always find a sympathetic ear at External Affairs. In a meeting with the deputy undersecretary of state for external affairs, Marcel Cadieux, the two discussed various
aspects of the situation in the Congo. In particular, the ambassador was
concerned the Soviets would attempt a takeover "unless the United States
and other friendly countries adopt publicly a firm position." The ambassador

must have left External Affairs somewhat disappointed. His government's views were only politely acknowledged and not wholeheartedly accepted. Cadieux, first and foremost, expressed faith in the UN and Hammarskjöld and, while accepting the possibility that communists might take advantage of anarchy in the Congo, he did not uncritically subscribe to the idea that the Soviets were plotting a takeover.[58]

Before long, the Belgians grew tired of Canada's lukewarm support. The Canadian ambassador to Belgium came to believe he exercised very little influence in Brussels. He reported: "I have whenever I could pressed the point with [Pierre] Wigny [the Belgian foreign minister] and others that Belgian cooperation with UN seemed wisest policy and best tactics but I didn't make any impression. I could hardly get a word in edgewise."[59] In some important respects, then, Canada was prepared at times to take an uncooperative approach with a NATO ally when there were political implications for Canada's relations with Africa.

Canada's difficult balancing act was also in evidence in the government's approach to Patrice Lumumba, who came to be seen increasingly by the West as unreliable and all too willing to turn to the Soviets for help. In July 1960, the Congolese prime minister visited North America. The Eisenhower administration warmly welcomed Lumumba but did not agree to provide direct bilateral assistance, the principal goal of the Congolese mission. After conferring with American secretary of state Christian Herter, Green decided Canada would take the same position: any Canadian aid would be channelled through the UN.[60] Neither the United States nor Canada wanted to open the door to direct bilateral Soviet assistance by setting a precedent, but this response ultimately disappointed Lumumba.

Even before the Congolese leader arrived in Ottawa, the Belgian chargé d'affaires there was lobbying External Affairs to downplay the visit. He emphatically labelled Lumumba a communist, elected to office using money provided by the Eastern bloc. While Canadian officials tried to limit the fanfare associated with Lumumba's visit, they were not convinced the Congolese prime minister was an avowed communist; instead, he was seen as an inexperienced and untrained leader, eager to grasp at anything that might consolidate his political position. They believed he played East and West against each other, politically and economically, and concurred with Hammarskjöld's view that he was "very responsive to friendship and to frankness, impressionable but apt to be swayed by changing influences ... ignorant, very suspicious, shrewd but immature in his ideas."[61] Lumumba's meeting with Diefenbaker proved to be an awkward affair that grew tense as the two leaders unsuccessfully attempted to convey to one another their respective positions on aid. Only after Lumumba suggested he was not expecting Canada to pay for Congolese civil servants did the conversation turn somewhat cordial.[62]

When the Congolese prime minister later accepted Soviet assistance, views in the West generally hardened against him. In mid-September 1960, with Western support, Colonel Joseph Mobutu successfully launched a military coup, and Lumumba was effectively placed under house arrest. UN peacekeepers surrounded his residence to protect him from Mobutu's forces, but Lumumba managed to escape. After he was captured by Mobutu's troops in December, Canada's position became even more ambiguous.[63] Non-aligned and East bloc members of the UN energetically raised Lumumba's plight in the UN General Assembly; the United States responded by trying to delay debate. Officials at External Affairs, however, opposed the American manoeuvre. "The present drift in the Congo situation," they argued, "could hardly be allowed to continue for three months without some United Nations action, unless we were prepared to contemplate a complete erosion of the United Nations position there." Canada was proving less strident than some of its allies, who advocated a wholly Western Congo policy. In fact, Ritchie believed it would be very difficult for Canada, given its participation in ONUC, to follow "the straight NATO line."[64]

Yet Canadian policy was not entirely favourable to Lumumba either. Ritchie expressed Canada's "shock and disgust" at the brutality of Mobutu's troops, who had savagely beaten Lumumba after his December capture, but he did not argue for the prime minister's release, suggesting instead that he "be brought to a fair and speedy trial in accordance with the guarantees which are normally given to accused persons."[65] In the House of Commons, Howard Green's reaction to Lumumba's treatment was half-hearted at best. When asked if the government had protested, the secretary of state for external affairs replied: "No ... there has been no protest launched. It would keep us very busy if we were to protest all the beatings which take place in the Congo. I agree that it was an unfortunate incident."[66] Neither Ritchie nor Green was aware that, by the date of their statements, Lumumba's political opponents had already assassinated him.

In the end, the Diefenbaker government's views of Lumumba were much less rigid than those held by its counterparts in Brussels and Washington. In Ottawa, he was perceived to be more a political opportunist than a hard and fast communist. Diplomacy at the UN demonstrated willingness, albeit grudging at times, to see Lumumba play a role in the resolution of the Congo's internal strife. This approach was clearly taken with an eye to Canada's role at the UN, its participation in ONUC, and its relations with Afro-Asian states more generally, even though this sometimes set Canada apart from important NATO allies. When news of Lumumba's assassination broke, the Cold War implications of his murder were apparent to everyone, including the Canadian cabinet, where Prime Minister Diefenbaker speculated on the likelihood that Lumumba's left-leaning successor, Antoine Gizenga, would strengthen his position in the Congo.[67]

One final point should be made about the Diefenbaker government's approach to UN peacekeeping in Africa. In the post-Cold War period, some UN operations became more muscular, enforcing rather than just keeping the peace. This shift to more robust peace enforcement has an important parallel from the past with ONUC. The Diefenbaker government was never entirely comfortable with the form of muscular peacekeeping that ultimately evolved in the Congo. When serious fighting broke out between ONUC and armed elements in the breakaway province of Katanga in the fall of 1961, Canada was compelled to consider UN requests for assistance while peacekeepers were engaged in open hostilities. The Canadian government was clearly ill at ease with developments in Katanga and was hardly enthusiastic when UN appeals for help arrived. On 20 September, the secretariat urgently requested transport aircraft, aircrews, maintenance personnel, and spare parts for airlifts within the Congo for three to five weeks. Officials warned Howard Green that there could be "armed resistance and renewed hostilities" if the UN moved to arrest mercenaries in Katanga. Cabinet considered the request, and Green acknowledged that the "decision was a difficult one." Although the aircraft would be at risk of attack, especially if an existing cease-fire ended, cabinet cautiously agreed on 23 September to send two C119s for one month.[68]

When the UN added jet fighters and light bombers to ONUC and requested additional Canadian technical support for the aircraft, the Diefenbaker government proved even more reluctant and initially turned down the request, reversing the decision at the ministerial level only after considerable high-level lobbying by the UN.[69] While not at all comfortable with these early forays into peacemaking rather than peacekeeping, the government guardedly supported more muscular peacekeeping in the Congo, partly to support Canadian and other peacekeepers already deployed with ONUC, and partly because of the significance of UN success in Katanga for the organization's future effectiveness. By the time hostilities came to a head in ending the secession of Katanga in early 1963, the Diefenbaker government was reluctantly resigned to the idea that some degree of force would be necessary to resolve the crisis. But, even as this premise was accepted, Ottawa maintained a cautious and hesitant view towards permitting Canadians to serve in ONUC during periods of heightened tension and in capacities that directly contributed to the peacekeeping operation's ability to exercise greater force. This was equally true with respect to Canadians serving as signallers, in ONUC headquarters, and as part of the RCAF contribution.

Participation in ONUC was Canada's first foray into peacekeeping in sub-Saharan Africa. Diefenbaker's government proved supportive of UN efforts in the Congo, even if it was less enthusiastic about how force was employed at times. Acknowledging the implications of the wider Cold War context, Canadian policy during the Congo Crisis clearly demonstrated an effort to balance interests in the West with the need not to alienate African and Asian governments by cooperating in a strictly NATO approach to Congolese developments.

Conclusion

There was considerable continuity in the Canadian approach to Africa before, during, and after Diefenbaker's time as prime minister. Anticipating the international and political implications of impending decolonization, the St. Laurent government and officials at External Affairs had set the stage for increased awareness of and engagement with Africa by the time the Progressive Conservatives arrived on the scene. The Diefenbaker government then increased representation abroad and implemented changes in departmental organization at External Affairs to better manage African relations.

Official thinking on the nature of African nationalism and its implications for European colonial powers, who happened also to be Canada's NATO allies, continued to develop under Diefenbaker in ways that recognized the intersections of decolonization and the Cold War. The interests of such important allies as Britain and France had to be balanced against the political aspirations of new African states, and Canada did not always come down on the side of its NATO allies, as seen with the Congo Crisis and Belgium in particular. Green, eager to garner new friends among the African states at the UN, could generally be counted on to take a not unsympathetic view of African objectives. The Progressive Conservative government did take a notable stand on the issue of apartheid and South Africa. Diefenbaker played a prominent role in the Commonwealth Conferences of 1960 and 1961, and while it would be overstating the case to suggest South Africa's departure was the result of the prime minister's actions, Diefenbaker's involvement did influence the outcome.

In the end, many issues associated with Canada's relations with African countries were already notable in the Diefenbaker years – the long-term political consequences of colonialism, the struggle against racial intolerance, distinctions between peacekeeping and muscular peacemaking – continued to shape Canadian approaches to Africa in subsequent decades. Apartheid persisted as a preoccupying issue. Ever more nations emerged from colonial status to achieve independence, but then the political tribulations experienced in the Congo were played out in many other parts of the continent. The signposts of future crises leading to later deployments of Canadian peacekeepers were clearly visible. The wind of change was forcefully thrusting Africa onto Canada's international agenda during the Diefenbaker years, and his government was the first to face the resulting opportunities and challenges. By devoting additional administrative and diplomatic resources to Africa, by setting precedents for how Canada would continue to navigate the complex associations between decolonization and the Cold War, and by demonstrating the capacity and willingness of Canada to play a peacekeeping role, the Diefenbaker government certainly proved itself willing, capable, and effective at paving the way for continuing engagement with Africa.

NOTES

1 See Roy MacLaren, *African Exploits: The Diaries of William Stairs, 1887–1892* (Montreal and Kingston: McGill-Queen's University Press, 1998); Roy MacLaren, *Canadians on the Nile, 1882–1898, Being the Adventures of the Voyageurs on the Khartoum Relief Expedition and Other Exploits* (Vancouver: UBC Press, 1978); Carman Miller, *Painting the Map Red: Canada and the South African War, 1899–1902* (Montreal: Canadian War Museum, 1993).
2 Douglas Anglin, "Towards a Canadian Policy on Africa," *International Journal* 15, 4 (1960): 293.
3 Ibid., 294.
4 For a full account of the development of Canadian diplomatic representation in Africa during the period under discussion here, see John Hilliker and Donald Barry, *Canada's Department of External Affairs: Coming of Age, 1946–1968* (Montreal and Kingston: McGill-Queen's University Press, 1995), 172, 176–77, 318–20.
5 Extract from Cabinet Conclusions, in Janice Cavell, ed., *Documents on Canadian External Relations*, vol. 27, *1960* (Ottawa: Foreign Affairs and International Trade Canada, 2007) (hereafter *DCER*, vol. 27), doc. 459, 900–2. It is worth noting that an amount of $15 million over three years was initially recommended by the secretary of state for external affairs and supported by the minister of finance, but cabinet reduced the amount by a third.

6   Hilliker and Barry, *Canada's Department of External Affairs*, 180–81.
7   Ibid., 176.
8   Richard A. Preston, *Canada in World Affairs 1959 to 1961* (Toronto: Oxford University Press, 1965), 229.
9   Ibid., 230.
10 Commonwealth Division to the Under Secretary of State for External Affairs (hereafter USSEA), Mr. Chapdelaine, Mr. Holmes, Mr. Ford, Mr. Ritchie, 15 November 1955, Library and Archives Canada (hereafter LAC), RG 25, vol. 7748, file 12354–40 pt. 1.
11 Expansion of Commonwealth Membership, 7 November 1955, LAC, RG 25, vol. 7748, file 12354–40 pt. 1.
12 USSEA to Secretary of State for External Affairs (hereafter SSEA), in Janice Cavell, ed., *Documents on Canadian External Relations*, vol. 28, *1961* (Ottawa: Foreign Affairs and International Trade Canada, 2009) (hereafter *DCER*, vol. 28), doc. 159, 806–7.
13 Extract of Report by Ambassador in France, *DCER*, vol. 27, doc. 662, 1274.
14 Ibid., 1280.
15 While the focus here is on the Commonwealth, Canadian diplomacy at the UN with respect to South Africa and apartheid during the Diefenbaker years follows a similar trajectory and demonstrates parallel themes. See Peter Henshaw, "Canada and the 'South African Disputes' at the United Nations, 1946–1961," *Canadian Journal of African Studies* 33, 1 (1999): 1–52.
16 In an account of these events, Frank Hayes gives some prominence to the role played by Canada and Diefenbaker. By comparison, Ronald Hyam emphasizes other factors to explain South Africa's departure from the Commonwealth. See Frank Hayes, "South Africa's Departure from the Commonwealth, 1960–61," *International History Review* 2, 3 (1980): 453–84; Ronald Hyam, "The Parting of the Ways: Britain and South Africa's Departure from the Commonwealth, 1951–61," *Journal of Imperial and Commonwealth History* 26, 2 (1998): 157–75.
17 John G. Diefenbaker, *One Canada: Memoirs of the Right Honourable John G. Diefenbaker – The Years of Achievement, 1956 to 1962*, vol. 2 (Toronto: Macmillan of Canada, 1976), 217. See also chap. 2.
18 Ibid., 209–10.
19 Memorandum from secretary to cabinet to prime minister, *DCER*, vol. 27, doc. 359, 730–31.
20 Note: prime minister's conversation with Mr. Louw, *DCER*, vol. 27, doc. 366, 739.
21 Diefenbaker, *One Canada*, 210–11.
22 Hyam, "Parting of the Ways," 164.
23 Ibid., 163.
24 High Commissioner in United Kingdom to SSEA, *DCER*, vol. 27, doc. 373, 749–50. See also Diefenbaker, *One Canada*, 212.
25 Extract from Cabinet Conclusions, *DCER*, vol. 27, doc. 374, 752.
26 Memo special assistant to SSEA to USSEA, *DCER*, vol. 27, doc. 378, 756.
27 SSEA to High Commissioner in United Kingdom, *DCER*, vol. 27, doc. 380, 758. Personal message from prime minister of United Kingdom to prime minister, *DCER*, vol. 27, doc. 382, 760–61, and chap. 2.
28 Alistair Horne, *Macmillan, 1957–1986*, vol. 2 (London: Macmillan, 1989), 392.

29 Special Assistant to SSEA to USSEA, *DCER*, vol. 28, doc. 459, 773.

30 Memo from secretary to cabinet to assistant USSEA, *DCER*, vol. 28, doc. 461, 779–80. Frank Hayes establishes Bryce's influence with Diefenbaker in "South Africa's Departure," 479.

31 Extract from Cabinet Conclusions, *DCER*, vol. 28, doc. 474, 805.

32 Memo by secretary to cabinet, *DCER*, vol. 28, doc. 475, 806–7.

33 See Hyam, "Parting of the Ways," 166–72, for a more detailed discussion of the conference proceedings.

34 Diefenbaker, *One Canada*, 218.

35 Hyam, "Parting of the Ways," 172.

36 Horn, *Macmillan*, 394.

37 As quoted in Hayes, "South Africa's Departure," 477.

38 High Commissioner in South Africa to USSEA, *DCER*, vol. 28, doc. 558, 950.

39 High Commissioner for Canada in Ghana to SSEA, 24 February 1959, LAC, RG 25, file 12684–40 pt. 1.2.

40 Ibid.

41 Notes of meeting, 23 April 1959, LAC, RG 25, file 12684–40 pt. 1.2. Interestingly, in his memoirs, Diefenbaker's recollections of Nkrumah, whom he claimed to know "reasonably well," also emphasized mysticism. He recounted a discussion with the Ghanaian leader about "mediums and extra-terrestrial communication." Diefenbaker made it clear he was not a believer, but he offered up William Lyon Mackenzie King's propensity in this regard. Diefenbaker, *One Canada*, 196.

42 Despatch No. 273 High Commissioner in Ghana to SSEA, in Michael Stevenson, ed., *DCER*, vol. 24, *1957–1958*, pt. 1 (Ottawa: Canadian Government Publishing, 2003) (hereafter *DCER*, vol. 24), doc. 469, 1099, 1101. Letter No. K-241 USSEA to High Commissioner in Ghana, *DCER*, vol. 24, doc. 470, 1103.

43 High Commissioner for Canada in Ghana to SSEA, 24 November 1958, LAC, RG 25, file 12684–40 pt. 1.1.

44 High Commissioner for Canada in Ghana to SSEA, 7 January 1959, LAC, RG 25, file 12684–40 pt. 1.1.

45 Ibid.

46 For a fuller assessment of the significance of race and racial issues in Canadian policy towards Africa at this time, see Kevin A. Spooner, "'Awakening Africa': Race and Canadian Views of Decolonizing Africa," in *Dominion of Race: Rethinking Canada's International History*, ed. Laura Madokoro, Francine McKenzie, and David Meren, 206–27 (Vancouver: UBC Press, 2017).

47 Robin S. Gendron, *Towards a Francophone Community: Canada's Relations with France and French Africa, 1945–1968* (Montreal and Kingston: McGill-Queen's University Press, 2006), 80.

48 Ibid., 47.

49 Ibid., 57.

50 Extract from memo UN Division to USSEA, *DCER*, vol. 27, doc. 113, 190.

51 Conversation between ambassador in France and President Charles de Gaulle, *DCER*, vol. 28, doc. 620, 1049.

52 Important accounts of the crisis are Catherine Hoskyns, *The Congo since Independence, January 1960–December 1961* (London: Oxford University Press, 1965); Ernest

Lefever, *Crisis in the Congo: A United Nations Force in Action* (Washington, DC: The Brookings Institution, 1965); and, more recently, Lise A. Namikas, *Battleground Africa: Cold War in the Congo, 1960–1965* (Washington, DC: Woodrow Wilson Center Press, 2013).

53 On Canada's role in UNEF, see Michael Carroll, *Pearson's Peacekeepers: Canada and the United Nations Emergency Force, 1956–67* (Vancouver: UBC Press, 2009).

54 H. Basil Robinson, *Diefenbaker's World: A Populist in Foreign Affairs* (Toronto: University of Toronto Press, 1989), 148.

55 Canada, House of Commons, *Debates*, 1 August 1960, 7327–48. Cabinet Conclusions, 5 August 1960, LAC, RG 2, vol. 2747. For a fuller discussion of the Canadian decision to contribute to ONUC, see Kevin A. Spooner, *Canada, the Congo Crisis, and UN Peacekeeping, 1960–64* (Vancouver: UBC Press, 2009), 31–62.

56 USSEA to SSEA, *DCER*, vol. 28, doc. 159, 233.

57 Sean Maloney, *Canada and UN Peacekeeping: Cold War by Other Means, 1945–1970* (St. Catharines: Vanwell Publishing, 2002), 105–6, 127. External to Brussels, 14 July 1960, LAC, RG 25, vol. 5208, file 6386–40 pt. 6.

58 Cadieux to USSEA, 20 July 1960, LAC, RG 25, vol. 5219, file 6386-C-40 pt. 1.

59 Brussels to External, 12 January 1961, LAC, RG 25, vol. 5221, file 6386-C-40 pt. 9.

60 Cadieux to USSEA, 27 July 1960; USSEA for PM, 29 July 1960, LAC, RG 25, vol. 5225, file 6386-D-40 pt. 1. Memorandum of conversation, in Harriet Dashiell Schwar and Stanley Shaloff, eds., *Foreign Relations of the United States, 1958–1960*, vol. 14, *Africa* (Washington, DC: United States Government Printing Office, 1992), doc. 153; Herter to Green, 28 July 1960, Dwight D. Eisenhower Library, Abilene, Kansas, Christian A. Herter Papers, 1957–61, box 13, CAH Telephone Calls, 7/1/60–8/31/60.

61 Cadieux to USSEA, 27 July 1960; USSEA to PM, 29 July 1960; Commonwealth Division to Smith, 22 July 1960. All in LAC, RG 25, vol. 5225, file 6386-D-40 pt. 1. PermisNY to External, 27 July 1960, LAC, RG 25, vol. 5209, file 6386–40 pt. 8.

62 Spooner, *Canada*, 57.

63 Ibid., 115–21.

64 UN Division to USSEA, 16 December 1960, LAC, RG 25, vol. 5221, file 6386-C-40 pt. 8.

65 PermisNY to External, 23 January 1961; Minutes of UN Advisory Committee on Congo, 20 January 1961. Both in LAC, RG 25, vol. 5221, file 6386-C-40 pt. 9.

66 Canada, House of Commons, *Debates*, 19 January 1961, 1217.

67 Cabinet Conclusions, 16 February 1961, LAC, RG 2, vol. 6176.

68 Spooner, *Canada*, 168.

69 Ibid., 170.

10

Tilting the Balance
Diefenbaker and Asia, 1957–63

JILL CAMPBELL-MILLER, MICHAEL
CARROLL, AND GREG DONAGHY

Asia was never one of John Diefenbaker's priorities, but the continent was simply too large and its postcolonial Cold War politics too turbulent for it to be ignored. For the most part, mindful of his own inexperience, Diefenbaker handled Asia gingerly, often heeding official advice and navigating pathways already well trod by his Liberal predecessors. His Progressive Conservative government continued to celebrate Canada's extensive postwar Commonwealth connections, made manifest in the Colombo Plan of 1950. It also reflected Liberal ambiguities on the question of recognizing the communist People's Republic of China, clinging safely to the status quo of non-recognition. And it steadily supported US efforts to defend the "free world" cause in Laos and Vietnam from communist aggression, while battling for regional peace. Yet, in subtle but significant ways, Diefenbaker's thumb weighed on the scales of Canadian policy, tilting the balance towards his priorities. His Commonwealth enthusiasms, his hawkish Cold War perspective, and above all his determination to promote prairie agriculture meant that Diefenbaker would leave his mark on Canada's place in Asia.

The People's Republic of China
Diefenbaker's foreign policy, especially in Asia, legitimately reflected his substantial domestic economic concerns. Though rarely appreciated fully in the literature, these are hard to overstate. Across the Canadian west, Prairie

voters raged in the 1950s as US agriculture, armed with Public Law (PL) 480 and government disposal policies that gave away American wheat as foreign aid, excluded Canadian producers from their traditional markets. Between 1954 and 1955, and 1956 and 1957, the Canadian share of the global wheat and flour market shrank from 27.4 percent to 20.6 percent, while the US share rose by over 10 percent to a whopping 41.9 percent.[1] By 1957, 700 million bushels of Saskatchewan wheat sat unsold as the province's net farm income dropped from $531 million in 1951 to $179 million in 1957, a level not seen since the Depression of the 1930s.[2]

The simultaneous collapse of the national economic boom that had sustained Liberal governments since 1945 amplified the impact of the wheat crisis. Canada plunged into recession in 1957 as commodity production declined and unemployment rates edged up to 4.7 percent. Though the economy rebounded the following year, it slid back into a second recession in late 1959, driving unemployment rates in 1960 above 8 percent, the highest level since the 1930s. Amid Liberal cries that "Tory times are hard times," Diefenbaker readily acknowledged that tackling the economy, especially the wheat surplus, was key to his government's survival.

In September 1957, commerce minister Gordon Churchill sent trade commissioner C.M. Forsyth-Smith to the communist People's Republic of China to prospect for a "market there for Canadian wheat and other commodities."[3] Early sales efforts, culminating in small contracts for forty-three thousand tons of wheat in March 1958, were quickly frustrated by Washington. Since Mao Zedong's communist forces had seized power in 1949, the US had led an unrelenting campaign to isolate Beijing. Washington refused to recognize Mao's government, denied it international legitimacy, and constrained its trade. American president Dwight Eisenhower redoubled these efforts in 1954, adopting the Foreign Assets Control (FAC) regulations to halt all exports to China by US companies and foreign companies controlled by American interests. As a result, Canadian grain and flour companies with significant US connections were forced to abandon their potential sales to China, upsetting the Diefenbaker government. The dispute festered quietly until the late spring of 1958, when Canadian members of the United Auto Workers union revealed that the Ford Motor Company had stopped its Canadian subsidiary from selling one thousand vehicles to China. A nationalist backlash propelled the question up the bilateral agenda on the eve of Eisenhower's first visit to Ottawa in July 1958.

The quarrel was easily resolved by the two North American leaders. Already worried by growing resistance to FAC regulations among the Western allies, US policy-makers were prepared to moderate their views. When Diefenbaker questioned him about the US restrictions, a sympathetic Eisenhower suggested that some kind of modus vivendi could be worked out. The next day, foreign secretaries John F. Dulles and Sidney Smith debated the merits of adopting "licencing procedures" to permit Canadian companies to trade with China. After discussion, "licencing" was replaced by "appropriate," a less precise term that did not imply that Canadian trade required US approval.[4]

Diefenbaker's determination to tap the China market was hardly surprising. Like the US, Canada did not recognize Mao's revolutionary government, and, after the Korean War began in 1950, Ottawa had backed US efforts to isolate Beijing by restricting trade and denying communist China a seat at the United Nations. But Canadian attitudes were shifting by the mid-1950s. Despite his strong anti-communism, Diefenbaker's own views reflected this change. Though American opposition would diminish only slowly, he welcomed a recommendation from Secretary of State for External Affairs Sidney Smith to move towards recognition by gradual stages.[5] He was nonetheless surprised when Eisenhower responded to a joke about China by shouting that "the day Canada recognized the Peking regime, he would kick the UN out of the US."[6]

Yet Diefenbaker approached his Asian tour in the fall of 1958 with an open mind. He was clearly frightened by Beijing's isolation during the Sino-American clash over the offshore islands of Quemoy and Matsu late in the summer of 1958. "More and more," he told UN secretary-general Dag Hammarskjöld in September, the prime minister was "coming to the very definite opinion that you can't continue to have six hundred million people in a corral."[7] But, in the Asia-Pacific region, he found no strong consensus favouring recognition. Indian prime minister Jawaharlal Nehru approved, but leaders in Malaya, Pakistan, Australia, and New Zealand did not. Worse, Canada's high commissioner to India, Chester Ronning, told him of Eisenhower's "emotional" reaction when St. Laurent raised the possibility of recognition in March 1957. "United States policy," Diefenbaker concluded after comparing presidential outbursts, "instead of becoming more flexible was becoming more rigid."[8] At a New Delhi press conference in November 1958, he firmly ruled out recognition but emphasized: "We want the contact between the Canadian and Chinese people to continue ... We are encouraging trade and other contacts with the Chinese people at the present time."[9]

Canadian policy and the trade rules worked out with Eisenhower were tested again. Mao's disastrous Great Leap Forward, a plan introduced in

1958 to encourage industrial over agricultural production, quickly led to famine and a sudden demand for Canadian grain. Despite unease in the Department of External Affairs about Washington's reaction, Agriculture Minister Alvin Hamilton sold 40 million bushels of grain worth $60 million to Beijing in late 1960.[10] Almost immediately, however, the deal was called into question when American multinational Imperial Oil indicated that its Canadian subsidiary would not fuel the ships carrying the wheat for fear of violating FAC regulations. China again topped the Canada-US agenda, just in time for Diefenbaker's inaugural meeting with the new US president, John F. Kennedy, on 20 February 1961.

Diefenbaker made his case, underlining the political and economic importance of the sales. Kennedy, pressed by Washington's formidable "China Lobby" to stand firm, was unhelpful, sending the prime minister back to Ottawa empty-handed.[11] But officials from the Department of the Treasury were more accommodating, offering a series of compromises that would exempt Canada from the FAC regulations provided Ottawa would informally enforce their provisions. Smith's successor, Howard Green, judged the proposals a "serious effort" by the US to sanitize the FAC regulations, but he worried that they still required Canada to police its commerce at the request of a foreign government. He recommended that no ground be conceded; Diefenbaker concurred, insisting that a "firm stand [be] maintained in principle and practice."[12] In the end, Washington watched powerlessly as Canadian vessels, fuelled by Imperial Oil, sailed off to China.

Even as Ottawa and Washington bickered over oil, Chinese officials offered a long-term deal for 6 million tons of wheat, the largest Western sale yet to Beijing. In contrast to earlier wheat sales, which were for cash, China wanted generous credit too. This departure in policy alarmed External Affairs, which reminded its minister of Beijing's decision to default on debts accumulated by the pre-1949 government. Undersecretary Norman Robertson was especially worried about vigorous opposition from the Kennedy administration. While the US had not protested the legality of the earlier cash purchase, he feared that it might view the extension of credit to China as a step towards recognition.[13]

Hamilton was undeterred. After threatening to resign, he won the prime minister's backing and easily persuaded his cabinet colleagues in March 1961 to authorize six months of credit. The complex and hard-fought negotiations that followed eventually forced cabinet to sweeten the pot by offering a $50 million credit for up to nine months. The final agreement, signed in April 1961, called for between 3 and 5 million tons of wheat and 600,000 to 1 million tons of barley, with a total value between $220 million and $365 million, to be purchased over a thirty-month period.[14]

For a third time, zealous American officials tried to kill the sale, invoking FAC regulations to block the export to Canada of US-made vacuators, suction devices for loading the grain onto tankers.[15] Alarmed at the prospect of another confrontation with Ottawa, Treasury Secretary Douglas Dillon told officials to find a solution.[16] The State Department eventually did, suggesting that the US unilaterally license the export of vacuators already ordered "as an accommodation to the Canadian government." This "extraordinary [US] effort," the embassy in Washington promptly insisted, should be accepted as a solution.[17] Green and Diefenbaker agreed, ending the controversy and US efforts to obstruct Canadian wheat sales to China.[18] For many Canadians, the victory prefigured a changing Canadian role in Asia, helping to legitimize China's global status and tilting Canada's Pacific axis towards Beijing. For the prime minister, it ensured his political base across the Prairies.

Bastions of the Free World

Diefenbaker and his priorities also had an important influence on how Canada responded to other regions of Asia. Policy sometimes shifted in response to the prime minister's broad interest in closer Commonwealth relations and his Cold War fears. This was certainly the case in Southeast Asia, where Canadian interests in early 1957 were poised between President Sukarno's Indonesia and Malaya. For most of the 1950s, St. Laurent's Liberals had favoured Indonesia, the fifth-largest country in the world, the largest Muslim-majority state, and a leading member of the postcolonial order.[19]

But Diefenbaker viewed revolutionary Indonesia with abiding suspicion. Sending Canadian aid to a country both outside the Commonwealth and "turning to communism," he warned cabinet in May 1958, "would be hard to justify politically."[20] In contrast, he warmly embraced the small Commonwealth country of Malaya, which was fighting a domestic communist insurgency, as an immediate priority. "If Malaya goes," he insisted, "everything goes."[21] He overturned a Liberal decision to delay appointing a high commissioner to Malaya, sending diplomat Arthur Menzies to Kuala Lumpur in December 1957. The following year, he spent four days of his Asian tour in Malaya, spurning pleas from his diplomats to visit Indonesia. Canadian aid followed him to Malaya, tripling from just $500,000 in 1958–59 to $1.8 million by 1959–60, despite the country's sizable foreign exchange surplus.[22] When aid experts cut the volume to a more manageable $1 million there was a chorus of cabinet opposition. "This should not be done," ministers insisted. "Malaya was a bastion against Communism and her share, instead of being $1 million, should be $2 million."[23] And so it soon was. "Malaya became Canada's chosen partner in Southeast Asia," concludes historian David Webster, "a role for which policy-makers had originally cast Indonesia."[24]

Economic factors also loomed large in the prime minister's Asian calculations, prompting a strengthened interest in closer relations with Japan. Canada and Japan shared a Cold War outlook centred on the US, but expanding economic linkages brought them closer together in the late 1950s than ever before. Since the two countries exchanged most-favoured-nation status in 1954 bilateral trade had soared, transforming Japan into Canada's third largest market.[25] Canadian exports, totalling just $97 million in 1954, climbed to $178 million in 1960, with wheat accounting for $82 million of the total. Low-cost Japanese imports, mostly textiles, flatware, and electronics, exploded as well, from $14 million in 1954 to $110 million in 1960, creating a complex trade relationship regulated by tough annual quota negotiations. At the same time, Japanese companies began examining investment opportunities in western Canada.[26]

During a visit to Ottawa in June 1961, Japanese prime minister Hayato Ikeda suggested establishing a joint ministerial committee to encourage more regular contacts by Canadian and Japanese cabinet ministers. Growing trade, the benefits of personal diplomacy, and free nation solidarity, Diefenbaker replied, clearly justified the effort.[27] In October, Diefenbaker himself headed to Japan for a five-day state visit. He blessed the new committee, announced relaxed immigration requirements for Japanese investors and technicians, and preached the Sunday lesson at Kwansei Gakuin University. "Out of our joint endeavours," he promised the Japan-Canada Trade Council, "will come not only lasting benefits for ourselves but the shining prospect of a world where the rising sun of international friendship will melt the icy grip which the Cold War has clamped on our generation."[28]

Nevertheless, Canada's traditional Commonwealth partners, India and Pakistan, remained the government's principal contacts in Asia. As Francine McKenzie illustrates (Chapter 1, this volume), Diefenbaker celebrated the "dynamic evolution" of the postcolonial, multi-racial Commonwealth, which was rooted in a set of shared liberal-democratic values inherited from Britain.[29] But there were important changes in emphasis. For most of the 1950s, Liberal policy-makers under St. Laurent had favoured India over Pakistan. Although mutual grievances over foreign aid, immigration, and the appropriate response to communism gnawed at relations, contacts between New

Delhi and Ottawa remained friendly. But, as Ryan Touhey makes clear, Diefenbaker would accelerate Canada's disengagement from India.[30]

There were few reasons to anticipate much change under Diefenbaker. "The change of Government in this country has not disturbed the excellent relations that India has had with Canada," reported the Indian high commission after the Progressive Conservative victory in June 1957, "and it is not likely to do so in the future."[31] Similarly, on the eve of his first Commonwealth prime ministers' meeting, Diefenbaker told his cabinet that he hoped to maintain "close relations" with Indian prime minister Nehru. But he didn't. A fiercely Western partisan in the cold war, Diefenbaker was quickly put off by Nehru's neutralism. Following their lengthy encounter during Diefenbaker's world tour visit, advisor Basil Robinson concluded that the "PM was impressed but he did not feel comfortable with Mr N." Arthur Menzies put it more bluntly: "Diefenbaker didn't like Nehru."[32]

In contrast, Diefenbaker was keen on Pakistan's president, General Ayub Khan, who seized power in a coup two weeks before Diefenbaker touched down in Karachi. Canadian high commissioner Herb Moran, a "tough-minded" veteran who admired Khan's military bearing and appreciated the stability associated with army rule, briefed the prime minister on the new president's sterling qualities.[33] Tall, handsome, and suitably mustached, Khan impressed Diefenbaker as "affable and charming," grateful for Western aid, and resolutely anti-communist in outlook.[34] These views were reinforced by voices in External Affairs, including Green's. The foreign minister compared feckless Indian diplomats with their Pakistani counterparts, who were "forthright, frank and willing to stand up and be counted."[35] Over the course of his premiership, Diefenbaker's views "never wavered."[36] Pakistan, he told Khan in 1962, is the "Asian bastion of the free world." And his government, he promised, would "do everything it can to help Pakistan ... this is a definite policy not merely an expression of goodwill."[37]

Diefenbaker tilted the balance of Canada's relations with India and Pakistan in other ways too. Most of the relationship with both countries was underpinned by Canada's contribution to the Colombo Plan, the Commonwealth aid program set up in 1950. Though Diefenbaker often embraced foreign aid in public as the very manifestation of the contemporary Commonwealth, he had his private doubts. He wondered uneasily how the money was spent amid soaring south Asian defence budgets and why there was so little direct benefit to Canada.[38] His tour of Asia reinforced these misgivings. During a visit to one signature aid project, the Warsak Dam in Pakistan, he was upset to encounter a senior Pakistani official who was utterly unaware of Canada's central role in the project.[39] In Sri Lanka, leftist prime minister S.W.R.D. Bandaranaike scandalized him by declaring that "he did not care where assistance came from as long as it arrived ... if Ceylon could not get what it wanted from the West they would turn to the USSR."[40] Getting value for Canada's contribution and tackling its wheat surplus emerged during the visit as Diefenbaker priorities.

Official government policy lagged slightly behind the prime minister. Trade Minister Gordon Churchill, a Manitoban MP and Diefenbaker's closest confidant, had floated the idea of using aid dollars to fund wheat gifts in the fall of 1957 but had encountered strong opposition. Officials in External Affairs and Finance were traditionally loath to divert money from industrial development projects to food aid. Asian aid recipients echoed these concerns. Indian finance minister T.T. Krishnamachari, for instance, insisted that gifts of Canadian industrial metals would be far more effective in relieving India's foreign exchange burden, especially given the generous terms offered by American PL 480.[41] His first initiative blocked, Churchill compromised with a loan scheme in November 1957, through which Canada provided India with $33 million worth of wheat, the first such Canadian loan to a developing country.[42]

Churchill returned to the charge in the summer of 1958, insisting that Colombo Plan funds be spent on wheat. Again, senior diplomat Doug LePan and his counterpart in Finance, A.F.W. Plumptre, warned their ministers that Colombo Plan funds should only be used for the "regular" aid program of technical assistance, development projects, and commodities that recipient countries *asked* to receive. Forcing wheat on Asian countries, they argued, jeopardized the goodwill that Canada had built up over the past decade.[43]

The debate simmered during the fall of 1958 and into the New Year. Churchill won the early rounds, when cabinet concluded in September that it was "unrealistic to provide aid [for other projects] when the basic problem facing Canada was to dispose of surplus agricultural products."[44] Buttressed with advice from Robertson, who feared that earmarking large sums of money for food aid would upset "the basic premise on which Canada's Colombo Plan operations have been conducted," Smith and Finance Minister Douglas Fleming fought back. By mid-January, cabinet was deadlocked.[45] But backed by the prime minister, Churchill easily prevailed in early February, when cabinet insisted that "efforts be made to ensure that the recipients take as much wheat and flour as possible."[46] Ministers set aside $15 million for gifts of wheat and flour in fiscal year 1958–59; in September, they added another $12.5 million, fully 25 percent of Colombo Plan fund, for wheat and flour in 1959–60.[47] Food aid had become a fundamental element of Canada's foreign aid program.

Indochina: Laos and Vietnam

Indochina was different. Diefenbaker mostly left the complicated diplomacy here to his foreign ministers, Smith and Green, and their diplomats. Like their Liberal predecessor, Lester B. Pearson, Smith and Green worked hard to reconcile Canada's Western loyalties with the task of reducing tension and advancing peace in Southeast Asia. Unfortunately for Diefenbaker's government, the circumstances had changed. The flagging US position in Southeast Asia, Washington's strategic uncertainties, and cack-handed US diplomacy generated tensions between Ottawa and Washington that were almost impossible to avoid. Peacekeeping in Asia did Diefenbaker no good at all.

Alongside communist Poland and neutral India, Canada had joined the three international control commissions supervising the 1954 Geneva peace settlements in Cambodia, Laos, and Vietnam, hopeful that it could play a useful role in promoting regional peace and defusing the Asian Cold War. In each of the former French colonies, Canadian diplomats and soldiers helped separate enemy combatants, repatriate prisoners-of-war, investigate cease-fire violations, and encourage political reintegration. This was frustrating work, and Canadian officials often found themselves stymied by their communist counterparts from Poland backed by the supposedly neutral Indians. Yet the results were not entirely discouraging. By 1955, Cambodia was quiescent, and its commission inactive. Vietnam had settled down by 1956, divided into two hostile but apparently permanent states, a communist North and a capitalist South. An elected government of national unity ruled in Laos, where the commission was adjourned *sine die* in July 1958. The whole arrangement, Canada's responsible assistant undersecretary, John Holmes, wrote in the spring of 1959, was a "surprisingly good bargain for the West."[48]

The bargain unravelled first in Laos. Starved of vital US financial support, neutralist prime minister Souvanna Phouma's unity government collapsed in July 1958 to be replaced by a succession of neutralist and right-wing regimes, each less successful than the last. By the following summer, displaced communist Pathet Lao forces, aided by North Vietnam (DRVN) and the USSR, had seized the northern Laotian province of Phongsali and the city of Sam Neua. At the same time, American money and arms flowed into Vientiane to prop up royalist prime minister Boun Oum. Over the next year, Laos slowly descended into civil war between its neutralist, communist, and royalist factions, threatening to engulf the entire region in conflict. As the Soviet Union, Britain, Poland, and India called for the International Control Commission (ICC) to reconvene and arrange a ceasefire, the US and its royalist allies fought on, rejecting a renewed ICC role. Though puzzled by the American strategy, External Affairs sensibly declined to referee a ceasefire that lacked stakeholder support, an approach that closely aligned Ottawa's policy with Washington's. "The Commission," Green briefed the prime minister at the end of 1960, "was never intended to function in conditions of civil war which now exists in Laos."[49]

Canadian diplomacy remained comfortably aligned with Washington's through the winter of 1961 as President Kennedy settled into the White House, wavering between armed intervention and negotiations.[50] When American ambassador Livingstone Merchant advised Diefenbaker in March that the United States might have to send troops to Laos, he found a sympathetic echo. "The US," Diefenbaker acknowledged, "could not go on indefinitely giving ground."[51] But Canadian policy-making became harder in the spring, when a royalist military setback drove a reluctant Kennedy to negotiate.[52] In May, representatives from fourteen countries, including the USSR, China, the US, Britain, and the three ICC members, met in Geneva with the three Laotian factions to establish a non-aligned Laos. Meanwhile, Canadian, Polish, and Indian diplomats assembled in Vientiane to reconvene the ICC and encourage a ceasefire.

Ottawa and Washington were soon at odds. Green and his diplomats, acutely aware of the ICC's limitations, took a narrow view of Canada's role in Geneva. They saw the talks as an American retreat and warned against hare-brained schemes on "the theme of 'how to defeat the Communists.'"[53] Moreover, they insisted that Canada was constrained by its quasi-judicial role. "As a member of the ICC," Green explained, "our future usefulness depends in part on conveying an impression of moderation and readiness to apply ourselves to our role." The prudent Canadian attitude enraged the chief American negotiator, Averell Harriman, and his boss, US secretary of state Dean Rusk, who asked Green outright if "the ICC now contained one Communist and two neutrals."[54]

Green was unfazed. "As far as the Canadian delegation is concerned," he instructed its head, High Commissioner Chester Ronning, "the essential points are to keep firmly before the Conference the question of equipment, freedom of access and suitable terms of reference ... and to leave others to take the lead in discussion about neutrality."[55] Indeed, Ronning was so focused on securing resources for the commission, including transportation, that other delegates dubbed him "Mr. Helicopter."[56]

The challenges for Green became no easier in the fall of 1962 as the ICC finally set about implementing the Geneva truce agreement reached over the summer. Progress was glacial. As ICC investigations of ceasefire violations required the consent of the tripartite Laotian government, neutralist and communist factions were readily able to block Western complaints. Consequently, Canadian commissioner Paul Bridle was forced to compromise with his Polish counterpart and the Indian chairman. Bridle's decision to support an investigation circumscribed by tight Laotian geographic restrictions and his handling of the resulting unanimous report critical of Washington infuriated Kennedy's team. Harriman tackled Canadian ambassador Charles Ritchie at a Washington dinner party in February 1963, sharply warning that "an over-conscientious exercise of judicial impartiality ... would be playing into Communist hands."[57]

The situation in Vietnam was just as difficult. The "good bargain" there had begun to unravel in January 1959 when North Vietnam, frustrated by South Vietnam's refusal to allow national elections, stepped up its support for the simmering communist insurgency in the South.[58] In response to Hanoi's efforts to promote rebellion, the US increased its military assistance to Saigon. By 1960, the pace of ICC work had picked up significantly. "General feeling here," warned commissioner Charles Woodsworth from Saigon, "is that period ahead may be extremely difficult."[59] He was right.

American aid to South Vietnam had a complicated history. When the ICC initially considered the issue in the mid-1950s, Canadian and American officials had quietly agreed to treat the first US military trainers as replacements for outgoing French troops, thus meeting the terms of the Geneva ceasefire, which allowed Saigon up to 888 foreign advisors. Happily, this legalistic view won India's support, and the US and South Vietnam escaped ICC condemnation for breaking the truce. Over Polish objections, Canada and India rallied behind this interpretation again in early 1960, when Saigon informed the ICC of US plans to increase its Military Assistance Advisory Group (MAAG) in South Vietnam to 685.[60]

The issue became more complex in May 1961, when Washington sought to add another one hundred advisors, with more increases clearly coming. The US, claimed State Department officials, still valued the Geneva settlement as a basis for a modus vivendi, but in view of communist subversion it no longer felt "bound to adhere literally to the terms of the Vietnam agreement."[61] The diplomats in External Affairs were doubtful. Canada, Robertson reminded his minister, "is in a different position [as an ICC member] and must insist on respect and observance of the Agreement." The unsettled crisis in Laos and the start of the Geneva Conference meant that American timing was "most unfortunate." Moreover, the Indians were unlikely to be helpful in preventing critical action by the ICC in view of the region's increasingly polarized politics. Perhaps, the undersecretary ventured, Ottawa ought to urge delay on Washington.[62]

Green demurred. During Kennedy's visit to Ottawa on 16–18 May, the president had appealed to Diefenbaker for help in "dramatizing" the crisis, insisting that Canada had "a special burden" as the Western representative on the ICC. The prime minister squirmed but stiffly acknowledged that "Canada had a duty to discharge its responsibility on the ICC more effectively."[63] Though Green thought the American proposal unwise, he feared that Canadian opposition would be "misunderstood";[64] instead, he instructed his officials to be "as co-operative as possible and to give the Americans what assistance we can."[65] Consequently, Ottawa advised Washington not to inform the ICC of the proposed increase in advisors.

Canadian policy was made more explicit in the fall, when the US indicated that it planned to further increase its military aid to South Vietnam well above the levels permitted under the accords. "We will do all we can to cooperate," Green replied again. In return, Canada expected the US to "recognize the difficulties and limitations of our position and ... [to] avoid placing us in a situation where we would be faced with [the] alternative either of voting against USA action or of taking a position clearly in violation of CFA [ceasefire agreement]."[66] Effectively, the minister explained, that meant avoiding press releases and moving troops and material "in such a way as to avoid an explicit demonstration that terms of 1954 are evaded."[67] In this way, Green hoped "to forestall an unfavourable decision." A week later, to the consternation of Canadian observers, the first flight of US military helicopters landed in Saigon amid a sea of international press photographers. North Vietnam immediately complained.

Communist subversion also had a long and complicated history. As insurgents backed by Hanoi increased their campaign of assassinations and terrorist bombings in 1959, South Vietnam and the US complained loudly to the ICC of truce violations, insisting that it investigate. But the ICC did little, paralyzed by Polish opposition and Indian doubts. Moreover, the available evidence was frequently sketchy, and South Vietnam refused to cooperate lest the ICC also examine its harsh treatment of communist activists. The ICC itself was unclear which provisions of the Geneva Accord were being transgressed and was uncertain of its own competence to act. When a documented case of subversion appeared in February 1960, Ronning in

New Delhi and Woodsworth in Saigon pressed the Indians to allow an ICC investigation. Sixteen months later, at its meeting of 24 June 1961, the ICC finally adopted an Indo-Canadian policy statement asserting the commission's right to investigate complaints of subversion.[68] In November, the high-profile murder of Colonel Hoang Thuy Nam, Saigon's liaison officer to the ICC, and eighty other subversion charges were sent to the ICC's legal committee for examination.

The ICC's investigations into DRVN subversion and US aid swung into gear in December 1961. Ottawa and Washington quickly clashed over the legal strategies used to deflect blame from the US. In the American view, delivered by Harriman to Canadian ambassador A.D.P. Heeney, DRVN subversion, having occurred first, effectively negated the truce provisions prohibiting US aid and precluded an ICC finding against either the US or SVN.[69] External Affairs and its minister sympathized – Green told the House of Commons in March that US aid was "a measure of defence against Communist action" – but Ottawa refused to endorse this unorthodox legal doctrine.[70] Nonetheless, the two allies agreed on the value of establishing a causal relationship between DRVN subversion and US aid. Consequently, when the Indian chairman announced in May 1962 that he had prepared a draft special report on subversion and aid, Canadian and US officials coordinated tactics closely. After consulting US ambassador to Saigon Frederick Nolting, Commissioner Frank Hooton reported to Ottawa that the draft was an "exceptionally useful document" whose "overall balance is clearly in favour of the South."[71] Additional consultations with Harriman and Sterling Cottrell, head of the US interdepartmental Vietnam Task Force, eased the way for Canada to endorse the Indian draft, isolating the Poles in opposition. A Canadian press release, drafted with help from Washington, made it clear that US aid was a legitimate response to sustained Northern aggression.[72]

Success in Saigon won scant praise in Washington, and even as Diefenbaker's government began its long topple, Southeast Asia only added to its misery. There was trouble in early 1963 when the Poles on the ICC in Laos demanded an investigation into Air America, a covert CIA airline carrying illicit arms to anti-communist forces in Southeast Asia. When US diplomats, who were repeatedly consulted on Western tactics, did not object, Bridle voted with the Indo-Polish majority to proceed. Two weeks later, under instructions, US embassy counsellor Rufus Smith called on dumbfounded officials in External Affairs to express the State Department's irritation "that the balance of Commission action was being shifted heavily against the US."[73] A full-court US diplomatic offensive followed. Rusk echoed the message a few days later in a meeting with Ritchie, issuing a "strong appeal to the Canadian Government to do whatever might be possible at this and succeeding stages to resist efforts by the Communist side to limit the Commission's effectiveness."[74] More demands – from Harriman and White House advisor Michael Forrestal – followed.[75] Green and his advisors hastened to make the ICC work as the Americans wanted, even as they grimly realized that "storm warnings may well be up in Southeast Asia."[76]

Diefenbaker and his Progressive Conservative government approached Asia much as did their Liberal predecessors – with one eye fixed on narrow Canadian opportunity, another focused on broader Western interests and values. It was, as Canadian diplomacy and foreign policy so often are, an effort to balance one legitimate interest against another. This meant shifts in emphasis but no dangerous, or even unseemly, upsetting of the established liberal international order. The prime minister's Commonwealth enthusiasms favoured Malaya over Indonesia as a Southeast Asian partner. A strong Cold War partisan, Diefenbaker backed Pakistan's firm military governor over India's subtle and compromising prime minister, accelerating an established trend away from cozy relations with New Delhi. Acutely attuned to Prairie hardships, he supported more food aid but not at the expense of the integrity of Canada's established aid programs. And, in keeping with the national mood of the mid-1950s, he carefully reordered relations with Communist China. He peddled vast amounts of wheat to Beijing, defying the US to do so, but declined to recognize China lest he upset relations with Washington. Balance was particularly important in Indochina. In Laos and Vietnam, he and his ministers struggled hard to reconcile their Cold War support for Washington with their country's long-term interest in a stable regional peace. In all of this, Diefenbaker's Pacific policy was far from unique. Indeed, it was quintessentially Canadian.

NOTES

The views expressed in this article are strictly those of the authors and do not represent the views of the Government of Canada. The authors would like to thank Michael D. Stevenson and Asa McKercher for their helpful comments. Jill Campbell-Miller's contribution to the chapter draws on her doctoral dissertation research, which was carried out with financial support from the Social Sciences and Humanities Research Council of Canada and the Shastri Indo-Canadian Institute.

1 Charles F. Wilson, *C.D. Howe: An Optimist Responds to a Surfeit of Grain* (Ottawa: Canadian Wheat Board mimeograph, 1980), 50. This section draws heavily on Greg Donaghy and Michael D. Stevenson, "The Limits of Alliance: Cold War Solidarity and Canadian Wheat Exports to China, 1950–1963," *Agricultural History* 83, 1

(2009): 29–50. For a helpful corrective, see Asa McKercher, "Diefenbaker's World: One Canada and the History of Canadian-American Relations, 1961–63," *Historian* 75, 1 (2013): 94–120.

2   F.H. Lacey, ed., *Historical Statistics of Canada*, 2nd ed. (Ottawa: Minister of Supply and Services, 1983), ser. M 119–28.

3   Holmes to Diefenbaker, 13 September 1957, in Michael D. Stevenson, ed., *Documents on Canadian External Relations*, vol. 25, *1957–58*, pt. 2 (Ottawa: Department of Foreign Affairs and International Trade, 2004) (hereafter *DCER*, vol. 25), 899–900.

4   Minutes of meeting, 9 July 1958, *DCER*, vol. 25, 14–20.

5   Memorandum from SSEA to the prime minister, 11 June 1958, *DCER*, vol. 25, 921–28.

6   Basil Robinson, *Diefenbaker's World: A Populist in Foreign Affairs* (Toronto: University of Toronto Press, 1989), 51; John G. Diefenbaker, *One Canada: The Memoirs of the Rt. Hon. John G. Diefenbaker*, vol. 2 (Toronto: Macmillan, 1976), 152.

7   H.B. Robinson to Norman Robertson, 1 November 1958, Library and Archives Canada (hereafter LAC), MG 31 E83, vol. 11, file 1.

8   Chester Ronning to Norman Robertson, 28 November 1958, LAC, RG 25, vol. 4721, file, 50055-B-40.

9   Cited in Robertson, memorandum for the prime minister, 2 January 1959, in Janice Cavell, Michael D. Stevenson, and Kevin Spooner, eds., *Documents on Canadian External Relations*, vol. 26, *1959* (Ottawa: Department of Foreign Affairs and International Trade, 2006) (hereafter *DCER*, vol. 26), 937.

10   Patrick Kyba, *Alvin: A Biography of the Honourable Alvin Hamilton, PC* (Regina: Canadian Plains Research Centre, 1989), 164. See also Peter Stursberg, *Diefenbaker: Leadership Gained, 1956–62* (Toronto: University of Toronto Press, 1975), 135.

11   Memorandum of conversation, 20 February 1961, *Foreign Relations of the United States, 1961–63*, vol. 13, *Western Europe and Canada*, ed. Charles S. Sampson and James E. Miller (Washington, DC: US Government Printing Office, 1994), 1140–9 (hereafter *FRUS*). On Kennedy's attitude, see Jean S. Kang, "Food for Communist China: A US Policy Dilemma, 1961–1963," *Journal of American-East-Asian Relations* 7, 1–2 (1998): 51.

12   H.B. Robinson marginal notation on Green to Diefenbaker, "United States Foreign Assets Control Regulations – Oil Bunkers for Grain Ships to China," 24 March 1961, LAC, RG 25, vol. 7607, file 11280-1-40, pt. 2.2.

13   Robertson to Green, 6 March 1961, LAC, RG 25, vol. 5280, file 9030–40.

14   Robertson to Green, 28 April 1961, LAC, RG 25, vol. 5280, file 9030–40.

15   Robertson to Green, 6 June 1961, LAC, RG 25, vol. 5280, file 9030–40.

16   Washington to Ottawa, Tel. 1816, 7 June 1961, LAC, RG 25, vol. 5280, file 9030–40.

17   Washington to Ottawa, Tel. 1820, 7 June 1961, LAC, RG 25, vol. 5280, file 9030–40.

18   Robinson, *Diefenbaker's World*, 268–71.

19   David Webster, "Eyeing the Indies: Canadian Relations with Indonesia, 1945–1999," in *Modern Canada: 1945 to the Present*, ed. Catherine Briggs, 218–29 (Toronto: Oxford University Press, 2014).

20   Cabinet Conclusions, 22 May 1958, in Michael D. Stevenson, ed., *DCER*, vol. 24, *1957–58*, pt. 1 (Ottawa: Canadian Government Publishing, 2003) (hereafter *DCER*, vol. 24), 951–53.

21 Cited in David Webster, *Fire and the Full Moon: Canada and Indonesia in a Decolonizing World* (Vancouver: UBC Press, 2009), 72.

22 Figures drawn from SSEA to Cabinet, 3 September 1958, *DCER*, vol. 24, 955–56; and Cabinet Conclusions, 21 July 1960, in Janice Cavell, ed., *Documents on Canadian External Relations*, vol. 27, *1960* (Ottawa: Foreign Affairs and International Trade Canada, 2007) (hereafter *DCER*, vol. 27), 892–95.

23 *DCER*, vol. 27, 893.

24 Ibid., 75.

25 "Briefing Note," 15 June 1961, in Janice Cavell, ed., *Documents on Canadian External Relations*, vol. 28, *1961* (Ottawa: Foreign Affairs and International Trade Canada, 2009) (hereafter *DCER*, vol. 28), 1300–01.

26 Figures drawn from Cabinet Document No. 368–60, 8 November 1960, *DCER*, vol. 27, 1126–32; and Briefing Note, 15 June 1961, *DCER*, vol. 28, 1299–1300.

27 Record of conversation between prime minister and prime minister of Japan, 26 June 1961, *DCER*, vol. 28, 1302–04.

28 "Mr. Diefenbaker Visits Japan," *External Affairs* 13, 12 (December 1961): 410. On immigration, see Patricia Roy, "Reopening the Door: Japanese Remigration and Immigration, 1945–68," in *Contradictory Impulses: Canada and Japan in the Twentieth Century*, ed. Greg Donaghy and Patricia E. Roy (Vancouver: UBC Press, 2008), 166.

29 "Diefenbaker and Nehru Agreed on Commonwealth Relationship," 20 November 1958, University of Saskatchewan Archives and Special Collections (USASC), Diefenbaker Papers, vol. 543, file 818.21.

30 Ryan Touhey, *Conflicting Visions: Canada and India in the Cold War World, 1946–76* (Vancouver, UBC Press, 2015), 138.

31 M.A. Rauf, 7 August 1958, National Archives of India (NAI), Ministry of External Affairs, AMS Section, F.28(6)/58, annual political report for the year 1957 from the high commissioner for India in Canada.

32 Both citations from Touhey, *Conflicting Visions*, 134–35.

33 Earl Drake, *A Stubble-Jumper in Striped Pants: Memoirs of a Prairie Diplomat* (Toronto: University of Toronto Press, 1999), 35, 37.

34 Cabinet Conclusions, 15 December 1958, *DCER*, vol. 24, 921.

35 Cited in Touhey, "Dealing in Black and White: The Diefenbaker Government and the Cold War in South Asia, 1957–1963," *Canadian Historical Review* 92, 3 (2011): 450.

36 Robinson, *Diefenbaker's World*, 72.

37 Henry Davis to Commonwealth Division, 28 September 1962, in Janice Cavell, *Documents on Canadian External Relations*, vol. 29, *1962–63* (Ottawa: Foreign Affairs, Trade and Development Canada, 2013) (hereafter *DCER*, vol. 29), 737–39.

38 Robinson, *Diefenbaker's World*, 71.

39 Ibid., 73.

40 Cabinet Conclusions, 15 December 1958, *DCER*, vol. 24, 921.

41 L.E. Couillard to Nik Cavell, 17 June 1947, and Nik Cavell to L.E. Couillard, 18 June 1957, LAC, RG 19, vol. 4334, file 8342/I39–1, pt. 2; Chester Ronning, Delhi to External, 5 September 1957, LAC, RG 19, vol. 4334, file 8343/I39–1, pt. 2; M.A. Rauf to J. Diefenbaker, and attachment, "Aide Memoire," 17 October 1957, LAC, RG 19, vol. 4334, file 8342/I39–1, pt. 2.

42 External to New Delhi, 26 November 1957, LAC, RG 25, vol. 6618, file 11302-B-40, pt. 2.1; A.F.W. Plumptre to the Minister, 24 July 1958, LAC, RG 25, vol. 7027, file 6000-R-40, pt. 1.1.

43 D.V. LePan, memorandum for the minister, "Allocation of Colombo Plan Funds," 4 September 1958, LAC, RG 25, vol. 7340, file 11038–1-40, pt. 11.1; A.F.W. Plumptre, memorandum to the minister of finance: wheat disposal, 16 September 1958, LAC, RG 19, vol. 4334, file 8342/I39–1, pt. 3.

44 Cabinet Conclusions, 7 September 1958, item no. 17453, Cabinet Conclusions Online, http://www.bac-lac.gc.ca/eng/discover/politics-government/cabinet-conclusions/Pages/cabinet-conclusions.aspx.

45 D.V. LePan (for Norman A. Robertson), memorandum for the minister, 30 January 1959, LAC, RG 19, vol. 4334, file 8342/I39–1, pt. 3; and Cabinet Conclusions, 10 January 1959, item no. 17879, Cabinet Conclusions Online.

46 Cabinet Conclusions, 3 February 1959, item no. 17968, Cabinet Conclusions Online.

47 Memorandum for cabinet, 26 August 1959, *DCER*, vol. 26, 313–14.

48 Holmes to Price Erichsen-Brown, 17 April 1959, *DCER*, vol. 26, 905. Holmes continued: "The détente achieved is admittedly precarious, but as the Communists hold so many advantages in the area, it is a major Western interest to hold onto even a precarious détente."

49 Memorandum from secretary of state for external affairs to prime minister, 30 December 1960, *DCER*, vol. 27, 1079–80.

50 Kennedy's approach to Laos "combined bluff with real determination in proportions he made known to *no one*." See William J. Rust, *Before the Quagmire: American Intervention in Laos, 1954–1961* (Lexington: University of Kentucky Press, 2012), 261.

51 Memorandum from head of Far Eastern Division to USSEA, 23 March 1961, *DCER*, vol. 28, 1127.

52 Arthur J. Dommen, *Laos: Keystone of Indochina* (Boulder, CO: Westview Press, 1985), 69–70; Telegram from the Department of State to the Embassy in Laos, 12 May 1962, in *FRUS, 1961–1963*, vol. 24, *Laos Crisis*, ed. Edward C. Keeper, doc. 361.

53 SSEA to Ambassador in the US, tel. G-201, 2 May 1961, *DCER*, vol. 28, 1154.

54 Secretary of State Rusk to Department of State, 14 May 1961, in *FRUS*, vol. 13, *Western Europe and Canada*, doc. 420.

55 SSEA to Chairman, Delegation to Conference on Laos, Geneva, 10 July 1961, *DCER*, vol. 28, 1176–77.

56 Brian L. Evans, *The Remarkable Chester Ronning: Proud Son of China* (Edmonton: University of Alberta Press, 2013), 191.

57 Counsellor, Embassy in the US, to Head, Far Eastern Division, 15 February 1961, *DCER*, vol. 29, 905.

58 See R.B. Smith, *An International History of the Vietnam War*, vol. 1, *Revolution versus Containment, 1955–61* (New York: St. Martin's Press, 1983), 161–69; William J. Duiker, *US Containment Policy and the Conflict in Indochina* (Stanford: Stanford University Press, 1994), 234–41.

59 Commission in Vietnam to SSEA, 29 November 1960, *DCER*, vol. 27, 1117.

60 A summary of the recent discussion on MAAG is in USSEA to SSEA, 1 March 1960, *DCER*, vol. 27, 1089–91.

61 SSEA to Delegation to Geneva Conference, 17 May 1961, *DCER*, vol. 28, 1204.
62 Ibid.
63 Cited in Asa McKercher, *Camelot and Canada: Canadian-American Relations in the Kennedy Era* (New York: Oxford University Press, 2016), 80. The authors owe Dr. McKercher a vote of gratitude for drawing this exchange to their attention.
64 O/SSEA to Far Eastern Division 27 May 1961, *DCER*, vol. 28, 1206.
65 USSEA to SSEA, 31 May 1961, and marginal note by Green, *DCER*, vol. 28, 1209–10.
66 SSEA to Ambassador in Washington, 2 December 1961, *DCER*, vol. 28, 1244–45.
67 Ibid.
68 See extract of letter from commissioner, ICSC Vietnam to USSEA, 14 July 1961, *DCER*, vol. 28, 1221–22.
69 Ambassador in Washington to SSEA, 15 December 1961, *DCER*, vol. 28, 1257–58.
70 SSEA to Ambassador in United States, 12 March 1962, *DCER*, vol. 29, 975–76.
71 Commissioner, ICSC Vietnam to SSEA, 19 May 1962, *DCER*, vol. 29, 988–89.
72 SSEA to Commissioner, ICSC Vietnam, tel. Y-239, 27 May 62, and Commission, ICSC Vietnam, Letter No. 171, 19 June 1962, both in *DCER*, vol. 29, 1000–01, 1003–07. See also, Canada, Department of External Affairs, press release no. 33, 25 June 1962, http://gac.canadiana.ca/view/ooe.sas_19620625EP/1?r=0&s=1.
73 Memorandum from AUSSEA to USSEA, 19 February 1963, *DCER*, vol. 29, 909.
74 Ambassador in the US to SSEA, tel. 677, 22 February 1963, *DCER*, vol. 29, 914.
75 Harriman to Green, 2 March 1963 and Record of Meetings with US Officials, 11 March 1963, *DCER*, vol. 29, 925–30.
76 Memorandum from USSEA to SSEA, 8 April 1963, *DCER*, vol. 29, 953–54.

11

The Winds of Change
Ellen Fairclough and the Removal of Discriminatory Immigration Barriers

ROBERT VINEBERG

Ellen Fairclough was the sixth woman elected to the Canadian House of Commons and the first woman to become a federal cabinet minister. She implemented regulatory changes eliminating discrimination in immigrant selection based upon race, colour, and nationality. Despite these achievements, there is remarkably little written about her. Her own memoirs are the sole book-length work,[1] and there have been only two scholarly papers, separated by thirty-three years. The earlier paper, by David Corbett,[2] focuses on whether the principles espoused by Prime Minister John Diefenbaker's 1960 Bill of Rights, that there be no discrimination "by reason of race, national origin, colour, religion or sex,"[3] were reflected during Fairclough's tenure as minister of citizenship and immigration. The more recent paper, by Margaret Conrad,[4] who also edited Fairclough's memoirs, summarizes her career from a feminist point of view. Corbett, writing in 1963, did not have the advantage of the perspective of time, and Conrad did not focus on Fairclough's policy stance as minister.

Fairclough and her officials in the Department of Citizenship and Immigration were not working in a vacuum. The world was rapidly decolonizing at the time, and new nations were vocally critical of developed nations espousing equality abroad but not at home. Fairclough inherited an immigration program that was out of step with the times. The unofficial but effective "white only" immigration policy was costing Canada "diplomatic legitimacy with newly independent former colonies" as Canada's advocacy of human rights in the new nations was at odds with its immigration policy.[5] Given the increasing international profile that Canada was assuming in the Caribbean, Africa, and Asia, it would be necessary, sooner or later, to bring immigration policy in line with foreign policy.[6]

The controversial story of Canada-United States relations between 1957 and 1963 has obscured the broad expansion of foreign relationships that took place during the Diefenbaker era. Prior to Diefenbaker's election, Canada had very few diplomatic missions outside of Europe and the US. However, his government established several Canadian missions in Latin America and Africa.[7] Furthermore, Diefenbaker's principled stand against apartheid in South Africa stood in marked contrast to Canada's immigration policy.[8] While immigration had not been considered in relation to foreign policy before Fairclough,[9] the elimination of Canada's discriminatory immigration barriers has to be understood within the broader context of a surprisingly active foreign policy.

Yet for all Diefenbaker's well-known commitment to human rights and the expanding activities of the Department of External Affairs in the developing world, the impetus for the new immigration policy did not come from either the prime minister or his secretaries of state for external affairs, Sidney Smith and Howard Green. The prime minister had never shown much interest in immigration, and, indeed, for the first year of his mandate he did not even appoint a full-time minister to this portfolio; instead the justice minister, E. Davie Fulton, filled the empty post on an acting basis. When Fairclough was appointed, Diefenbaker may well have expected her to be rather passive and to avoid innovation. If so, he had forgotten her long history of introducing private members' bills to eliminate discrimination in the Federal Labour Code. Fairclough and civil servants in her department, most notably George Davidson, were almost solely responsible for crafting a major policy revision that brought the neglected area of immigration in line with the Diefenbaker government's broad approach to the decolonizing world.

This chapter examines the failure of Fairclough's early attempts to develop an effective immigration program due to a recalcitrant deputy minister and an indifferent cabinet. Then it describes the alignment of younger policy officers in Citizenship and Immigration and a new, socially activist deputy minister (Davidson) with domestic and international pressures. The result, despite the indifference of the prime minister and Green's lack of sympathy with the plan, was Canada's first non-discriminatory immigration policy. The chapter also briefly describes Fairclough's life before becoming a cabinet minister. As Margaret Conrad has written, she was an "exceptional woman" for her time, who "was a pioneer in virtually everything she did."[10]

Early Years

Ellen Louks Cook was born on 28 January 1905 in Hamilton, Ontario. In her teens, during the post-First World War depression of the early 1920s, she found work when her father could not, thus becoming the family's sole breadwinner. After secondary school, she became a bookkeeper and, later, one of Canada's first female certified accountants. The Cooks were practising Methodists. The Methodist Church supported the social gospel movement, and Ellen embraced the belief that people's worldly condition ought to be improved. She and Gordon Fairclough eloped in 1931 to save her family the cost of a wedding it could not afford. Their only child, Howard, was born ten months later.[11]

Ellen Fairclough gravitated early to Conservative politics and worked behind the scenes for many years. She was persuaded to run for civic politics and was elected to Hamilton City Council in 1946 and, in 1949, became deputy mayor. She first ran for Parliament in Hamilton West in 1949, losing to a popular Liberal incumbent, but the following year, when the latter was appointed to the Bench, Fairclough won the by-election.

Member of Parliament

Fairclough was the sixth woman to be elected to the Canadian Parliament, but in 1950 she was the sole sitting woman MP. In 1953 she was joined by Margaret Aitken, Conservative member for the riding of York-Humber. Fairclough sat on the Opposition benches for seven years, first under George Drew and then under John Diefenbaker. Drew had great confidence in Fairclough and made her Opposition labour critic.[12] From this position, in June 1951, she began her "campaign for a fair employment practices bill that would prohibit discrimination in hiring on the basis of race, colour, sex, nationality or place of origin."[13] In doing so, she demonstrated her commitment to women's rights and decolonization well before they were popular ideas in Canada. Her private member's bill went nowhere, nor did her subsequent attempts in 1953, 1954, and 1955. However, in 1956 the governing Liberals introduced her proposals as a government bill, which was passed. Her determination had finally resulted in success.[14] Greater success was to come in the election of 1957.

Minister

In the campaign of 1957, Diefenbaker promised to put a woman in cabinet if he was elected. Following the election, he had two female MPs from which to choose – Fairclough and Aitken – and he chose the more experienced

Fairclough. As she had chaired the caucus committee on labour since 1951, Fairclough expected to be offered labour or another senior portfolio. However, the prime minister-elect offered her the position of secretary of state, one of the least important portfolios. The following year, sensing the time was propitious, Diefenbaker called an election and was rewarded with the largest majority in Canadian history up to that time. He then gave Fairclough a promotion to a more challenging portfolio, citizenship and immigration.[15] The *Globe and Mail* wrote: "Fairclough is an excellent choice for her post. Her service in Parliament has marked her as one of the ablest members of her party."[16]

According to Conrad, Fairclough came to office without an agenda but was able to quickly sense what needed to be done.[17] The immigration portfolio was in need of major policy and administrative modernization. The Immigration Act, dating from 1952,[18] still discriminated on the basis of "nationality, citizenship, ethnic group, occupation, class or geographical area of origin" as well as on the basis of "peculiar customs, habits, modes of life or methods of holding property" and "unsuitability having regard to the climatic, economic, social, industrial, educational, labour, health or other conditions or requirements existing" in Canada.[19] The selection criteria in the 1953 Immigration Regulations,[20] last amended in 1956, gave preference to British subjects from the "old Commonwealth" and persons from France and the United States, followed by the rest of Western Europe.[21] The repeal of the Chinese Immigration Act in 1947 had allowed Chinese residents to bring their wives and children to Canada, but all other immigration from that country was still effectively closed down.[22] Similarly, while absolute bars to non-family immigration from the Indian sub-continent were lifted in 1951, the quotas imposed were incredibly low: 150 per year from India, 100 from Pakistan, and 50 from Ceylon.[23] Fairclough recognized that in "the postwar period momentum was developing to change the criteria for immigration to Canada away from country of origin and family relationships and toward individual attributes such as education, skills, and work experience."[24] She had already shown her personal attitude towards discrimination in her efforts to eliminate it from hiring practices under the Labour Code.

Fairclough recalled that Diefenbaker did not take much interest in immigration and that, "generally speaking, the Prime Minister left me to run the department."[25] However, one exception came when Fairclough attempted to solve a problem inherited from the Liberal administration. A backlog of some sixty thousand applications had developed at the Rome visa office due to provisions allowing residents of Canada from Europe to sponsor siblings and married children. Most of the backlog consisted of relatively unskilled workers from southern Italy. Early in 1959, Fairclough proposed to cabinet revisions to section 20 of the Immigration Regulations "by deleting brothers and sisters and married sons and daughters from the admissible classes of close relatives. This would apply to immigrants from all countries but was intended to reduce the movement of Italian Immigrants." In the cabinet discussion, some ministers felt that a program regarded as "too restrictive ... would be politically dangerous." However, the consensus was that "it was good housekeeping for Canada, under the present economic conditions," and Cabinet ordered that Regulation 20 (c) be amended accordingly.[26] Given the foreign policy implications of the issue, European ambassadors were advised prior to the implementation of Order-in-Council PC 1959–0310, passed on 19 March 1959.[27]

Fairclough recalled that the "controversial measure had been well thrashed out in Cabinet," but it took effect simultaneously with a provincial election in Ontario and the decision became a major political issue for the governing Conservatives in that province. The "provincial minister in charge of immigration was raising particular hell" and characterized the decision as discrimination against Italians.[28] Diefenbaker was deluged with letters.[29] Even the *Saskatoon Star-Phoenix*, in the PM's own province, opposed the changes, writing that "the federal government remains restriction-minded when it comes to admitting New Canadians to this country."[30]

On 14 April, Cabinet revisited the issue and Fairclough observed that she "had been surprised at the strength of the opposition propaganda machine against the changes." Ministers considered the issue "to be one of the most important politically that the government had had to face. The change in regulations appeared to be have been a mistake, but it should be made to appear that the discriminatory features of the regulations went back" to the Liberal era. Cabinet directed Fairclough to announce that cabinet agreed to rescind the Order-in-Council and that the government intended to "completely re-examine the Immigration Act and Regulations with a view to bringing in a revised Act in the next session."[31] Fairclough recollected, "Of course, yours truly got the blame and there was plenty of it."[32]

In the House of Commons the Liberal immigration critic and former minister of citizenship and immigration, Jack Pickersgill, pummelled Fairclough and the government, calling the amendment "an unnecessary and cruel act" and stating that it was evidence of the government's "bad management and bad faith."[33] Fairclough tried gamely to parry Pickersgill's arguments before, as cabinet had decided, pledging to "produce a new deal in immigration matters: positive approaches, democratic programming, raising of standards, flexible practices for selective immigration to replace rigid restrictions in the present act and regulations." Fairclough stated that she had "no aversion to changing my mind if circumstances make such action advisable" and announced that the amendment would be rescinded "until such time as the discriminatory section 20 can be replaced."[34] Cabinet passed Order-in-Council PC 1959–0507 on 23 April 1959 reinstating the old regulations.[35]

The *Globe and Mail* was very supportive of Fairclough's efforts. In a 24 April editorial, it wrote:

> Immigration Minister Fairclough displayed commendable courage in reversing the decision which restricted the sponsorship of certain immigrants' relatives ... The initial decision to withdraw priority for all but close relatives was, in theory, a good one; Mrs. Fairclough should at least have been given the opportunity to prove that it was sound in practice.[36]

After condemning the government for half-hearted efforts to sell its policy, the *Globe* welcomed Fairclough's pledge to review the legislation, saying, "This country's immigration policy – if it can be called a policy – is badly in need of a revision," and calling for a "review before a Parliamentary Committee, where the public can observe what is going on."[37]

J.B. (Joe) Bissett, who was coordinator between Fairclough's office and the department from 1958 to 1960, recalls that Fairclough "could make courageous decisions even when they were politically dangerous" but "understood that politics often over ruled good policy."[38] As to her hope that she could move quickly to bring forward new immigration legislation, consistent with the principle of equality, Fairclough was frustrated by a total lack of interest among her cabinet colleagues. She recalled:

> It is true that Citizenship and Immigration was a terrible department to administer. One of the reasons that it came into such disrepute was the lack of a good, firm policy. I tried for months after assessing the portfolio to get the cabinet to consider my suggestions for reform, but I was brushed off – so many other things were considered more important. I also found my Deputy Minister [Colonel Laval Fortier] difficult to work with. Although we got along on a personal basis, he was a rigid man, used to military discipline, who would stubbornly resist my efforts to introduce change in departmental policy.[39]

Bissett confirmed that Fairclough did not have a close relationship with Fortier. Fortier's "formal ... and old school" approach probably extended to his relations with his deputy minister colleagues and was a major reason Fairclough had difficulty exerting influence on her fellow cabinet ministers, all of whom were being briefed on immigration issues by their own deputies.[40]

Following the fiasco of the rescinded regulations, Fairclough decided she needed a new deputy minister. She was impressed by George Davidson, who had been deputy for the welfare side of the Department of Health and Welfare since 1944. He had a PhD in classics from Harvard University but had made his career in public welfare, first in British Columbia and then as executive director of the Canadian Welfare Council, prior to joining the federal civil service. Davidson piloted through the bureaucracy many of the elements of today's social security net, including family allowances, old age security, old age assistance, unemployment insurance, and hospital insurance. Sensing Davidson was ready for a change, and would bring his social-activist attitude to a new job, Fairclough "told Diefenbaker that [she] wanted a new deputy minister and suggested George Davidson."[41] It took until the following year, 1960, to get Davidson on board.[42]

Rumours about Fortier's departure began circulating in early 1960. Bissett, who kept a daily journal throughout 1960, thought that "whoever it may be, his task will be difficult for it is clear the Minister is a difficult person to work for. Moreover the whole Department is woefully weak in certain key positions." In Bissett's view, a new act and a workable policy were needed but he didn't expect that it would happen in 1960: "too much legislation to deal with and immig[ration] such a controversial subject."[43] Bissett felt the "situation had become intolerable not only vis a vis the DM and Fairclough but also because Fortier had lost confidence in his senior officials and they with him." As for Davidson, Bissett heard that he was "a very good man and capable of doing a good administrative job. I have hopes for a completely new approach to our problems now."[44] Concluding his remarks for the day, Bissett hoped for better times:

> I feel the Minister with [Fortier] her "problem child" (as she calls him) out of the way will really begin to shine. Let us hope Davidson can meet her approval. If so the Dept can look upon the future with great hope and Canadian immigration may become a respected word, which now it is definitely not.[45]

Meanwhile, in autumn 1959, as promised in the House, Fairclough proceeded with a reform agenda and prepared a memorandum to cabinet (MC)

on the subject. Knowing that Diefenbaker was skittish about immigration reforms after the debacle of the rescinded regulations, Fairclough told cabinet
on 6 January 1960 that she had prepared recommendations for amendments
to the Immigration Act and that she had considered two approaches. The
first was to amend the act, but that "would unleash a storm of controversy
both from those wishing for more and those wanting less immigration ...
In this event, the Government would then face public criticism ... without
receiving kudos for having taken action."[46] The second option, which Fairclough proposed, was to appoint a Royal Commission to examine the issue.

Fairclough stated she supported this option because a Royal Commission "would need several years to complete its assignment. The government
would by this means be able to fulfil its commitment to take action on the
Immigration Act, and ought to be in a position to introduce a comprehensive revision at the Session following the next general election." She went on
to observe that a Royal Commission

> would help to make the public aware of the difficulties inherent in the ad-
> ministration of an immigration policy, would enable the public to make
> its opinions known, and should, in particular, obtain the views of the
> public concerning the numbers of immigrants to be admitted annually and
> as to the classes and nationalities of persons that Canada should seek as
> immigrants.[47]

Fairclough probably made this recommendation because she felt she had no
support in cabinet for immediate change and hoped that a Royal Commission could generate momentum.

Cabinet debated the options but could not come to agreement, so a committee was struck to study the issue. It reported to cabinet on 20 January, and
while a majority of the committee favoured a Royal Commission, the minister of justice, Davie Fulton, had strong reservations. Fulton's view was that

> a Royal Commission could do little to assist in the determination of the
> appropriate volume of immigration, because this was really a political or
> executive decision. The chief difficulties of the Department of Citizenship
> and Immigration did not arise out of the general policy on the amount of
> immigration but from procedural questions.[48]

Fulton had acted as minister of Citizenship and Immigration for eleven
months before Fairclough's appointment, but, as he was substantively min-

ister of justice, he had paid little attention to immigration.[49] Likely, his intervention at cabinet was mainly political, given the relatively large Asian population in British Columbia, his home province. Cabinet decided not to establish a Royal Commission but ordered a review of immigration policy leading to a general policy statement from the minister and, possibly, legislative and regulatory changes.[50]

Fairclough wanted to return to cabinet quickly with proposals that avoided major policy changes but that would improve the administration of the immigration program, and she asked Fortier to prepare an MC. Fortier assigned the task of drafting it to the department's recently established Economic and Social Research Branch.[51] The author, Jack Manion, was a young policy officer, one of the new generation of university graduates who, like Bissett, were bringing new attitudes to the department.[52] Bissett felt that Manion was "the key player and he was the driver for policy reform."[53] Bissett commented on the strange way in which the document was developed:

> The origin of the memo is interesting in itself. It was prepared chiefly by Manion and approved by the Director but shot down by DM and C.E.S. Smith [Director of Immigration] who submitted their own version to the Min[ister]. She objected to this on ground[s] their memo contained nothing new or positive. I told her Manion had prepared something quite different and she asked me to get it, which I did. She liked it & took it to Hamilton on [the] weekend and rewrote it. It was then sent to PM and today sent to Privy Council office for presentation for Cabinet consideration.[54]

Fairclough wanted changes and ignored Fortier. Bissett noted that Fortier was "later ... given [the] opportunity of commenting upon [the memo], which he did very critically."[55] Notwithstanding Fortier's objections, Fairclough signed the MC on 15 February. This genesis of an MC, through excluding the deputy minister, was highly unusual.

The MC started from the premise that the "policy of national development, to which this Government is dedicated, necessarily involves population planning" and that, "for Canada, immigration is the most acceptable and most immediately effective means of population planning." It listed the economic arguments for immigration and examined recent population and migration trends, concluding that Canada had to abandon the "tap on and off" approach to immigration in favour of a planned and predictable system. It recommended "an average flow equal to one per cent of the Canadian population with annual movements of from .75 per cent to 1.25 per cent."[56]

Echoing Liberal prime minister Mackenzie King's 1947 statement to Parliament on immigration,[57] the recommendations concluded that the system had to select "suitable, desirable and adaptable immigrants who will be of economic benefit to Canada."[58] There was no mention of eliminating the discriminatory provisions.

As is normal, the prime minister received advice on the MC from his deputy, the secretary to cabinet, R.B. Bryce. On 4 April, Bryce wrote to Diefenbaker to express strong criticism of Fairclough's proposals. He opposed the "numerical objective" and recommended a "more flexible, less precise, more moderate and more selective" policy. Bryce's opposition to large-scale immigration was clear from his later comment: "We are going to have trouble enough with our foreign policy in the 1960's without complicating it further by large numbers of new Canadians from Europe who have European rather than Canadian attitudes on questions of the greatest importance." He opined that Canada should "plan, quietly, gradually to taper off our efforts to attract immigrants from Europe and devote more effort to the re-employment of Canadians." However, he did suggest that the lower immigration targets "should include a fairly substantial sprinkling of coloured people deliberately included to make evident that we do not object to them in principle."[59] Bryce recognized the need for a colour-blind immigration policy but was not ready to endorse it wholeheartedly. He also identified foreign policy implications, not of immigration policy itself, but from the views of immigrants who might disagree with Canada's existing foreign policies. There does not appear to have been a written response from the prime minister.

Bryce's comments were shared with Fairclough, and she, according to Bissett, was "definitely not impressed with Bryce's ideas and I feel she will convince her colleagues that Bryce is wrong not only from a practical point of view but also economically."[60] Fairclough believed that higher immigration levels would be beneficial to Canada and rejected Bryce's overall argument about numbers. She also did not want a mere token policy for non-white people. She wanted to eliminate discrimination entirely, but she appreciated that the proposal on levels was more than enough for her Cabinet colleagues to digest in one sitting.

Bissett's assessment of his minister's ability to convince her colleagues was overly optimistic. Without the active support of Fortier lobbying his deputy ministerial colleagues, and given Bryce's opposition, the MC stood little chance of approval. When cabinet considered the memo on 12 April, Fairclough reminded her colleagues that the current policy, "with minor

modifications, was substantially the one set out by the previous administration under the Mackenzie King regime" and that, because the Conservative government had promised to amend the Immigration Act and was
dedicated to "national development," it was time to "activate immigration."
She stated that her department now had the capacity to process 200,000
immigrants annually and argued that, for "economic, political and moral
reasons, Canada should accept a substantial flow of immigrants." Cabinet
discussion was animated but no consensus could be reached. Some did not
like the "percentage basis" system but others felt that, "if this principle was
not accepted, there would be nothing new in the immigration policy of the
government."[61] Ultimately, cabinet left Fairclough with two short paragraphs
of guidance stating that Canada's national immigration policy should allow
a substantial flow of immigrants and that the department should be given
the authority to adopt procedures designed to select "suitable, desirable and
adaptable immigrants who would be selected on the basis of being able to
establish themselves in Canadian social, cultural, political and economic
life without undue hardship to themselves or hardship and dislocation" to
Canadians.[62]

Despite hopes that the new policy would be different from the Liberals'
post-Second World War policy, it still looked remarkably similar. It would
be late the following year before Fairclough succeeded in taking a major step
not only to differentiate her immigration policy from that of the Liberals but
also to clear the way for a modern immigration policy consistent with other
foreign policy initiatives supportive of racial equality.

Meanwhile, Fairclough continued to await her new deputy. On 18 March,
Bissett noted: "Still no word as to when DM will leave us. I do know the
Minister is pressing the matter with Bryce."[63] On 9 May, Davidson finally
became deputy minister of citizenship and immigration. From the beginning, Davidson demonstrated that he took a very different approach from
his predecessor. Bissett recorded that Davidson "called a meeting of the
various Directors and made it quite clear he would not be bogged down by
detail. The Directors will become Directors again and responsibility will be
discharged properly." Bissett concluded his journal entry with a wish that
"Fairclough [would] get along well with him: for surely this is the key to successful operation."[64]

Fairclough recalled: "It was a happy day for me when George joined
the department. George was an exceptional person who stood firm on
principle – I could never budge him on a matter of principle – but was flexible in administrative matters."[65] Davidson was just the deputy Fairclough

needed to advance her agenda. He understood government beyond his own department and he focused on the big picture. Furthermore, he was respected by his deputy ministerial colleagues and could enlist their support for immigration policy changes. In October 1960, Fairclough told Bissett, "now that Dr. Davidson was D.M. she felt she could really make something of the Dept."[66] In her memoirs, she wrote:

> With George Davidson's help our government was able in 1962 to bring in new immigration regulations, which at least marked the beginning of reform. Essentially we were attempting to make education, training, and skills the primary criteria for immigration, rather than family relationships and country of origin.[67]

The time was right for pursuing immigration reforms. With approval of the Bill of Rights, basic rights were enshrined in law, at least within the federal jurisdiction. Canada had largely caught up with the noble objectives of the Universal Declaration of Human Rights, Article 2 of which states: "Everyone is entitled to all the rights and freedoms set forth in this Declaration, without distinction of any kind, such as race, colour, sex, language, religion, political or other opinion, national or social origin, property, birth or other status."[68] For twelve years following adoption of the Declaration, Canadian law had been lagging behind global ideals, and even with the Bill of Rights, Canada's immigration legislation remained blatantly discriminatory.

World events, in which Canada played a major part, were also influential in helping Fairclough to move forward with immigration reforms. The World Council of Churches held a migration conference in Leysin, Switzerland, in June 1961 that advocated "the need to avoid any exclusion of migrants on the basis of race, nationality or religion."[69] Within the Commonwealth, the twin issues of apartheid in South Africa and the push for equality from the countries of the "New Commonwealth" were front and centre.[70] On 16 January 1961, Howard Green, the secretary of state for external affairs, advised the prime minister as follows:

> The argument that migration should not be limited by racial discrimination has been prominent and is currently illustrated by criticisms in the West Indies of Canadian immigration policy. Of the old Commonwealth members the United Kingdom alone has opened its doors to Commonwealth citizens regardless of race. The results of this policy are conspicuous, with non-white areas in all the large cities and with the market for

unskilled labour flooded, and largely supplied, by non-white persons. It is questionable whether it would be in the interests of Australia, New Zealand or Canada to follow the United Kingdom example.[71]

While Green did not foresee the inevitability of a non-discriminatory immigration policy, Canadian opinion was changing. On 26 September 1960, Leonard Hatfield, general secretary of the Council for Social Services of the Anglican Church of Canada, wrote Diefenbaker warning against "the danger of Canadian hypocrisy when discrimination abroad is deplored and oftentimes overlooked at home."[72] Similarly, early in 1961, historian Kenneth McNaught wrote in *Saturday Night*, then Canada's major political and news magazine: "If in addition [to condemning apartheid], Canada were to announce a revision of her own immigration policy to eliminate race as a criterion of admission, she would add still more lustre to her role."[73] Donald Gordon, *Saturday Night's* London correspondent, noted that, without a more open immigration policy, Canada's "lustre" would begin to tarnish. He quoted a West Indian working in Ghana:

> Canada is becoming known throughout the colored world. We hear your professions of friendship and see your political leaders taking firm stands on racial issues. But we also see your huge land with all its space and resources refusing entry to non-whites. You'll get little lasting goodwill that way. We're all pretty sick of words and empty promises.[74]

Meanwhile, the UK was increasingly concerned that it was bearing a disproportionate share of immigration from the Commonwealth Caribbean and pressured Canada to accept more West Indian immigrants. In the 13 May 1961 issue of *Saturday Night*, Gordon explained that, after averaging about thirty thousand per year in the 1950s, some sixty thousand West Indians moved to the UK in 1960 and the British were looking for some burden-sharing by other Commonwealth counties, in particular Canada, given its close ties with the Caribbean. Gordon was advised, unofficially, by the Commonwealth Office that British prime minister Harold Macmillan had raised the issue with Diefenbaker during his visit to Ottawa in April 1961. Macmillan had reportedly expressed the issue in broad terms, arguing that relations with the emerging Afro-Asian nations would be dependent on keeping channels open between the old, white Commonwealth and its new members. Gordon warned *Saturday Night's* readers that these efforts would fail "if, even by appearance alone, the white members erect racially-based barriers. 'It's up to your Mr. Diefenbaker,' summed up one carefully anonymous [Commonwealth Office] official."[75] Perhaps Britain went public because Diefenbaker had not seemed to comprehend Macmillan's hints during his visit to Ottawa. (The minutes of the meeting of the two prime ministers do not even refer to immigration.[76])

Despite Diefenbaker's indifference, the stars were beginning to align as Fairclough and the new leadership in her department proceeded with proposals that would change the face of Canadian immigration policy, steadily encouraged by the media, the churches, and diplomatic pressure. On 18 October 1961, Fairclough presented to cabinet new draft regulations designed to eliminate "racial or colour discrimination." Referring to Regulation 20, she said:

> This was the heart of Canada's immigration law and, in its present form, provided the main source of criticism that Canadian immigration law had within it concealed elements of discrimination. The present 20(a) and (b) listed the countries from which immigrants might come to Canada freely on the basis of their training, skills etc., without reference to their having close relatives in Canada and all the countries so selected had a predominantly white population except South Africa. The new draft attempted to eliminate this discriminatory feature by omitting all reference to questions of nationality, geography or regions of the world. The new regulation put primary stress on selection based on skills and qualifications.[77]

The draft regulations also proposed amendments to Regulation 31(d), eliminating the advantage that those from Europe, the Western hemisphere, Israel, Lebanon, and Egypt had of being able to sponsor their extended families (including fiancés or fiancées, unmarried brothers and sisters, and minor orphan nephews and nieces). Cabinet deferred its decision until 18 January 1962 and, ultimately, considered it preferable to "move the less favoured groups forward by progressive steps to a position of complete equality with more favoured groups, rather than achieve equality by withdrawing privileges from more favoured groups." Cabinet recognized that this "would perpetuate the discrimination against people from the less preferred countries" but felt that complaints on this score "would be less serious than those which would arise from restricting Europeans."[78] Cabinet seemed more interested in domestic political fallout than in the importance of implementing a totally non-discriminatory immigration policy.

Cabinet approved the amended *almost* non-discriminatory package, which was implemented by Order-in-Council PC 1962–0086 of 18 January 1962.[79] The regulations became effective on 1 February 1962, and Canada took a major step towards a totally non-discriminatory immigration system. The cabinet record shows no indication that the ministers appreciated the importance of their decision. Immigration historian Freda Hawkins has observed that cabinet, as a whole, was not generally engaged with immigration policy and that, when it did engage, it was in a negative way. She concluded that the changes had their origin in the department itself,[80] a conclusion that is borne out by the evidence in this chapter. Bissett recalls that Davidson and Fairclough "shared essentially the same liberal thinking about the need to bring immigration policy in line with a changing world but it was Ellen who was the primary force and Davidson was in support."[81] Without Fairclough's determination, the changes would not have happened.

Fairclough tabled the new regulations in the House of Commons on 19 January and underlined their significance: "any suitably qualified person from any part of the world can be considered for immigration to Canada entirely on his own merits without regard to his race, colour, national origin or the country from which he comes."[82] The announcement was big news. A banner front-page headline in the *Globe and Mail* read: "Canada Unlocks Its Doors to All Who Possess Skills – Bias Ends – On Paper at Least."[83] The *Winnipeg Free Press* declared: "White Canada Policy Killed: New Immigrant Selection Rules Hinge on Skills, Not Color."[84] The *Globe* followed with an editorial on 22 January, pointing out that the change "should go a long way to clear Canada of the reproach of practicing racial discrimination in its immigration policy." It went on to observe: "If Canada is to survive, to grow and be prosperous, its first requirement is more people, and they can come in time only through immigration."[85] In the following months the *Globe* published a half dozen more editorials on immigration, indicating the importance its editors attached to the subject.[86] While some commentators wondered whether the new regulations would really make a difference, the numbers show that they did. Between 1961 and 1965, annual immigration from India jumped from 568 to 2,241; from the West Indies from 1,126 to 2,926; from Hong Kong from 710 to 4,155; and from non-Commonwealth Asia from 270 to 2,157.[87]

Diefenbaker called an election for 18 June 1962, and the Conservatives lost their majority. He laid a share of the blame on Fairclough. Citizenship and Immigration, assisted by the Department of Justice, had been trying to break up widespread fraudulent Chinese immigration from Hong Kong. Justice sought

prosecutions but Citizenship and Immigration preferred admissions of mis-
doing, after which the illegal immigrants could obtain permanent residence.
This pursuit of prosecutions resulted in the loss of some ridings with a high
Chinese Canadian population. Though it was hardly her fault, Fairclough
was blamed and demoted to a lesser portfolio. She was sworn in as postmaster general on 9 August 1962. Three days later, Diefenbaker attempted
to justify his action in a secret memo, writing:

> One of the most serious problems that was faced by the Government dur-
> ing the election was the question of immigration. Mrs. Fairclough had done
> well in her position but ethnic peoples do not feel that a woman should
> have a responsible position and never fully accepted her. I so advised her,
> and pointed out that we had lost two constituencies and possibly three
> because of the action taken against the Chinese ... After some discussion,
> all in good spirits, she agreed to the transfer.[88]

While Fairclough was miffed by Diefenbaker's excuses for her demotion, in
retrospect she realized that it was a blessing to have been relieved from the
continued stress of dealing with a very difficult portfolio – stress to which
the prime minister no doubt contributed by expressing concern about immigration only when problems threatened his government's popularity.[89]

As described in other chapters in this volume, the government had been
wavering over the issue of arming Canadian weapons systems with nuclear
warheads. Fairclough believed that Green, who opposed acquisition of the
warheads, was being "overly idealistic," but she also believed that Douglas
Harkness, who supported it, "was having difficulty developing an objective
perspective on defence policy."[90] Despite Diefenbaker's vacillation, Fairclough remained loyal to her prime minister. The government stumbled to
defeat in the House on 5 February 1963 and in the subsequent election Fairclough lost her seat.

Conclusion

Fairclough was justifiably proud of her accomplishments as immigration
minister. In a March 1962 speech she stated:

> The newly-emerging nations of the world will be watching with interest to
> see how sincere we are in applying our new immigration policy and the re-
> ception the Canadian people give to the newcomers. We have here a golden
> opportunity – perhaps there may not be too many more – to demonstrate

to these people that Canadians too realize that the winds of change are blowing.[91]

Canadians did recognize the winds of change. The subsequent Liberal government issued a White Paper on immigration in 1966,[92] leading to the 1967 regulations that implemented the famous "Points System," which applied objective criteria to the selection factors in Fairclough's 1962 regulations. However, Fairclough's proposal of 1 percent immigration was not adopted by any government or party until the Liberal *Red Book* policy platform for the 1993 election.

Annual immigration levels continue to be below 1 percent of the Canadian population. Nevertheless, the core of Canada's current immigration policy remains based upon Fairclough's ground-breaking reforms. Similar reforms were implemented in the United States in 1965 and in Australia in 1973. Unlike her predecessors – and unlike Diefenbaker and her cabinet colleagues – Fairclough sensed that the time for immigration reform had come. As David Corbett wrote in 1963, she thereby placed immigration policy squarely "in its proper context as part of foreign policy."[93]

NOTES

1 Ellen Louks Fairclough, *Saturday's Child: Memoirs of Canada's First Female Cabinet Minister*, ed. Margaret Conrad (Toronto: University of Toronto Press, 1995).
2 David Corbett, "Canada's Immigration Policy, 1957–1962," *International Journal* 18, 2 (1963): 166–80.
3 *Canadian Bill of Rights*, SC 1960, c. 44, sec. 1.
4 Margaret Conrad, "'Not a Feminist, But ...': The Political Career of Ellen Louks Fairclough, Canada's First Female Federal Cabinet Minister," *Journal of Canadian Studies* 31, 2 (1996): 5–28.
5 Ninette Kelley and Michael Trebicock, *The Making of the Mosaic: A History of Canadian Immigration Policy*, 2nd ed. (Toronto: University of Toronto Press, 2010), 337.
6 Ibid., 351.
7 Asa McKercher, "Southern Exposure: Diefenbaker, Latin America, and the Organization of American States," *Canadian Historical Review* 93, 1 (2012): 57–80. See also McKercher Chapter 8 (this volume).
8 Laura Madokoro, "'Slotting' Chinese Families and Refugees, 1947–1967," *Canadian Historical Review* 93, 1 (2012): 32, 33.
9 Ibid., 46.
10 Conrad, introduction to Fairclough, *Saturday's Child*, xii, xiii.
11 Conrad, "Not a Feminist," 3, 4.
12 Fairclough, *Saturday's Child*, 71.
13 Ibid., 86.

14 Ibid., 87.

15 Ibid., 109.

16 *Globe and Mail*, 15 May 1958.

17 Conrad, "Not a Feminist," 12.

18 Immigration Act, Chapter 325, Revised Statutes of Canada, 1952.

19 Immigration Act, 1952, s. 61(g).

20 Immigration Regulations, Order in Council PC 1953–0895, 26 May 1953.

21 Immigration Regulations, Order in Council PC 1956–0785, 24 May 1956, s.20.

22 Cabinet Conclusions, Library and Archives Canada (hereafter LAC), RG 2, vol. 2639, 13 February 1947, 2, available online at http://www.bac-lac.gc.ca/eng/discover/politics-government/cabinet-conclusions/Pages/cabinet-conclusions.aspx. All further references to Cabinet Conclusions are from this site.

23 Cabinet Conclusions, LAC, RG 2, Vol. 2647, 24 January 1951, p. 6.

24 Fairclough, *Saturday's Child*, 110.

25 Ibid., 111.

26 Cabinet Conclusions, LAC, RG 2, Vol. 2744, 12 February 1959, 7, 8.

27 Cabinet Conclusions, LAC, RG 2, Vol. 2744, 14 April 1959, 5.

28 Fairclough, *Saturday's Child*, 115.

29 Diefenbaker Fonds, University of Saskatchewan Library, Privy Council Office Files, MG01/VI, file 571 – Immigration and Citizenship – Immigration Policy and Administration, 1957–59 (reel M7964), 315440, 315442, 315453.

30 *Saskatoon Star-Phoenix*, 4 April 1959, in Diefenbaker Fonds, University of Saskatchewan Library, Privy Council Office Files, MG01/VI, file 571, Immigration and Citizenship, Immigration Policy and Administration, 1957–59 (reel M7964), 315449.

31 Cabinet Conclusions, LAC, RG 2, Vol. 2744, 14 April 1959, 5, 6.

32 Fairclough, *Saturday's Child*, 115.

33 Canada, House of Commons, *Debates*, 15 April 1959, 2711.

34 Ibid., 22 April 1959, 2937, 2938.

35 Cabinet Conclusions, LAC, RG 2, Vol. 2744, 23 April 1959, 6.

36 "Overhaul the Whole Policy," *Globe and Mail*, 24 April 1959.

37 Ibid.

38 J.B. Bissett, e-mail to author, 31 October 2014. Bissett went on to head the Immigration Foreign Service, become assistant deputy minister, immigration, and later, Canadian high commissioner to Trinidad and Tobago and ambassador to Yugoslavia with cross appointments to Albania and Bulgaria.

39 Fairclough, *Saturday's Child*, 118.

40 Bissett, e-mail to author, 31 October 2014.

41 Fairclough, *Saturday's Child*, 119.

42 Davidson would go on to be secretary to the Treasury Board, president of the CBC, and undersecretary general of administration and management at the United Nations, the highest position ever held by a Canadian at the UN. See Richard B. Splane, *George Davidson: Social Policy and Public Policy Exemplar* (Ottawa: Canadian Council on Social Development, 2003).

43 J.B. Bissett, unpublished journal, 4 February 1960. The journal remains in Bissett's possession.

44 Ibid., 12 February 1960.

45 Ibid.
46 Cabinet Conclusions, LAC, RG 2, vol. 2746, 6 January 1960, 6–8.
47 Ibid.
48 Ibid.
49 Freda Hawkins, *Canada and Immigration: Public Policy and Public Concern*, 2nd ed. (Montreal and Kingston: McGill-Queen's University Press, 1988), 120.
50 Cabinet Conclusions, LAC, RG 2, vol. 2746, 20 January 1960, 2–4.
51 Department of Citizenship and Immigration, *Immigration Policy,* unpublished manual (in author's possession), 1964, C11.
52 John L. (Jack) Manion (1931–2010) spent most of his career dealing with immigration and employment issues, becoming deputy minister of employment and immigration in 1977. He became secretary to the Treasury Board in 1979, associate secretary to cabinet in 1986, and principal of the Canadian Centre for Management Development in 1988. He retired from the Public Service in 1991.
53 Bissett, e-mail to author, 26 December 2015.
54 Bissett, unpublished journal, 5 February 1960.
55 Ibid., 12 February 1960.
56 Bissett indicated in his journal on 15 February 1960 that the 1 percent target and the abandonment of the "tap on-tap off" policy had their origin in a paper he wrote in 1957, of which Manion was aware.
57 Canada, House of Commons, *Debates*, vol. 3, 1 May 1947, 2644–46.
58 Cabinet Document 46–60, in Janice Cavell, ed., *Documents on Canadian External Relations*, vol. 27 (Ottawa: Foreign Affairs and International Trade Canada, 2007) (hereafter *DCER*, vol. 27), doc. 666.
59 Memorandum from secretary to cabinet to prime minister, 4 April 1960, *DCER*, vol. 27, doc. 668.
60 Bissett, unpublished journal, 5 April 1960.
61 Cabinet Conclusions, LAC, RG 2, Vol. 2746, 12 April 1960, 5–8.
62 Ibid.
63 Bissett, unpublished journal, 18 March 1960.
64 Ibid., 9 May 1960.
65 Fairclough, *Saturday's Child*, 119.
66 Bissett, unpublished journal, 10 October 1960. Bissett received a promotion and left the Minister's office later in October 1960.
67 Fairclough, *Saturday's Child*, 119, 120.
68 United Nations, *The Universal Declaration of Human Rights*, 1948, United Nations documents, http://www.un.org/en/documents/udhr.
69 "Migration Conference," *Ecumenical Review* 14, 1 (1961), 92–109, 101.
70 See documents 459–83 and 557–63 in Janice Cavell, ed., *Documents on Canadian External Relations*, vol. 28 (Ottawa: Foreign Affairs and International Trade Canada, 2009) (hereafter *DCER*, vol. 28).
71 Memorandum from secretary of state for external affairs to prime minister, 16 January 1961, *DCER*, vol. 28, doc. 460.
72 Diefenbaker Fonds, University of Saskatchewan Library, Privy Council Office Files, MG01/VI, file 571, Immigration and Citizenship, Immigration Policy and Administration, 1960–61 (reel M7964), 315725, 315726.

73 Kenneth NcNaught, "Verwoerd Challenges the Commonwealth," *Saturday Night*, 4 March 1961, 11.

74 Donald Gordon, "Puppy Love at Ottawa: Canada's Immature Afro-Asian Romance," *Saturday Night*, 15 April 1961, 16.

75 Donald Gordon, "West Indian Immigration: Britain Puts the Pressure on Canada," *Saturday Night*, 13 May 1961, 37, 38.

76 Minutes of meeting between prime minister of United Kingdom and prime minister, 10 April 1961, *DCER*, vol. 28, doc. 554.

77 Cabinet Conclusions, LAC, RG 2, 18 October 1961, 6, 7.

78 Cabinet Conclusions, LAC, RG 2, vol. 6192, 18 January 1962, 4, 5.

79 Ibid., 5. The cabinet record misidentifies the order-in-council as 1962–82 whereas in fact it was 1962–86.

80 Hawkins, *Canada and Immigration*, 130.

81 Bissett, e-mail to author, 26 December 2015.

82 Canada, House of Commons, *Debates*, 19 January 1962, 9.

83 *Globe and Mail*, 20 January 1962.

84 *Winnipeg Free Press*, 20 January 1962.

85 "The Opening Door," *Globe and Mail*, 22 January 1962.

86 "Race Prejudice," 23 January 1962; "Declining Immigration," 12 February 1962; "Selective Immigration," 12 March 1962; "Publicizing the Rules," 29 March 1962; "The Search for Immigrants," 11 July 1962; "A Practical Look at Immigration," 21 November 1962. All in *Globe and Mail*.

87 Dominion Bureau of Statistics, *Canada Year Book 1965* (Ottawa: Queen's Printer, 1965), 209; and *Canada Year Book 1967* (Ottawa: Queen's Printer, 1967), 220.

88 Diefenbaker Fonds, University of Saskatchewan Library, Privy Council Office Files, MG01/XII/C/171, vol. 60, 041926.

89 Peter Stursberg, *Diefenbaker: Leadership Gained, 1956–62* (Toronto: University of Toronto Press, 1975), 71.

90 Fairclough, *Saturday's Child*, 129.

91 Ellen Fairclough, speech to the Social Planning Council of Metropolitan Toronto, 9 March 1962. Cited in Corbett, "Canada's Immigration Policy," 179, 180.

92 Jean Marchand, *Canadian Immigration Policy* (Ottawa: Information Canada, 1966).

93 Corbett, "Canada's Immigration Policy," 179.

PART 5

The Role of the Foreign Minister

12

Sidney Smith, Howard Green, and the Conduct of Canadian Foreign Policy during the Diefenbaker Government, 1957–63

MICHAEL D. STEVENSON

The conduct of Canadian foreign policy between 1957 and 1963 has been analyzed extensively, with Prime Minister John Diefenbaker being the primary focus of much of this scrutiny. Biographical accounts of Diefenbaker emphasize the pre-eminent role he played in foreign affairs and focus on his complex and frequently contentious interactions with American presidents and other world leaders. Denis Smith's *Rogue Tory*, Knowlton Nash's *Kennedy and Diefenbaker*, and Peter Newman's *Renegade in Power* most effectively represent this vein of writing.[1] Policy appraisals of specific topics in Canada's foreign affairs dossier again frequently concentrate on the role of Diefenbaker. Patricia McMahon's *Essence of Indecision* documenting the nuclear weapons question in the Diefenbaker period and Kevin Spooner's *Canada, the Congo Crisis, and UN Peacekeeping* are representative of this academic literature.[2] Finally, memoirs of key Conservative politicians and senior civil servants frequently accentuate Diefenbaker's influence in the foreign policy arena. Basil Robinson's *Diefenbaker's World* (possibly the best account of the period), Donald Fleming's multi-volume *So Very Near*, and Arnold Heeney's *The Things That Are Caesar's* stand out in this literature, with Diefenbaker's own *One Canada* memoirs also contributing to this autobiographical strand of analysis.[3]

In all of these accounts, the role of Diefenbaker's two foreign ministers – Sidney Smith and Howard Green – in formulating and administering Canadian external relations policy is largely marginalized or ignored. In comparative terms, this paucity of scholarship is puzzling considering the comprehensive analyses that have been written about Liberal secretaries of state for external affairs in the 1950s and 1960s. John English has examined Lester Pearson's tenure as foreign affairs minister in Louis St. Laurent's government in the second volume of *The Life of Lester Pearson*, as has Robert Bothwell in *Pearson: His Life and World*.[4] Similarly, Greg Donaghy, in *Grit: The Life and Politics of Paul Martin Sr.*, has carefully scrutinized the career of Paul Martin as foreign minister from 1963 to 1968 in Pearson's government.[5] In contrast, no serious academic biographies have ever been published focusing on Smith or Green.[6] Archival sources are not an impediment in producing appraisals of the foreign policy legacies of either Conservative minister, particularly for Green, who left two significant archival repositories.[7]

An examination of the tenure of Smith and Green provides new perspectives on the conduct of Canadian foreign policy during the Diefenbaker government. The two men came from disparate backgrounds. Smith entered cabinet with no political experience after enjoying a distinguished career in university administration, and he proved incapable of carving out an independent role in the foreign affairs portfolio before his untimely death in March 1959. Green assumed the position of secretary of state for external affairs in June 1959 and proved to be one of the most influential and independent foreign ministers in Canadian history. Extensive political experience, close personal relations with Diefenbaker, and the ability to mobilize the diplomatic resources of the Department of External Affairs (DEA) allowed Green to leave a distinct mark on Canada's diplomatic history. Removing the focus from the actions of Diefenbaker and placing it on the activities of Smith and Green can provide fresh insight into Canada's relations with other countries – most notably the United States.

Following the Progressive Conservative victory in the June 1957 federal election, Diefenbaker temporarily assumed the role of secretary of state for external affairs while a permanent minister could be found. He eventually appointed Smith, an exceptionally gifted university administrator and a prominent Progressive Conservative supporter who had been considered a strong candidate for the leadership of the party in 1942.[8] A veteran of the First World War, Smith was appointed dean of the Dalhousie Law School in 1929 before serving as the president of the University of Manitoba from 1934 to 1944 and the University of Toronto from 1945 to 1957. Although Diefenbaker claimed Smith was "a profound student of international relations,"[9] his legal background did not touch on matters of foreign affairs;

instead, he was an expert in business law and trusts.[10] Initially, Diefenbaker's idea to appoint an outsider such as Smith was viewed as a masterstroke. Donald Fleming, the newly appointed minister of finance, recalled: "Dief called me in to ask me what I would think of the appointment of Sidney Smith. I immediately replied, 'That would be a ten-strike.' The wide respect in which he was held throughout Canada and his academic eminence would win strong acceptance even though he bore the handicap of having no experience in Parliament."[11] Smith admitted privately that accepting the external affairs portfolio was "contrary to my truly personal wishes," but the "unique type of public service" being offered forced him to accede to Diefenbaker's request.[12]

Smith, unfortunately, never adapted to the demands of one of the most taxing cabinet posts, and his genuine skill in university administration did not seem to transfer to government and the rough-and-tumble environment of Parliament. Robert Bryce, the influential clerk of the Privy Council and secretary to the cabinet during the Diefenbaker government, expressed sympathy for Smith because of his "inexperience and exaggerated build-up," but he believed that Smith was "not gifted to make the kind of decisions he had to" and that he "never would have made a great minister."[13] Examining External Affairs files demonstrates that he did not take a keen interest in material prepared for him by DEA officials. Handwritten marginalia often demonstrate the level of engagement of foreign ministers with policy questions. Smith almost without fail did not comment on memoranda received from his undersecretaries, Jules Léger and (from October 1958) Norman Robertson, usually just initialing "OK" on these documents. Basil Robinson, Diefenbaker's DEA liaison officer, noted that the foreign affairs portfolio "had exposed the minister's experience and taxed his powers of concentration. The openness of his mind did not seem to be matched by a capacity to put his own imprint on new information or advice."[14] Charles Ritchie, Canada's permanent representative to the United Nations in New York, was somewhat less nuanced in his evaluation of Smith's talents:

> He has been extremely kind and understanding in his dealings with me and I like him. He is shrewd enough too, but all the same I ask myself what can be the secret of his success. It is certainly not force of intelligence or grasp of issues. And he does talk such nonsense. Last night he began comparing Canada to his thirteen-year-old daughter, "both adolescents at a difficult age." He says, "We must not let ourselves be treated like Tunisians." What can he mean?[15]

Ultimately, Smith had difficulty escaping from Diefenbaker's considerable shadow and failed to carve out an independent role for himself in cabinet. This problem had been evident since the day of his swearing-in in September 1957, when Smith, in answer to a reporter's question, praised the handling of the 1956 Suez Crisis by the St. Laurent government and was immediately corrected and reprimanded by Diefenbaker, who was present during the press scrum. There was little rapport between the two men and they never established a solid working relationship. "Smith was awed by Diefenbaker," Basil Robinson noted, "reluctant to bother him, afraid to provoke his disapproval ... Their contacts, apart from Cabinet meetings, were sporadic and fitful, and not sufficiently thorough to shape the foundation of a coherent foreign policy."[16] Smith, therefore, was not allowed and was not temperamentally suited to develop a bold foreign policy. More experienced ministers such as Donald Fleming assumed control of critical policy files such as Commonwealth trade, and Diefenbaker took responsibility for crucial files such as NORAD and other defence initiatives. Smith performed passably and competently when called upon to do so, but he could only have an impact in areas where his thinking mirrored Diefenbaker's.

An overview of four important foreign policy files demonstrates the relatively low profile Smith maintained during his sixteen-month tenure as secretary of state for external affairs. First, Smith played virtually no role in directing or coordinating Canadian activities at the first United Nations Conference on the Law of the Sea in Geneva during March and April of 1958.[17] This was arguably one of the most important matters the Diefenbaker government faced, since decisions taken at the conference had a potentially enormous economic impact on issues such as territorial sea width and coastal fishing rights, both important to Canada. Canadian policy for the UN conference was formulated by the Cabinet Committee on Territorial Waters under the direction of the minister of northern development and national resources, Alvin Hamilton, and not Smith. The Canadian delegation to the conference was led by George Drew, the high commissioner in London and Diefenbaker's personal political appointee, and Marcel Cadieux, the DEA's legal advisor, largely handled the file within External Affairs in Ottawa. The matters involved in the law of the sea debate were highly technical and complex, and Smith perhaps justifiably could not play an active role apart from reporting to cabinet on the progress of the Geneva meetings. But Smith's seeming detachment from the policy-making process on this topic nonetheless stands out.

If Smith played no role in the international law of the sea deliberations, he secured his greatest diplomatic success in important United Nations deliberations arising out of the 1958 crisis in the Middle East. The United Nations Observation Group in Lebanon (UNOGIL) had been formed in June 1958 to report on the Lebanese government's complaint about outside interference in its affairs by the nationalistic government of the United Arab Republic. The subsequent overthrow of the pro-Western Iraqi government on 14 July 1958 precipitated American military intervention the next day after Lebanese president Camille Chamoun appealed for assistance. Canada played a strong role in solving this emergency. Feverish activity in capitals around the world eventually resulted in the convening of an emergency session of the United Nations General Assembly from 8 to 21 August. Supported by External Affairs personnel, Smith worked energetically in New York with Norwegian officials to craft a seven-power resolution calling for the withdrawal of US troops following the establishment of UN mechanisms to guarantee the political integrity of Lebanon. Ultimately, this resolution spurred Arab nations to sponsor their own ten-power resolution that adopted several provisions of the seven-power draft. *"Mirab[i]le dictu,"* Smith reported from Washington on the last day of the session, "the Assembly unanimously adopted the Arab resolution ... I am delighted by the success of this first really important meeting of the Assembly that I have attended. I am not ashamed of Canada's contribution."[18] Basil Robinson subsequently concurred with Smith's evaluation of his personal role, noting that the Canadian foreign minister played "a persevering part" in ending the Lebanon Crisis and that it "brought the Prime Minister and Sidney Smith to work more effectively together than at any previous time."[19]

Smith built on this success in the international arena by playing a constructive role in the creation of Commonwealth education exchanges. As part of the Commonwealth Trade and Economic Conference held in Montreal from 15 to 26 September 1958, a proposal for a Commonwealth scholarship program emerged from detailed interdepartmental consultations, with one hundred scholarships to be offered by Canada at an annual cost of $750,000. Smith coordinated the consultation efforts in various Commonwealth capitals before the conference about the viability of the proposed scholarship program, and he spoke forcefully at the conference supporting the initiative, noting that the scheme sought to go beyond Canada's traditional support for the technical training of experts under the terms of the Colombo Plan. Comfortably employing the oratorical flourishes honed in a university environment, Smith emphasized that "an increasingly complex economic and social organism called for trained people of more general skills and aptitudes to exercise the qualities of judgment, insight, sympathy, and intelligent synthesis that were clearly required in the process of economic growth."[20] Before his death, Smith continued to monitor and encourage the development of the educational exchanges, and the Commonwealth Education Conference held in July 1959 formally established the Commonwealth Scholarship and Fellowship Plan.

Despite these two successes in UN and Commonwealth venues that allowed Smith to demonstrate his worth as a helpful fixer, his inability to influence and shape Canadian policy during the 1958–59 Berlin Crisis illustrated his subservient role to Prime Minister Diefenbaker in the formulation of major elements of Canadian foreign relations. Renewed East-West tensions over Berlin in 1958 provided DEA officials with the opportunity to break out of the traditional Canadian passive stance of allowing the US, Britain, and France to speak for the NATO alliance. A detailed departmental memorandum completed in January 1959 called for five "lines of enquiry" to be made by Canada in NATO circles that included increasing contacts with East Germany, a separate solution on Berlin divorced from the question of unification, and the scaling back of the Western demand that the first step in any settlement be free elections across both Germanys.[21] Smith sent this memorandum to Diefenbaker with a handwritten covering note:

In this Department, we have recently been seeking for a role for Canada in the Berlin situation – a role that could be helpful and constructive. The deliberations during the past few weeks in the NATO Council have not been encouraging. I do not like the possibility of the USA, France, the United Kingdom, and West Germany taking the view that they should decide what should be done ... Herewith is a memorandum into which we have put much thought.

But Diefenbaker rejected Smith's counsel that a bold Canadian initiative be undertaken over Berlin. Canadian missions in NATO capitals would only be allowed to float the ideas contained in the DEA memorandum informally. The prime minister believed that by even following this cautious course, though, that "there was a danger that if our explanatory enquiries followed closely the questions and the argumentation in the memorandum, other governments might infer that the direction of thought implied therein had become, or was on the verge of becoming, Canadian policy."[22] Basil Robinson noted that Diefenbaker believed that the bold DEA initiative "was Pearsonian territory and he was apprehensive that Sidney Smith would not be able to control the 'Pearsonalities'" in External Affairs.[23] Desultory consultations in NATO countries did take place, but Smith could not direct any comprehensive diplomatic offensive over Berlin without Diefenbaker's imprimatur.[24]

Sidney Smith died suddenly of a heart attack on 16 March 1959; all observers – including John Diefenbaker – believed his death came as a result of overwork. Although Donald Fleming observed that Smith "had not found the adjustment to the parliamentary arena easy," he nonetheless believed that Smith's status in the university and professional sectors had helped the Conservative cause. "To me it was noticeable after his death," the minister of finance concluded, "that we seemed to draw less support and respect from that important stratum of Canadian society."[25] Howard Green also privately noted Smith's growth in familiarity with his portfolio: "Sidney Smith died suddenly today – first break in our Cabinet ranks and a grand person – beginning to make a name as Secretary of State for External Affairs. PM very upset."[26] Despite this acknowledgment of Smith's slow maturation in his cabinet portfolio, the authors of the DEA's official history politely sum up his limited impact by noting that "the experience with Smith had alerted the department to the need for attention to the requirements of a minister without a background in foreign affairs."[27]

Diefenbaker delayed naming Smith's successor for more than two months, and speculators believed that Fleming or Justice Minister Davie Fulton would obtain the plum external affairs post. But Diefenbaker again surprised the political cognoscenti by naming Green as secretary of state for external affairs on 3 June 1959. Green served in the Canadian Expeditionary Force during the First World War and subsequently established a law practice in Vancouver before entering Parliament as the only Conservative to win a new seat in the face of the Liberal landslide in the election of 1935. In twenty-two years on the Opposition benches, Green developed a reputation as an exceptionally skilled debater who played a key role in skewering the Liberal government's record during the 1956 Suez Crisis and the bruising pipeline debate. Green held the public works portfolio and served as House leader and deputy prime minister in Diefenbaker's minority government after the June 1957 federal election.

Green's appointment generated considerable controversy. Many political friends and foes alike viewed him as narrow in his worldview and lacking in international affairs experience. The US embassy in Ottawa, for example, forwarded to Washington an opinion from a Canadian source that, despite Green's "high principle, complete integrity, and real stature," he possessed "some old fashioned, practically antediluvian ideas on foreign affairs which could be expected to cause problems."[28] Donald Fleming – who described Green as "a painstaking, hard working, but colourless" foreign minister – articulated an additional common concern that Green's strong commitment to the British Commonwealth automatically meant that "he was suspected of harbouring an anti-American bias."[29] Furthermore, Green was initially viewed as Diefenbaker's "charming stooge" by critics of the appointment whose "very innocence in foreign affairs is unlikely to dispose him to argue much with his boss."[30] Finally, some political opponents viewed Green as insular, naïve, and narrow-minded and whom C.D. Howe, the powerful Liberal cabinet minister, wittily described as a member "who goes around the Parliament buildings with a smirk on his face, a Bible in his hand, and a stiletto up his sleeve."[31]

These contemporary descriptions of Green have fermented for many decades and consistently colour academic appraisals of Green's tenure in the foreign affairs portfolio. The most infamous case of Green's alleged unworldliness and simplicity, unfortunately still in current circulation, involves the visit of Congolese prime minister Joseph Lumumba to Ottawa from 29 to 31 July 1960. Political commentator Lawrence Martin routinely refers to a defamatory story supposedly linking Green and Lumumba during the visit:

> The African leader had the reputation of a notorious fornicator. In a meeting with Green, he asked that a girl be sent over to his Chateau Laurier suite. The churchgoing Green thought he meant a typist. When the unsuspecting stenographer entered Lumumba's room all hell broke loose.[32]

Journalist Charles Lynch provided his own embellishment to the story currently propagated by Martin:

> He brought an entourage of 30 to Ottawa, and no sooner were they ensconced in suites in the Chateau Laurier than they sent a message to Howard Green, the austere secretary of state for external affairs, asking, "Where are the women?" Green, a prim and proper man with a minimal knowledge of the world outside Canada and no knowledge at all of Africa, sent back word that the Canadian government did not deal in such matters. One of Green's aides, in delivering the reply, let slip on the sly that maybe the distinguished guests could try the By Ward Market, the hangout for hookers, just two blocks down the street. Upon receipt of these tidings, Lumumba

went into a snit, and when it came time for the welcoming reception in the hotel that evening, with Howard Green as the host, he refused to show up. Finally, he was persuaded to come, but the party had all the makings of a major fizzle, with Congolese and Canadian men standing around in surly silence and Howard Green staring into his perpetual glass of orange juice, of which he consumed hundreds of barrels during his years at the diplomatic trough.[33]

The plain fact is these scurrilous accounts linking Green with Lumumba are completely false and unfairly denigrate and prejudice Green's diplomatic record, despite their acceptance as the gospel truth by two generations of Canadian historians and journalists. As shown by archival documents and attested by his advisors, Green never met Lumumba. He left Ottawa on Friday, 29 July, to attend a Conservative political event in Alberta before Lumumba arrived in the city. Attendance records at two cabinet meetings held on Saturday, 30 July, confirm Green's absence, as does the record of the conversation Lumumba had with DEA officials the same day.[34] Lumumba cut short his visit and left Ottawa on Sunday, 31 July, before Green returned that evening. The facts of the case are straightforward and have nothing to do with Howard Green. Lumumba arrived in Ottawa and, at one point, asked for female company. External Affairs arranged with the hotel where he was staying that he would be supplied with the same. After consultation between the staff of the hotel and a departmental representative, the outlay for this service was subsequently charged as "flowers" on the hotel's invoice.[35] The bare bones of the story appear to have taken on a distorted and exaggerated life of their own through journalistic imagination and the dissemination of the false account by American officials seeking to undermine Green's authority.

These critiques of Green's personality and temperament are frequently augmented by a more serious charge of anti-Americanism in matters of policy. There is certainly an element of truth in scholarly evaluations of Green's ministerial record in this regard. Green did adopt a distinctly nationalist position that frequently placed him at odds with Washington. But there was little or no personal animus towards American government officials, particularly those in the Eisenhower administration. After meeting US secretary of state Christian Herter and his assistant undersecretary (and former US ambassador in Ottawa) Livingston Merchant on multiple occasions, Green privately reported to his son: "I like Herter very much – and as you know have always liked Merchant."[36] Green did prove inflexible on the total integration of Canadian and American continental defence, earning increasing condemnation from the Kennedy administration after Eisenhower left office in January 1961. He steadfastly refused to succumb to increasing pressure from Washington – and from some elements in the Diefenbaker cabinet and the Department of External Affairs – to supply American nuclear warheads to Canadian Bomarc squadrons and RCAF interceptor aircraft. Green's perceived anti-Americanism was also magnified by his willingness to use his advocacy of disarmament and nuclear non-proliferation for political purposes. Green's courting of public opinion exasperated senior officials in the Kennedy administration and caused them to repeatedly complain about his "great sensitivity to domestic political breezes"[37] and "propensity for playing to the galleries."[38]

Green enjoyed three advantages over Sidney Smith in pursuing an independent course of action. First, he enjoyed the complete confidence of Prime Minister Diefenbaker and the two men had similar views on most policy matters. Despite running against Diefenbaker in 1942 for the party leadership and preferring Donald Fleming over him in the 1956 leadership race, Green and Diefenbaker had a long and deep relationship based on mutual respect, Diefenbaker's trust in Green, and Green's unwavering loyalty to his leader. Shortly before assuming the external affairs portfolio, Green told his mother about being asked to share the expansive lunch that Olive Diefenbaker provided for her husband. "He seems to like to chat with me," Green noted, "and we really get along excellently together."[39] Green also routinely spent time with Diefenbaker at the prime minister's retreat at Harrington Lake. It is clear in all of this that Diefenbaker trusted the experienced Green not to be captured by the much-feared "Pearsonalities" in External Affairs.

Second, Green possessed a commanding presence in Parliament and in articulating government policy to the general public. He earned the respect of most House of Commons members for his performance on the front benches, with Paul Martin commenting that Green was the government's "best House of Commons debater."[40] Green campaigned tirelessly for the Conservative cause, conducting a remarkable range of speaking engagements despite his busy External Affairs ministerial schedule to attend international meetings. In the 1962 election campaign, for example, Green travelled throughout the country on a gruelling schedule trying to shore up party fortunes. In one five-day swing through the Prairies and Ontario that began in Alberta on 4 June, Green spoke in Redwater, Edmonton, and Calgary in Alberta; in Regina, Moose Jaw, and Davidson in Saskatchewan; in

Flin Flon, Winnipeg, and Selkirk in Manitoba; and in Toronto before returning to Ottawa on 9 June.

Finally, Green exercised strong control over the Department of External
Affairs and demonstrated a complete command of the political and policy
agenda Canada sought to adopt in the conduct of foreign policy. He involved
himself intimately with policy formulation, as evidenced by his remarkably
detailed, lawyerly dissection of memoranda and drafts of cabinet documents that crossed his desk. Green excelled in establishing interpersonal
relationships within his department, and even if civil servants opposed
some of his signal initiatives in disarmament or bilateral defence relations
with the United States, he gained the full respect and confidence of many of
his senior officials, including Norman Robertson, the departmental undersecretary. In the pursuit of his goals, he frequently surprised both political
friends and foes by his tireless advocacy of Canada's position and his ability
to achieve his aims. Charles Ritchie – no strong admirer of the Diefenbaker
government – provided a synopsis of Green's effectiveness, for example, in
securing a strong resolution passed by the United Nations Disarmament
Commission in August 1960:

> The first morning that I can breathe again after five days of the Minister's
> presence in New York, during which he pulled off a very neat little ploy on
> disarmament, sent up his prestige, and got what he wanted by a mixture of
> toughness and shrewdness that surprised his fellow professional politician,
> Cabot Lodge, while at the same time stealing the show from him. I think
> Cabot may have thought he was dealing with a nice old boy from the sticks
> who was a little slow on the uptake and could be patronized with his usual
> effortless effrontery – but it did not work out like that. This exercise dem-
> onstrated the advantage of taking an inflexible and clear-cut position at the
> start, in our case a middle position to which the "uncommitted" countries
> in the UN gyrated.[41]

Four major policy initiatives demonstrate the strong influence Green
exerted as secretary of state for external affairs from 1959 to 1963. First,
Green's role in the scuttling of Operation Skyhawk – the first major
Canada-US test of NORAD's defence perimeter – in August and September
1959 revealed the similarity of his and Prime Minister Diefenbaker's thinking on bilateral military affairs. Both Green and Diefenbaker had expressed
concern about the growing number of American requests for military integration, with Green informing Arnold Heeney, the Canadian ambassador in

Washington, in the summer of 1959 that "the United States should be 'held down' in these matters and should not be given all they asked for."[42] Operation Skyhawk was a comprehensive defence exercise scheduled to occur on 3 October 1959 that would test the NORAD response to a Soviet bomber attack and require the grounding of all commercial aircraft in the US and Canada for six hours. Planning for Skyhawk had started in January 1959 and US cabinet secretaries and President Eisenhower were aware of the exercise, but Canadian defence minister George Pearkes did not learn of the exercise until 11 August 1959 and Green was not briefed on the matter until 21 August. The Canadian foreign minister conveyed particular concern to his officials about a draft press released prepared by the US Department of Defense that clearly emphasized the air defence exercise was to simulate an attack on Canada; he subsequently expressed his feelings about the matter in a margin note of a DEA memorandum: "Totally inappropriate and provocative now – reserve right to consider proposal further."[43]

At a Cabinet meeting on 26 August, Green joined with Diefenbaker to scuttle the exercise despite impassioned lobbying from Pearkes and Transport Minister George Hees. In a climate of Cold War thaw symbolized by the scheduled upcoming exchange of visits between Eisenhower and Soviet premier Nikita Khrushchev, anti-Skyhawk Conservative members argued that the exercise would be viewed by Moscow as an attempt "to show the iron fist."[44] A diplomatic note delivered on 28 August to Washington announcing Canada's withdrawal from Skyhawk roused a furious campaign led by Eisenhower himself to convince Diefenbaker to reconsider the decision. The US ambassador in Ottawa, Richard Wigglesworth, also pressed the issue with Green, but these representations were to no avail, and Diefenbaker informed Eisenhower on 6 September that Canada would not budge. Green refused to be cowed by US officials in the aftermath of Skyhawk's cancellation. He bluntly informed his American counterpart, Christian Herter, that "marked differences" existed between Ottawa and Washington over defence cooperation.[45] Furthermore, he informed the American delegation at the November 1959 meeting of the Ministerial Committee on Joint Defence that he remained adamant in his view that "appropriate political control" needed to be exercised over the staging of any future large-scale defence exercises.[46] Green's first major policy decision demonstrated the sway he held in the formulation of Canadian foreign policy, and the State Department post-mortem of the matter emphasized that Green played "the key role" in scuttling the exercise and noted his "particularly important position because of his influence with the Prime Minister."[47]

The second policy file demonstrating Green's importance concerns financial aid to and diplomatic recognition of developing countries. Green sought to establish improved connections with developing countries in South America and Africa both in an effort to bolster support for Canada's diplomatic initiatives at the United Nations and from a firm belief in assisting disadvantaged populations. He undertook one of the longest ministerial tours during the Diefenbaker government when he visited Central and South America for ten days between 22 and 29 May 1960 seeking to improve Canada's hemispheric trade relations. Green also fully supported the establishment of an external aid office in August 1960 that centralized control of Canada's economic assistance programs under his own authority as secretary of state for external affairs; it was the first such agency or ministry in the OECD.[48] Green kept a close watch on the External Aid Office and often met with its first director-general, Herbert Moran. Nevertheless, he once castigated him, in 1961, when Moran informed Parliament's External Affairs Committee that he supported cutting down the vote for Canadian aid to developing countries because he could not spend the money. "I thought he was very good," Green complained humorously to his son, "but he may just end up as consul-general in Timbuktoo!"[49]

Green's strong influence in shaping Progressive Conservative policy is further evident in the complex negotiations to develop the Columbia River. Protracted consultations with Washington resulted in a treaty signed between Canada and the United States on 17 January 1961 that contained the broad parameters of an agreement to harness the hydroelectric capacity of the Columbia. But a sharp disagreement between W.A.C. Bennett, the Social Credit premier of British Columbia, and the Diefenbaker government subsequently arose on two issues. Bennett wanted Ottawa to take on a greater share of the capital costs of the project, and he also wanted to sell his province's share of the power developed downstream in the United States to American consumers and not to British Columbia's Lower Mainland. Bennett meant to supply its needs by a great power project on the Peace River. Howard Green forcefully opposed Bennett's plans. He held that British Columbia needed cheap Columbia River power for its development instead of the more expensive hydroelectricity expected from the Peace River project. Furthermore, he refused to let Bennett set the terms of any Canadian agreement with the United States. His mistrust of the BC premier was in part political: originally a Progressive Conservative in the provincial legislature, Bennett had defected to the Social Credit Party in 1951. Over the duration of the Columbia negotiations, Green described Bennett variously as "a menace,"[50] "bumptious and objectionable,"[51] "a bit of a Mussolini,"[52] and "a slippery customer,"[53] and he steadfastly held firm to his position that downstream benefits would not be sold for any price.

The Kennedy administration and some senior members of the Canadian cabinet, however, did not share Green's views and clamoured for a deal. Impatient American negotiators proposed in April 1962 that the United States would be willing to buy Canadian downstream power benefits at a reasonable price of five mills per kilowatt hour for a period of twenty years, a position supported in principle by the BC government and many of Green's cabinet colleagues. Green, nevertheless, carried the day, refusing to consider the American offer. Despite personal entreaties from Diefenbaker in August 1962 to reverse his position, Green bluntly informed the prime minister that the "one thing above everything else that he valued was his reputation and that he could not do other than withdraw from the Cabinet" if the government accepted Washington's terms.[54] Desultory negotiations dragged on before the Diefenbaker government fell in 1963, and the incoming Liberal government of Lester Pearson quickly signed an agreement on the Columbia that did not differ significantly from the 1962 American proposal. Donald Fleming reported in his memoirs on Green's single-handed obstruction:

> In refusing at the behest of one stubborn man to grasp the opportunity for agreement I believe Dief and the Cabinet acted irresponsibly. We exposed ourselves to the accusations that we were incapable of making essential decisions. We squandered an opportunity to prove we were quite able to make the biggest decision of all and to open a new chapter in the development of Canada's natural resources. We paid dearly for that tragic failure. Howard had frustrated the development of the Columbia.[55]

Finally, Green demonstrated his ability to shape Canadian foreign policy and influence international relations by securing the passage of a major United Nations resolution in November 1962 calling for a nuclear test moratorium. This capped the effort he started during his first UN session as SSEA in 1959 to gradually bring nuclear weapons under international arms control. At the autumn 1962 session of the United Nations, the General Assembly debated the issue of an uninspected suspension of nuclear tests, a plan that Canadian defence minister Doug Harkness warned Green posed "grave risks" to the Western defence position.[56] Green nonetheless instructed Canadian officials in New York to accept a potential resolution with an unpoliced testing moratorium clause commencing 1 January 1963 with follow-up agreements to be negotiated to ensure compliance, and he "laid into the nuclear powers for continued nuclear testing" in a UN speech delivered on 11 October.[57] When neutral countries subsequently submitted an eight-power resolution calling for a moratorium to compete with a resolution sponsored by the US and the UK with no moratorium starting date, Canada made no effort to oppose its terms. Canada's independent stance caused President Kennedy to warn John Diefenbaker on 20 October that the Canadian position "can only damage, and damage seriously, the Western position on an essential issue of Western security."[58] The Cuban Missile Crisis added fuel to the moratorium debate and widened the split between Green and Douglas Harkness over defence issues, with Harkness furiously lobbying Diefenbaker to rein in Green and prevent Canada from voting for a testing moratorium without inspection clauses.

Green travelled to New York on 28 October to personally handle the testing suspension debate. Nikita Khrushchev's walk-back on Cuba allowed Canada to propose amending the neutral resolution to specifically call for the US, UK, and USSR to settle their differences over testing and urge an immediate agreement to ban all tests in the atmosphere, underwater, and in outer space if a complete test ban could not be agreed to by 1 January 1963. Green counselled US secretary of state Dean Rusk that the amended resolution was "in as good a shape as it was possibly going to get" and he hoped the United States could at least see clear to abstain on the matter.[59] Ultimately, on 6 November the General Assembly passed the neutral resolution with the Canadian amendments with seventy-five votes of support, zero votes against, and twenty-one abstentions. Green's performance at the UN marked the high point of his diplomatic career and received wide praise in Canadian political and press circles.

Green's indelible stamp on the crafting of Canadian foreign policy continued to play a role in the course of the final months of the Diefenbaker government. In November 1962, the Canadian cabinet attempted to address the long-simmering question of the acquisition of nuclear weapons by offering to open high-level diplomatic political talks with the United States.[60] Green carefully monitored Canadian negotiators as they attempted to arrange a "missing part" agreement that would conform to Green's wish that complete operational nuclear warheads not be stored on Canadian soil, with an essential element of warheads stored in the US and moved across the border when an international crisis occurred. But the decision by Lester Pearson in January 1963 to commit the Liberal Party to accept US nuclear tips and Diefenbaker's mishandling of the nuclear weapons file through his public revelation of the top-secret bilateral talks and refusal to come down on one side or the other of the nuclear debate caused the collapse of the Progressive Conservative government and the election of a minority Liberal government in April 1963. Green once again travelled the country during the election campaign and relied heavily on his commitment to disarmament and opposition to nuclear weapons acquisition to argue that voters would decide whether Canada "will be a great nation or a satellite."[61] On this occasion, even voters in his Vancouver Quadra riding surprisingly turned against Green and narrowly returned a Liberal candidate. Nonetheless, the veteran Conservative parliamentarian accepted the defeat with grace and simply commented – "That's politics."[62]

Scrutinizing the record of Sidney Smith and Howard Green reveals two widely different styles of foreign policy leadership. Smith never overcame his lack of political experience and his lack of a close working relationship with John Diefenbaker and usually remained in the prime minister's diplomatic shadow. Furthermore, he did not seem to possess a personal vision or blueprint to follow in the advancement of Canada's external affairs agenda. Nonetheless, supported by his officials, he played a constructive, if unspectacular, role in a number of key policy areas and performed competently when given the freedom and opportunity to do so. Green, on the other hand, built on a distinguished parliamentary record, his personal connection with Diefenbaker, and a clearly articulated vision of Canada's place in the international arena to wield a disproportionate influence in the Conservative government. Green frequently became a polarizing figure for his passionate advocacy of policy stances that placed him at odds with members of his own government and Western allies. But his influence in formulating Canadian foreign policy from 1959 to 1963 cannot be disputed. Few Canadian foreign ministers have played such a preponderant role in determining Canada's foreign policy agenda.

An overview of the ministerial careers of Smith and Green provides important new perspectives on the conduct of Canadian foreign policy from 1957 to 1963. Of foremost importance is the demonstrated need to integrate both foreign ministers into the narrative of external affairs policy formulation and to reduce and qualify John Diefenbaker's part in it. The Conservative prime minister certainly played a major role that cannot be ignored, but placing him at the centre of most policy debates diminishes the records of Smith and particularly Green and frequently distorts the history of Canada's diplomacy during this period. Furthermore, the lack of existing scholarship examining the careers of Smith and Green in politics points to the considerable opportunities that exist to reinterpret Canadian diplomacy during the 1950s and 1960s. Although specific aspects of Canada's foreign policy at that time have been covered adequately, a significant amount of archives-based research remains to be undertaken; such work will replace older journalistic accounts of Progressive Conservative foreign policy that have so often been used authoritatively by historians. Finally, research on the impact of Smith and Green on promoting Canada's international interests may allow for a more balanced picture to be gained of the entire sweep of Canadian diplomacy in the post-World War era, a diplomatic history that has disproportionately emphasized Liberal initiatives during the St. Laurent, Pearson, and Trudeau governments while downplaying the achievements of the Diefenbaker government.

NOTES

1 Denis Smith, *Rogue Tory: The Life and Legend of John G. Diefenbaker* (Toronto: Macfarlane Walter and Ross, 1995); Knowlton Nash, *Kennedy and Diefenbaker: Fear and Loathing across the Undefended Border* (Toronto: McClelland and Stewart, 1990); Peter Newman, *Renegade in Power: The Diefenbaker Years* (Toronto: McClelland and Stewart, 1963).

2 Patricia McMahon, *Essence of Indecision: Diefenbaker's Nuclear Policy, 1957–1963* (Montreal and Kingston: McGill-Queen's University Press, 2009); Kevin Spooner, *Canada, the Congo Crisis, and UN Peacekeeping, 1960–1964* (Vancouver: UBC Press, 2009).

3 Basil Robinson, *Diefenbaker's World: A Populist in Foreign Affairs* (Toronto: University of Toronto Press, 1989); Donald Fleming, *So Very Near, the Rising Years: The Political Memoirs of the Honourable Donald M. Fleming,* vol. 1 (Toronto: McClelland and Stewart, 1985); Donald Fleming, *So Very Near, the Summit Years: The Political Memoirs of the Honourable Donald M. Fleming,* vol. 2 (Toronto: McClelland and Stewart, 1985); Arnold Heeney, *The Things That Are Caesar's: Memoirs of a Canadian Public Servant* (Toronto: University of Toronto Press, 1973); John G. Diefenbaker, *One Canada: Memoirs of the Right Honourable John G. Diefenbaker,* vol. 2, *The Years of Achievement, 1956–1962* (Toronto: Macmillan Canada, 1976); John G. Diefenbaker, *One Canada: Memoirs of the Right Honourable John G. Diefenbaker,* vol. 3, *The Tumultuous Years, 1962–1967* (Toronto: Macmillan Canada, 1977). Diefenbaker's memoirs should be used with caution in terms of their accuracy and objectivity. See Asa McKercher, "Diefenbaker's World: One Canada and the History of Canadian-American Relations, 1961–63," *Historian* 75, 1 (2013): 94–120.

4 John English, *The Life of Lester Pearson,* vol. 2, *The Worldly Years, 1949–1972* (Toronto: Knopf Canada, 1972); Robert Bothwell, *Pearson: His Life and World* (Toronto: McGraw-Hill Ryerson, 1978).

5 Greg Donaghy, *Grit: The Life and Politics of Paul Martin Sr.* (Vancouver: UBC Press, 2015).

6   E.A. Corbett's *Sidney Earle Smith* (Toronto: University of Toronto Press, 1961) provides only a brief, unscholarly, retrospective account of Smith's career.

7   The first of these, in the City of Vancouver Archives, contains Green's private papers covering his entire life and includes thousands of detailed personal letters written and received by Green from his adolescence to the last years of his life. A second collection held by Library and Archives Canada contains detailed official records chronicling Green's ministerial career and a substantial newspaper clipping collection.

8   As it turned out, Smith did not seek the party leadership in 1942; both John Diefenbaker and Howard Green stood in the Progressive Conservative leadership convention but lost to John Bracken. See Hugh Segal, *The Right Balance: Canada's Conservative Tradition* (Vancouver: Douglas and McIntyre, 2011), 122–24.

9   Diefenbaker, *One Canada: The Years of Achievement*, 45.

10 See, for example, John D. Falconbridge and Sidney Earle Smith, *Manual of Canadian Business Law* (Toronto: Sir Isaac Pitman, 1930).

11 Fleming, *So Very Near, the Rising Years*, 371.

12 Smith to Small, 12 September 1957, Sidney Earle Smith Papers, vol. 18, file 60, Thomas Fisher Rare Book Library, University of Toronto.

13 John Hilliker interview with R.B. Bryce, 23 May 1980, Oral History Interview Collection, Historical Section, Global Affairs Canada.

14 Robinson, *Diefenbaker's World*, 41.

15 Charles Ritchie, *Diplomatic Passport: More Undiplomatic Diaries, 1946–1962* (Toronto: McClelland and Stewart, 1981), 122.

16 Robinson, *Diefenbaker's World*, 42.

17 For an overview of Canada's preparation for and participation in the 1958 UN Law of the Sea Conference, see Michael D. Stevenson, ed., *Documents on Canadian External Relations* (hereafter *DCER*), vol. 24, 1957–58, pt. 1 (Ottawa: Department of Foreign Affairs and International Trade, 2003), docs. 37–87.

18 New York Telegram 1282, 21 August 1958, in Michael D. Stevenson, ed., *DCER*, vol. 25, *1957–58*, pt. 2 (Ottawa: Canadian Government Publishing, 2004), doc. 382.

19 Robinson, *Diefenbaker's World*, 52–53. See Greg Donaghy, Chapter 4, this volume, for a complete analysis of Canada's role in solving the 1958 crisis in the Middle East.

20 Extract from minutes of meeting of the Eighth Plenary Session of the Commonwealth Trade and Economic Conference, 19 September 1958, in *DCER*, vol., 24, doc. 384.

21 Smith to Diefenbaker, 23 January 1959, in Janice Cavell, Michael D. Stevenson, and Kevin Spooner, eds., *Documents on Canadian External Relations, 1959*, vol. 26 (Ottawa: Department of Foreign Affairs and International Trade, 2006) (hereafter *DCER*, vol. 26), doc. 78.

22 Robinson to Smith, 26 January 1959, *DCER*, vol. 26, doc. 79.

23 Robinson, *Diefenbaker's World*, 89.

24 For a policy file in which Smith proved able to carry the day in the face of Diefenbaker's opposition, see Jill Campbell-Miller's analysis of foreign assistance to India in Chapter 10, this volume.

25 Fleming, *So Very Near, the Summit Years*, 27.

26 Datebook Entry, 17 March 1959, Howard Green Papers (hereafter HGP), box 605-G-3, file 10, City of Vancouver Archives (hereafter CVA).
27 John Hilliker and Donald Barry, *Canada's Department of External Affairs*, vol. 2, *Coming of Age, 1946–1968* (Montreal and Kingston: McGill-Queen's University Press, 1995), 148. For a detailed account of the interaction of both Smith and Green with Diefenbaker, see John Hilliker, "The Politics and the 'Pearsonalities': The Diefenbaker Government and the Conduct of Canadian External Relations," *Historical Papers* 19, 1 (1981): 151–67.
28 Ottawa Telegram 961, 4 June 1959, RG 59, State Department Records, Central Files, 1950–63, box 3216, file 742.13/3–1358, United States National Archives (hereafter USNA).
29 Fleming, *So Very Near, the Summit Years*, 29.
30 "Everybody Likes Howard Green But ...," *Toronto Daily Star*, 6 June 1959.
31 Canada, House of Commons, *Debates*, 15 May 1950, vol. 2, 2488.
32 Lawrence Martin, "Camelot on the Rideau? Don't Wait for It," *Globe and Mail*, 19 February 2013.
33 Charles Lynch, *You Can't Print THAT! Memoirs of a Political Voyeur* (Toronto: Harper-Collins, 1988), 197.
34 Robertson to Green, 1 August 1960, in Janice Cavell, ed., *Documents on Canadian External Relations*, vol. 27, *1960* (Ottawa: Foreign Affairs and International Trade Canada, 2009), doc. 16.
35 George Ignatieff, *The Making of a Peacemonger: The Memoirs of George Ignatieff* (Toronto: University of Toronto Press, 1985), 191.
36 Green to Lewis Green, 12 July 1959, HGP, box 593-F-1, file 2, CVA.
37 Ottawa Telegram 960, 30 March 1962, National Security Files, box 18, file general 2/62–3/62, John F. Kennedy Library (hereafter JFKL).
38 Ottawa Telegram 1328, 15 April 1963, National Security Files, box 18A, file general 4/11/63–5/3/63, JFKL.
39 Green to Mother, 12 April 1959, HGP, box 593-E-5, file 5, CVA.
40 Martin to Green, 3 March 1961, HGP, box 605-D-6, file 4, CVA.
41 Ritchie, *Diplomatic Passport*, 122. See Nicole Marion (Chapter 7, this volume) for a discussion of the Diefenbaker government's disarmament policy.
42 Heeney memorandum for file, 30 June 1959, Arnold Heeney Papers, Library and Archives Canada (hereafter LAC), MG 30, E 144, vol. 1, file 14.
43 Holmes to Green, 25 August 1959, LAC, RG 25, vol. 6050, file 50309-D-40.
44 Cabinet Conclusions, 26 August 1959, LAC, RG 2, vol. 2745.
45 Washington Telegram 2266, 22 September 1959, *DCER*, vol. 26, doc. 211.
46 Minutes of meeting of Canada-United States Ministerial Committee on Joint Defence, 8 November 1959, *DCER*, vol. 26, doc. 229.
47 Wigglesworth to Merchant, 14 October 1959, RG 59, Bureau of European Affairs Files, Alphanumeric Files Relating to Canadian Affairs, 1957–63, Records Relating to Military Matters, vol. 3, file 3-C-3 Skyhawk, NORAD-SAC Exercises, 1959, USNA.
48 Cabinet Document 272–60, 15 August 1960, *DCER*, vol. 26, doc. 670.
49 Green to Lewis Green, 4 June 1961, HGP, box 593-F-1, file 4, CVA.

50 Green to Mother, 16 November 1958, HGP, box 593-E-5, file 4, CVA.

51 Green to Lewis Green, 26 July 1959, HGP, box 593-F-1, file 2, CVA.

52 Green to Lewis Green, 7 August 1961, HGP, box 593-F-1, file 4, CVA.

53 Green to Mother, 14 January 1962, HGP, box 593-E-6, file 4, CVA.

54 Memorandum by Prime Minister, 20 August 1962, in Janice Cavell, ed., *Documents on Canadian External Relations*, vol. 29, *1962–63* (Ottawa: Foreign Affairs, Trade and Development Canada, 2013), doc. 286.

55 Fleming, *So Very Near, the Summit Years*, 471.

56 Harkness to Green, 17 October 1962, Howard Green Papers, LAC, MG 32 B 13, vol. 11, file 2.

57 Burns diary entry, 11 October 1962, E.L.M. Burns Papers, LAC, MG 31 G 6, vol. 8, file diaries 1962.

58 White to Diefenbaker, 20 October 1962, Howard Green Papers, LAC, MG 32 B 13, vol. 11, file 2.

59 Bow to Green, 2 November 1962, Howard Green Papers, LAC, MG 32 B 13, vol. 11, file 2.

60 For a detailed overview of these talks that led ultimately to the collapse of the Diefenbaker government, see Michael D. Stevenson, "'Tossing a March into Dry Hay': Nuclear Weapons and the Crisis in US-Canadian Relations, 1962–1963," *Journal of Cold War Studies* 15 (4): 5–34. See also Isabel Campbell (Chapter 6, this volume) for an overview of defence policies championed by Diefenbaker and Green.

61 "Canada: Great Nation or Satellite?," *Victoria Times*, 5 April 1963.

62 "Green's Defeat 'Shocking,'" *Edmonton Journal*, 9 April 1963.

PART 6

The End of the Diefenbaker Era

13 A Complex Reckoning
A Personal Reflection on the 1963 Election

HUGH SEGAL

The election that ended John Diefenbaker's time as prime minister on 8 April 1963 took place a little short of six years after the surprising Diefenbaker breakthrough of 10 June 1957. To the astonishment of many, in 1957 the Progressive Conservative Party gained sixty-one seats, while the establishment, long-in-the-tooth Liberals lost sixty-four seats. The percentage swing to the Tories was precisely the same as the percentage swing away from the Liberals. Over two decades of Liberal rule came to an unexpected end, despite the perceived competence and avuncular popularity of Prime Minister Louis St. Laurent. In 1948 St. Laurent had succeeded the less avuncular and far less sunny Mackenzie King who, after regaining office in 1935, led the country through the height of the Depression and the challenges and vicissitudes of the Second World War.

Diefenbaker, often defeated in his quests first for a parliamentary seat and then to become party leader, had received an unexpected opportunity to realize the second goal after George Drew's illness took him from the leadership role in August of 1956. The stage had already been partly set for a Liberal electoral defeat. A few months before his resignation, Drew had led a spirited fight against the Liberal use of closure on the famous "Pipeline Bill" and the "who-can-stop-us" arrogance of the minister of trade and commerce, the brilliant and efficient C.D. Howe. As Diefenbaker's biographer Denis Smith has written, "It was high political theatre, conducted with instinctive skill by an opposition confident that it had both propriety and public support on its side."[1]

Then, while the party was under the interim leadership of Earl Rowe, came the Suez Crisis. Diefenbaker, as Opposition foreign policy critic for the Tories, did not embrace the inspired creativity of Lester Pearson's diplomatic engagement on the Suez Crisis and the creation of the United Nations peacekeeping force quite as gratefully as the Liberal and media establishment might have wished. Instead, he portrayed Pearson as being an agent of US interests versus those of the United Kingdom. This strategy revealed more than could then be guessed about the nuclear weapons controversy that would contribute to Diefenbaker's defeat in 1963.

In December 1956, Diefenbaker easily won the Conservative Party leadership on this, his third try, knowing that he would soon face an election campaign. The arrogance of the Liberals in imposing closure on the Pipeline Bill debate – one of many Liberal blind spots when it came to the self-serving American-Canadian corporate economic initiatives in that postwar period – resulted in a 1957 election campaign that focused on the political process as opposed to its outcomes. This played right into the Diefenbaker style of campaigning. Tory fortunes became identified with a mix of nationalism and advocacy of both the rights of Parliament and the right of ordinary Canadians to be heard. Such themes fed into his populist support of greater pensions for widows, subsidy support for farmers, and long-time championing of human rights. For a master of rhetoric like Diefenbaker, well-schooled in the appropriate histrionics of a defence lawyer, the situation was tailor-made. St. Laurent, a superb former minister of justice, and Pearson, a buttoned-down and completely reasonable diplomat and public servant, were no match for him.

Diefenbaker came from the progressive, more left-wing Prairie section of the party – in other words, he had the same western roots as the Co-operative Commonwealth Federation of M.J. Coldwell and Tommy Douglas and the populism of Bible Bill Aberhart and Social Credit. More populist than socialist, and more progressive than conservative, the Diefenbaker message was shaped on the appeal of a "new broom" (which, after five Liberal governments in a row since 1935, was not a hard argument to make) and opposition to "massive Liberal arrogance" (also not hard to do after the Pipeline Debate). Diefenbaker's fiery charisma filled halls and made television a new and convincing campaign tool for the first time ever.

The ensuing six years of Diefenbaker government were not, by any means, a period of either stunning success or abject failure. In both domestic and foreign policy, the record was mixed – even though Diefenbaker's personal popularity remained quite compelling. At first, the self-reverential Liberals found it hard to believe that they had actually been defeated, or that Canadians could have purposely meant to do so. The continued arrogance of the

Liberals resulted in a massive majority for the Tories in 1958 (208 out of 265 seats). After the 1958 election, a plethora of controversial domestic and foreign policy events clouded not only Diefenbaker's prospects for victory in 1963 but also, although to a lesser extent, those of Pearson.

I once overheard Keith Davey (a Liberal senator who led the Pearson and Trudeau campaigns) joke that it took "two elections to get 'Dief' elected and two to get rid of him." Much of this difficulty stemmed from the nationalist and anti-establishment tilt of Diefenbaker's initial surge in 1957 and 1958. The same political posture contributed to his political decline in 1962–63. Yet the perception that Diefenbaker was fighting against powerful vested interests, his dynamic campaign persona, and the loyalty he still commanded in vast segments of rural English-speaking Canada combined to produce a remarkably close outcome in 1963.

The hold that "The Chief," as Diefenbaker was affectionately called by so many, had on Canadians was not solely of his own making. I argue in this final chapter that much of the loyalty he retained, and of the "heroic" status he was often accorded, was evoked by the forces arrayed against him between 1961 and 1963 in the disputes over foreign and defence policy: the establishment circles of the country, US president John F. Kennedy, large swathes of Kennedy's Democratic administration, and the US media.

There was unprecedented direct intervention, both public and covert, in Canadian domestic politics by the White House, the US embassy in Ottawa, and the US media, which put forward a White House-induced "spin" on Canadian politics. Shortly before the campaign began, several senior Conservative ministers resigned. That these factors could not produce a Liberal majority victory speaks volumes about the sense of unease voters had with the Pearson Liberals and the broader issues in Canada-United States relations at the time. Progressive Conservative, Social Credit, and New Democrat support totalled almost 60 percent of votes cast. This is not, in and of itself, surprising in a multi-party political system. But, since two of these three parties were opposed to the acquisition of nuclear weapons and the other was divided on the issue,[7] it did point to a general unease, Nobel Peace Prize notwithstanding, about Diefenbaker's main opponent in the 1963 election and his policies.

In his usual compelling literary style, Charles Ritchie, our ambassador to Washington during that era, summed up the central problem of nuclear weapons. In his diary entry for 30 September 1962, Ritchie wrote:

The Canadian government has certainly made it abundantly plain that we are against nuclear arms as one is against sin, and the moral attitude is shared by the most sophisticated (Norman Robertson) and the least so among Canadians. It is exemplified in the figure of Howard Green. It is not only a moral attitude, but also hygienic; the two often go together in Canada. Fall-out is filthy in every sense of the word. This reaction, strong in many parts of the world, is particularly strong at home. It is from this source that our disarmament policy comes. That policy may not be rational but it is very Canadian. Don't forget that for much of our history we were protected by the British Navy and now we are protected by the United States' nuclear bomb. All this may be peculiar, it may be unjustifiable, it may be irrational, it may be irresponsible, but no political leader of any stamp is prepared to go to the Canadian people and tell them that they must have nuclear arms or store nuclear arms. This may change with a change of government; if so, gradually. This is a deep policy difference between us and the United States. At any rate, so long as the present government lasts, a) we will not fill the Bomarc gap; b) we don't want nuclear arms for the RCAF ourselves; c) we will not store nuclear weapons; d) we are against the resumption by the United States of nuclear tests. The United States wants all four of these from us. They are exasperated by our attitude, but so far they are holding their hand. It remains to be seen how long they will resist the temptation to bring pressure upon us of a kind that might bring about a change of government.[3]

A few months after this entry was written, the American attacks on Diefenbaker began in earnest. For example, no less a person than Arthur Schlesinger, senior advisor and speechwriter to the president, stopped in Vancouver on his way to Japan at the end of January 1963. Angered by Canada's principled maintenance of ties with Cuba and its sale of much-needed grain to the People's Republic of China, as well as its clear resistance to nuclear arms – all frustrating the Kennedy view of America's rights – Schlesinger blasted Diefenbaker's refusal to join the Organization of American States and his trade policies involving Cuba and China, "saying these rendered Canada an unreliable ally. Anything that helps Castro, he said, hurts the Western Alliance."[4]

One historian of this intense US political intervention, John Boyko, summarized the event in this way: "It was a blunt formal attack made doubly shocking by the fact that Schlesinger delivered it on Canadian soil. It is hard to imagine that he acted without Kennedy's knowledge or approval."[5] Setting aside the question of the Diefenbaker government's competence in executing its foreign policy, Canada was being attacked for having its own foreign policy at all rather than simply mirroring US geostrategic preferences. The affable, diplomatically skilled Ritchie, who had been astonished by the hostility towards Canada in the US capital ever since his arrival there, asked in his diary: "Do the Americans realize that our differences of outlook from them in international affairs make us more valuable to them than if we were mere satellites? I sometimes doubt it."[6]

The following are examples, but not an exhaustive list, of the Kennedy administration's interventions on behalf of Pearson and his Liberals to help defeat the Diefenbaker government. While the Americans' concerns were in some ways understandable, their interventions were nevertheless extraordinary.

- From early 1962 onwards, the US ambassador, Livingston Merchant, and his successor, Walton Butterworth, held clandestine briefings for Canadian journalists, with the aim of influencing them in favour of nuclear weapons.[7]
- In April 1962, Kennedy invited Pearson to a dinner for Nobel Prize winners at the White House. Pearson had a private, personal meeting with the president, and this meeting was revealed to the American and Canadian press. On the same occasion, Kennedy arranged for Pearson to receive an honorary doctorate from Boston College.[8]
- On 18 February 1963, *Newsweek* magazine (which was edited by a friend of Kennedy's) carried an extremely unflattering cover photo of Diefenbaker, along with a story that ridiculed the prime minister.

Then there was the remarkable visit to Canada in early January 1963 by US general Lauris Norstad, who had been the military commander at Supreme Headquarters, Allied Powers, Europe (SHAPE). After complimentary remarks from Norstad about the calibre of Canadian Forces serving with NATO in Germany came a battery of questions about nuclear weapons. Southam's Charles Lynch (primed, as he later admitted, by Merchant's briefings), asked: "Does it mean, sir, that if Canada does not accept nuclear weapons for their aeroplanes, she is not actually fulfilling her NATO commitments?" Norstad answered, "I believe that is right. She would be meeting it in force but not under the terms of the requirements that have been established by NATO ... We are depending upon Canada to produce some of the tactical atomic strike forces." As Lynch summed it up, "Norstad said in public what Merchant had been saying in private."[9]

Norstad's assertion – which, to be fair, came after a long series of questions and was not a formal statement – sparked a massively pro-Pearson and anti-Diefenbaker cascade of stories and editorials in the *Montreal Gazette* and the *Toronto Telegram* (both traditionally Conservative newspapers), plus a broadside of anti-Diefenbaker attacks from the Opposition benches in the House of Commons. Even the *Globe and Mail*, which had steadfastly opposed the acquisition of nuclear weapons by Canadian forces, swung around after the Norstad press conference.

With presidential pollster Harris reporting directly to the Liberals that about 54 percent of voters now supported acquisition of nuclear weapons, with Quebec coming in at 58 percent and Ontario at 70 percent, Pearson's general dislike of nuclear weapons came under the pressure of intense partisan self-interest. In a speech made on 12 January 1962, Pearson set aside his long-standing opposition to nuclear weapons. The die was now cast for the no-confidence motion in the minority Parliament elected in 1962 that would bring the Diefenbaker government down. As Pearson's biographer John English reported, Pearson himself admitted that the day he embraced nuclear weapons was "when I really became a politician."[10]

The Liberals' 41 percent of the popular vote, usually enough in our distorted first-part-the-post system to produce a majority, failed to do so in this case. The Tories hung on to ninety-five seats and just under 33 percent of the vote. That the Social Credit Party under Robert Thompson and the recently created and strongly anti-nuclear New Democratic Party, led by Tommy Douglas, together held just under 25 percent of the vote spoke to the indecision of the country as a whole. Pearson's minority victory would serve him well, and his subsequent service to Canada was of great significance and value. But, unlike King, Diefenbaker, and St. Laurent, he would never win a majority government.

In my early teens, I was mesmerized by Diefenbaker, being particularly impressed by his nationalist anti-nuclear stance and his Bill of Rights. Diefenbaker had come to tour the school I attended (United Talmud Torahs Hebrew School in west end Montreal) during the 1962 election campaign, and he had made an emotional speech about the Bill of Rights. During the 1963 election, I remembered the fear and angst as the air raid sirens rang out only half a block from our home during the Cuban Missile Crisis. It was easy to choose Diefenbaker's nationalism over the "pro-American" Pearson's willingness to accept nuclear weapons. At only thirteen years of age, I had no understanding of the factors that make for a successful foreign policy. My youthful enthusiasm for Diefenbaker's stance on nuclear weapons was not wrong. It was just seriously under-informed.

It would, of course, be a mistake to characterize Diefenbaker as purely a political martyr bravely defending a nuclear-free world and the sovereign rights of an independent Canadian foreign policy. His lack of cabinet management skills; his inability to build consensus with estimable senior ministers such as Douglas Harkness (national defence) and George Hees (trade and transport), whose resignations deeply wounded his administration; and his insensitivity to the need for prompt and active cooperation between Canadian and American forces during the Cuban Missile Crisis in the fall of 1962 all led to broad and justified dissent within his cabinet.

It was not that the successes of Diefenbaker's government were massively outweighed by its setbacks. True, there had been serious economic difficulties, including a run on the Canadian dollar, unemployment, and a quite unnecessary tussle with the governor of the Bank of Canada, James Coyne. But on the other side of the ledger were the Bill of Rights, increased old age pensions, de-racialization of immigration and citizenship policy, the first woman cabinet minister, the assurance of First Nations right to vote, and the very first appointment of a First Nations leader to the Senate, along with infrastructure projects like the Roads to Resources approach to development in the Canadian North. The problem was that the leader appeared erratic and unsteady in holding it all together. Over our history, the Liberal Party has been the default choice when there was an apparent Tory deficit in managerial competence. This factor worked in Pearson's favour, even among those who did not support his about-face on the nuclear issue.

As a young man and young Tory, I dismissed Peter C. Newman's *Renegade in Power: The Diefenbaker Years* as a rant that never even tried to find something constructive about Diefenbaker's record in office – a view I largely maintain. However, some of Newman's comments about Diefenbaker's shortcomings ring true. "The effectiveness of external policy," he wrote,

> depends ultimately on the health of a country's internal affairs, and it was the domestic crisis of confidence during the Diefenbaker Years that contributed most heavily to the tarnishing of the nation's image abroad. The carnage of the Coyne affair, the absence of clear fiscal and monetary policies, the government's shifty defence stand, and the mishandling of devaluation [of the dollar] affected Canadian prestige at least as much as the Prime Minister's combative behaviour.[11]

As for foreign policy itself, Newman quoted Peyton Lyon, a former diplomat and thoughtful analyst, whose major criticism was that the Diefenbaker government had "reversed the previous Canadian policy of seeking the maximum of diplomatic achievement with the minimum of publicity."[12] As the chapters in this volume so clearly underline, this need not have been the case. For example, if the government had undertaken a thorough study of defence issues early in its mandate and then formulated a consistent policy on nuclear weapons, there would never have been such rancorous and damaging public debates on the subject.

The core frustration in looking at the populist, progressive, and anti-establishment values that fuelled Diefenbaker's election victories is his failure to use all of these values to shape clear, effective foreign and defence policies. Half-baked initiatives and self-indulgent, over-the-top rhetoric consistently undermined even the most noble of policy purposes. Execution and competence matter. The Diefenbaker government's downfall was not a tragedy involving huge failure or calamitous collapse; rather, the tragedy lay in the unmet expectations shared by so many who came out to vote and make a new beginning in 1958.

NOTES

1 Denis Smith, *Rogue Tory: The Life and Legend of John G. Diefenbaker* (Toronto: Macfarlane Walter and Ross, 1995), 202.

2 The Social Credit leader, Robert Thompson, declared that he would accept nuclear weapons if a non-partisan parliamentary committee recommended doing so. However, the deputy leader, Réal Caouette, was strongly opposed to acquisition. See "Real Caouette: Will Battle Anyone Bringing in A-Arms," *Globe and Mail*, 4 March 1963.

3 Charles Ritchie, *Storm Signals: More Undiplomatic Diaries* (Toronto: Macmillan, 1983), 22.

4 Robert W. Reford, *Canada and Three Crises* (Toronto: Canadian Institute of International Affairs, 1968), 165.

5 John Boyko, *Cold Fire: Kennedy's Northern Front* (Toronto: Knopf Canada, 2016), 147–48.

6 Ritchie, *Storm Signals*, 2, 16.

7 Knowlton Nash, *Kennedy and Diefenbaker: Fear and Loathing across the Undefended Border* (Toronto: McClelland and Stewart, 1990), 146–47.

8 Jocelyn Maynard Ghent, "Canadian-American Relations and the Nuclear Weapons Controversy, 1958–1963" (PhD diss., University of Illinois at Urbana-Champaign, 1976), 132, 133.

9 Charles Lynch, *You Can't Print THAT! Memoirs of a Political Voyeur* (Edmonton: Hurtig, 1983), 150; Nash, *Kennedy and Diefenbaker*, 223. Nash states that Lynch's question was the first; in fact, it was the seventh. For a fuller account, see Peyton V. Lyon, *Canada in World Affairs, 1961–1963* (Toronto: Oxford University Press, 1968), 130–37.

10 John English, *The Worldly Years: The Life of Lester Pearson*, vol. 2 (Toronto: Knopf Canada, 1992), 262. Pearson made this admission in a 1972 interview with Denis Smith.

11 Peter C. Newman, *Renegade in Power: The Diefenbaker Years* (Toronto: McClelland and Stewart, 1963), 249–50.

12 Ibid., 252.

Conclusion

RYAN M. TOUHEY

No other Canadian prime minister is equated with abject failure in the conduct of foreign relations in quite the same way as John G. Diefenbaker. In the long history of Canadian diplomacy, the Diefenbaker era is regarded as a troubled time, particularly when juxtaposed against the so-called "golden era" of Canadian foreign policy in the 1940s and early 1950s. Studies of Diefenbaker's diplomacy have focused on his role in the collapse of Canada-US relations during the second half of his mandate and the simultaneous tensions in Canada-UK relations. A frequent point of emphasis is the tense, even sulphurous, relationship between Diefenbaker and American president John F. Kennedy. The Diefenbaker-Kennedy relationship is almost operatic in its arc, characterized by loathing, distrust, and allegations of political impropriety. Many historians have found Diefenbaker wanting as a statesman and ill-suited for diplomacy. Jack Granatstein harshly concluded his study of the Diefenbaker-Pearson era by dismissing the Progressive Conservative leader and his foreign policy as "aberrations."[1] Robert Bothwell contended that "Diefenbaker was not a diplomatic asset."[2]

However, as this book makes clear, it is simply not enough to view this period solely through the lenses of diplomatic decline and personal conflict. The Diefenbaker government entered office during a period of enormous challenge that bedeviled all Western governments. Public fear of nuclear Armageddon was soaring and the rapid pace of decolonization was transforming Canada's world, especially in the Commonwealth and at the United Nations. Pressing American defence demands in response to a confident and technologically ascendant Soviet Union also unnerved Canadians as nationalists questioned to what extent Canada remained an independent nation. Most of the authors in this collection demonstrate that Diefenbaker's response to these challenges was more nuanced and successful than his critics have acknowledged. Diefenbaker came to power with a unique but untested worldview. He had condemned Canada's position during Suez but once elected he also held steadfast to many of the pillars of Liberal foreign policy. He could be both contradictory and pragmatic, as this collection suggests. While some of its chapters acknowledge that his personal traits and poor decision making affected his statecraft, many of them use new sources to pose new questions, reframing how historians consider Diefenbaker's foreign relations. This is especially true of his government's diplomacy in Asia, Latin America, and the Commonwealth, and in his relationships with such prominent cabinet ministers as Ellen Fairclough, Sidney Smith, and Howard Green.

A number of key themes emerge from this collection that better inform and shape our understanding of this era in Canadian foreign relations. First, several contributors demonstrate that Diefenbaker, despite his flaws, was indeed capable of successful diplomacy. Second, the collection reminds us that historians need to acknowledge the tumult of the period, recognizing that there is greater continuity between the policies of Liberal prime minister Louis St. Laurent and Diefenbaker than generally understood. Third, and a methodological point, these chapters illustrate the importance of using foreign archival sources and the international literature to interrogate the Diefenbaker era.

Obviously, new questions and new sources will not eliminate the controversy that surrounds Diefenbaker and his diplomacy. For instance, in their assessments of Diefenbaker's approaches to the Commonwealth, Francine McKenzie and Norman Hillmer utilize British documents to show that Diefenbaker's efforts to revitalize a flagging Commonwealth were greeted with hope and optimism in London. Yet these two scholars arrive at different conclusions about Diefenbaker's success. According to McKenzie, Diefenbaker's Commonwealth foreign policy, while not without fault, broadened the scope of Canadian foreign policy towards transforming the white Commonwealth into a multiracial body. In Hillmer's view, however, Anglo-Canadian relations suffered significantly due to Diefenbaker's combative stance towards

Britain's tilt towards the European Economic Community – earning the enmity of British prime minister Harold Macmillan – and due to his unwillingness to follow London's lead in reconciling apartheid South Africa with the Commonwealth.

Continental relations between Canada and the United States during the Diefenbaker period have received considerable attention from Canadian historians. Anti-Americanism lurked darkly below Diefenbaker's surface – or so many standard interpretations of the early period from 1957 to 1960 suggest – only to be unleashed from 1960 to 1963 as bilateral defence tensions escalated. Janice Cavell's chapter questions the notion that a suspicious Diefenbaker was eager to exploit anti-American sentiment. Rather, she suggests that the aftermath of the Suez Crisis prompted Canadians to ask if the continental relationship had become too integrated for their comfort. For much of the media and general public, the Liberals appeared too close, too comfortable with the status quo, and too happy to travel the "American Road." By contrast, Diefenbaker in his election campaigns of 1957 and 1958 championed a "Northern Vision" that offered a distinct path for Canadian nationalists to follow. And follow the Canadian public did. In Cavell's reading, Diefenbaker did not cause or inflame anti-Americanism, though his political fortunes benefited from the mounting anti-continentalist zeitgeist.

Like Cavell, Greg Donaghy looks at the early years of the Canada-US relationship. US president Dwight Eisenhower managed Diefenbaker's sensitive nature with aplomb, treating his colleague with mutual respect and courtesy. Using Canada's role during the 1958 Lebanon Crisis as a case study, Donaghy reveals that Diefenbaker put just as much effort into maintaining a harmonious relationship with the American president, showing, like McKenzie, that the Canadian was indeed capable of successful personal diplomacy. This is an important insight that challenges the caricature of Diefenbaker as simply being "played" by the courtly Eisenhower from 1957 to 1960.[3]

As Canada-US tensions mounted during the Kennedy years, much of the blame has been placed on Diefenbaker. Stephen Azzi's chapter, however, will surely force historians to revisit long-held conclusions that Kennedy acted reasonably towards his Canadian counterpart, while Diefenbaker proved stubborn, petulant, and irrational. Azzi's selection of sources and methodology reflects many of the new historiographical trends in the writing of Canadian international history. Drawing on an array of US archival sources and recent American literature, Azzi incorporates the role of gender into his analysis to challenge this conventional account. Kennedy and his advisors looked upon foreign policy through a masculine lens whereby toughness and vigour were vital characteristics. They regarded men like Diefenbaker, who seemed to lack those traits, as childish, irrational, and weak. As a result, as Azzi makes clear, Kennedy's White House was too quick to dismiss Ottawa's concerns about inadequate consultation on bilateral defence matters.

Similarly, Kennedy's administration believed that immaturity partly explained Diefenbaker's indecision on accepting US Bomarc nuclear missiles in Canada. The Bomarc episode has widely been considered a classic case of Diefenbaker working at cross purposes with his cabinet and his officials, unsure of his government's defence commitments and unable to make a decision. Isabel Campbell and Nicole Marion disagree. Campbell shows that Diefenbaker's concerns reflected both his personality and his understanding that shifting debates on nuclear strategy and military thinking meant that Bomarc missiles might have a detrimental impact on Canadian security. This Diefenbaker is not a vacillating politician but a prime minister who put much consideration into the value of nuclear weapons for national defence.

Nicole Marion challenges recent charges that Diefenbaker hesitated to obtain nuclear weapons for cheap political purposes, seeking votes from such nuclear disarmament groups as the Voice of Women. Marion insists that public opinion is only one of many reasons that explain Diefenbaker's approach towards nuclear weapons. In her estimation, the prime minister shrewdly used public opinion, and even appeared to encourage disarmament groups, to justify his guarded approach to making a decision on the file, worried that a hasty decision could suborn Canadian sovereignty. Like Campbell, Marion provides a complex picture of a prime minister who should not be caricatured as a bumbler who didn't know his own mind. In sum, Azzi, Campbell, and Marion insist that scholars of Canada-US relations reconsider their long-held assumptions about this period.

Diefenbaker's approach towards the developing worlds of Africa, Latin America, and Asia also reveals a more complex and practical side to his diplomacy. Accelerating decolonization in the late 1950s presented unexpected opportunities and challenges to the Diefenbaker government. From 1957 to 1960, the number of newly independent countries joining the UN soared. In 1960 alone, seventeen former African and Asian colonies were granted membership. While the UN General Assembly became more representative, it was also more factionalized. Within a few short years the West had lost its ability to control the agenda in New York, where denunciations of Western imperialism forced many NATO allies onto the defensive. Though an unabashed Cold Warrior who was deeply suspicious of the non-aligned tendencies of the postcolonial Global South, Diefenbaker hoped Canada could bridge the divide between the West and its former colonies lest Moscow gain footholds in Africa and Asia. While more clearly needs to be done to fully understand Canada's role, both bilaterally and multilaterally at the UN, the Commonwealth, and in NATO, as this collection demonstrates, Diefenbaker's role in addressing decolonization and its implications is one of his underappreciated legacies.

Asa McKercher reminds us that Diefenbaker and his foreign ministers paid more attention to the economic and geopolitical potential of Latin America than any previous Canadian government. Diefenbaker lamented the fact that Canada had not done enough to build links with Latin America, and he became the first prime minister to visit the region when he travelled to Mexico in 1960. Both foreign ministers, Sidney Smith and Howard Green, took prolonged tours of South America. Diefenbaker's government established a Latin American division in the Department of External Affairs to strengthen Canadian capacity to participate in regional affairs. When Cold War tensions increased throughout Latin America following the Cuban revolution, Diefenbaker's confidence gave way to measured caution as he halted diplomatic expansion even as doing so limited trade opportunities. McKercher argues that Diefenbaker was not wavering; rather, the prime minister concluded that Canadian interests were not well served by becoming embroiled in a potential Cold War battleground.

Africa, too, was on the periphery of Canadian interests when Diefenbaker came to power in 1957. Over the next six years, argues Kevin Spooner, Diefenbaker's government laid the diplomatic foundations for future Canadian engagement with the giant, impoverished continent. Decolonization prompted Ottawa to confront the rapid changes sweeping across Africa. Missions were opened in newly independent Ghana and Nigeria, and when Belgium abandoned the Congo to civil war, Diefenbaker dutifully sent Canadian peacekeepers. Apartheid South Africa was even more important. A champion of civil rights at home, Diefenbaker was uncertain if the Commonwealth could maintain ties with a nation that denied basic rights to the majority of its citizens on the basis of race. Much to the chagrin of London

and Pretoria, Canada stood with the Commonwealth's non-white majority to oppose South Africa's continued membership. Although Diefenbaker
won plaudits from the new Commonwealth states, Norman Hillmer cites
the episode as one more self-inflicted blow to his cherished policy of rebuilding the Commonwealth. Nonetheless, it had to be done, and Diefenbaker's
handling of the complex files linked to decolonization, peacekeeping, and
racial politics established the framework for Canada's African diplomacy for
the next two decades.

Asia, too, attracted significant attention from Diefenbaker and his
government. Jill Campbell-Miller, Michael Carroll, and Greg Donaghy begin their chapter on this region with an analysis of Diefenbaker's ground-
breaking wheat sales to China, emphasizing the domestic political and
economic imperatives behind these sales. Even as Diefenbaker delicately
pursued trade opportunities in Communist China, his antipathy for communism tilted Canada away from favoured Liberal allies, India and Indonesia, and towards Pakistan and Malaya, countries with strong pro-Western
sympathies. Clearly, as this chapter demonstrates, Diefenbaker was willing
to chart his own path in Asia.

There were careful limits to Diefenbaker's independent policy-making.
On the complicated Canadian role on the International Control Commission in war-torn Indochina, Campbell-Miller, Carroll, and Donaghy
highlight Diefenbaker's careful regard for established Western Cold War
interests and illustrates the diplomatic continuity that existed between the
St. Laurent and Diefenbaker governments. Diefenbaker's Progressive Conservative government largely pursued the ICC policies established by
St. Laurent, leaving the details in the safe hands of the professional diplomats at External Affairs. The authors challenge the view that Diefenbaker
distrusted the so-called "Pearsonalities," suggesting instead that he was willing to defer to his officials on complex files.

Historians have rarely assessed the influence of Diefenbaker's cabinet
ministers with regard to sculpting foreign policy. Chapters by Michael Stevenson and Robert Vineberg help correct this oversight. Stevenson notes
that much of the existing literature emphasizes the pre-eminent role Diefenbaker played in foreign affairs, thereby marginalizing the roles of his two
SSEAs, Sidney Smith and Howard Green. Stevenson admits that the politically inexperienced Smith did not have a close relationship with his prime
minister and tended to stay in his shadow, but he argues that Smith played
a constructive policy role when the opportunity arose. Green, a respected
and capable politician, who shared a personal connection with Diefenbaker,

was more important. He possessed a distinct and confident worldview that permitted him to exercise a "disproportionate influence" on government policy.

Ellen Fairclough has remained even more absent in discussions of Diefenbaker and foreign affairs. Little scholarly literature tackles Fairclough, the first female cabinet minister in Canadian history. Vineberg's important chapter begins to remedy this. As minister of immigration and citizenship, it argues, Fairclough modernized Canada's immigration regulations, removing barriers and quotas affecting non-white immigration that irked many newly independent Commonwealth states in Africa, Asia, and the Caribbean. Like Green, Fairclough made her mark on her department. Consideration of these cabinet ministers reminds us of the shortcomings of situating Diefenbaker as the sole determining figure who affected the practice and conduct of foreign affairs from 1957 to 1963.

John Diefenbaker and his foreign policy legacy provoke polarizing perspectives and will continue to do so. Diefenbaker's cautious temperament, strong personality, and deep longing for a Britain that was still "Great" seriously compromised his statecraft. However, it is simply not good enough to treat the era as an aberration in Canada's liberal internationalist tradition dominated by an unhinged leader who was out of his depth. It is also a mistake to extrapolate the poor state of triangular relations between Diefenbaker's Ottawa, Macmillan's London, and Kennedy's Washington onto Canadian foreign policy writ large for the entire 1957–63 period. Doing so ignores new questions around decolonization, geography, gender, and race, themes important to the history of Canada's foreign policy at this time.

Rather, it is vital to acknowledge, as this collection does, that Diefenbaker's era dovetailed with profound global changes that tested the international order. Diefenbaker, a leader with little foreign policy experience, contended with the multiracial transformation of the Commonwealth, the expansion of the UN, and the rise of the European Economic Community amid mounting global fears of nuclear crisis and fresh conflict across the developing world from Africa to the Caribbean to Indochina. In navigating through these challenges, Diefenbaker's foreign policy was more thoughtful and shrewd on foreign affairs than has been acknowledged. Rather than simply dismissing him as a "Rogue Tory" on the world stage, this collection clearly emphasizes the need for all students of Canadian foreign relations to push beyond the conventional and to reassess John Diefenbaker's record with fresh eyes.

NOTES

1 J.L. Granatstein, *Canada 1957–1967: The Years of Uncertainty and Innovation* (Toronto: McClelland and Stewart, 1986), 301.

2 Robert Bothwell, *Alliance and Illusion: Canada and the World, 1945–1984* (Vancouver: UBC Press, 2007), 136.

3 J.L. Granatstein, *Yankee Go Home? Canadians and Anti-Americanism* (Toronto: HarperCollins, 1996), 126.

Contributors

Stephen Azzi is an associate professor and the director of the Clayton H. Riddell Graduate Program in Political Management, Carleton University.

Isabel Campbell is a historian working in the Directorate of History and Heritage, Department of National Defence.

Jill Campbell-Miller is a postdoctoral fellow at the Gorsebrook Research Institute, St. Mary's University.

Michael Carroll is an associate professor of history at Grant McEwan University.

Greg Donaghy is head of the Historical Section, Global Affairs Canada.

Norman Hillmer is Chancellor's professor of history and international affairs at Carleton University.

Nicole Marion received her PhD from Carleton University in 2017.

Francine McKenzie is a professor of history at Western University.

Asa McKercher is an assistant professor of history at the Royal Military College of Canada.

Hugh Segal is a former member of the Senate of Canada and principal of Massey College.

Kevin A. Spooner is an associate professor of North American studies and history at Wilfrid Laurier University.

Michael D. Stevenson is an associate professor of history and interdisciplinary studies at Lakehead University (Orillia campus).

Robert Vineberg, formerly a senior civil servant, is an independent scholar.

Index

Note: Abbreviations used in index follow the list on page x.

Aberhart, William, 272
Abbott, Douglas, 125
Acheson, Dean, 109
Adenauer, Konrad, 28
Africa, 6–7, 186–205, 282–84; Canada's
  early relations with, 187–90;
  communist threat in, 7, 186, 194–97,
  199, 200–3, 205, 283; Congo Crisis
  in, 7, 187, 199–204, 205, 283;
  decolonization in, 173, 194–99;
  French-speaking nations of, 194–95,
  197–99. *See also entry below;*
  decolonization, in Africa; *specific*
  countries
Afro-Asian countries, 37, 203, 239; and
  Commonwealth, 33, 51–52; and
  Congo Crisis, 202–4; and non-
  aligned movement, 30, 188, 202, 218,
  283; and South Africa, 8, 38, 56, 59,
  190–94, 204–5; at UN, 97, 198
Air America, 221
Aitken, Margaret, 229
Algeria, 194–95, 197–98, 199
All-African Peoples' Congress, 196

Allard, Hector, 171
Alliance for Progress, 168, 176, 177,
  178–79
Aluminum Limited, 187
Anderson, Allan, 171
Anglican Church of Canada, 239
Anglo-American relations. *See* British-
  US collaboration/cooperation
Anglo-Canadian relations. *See* British-
  Canadian issues/irritants; United
  Kingdom
anti-Americanism: and Canadian
  nationalism, 69–71, 82*n*16, 87, 276;
  of Diefenbaker, 3, 30–31, 39, 77, 80,
  85, 155, 281; Green as suspected of,
  256, 257–58; and nuclear
  disarmament issue, 145, 155; in
  Pearson years, 4, 16; and Suez
  Crisis, 5–6, 8, 67–80, 281. *See also*
  Suez Crisis, anti-Americanism
  following
apartheid. *See* South African apartheid
Arden-Clarke, Charles, 195
Argentina, 167, 173, 177, 178, 179

Armstrong, Willis C., 106, 111,
    112–13, 114
Asia, 6–7, 209–22, 282–83, 284;
    Canada-US tensions over, 108, 111,
    218–22; communist threat in, 7,
    29–32, 38, 40, 88, 168, 194, 213–16,
    217, 219, 220–21, 283; Diefenbaker's
    tour through, 6, 25–40; immigrants
    from, 230, 235, 241–42, 285; and
    non-aligned movement, 30, 218,
    283. *See also* Afro-Asian countries;
    specific countries
Australia, 155, 211; Diefenbaker's visit
    to, 6, 26, 27, 28, 29, 31, 34, 37;
    immigration to, 34, 59, 239, 243;
    and South Africa, 38, 54, 193
Avro CF-105 Arrow, 9–10, 126–27

Baird, John, 85
Ball, George, 111
ballistic missiles: in Cuba, 153;
    intercontinental, 9, 10, 18*n*13,
    125–26; Polaris, 10, 124, 130–32,
    135–36, 137, 154
Bandaranaike, S.W.R.D., 31, 32,
    42*n*41, 216
Bandung Conference (1955), 30
Barnet, Richard J., 110
Bartlett, Charles, 107
Batista, Fulgencio, 171
Bay of Pigs (Cuba), US invasion of, 107,
    176–77
Beaulieu, Paul, 89, 91–92
Belgian Congo, 199. *See also* Congo,
    Republic of the; Congo Crisis
Bennett, W.A.C., 261–62
Berlin: division of (Berlin Wall), 12, 129,
    133–34, 136, 150, 254–55
Betancourt, Romulo, 175
Bikini Atoll: US nuclear testing at,
    151–52
Bissett, J.B. (Joe), 232–33, 235, 236,
    237–38, 241, 244*n*38
Bolivia, 175, 184*n*43
Bomarc missiles, 123–37; conventional
    warhead option for, 132, 138*n*17;

internal wrangling over, 130–32;
    nuclear warheads for, 9–10, 12, 14,
    112, 126–27, 132–37, 145–46,
    155–56, 282; problems of, 18*n*3,
    126, 130, 155–56; as superseded by
    Polaris missiles, 10, 124, 130–32,
    135; US responses to decision-
    making on, 111–15, 133–37, 258,
    274, 282. *See also* defence policy, in
    nuclear era; nuclear weapons;
    specific weapons and aircraft
Borden, Robert, 78
Bothwell, Robert, 15, 86, 250, 279
Boun Oum, Prince of Laos, 217
Bow, Brian, 144
Bower, Richard, 179
Boyko, John, 274
Bradlee, Ben, 113
Brazil, 167, 169, 170, 171–72, 174, 177, 179
Bridle, Paul, 18*n*7, 219, 221
Britain. *See* United Kingdom
British-Canadian issues/irritants:
    Canadian trade diversion proposal,
    34, 49–50; proposed EEC free trade
    area, 47, 48, 50–51, 57; South
    Africa, 53–57, 59, 191–92, 281,
    283–84; Suez Crisis, 5–6, 69–70,
    72–76; UK's application to join
    EEC, 8, 38, 57–58, 59, 280–81; UK's
    nuclear agreement with US, 124,
    135–36, 137, 154
British-US collaboration/cooperation:
    Canada's exclusion from, 58, 87; on
    joint control of nuclear weapons,
    147–48; in Middle East/Lebanon
    Crisis, 89–97; in opposing pan-
    Arab nationalism, 88–90; on
    Polaris missiles, 124, 135–36,
    137, 154
Bryce, Robert B.: and nuclear weapons
    issue, 130, 131, 132; on Smith, 251;
    on South Africa, 190–91, 192, 193;
    views on immigration reform,
    236–37
Bull, Odd, 91
Bundy, McGeorge, 107, 114, 116*n*6

Burns, E.L.M.: as advisor to Green, 128–29, 132; as UNEF commander, 73, 74, 199
Butterworth, W. Walton (Walt), 103, 104, 106, 108, 113, 114, 155, 275

Cabinet Defence Committee (CDC), 129, 130
Cadieux, Marcel, 5, 200–1, 252
Callan, Les, 76
Cambodia, 217
Campbell, Hugh, 129
Campbell, Norman, 73
Campbell, Ross, 89
Canada-US Ministerial Joint Committee on Defence, 1960 meeting of (Montebello, QC), 11–12, 174–75
Canadian Bill of Rights, 53, 193, 227, 238, 276, 277
Canadian Committee for the Control of Radiation Hazards (CCCRH), 146, 151–52
Canadian Peace Congress (CPC), 146, 155
Canadian Welfare Council, 233
Caouette, Réal, 278*n*2
Castro, Fidel, 11–12, 14, 111, 174–79, 274; Cuban revolution led by, 167–68, 171; and communism, 171, 174, 176, 178–79; as fomenting regional unrest/instability, 171, 178. *See also* Cuba; Cuban Missile Crisis
Central Intelligence Agency (CIA), 88, 110, 221
Ceylon, 230; Diefenbaker's visit to, 6, 27, 28, 31, 42*n*41, 216
Chamoun, Camille, 88–93, 253
Chiefs of Staff Committee, 127, 130, 132
Chile, 173, 179
China, People's Republic of (PRC): as communist threat, 7, 29, 30, 35, 196; immigration from, 230, 241–42; and Laos, 218; recognition of, 30–31, 209, 210–12; US concerns over Canadian trade with, 79, 93, 210–13, 274; wheat sales to, 7, 209–13, 222, 274, 284

Chinese Immigration Act (1923): repeal of, 230
Churchill, Gordon, 154, 210, 216
Churchill, Winston, 86
Citizenship and Immigration, Department of, 227, 228, 230, 231, 232, 234. *See also* Fairclough, Ellen, *and entry following*; immigration policy, Fairclough's reforms to
Cohen, Andrew, 85
Cohen, Maxwell, 67–68, 69–70, 75
Cold War. *See* communism, Cold War against
Coldwell, M.J., 272
Colombia, 167, 179
Colombo Plan, 36–37, 209, 253; and sale of Canadian wheat/flour, 36, 51–52, 215–17
Columbia River: hydroelectric development of, 261–62
Combined Universities Campaign for Nuclear Disarmament (CUCND), 146
Commonwealth of Nations: Colombo Plan of, 36–37, 51–52, 209, 215–17, 253; Diefenbaker's vision for, 26, 28–29, 37–39, 52; Diefenbaker's tour of, 6, 25–40, 169, 186, 280; Macmillan's turning away from, 7–8, 35, 38, 45, 47–48, 52–53, 57–59, 280–81; and UK's application to join EEC, 7–8, 35, 38, 45, 47–48, 52–53, 57–59, 280–81. *See also* Africa; Afro-Asian countries; Asia; British-Canadian issues/irritants; decolonization, *and entry following*; South Africa, *and entry following*; Suez Crisis, *and entry following*; United Kingdom
Commonwealth Scholarship and Fellowship Plan, 51, 254
Commonwealth tour by Diefenbaker, 6, 25–40, 169, 186, 280; British attitudes toward, 27; DEA anxieties about, 28; failings of, 26, 30, 33–34, 35–36, 39; itinerary of, 26–29;

press coverage of, 26, 35, 37;
speeches given on, 26, 28, 25, 52.
See also entry below
Commonwealth tour by Diefenbaker,
issues arising during: communist
threat, 29–32, 38, 40, 213–16;
decolonization, 32, 40, 198–99;
improvement in post-Suez Crisis
relations, 25, 27; racial diversity/
equality, 32–34, 38, 39–40;
recognition of PRC, 30–31, 211;
trade promotion, 35–36, 38; trade
tied to aid, 36–37
Commonwealth Trade and Economic
Conference (1958), 253
communism, Cold War against, 8, 16,
36–37, 38, 70, 104, 110, 260; in
Africa, 7, 186, 194–97, 199, 200–3,
205, 283; in Asia, 7, 29–32, 38, 40,
88, 168, 194, 213–16, 217, 219, 220–21,
283; in Berlin, 12, 129, 133–34, 136,
150, 254–55; Commonwealth and,
29–32, 46–47, 52; in Cuba/Latin
America, 167–68, 171, 174–80; in
Middle East, 71–72, 75, 87–97; in
PRC, 7, 29, 30, 35, 196. *See also*
Cuban Missile Crisis; Lebanon
Crisis; Suez Crisis; USSR; Vietnam,
ICC's work in
Congo, Republic of the, 199; Belgian
military bases in, 199, 200;
communist threat in, 200–3
Congo Crisis, 7, 187, 199–204; and
Canada-Belgium relations, 200–2;
and Canada's view of Lumumba,
201–3; Canadian peacekeeping in,
199–204, 205, 283; and violence in
Katanga, 203–4
Conrad, Margaret, 227, 228, 230
conventional forces/weapons, 123–36;
flexibility of, 124, 128–29, 134, 136;
Kennedy and McNamara on, 12,
124, 129, 133–34, 135, 136, 150;
NATO's changing views of, 123,
125, 127–30, 131–32, 135, 150; as
opposed by National Defence staff,

10, 123–24, 126–27, 129–32, 134,
136, 140*n*46; as supported by DEA,
124, 127–29, 132, 136. *See also*
defence policy, in nuclear era;
nuclear weapons
Corbett, David, 227, 243
Costa Rica, 171, 173, 175
Costigliola, Frank, 108
Cottrell, Sterling, 221
Coyne, James, 277
Cuba, 7, 16, 111; Castro's revolution in,
167–68, 171; as communist threat,
168, 171, 173, 174, 176–80, 274; and
OAS, 178; US military blockade of,
153; US-sponsored invasion of,
107, 176–77; US trade embargo
against, 11–12, 174–75. *See also
entry below*
Cuban Missile Crisis, 98, 134, 153–54,
186, 263, 276–77; and Diefenbaker's
criticism/non-support of US, 38, 85,
109; and lack of US consultation
with Canada, 14, 108–9, 153
Cumming-Bruce, F.E., 27
Cuordileone, Kyle, 110

Davey, Keith, 273
Davidson, George, 228, 233, 237–38,
241, 244*n*42
Dean, Robert, 110
decolonization, 5, 285; and Arab
nationalism, 90; and Canada's
immigration policy, 7, 227–28, 229;
and Commonwealth/UN, 6, 32, 52,
187–97, 279–80, 282–84; and
expansion of Canadian diplomatic
missions, 173, 283. *See also entry
below*
decolonization, African, 173, 194–99;
and Canada's relations with NATO
allies, 198–204; and Commonwealth,
52, 187–88, 194–97, 283–84; and
communist threat, 186, 194–97, 199,
201, 202–3, 205; in French-speaking
nations, 194–95, 197–99; St. Laurent
government and, 188–89, 194, 204

defence policy, in nuclear era, 123–37;
Bomarc missile controversy and,
9–10, 12, 14, 112, 126–27, 132–37,
145–46, 155–56, 282; massive
retaliation strategy and, 123–24,
125, 129; NORAD program and, 9,
15, 145, 259–60; Soviet threats/
technology and, 9, 12, 125–36.
See also Bomarc missiles;
conventional forces/weapons;
nuclear disarmament, *and entry
following*; nuclear weapons
Dexter, Grant, 76
Diefenbaker, Elmer, 28, 151
Diefenbaker, John G., 3–17, 271–85;
anti-Americanism of, 3, 30–31, 39,
77, 80, 85, 155, 281; becomes
Progressive Conservative leader, 76,
272; and Bill of Rights, 53, 193, 227,
238, 276, 277; character of, 4, 12,
42*n*41, 54, 103, 144–45, 153, 276–77,
281; Commonwealth tour of, 6,
25–40, 280; and Eisenhower, 8–9,
12, 73, 80, 85–98, 201, 281; election
defeat of (1963), 3, 4, 124, 144, 155,
242, 262, 264, 271–78; foreign
ministers of, 249–65, 284–85; and
Kennedy, 12–13, 18*n*6, 105–6, 107,
108–9, 110–12, 117*n*15, 133–34, 144,
150–53, 154; and Macmillan, 18*n*6,
25, 27, 47–48, 50, 54–55, 58–59;
majority government of (1958), 3,
271, 272–73; minority governments
of (1957, 1962), 3, 13, 78; "Northern
Vision" of, 70, 78–80, 281;
scholarship on, 14–17, 249, 279.
See also specific topics; foreign
policy, in Diefenbaker era
Diefenbaker, Olive, 28, 148, 258
Dilks, David, 48
Dillon, Douglas, 213
disarmament, nuclear. *See* nuclear
disarmament, *and entry following*
Dominican Republic, 171, 175, 179
Donaghy, Greg, 250
Douglas, T.C. (Tommy), 272, 276

Douville, Bruce, 152
Drew, George, 229, 252, 271
Duke, Angier Biddle, 111
Dulles, John Foster, 86, 211; and
Lebanon Crisis, 88–89, 92, 95–97;
and Suez Crisis, 68, 71–72
Dupuy, Pierre, 189–90, 194, 198

Ecuador, 175, 178–79
Eden, Anthony, 48, 71–73
Egypt: and Lebanon Crisis, 88, 90, 91,
92, 253; and Suez Crisis, 8, 46,
71–76
Eisenhower, Dwight D.: and PRC, 30–31,
210–12; and Congo aid request,
201–2; and Cuba, 11–12, 174–75;
Diefenbaker's relationship with,
8–9, 12, 73, 80, 85–98, 201, 281;
and Green's scuttling of planned
NORAD test, 259–60; and
Lebanon Crisis, 87–98, 281; and
nuclear weapons issue, 86–87,
129–30, 131; and summit with
Khrushchev, 95–96. *See also*
Lebanon Crisis
election campaigns: in 1957, 6, 47, 69,
77–78, 229, 272; in 1958, 69–70,
78–79; in 1962, 13, 58, 152, 241–42,
258–59; in 1963, 3, 19*n*26, 113–14,
155–56, 264, 271, 273, 276
Elizabeth II, 45, 46, 59
Emerson, Gloria, 107
Engen, Hans, 97
English, John, 259, 276
European Economic Community (EEC),
35; 285; proposed free trade area
with, 47, 48, 50–51, 57; UK's
application to join, 8, 38, 57–58, 59,
280–81
External Affairs, Department of (DEA),
15–16, 26–28, 228, 249–50; and
Africa, 187–89, 196–97, 198, 200–3,
204, 283; and Asia, 211–12, 215–16,
218–22, 284; Diefenbaker as
temporary minister of, 9, 27, 250;
external aid office of, 261; and Latin

America, 171, 173–74, 175, 177,
178–79, 228, 261, 280, 283; and
Middle East, 89–90; and nuclear
disarmament, 144–49; and split
with National Defence on nuclear
weapons, 10, 123–36; "Pearsonalities"
in, 255, 258, 284. *See also* Green,
Howard; Smith, Sidney

Fairclough, Ellen: early family life/
career of, 229; election of/work as
labour critic, 227, 228, 229; as first
woman cabinet minister, 227, 229–30,
277; and immigration portfolio,
230–42; later change of portfolio/
election defeat of, 242. *See also
entry below*
Fairclough, Ellen, as immigration
minister, 227–43; attempt of, to
amend regulation affecting Italian
immigrants, 230–32, 234; Bissett's
recollections of, 232–33, 235, 236,
237–38, 241; Bryce vs, 236–37;
cabinet's responses to work of,
231–41, 243; and Canada's
discriminatory immigration policy,
227–28, 230, 240, 241, 285; and
Chinese immigration fraud, 241–42;
and Davidson as deputy minister,
228, 233, 237–38, 241; development
of non-discriminatory policy by, 7,
233–41, 285; Diefenbaker and, 7,
230, 239–40, 241–42, 280; and
emphasis on education/skills, 230–31,
238, 240; and Fortier as deputy
minister, 232–33, 235, 236; Green
vs, 238–39; legacy of, 243;
predecessors of, 228, 231–32, 234–35;
and recognition of post-colonial
world, 228, 239, 241, 242–43
Fairclough, Gordon, 229
Feinberg, Abraham, 148
Fleming, Donald, 49, 51, 111, 249, 255–56,
258; and Smith, 18n14, 216, 251,
252, 255
Ford, Robert, 89, 167, 170

Ford Motor Company of Canada,
79, 210
Foreign Assets Control (FAC)
regulations (US), 79, 210–13
foreign ministers. *See* Green, Howard;
Pearson, Lester; Smith, Sidney
foreign policy, in Diefenbaker era, 3–17,
271–85; on Africa, 6–7, 186–205,
282–84; on Asia, 6–7, 209–22,
282–83, 284; Commonwealth
relations and, 6, 25–40, 280;
continuity of, with Liberals' policy,
16–17, 188–89, 204, 280, 284; on
Cuba/Latin America, 7, 11–12, 14,
167–80, 283; Eisenhower
administration and, 8–9, 11–12,
85–98, 281; with Green as minister,
10–11, 255–65, 284–85; historians
on, 14–17; immigration reforms
and, 7, 227–43, 285; Kennedy
administration and, 3–4, 8, 12–14,
15, 103–15, 273–76, 281–82; vs
Liberal "golden age," 4, 5–6, 16,
25–26, 169, 250, 279; on nuclear
defence, 9–10, 12–14, 15, 123–37,
282; on nuclear disarmament,
10–11, 143–57, 282; post-Suez
anti-Americanism and, 3, 5–6, 8,
67–80, 281; with Smith as minister,
10–11, 217, 228, 250–55, 264–65,
280, 284–85; on South Africa, 8,
53–57, 190–93, 204–5; UK and, 7,
45–59, 280–81. *See also specific
topics;* communism, Cold War
against
Forrestal, Michael, 222
Forsyth-Smith, C.M., 210
Fortier, Laval, 232–33, 235, 236
Foulkes, Charles, 125, 130
Frondizi, Arturo, 173, 177, 179
Fulton, E. Davie, 228, 234–35

Galbraith, John Kenneth, 107–8
Garner, Lord (Joseph John Saville
Garner), 26, 35, 39, 46, 49–51,
55–56, 57, 59

Gaulle, Charles de, 28, 58, 86, 109, 198
Ghana, 33, 52, 188, 194–97, 239, 283
Ghent, Jocelyn Maynard, 15
Gill, Evan, 195–97
Gizenga, Antoine, 203
Gladstone, James, 34
Glazebrook, George, 195–96
Gordon, Charles, 187
Gordon, Donald, 239–40
Gordon, Walter, 114
Granatstein, J.L., 15, 279
Grant, George, 14–15
Green, Howard, 10–11, 156, 249–50,
    255–65; and Africa, 188, 194, 198,
    201–4, 261; and Asia, 212–13, 215,
    217–22; and Columbia River
    project, 261–62; and DEA, 149,
    259; Diefenbaker's support of, 11,
    149, 250, 258, 264, 284–85; as
    disarmament advocate, 11, 110, 115,
    124, 136, 148–50, 154–56, 173, 194,
    258, 259, 262–64; vs Harkness, 132,
    149–50, 154, 242, 262–63; and
    immigration, 228, 238–39; and
    Latin America, 14, 168, 169, 171–80,
    261, 283; and nuclear weapons
    issue, 10–11, 124, 127–29, 130, 132,
    136, 147, 154–56, 242, 257–58,
    263–64; as parliamentarian, 11,
    258–59; on Pearson's handling of
    Suez Crisis, 68, 75, 255; Ritchie on,
    259, 273–74; scurrilous story about,
    256–57; and scuttling of NORAD
    test, 259–60; and UN nuclear test
    moratorium, 262–63; US officials
    and, 12, 107, 109, 110, 257–60
Gromyko, Andrei, 97

Halberstam, David, 104, 107, 110
Hamilton, Alvin, 212, 252
Hammarskjöld, Dag, 28, 211; and
    Congo Crisis, 199–200, 201; and
    Lebanon Crisis, 91–92, 95, 97
Harkness, Douglas, 109, 112, 134, 153–56;
    vs Green, 132, 149–50, 154, 242,
    262–63; as poorly informed by

staff, 131–32; resignation of, 113,
    124, 136, 276–77
Harriman, Averell, 116n6, 218–19,
    221–22
Harris, Lou, 114, 276
Hatfield, Leonard, 229
Hawkins, Freda, 241
Heeney, Arnold, 12, 105, 106, 145, 221,
    249, 259–60
Hees, George, 111, 260, 276–77
Heidt, Daniel, 16
Heiss, Mary Ann, 110
Hellyer, Paul, 134
Herter, Christian, 87, 96, 201, 257, 260
Heusinger, Adolph, 129
Hilliker, John, and Donald Barry, 15,
    144–45
Hillmer, Norman, 15
Hoang Thuy Nam, 221
Hoganson, Kristin, 110
Holmes, John W., 69, 89, 98, 217
Home, Lord (Alexander Douglas-
    Home), 53
Honest John missiles, 10, 125, 128,
    137n7, 138n14
Hooton, Frank, 221
Horne, Alistair, 192
Howe, C.D., 169, 256, 271
Hussein, King of Jordan, 93
Hutchison, Bruce, 68, 70
Hyam, Ronald, 191, 193

Igartua, José, 69
Ignatieff, George, 149
Ikeda, Hayato, 214
immigrants to Canada, 230, 241;
    Chinese, 230, 241–42; from
    Indian sub-continent, 230, 241;
    Italian, 230–32, 234; West Indian,
    238–39, 241
Immigration Act, 230, 231–32, 234,
    237; Regulations of, 230–32, 233,
    234, 238, 240–41
immigration policy, Fairclough's
    reforms to, 7, 233–41, 285; and
    attempt to amend regulation

affecting Italian immigrants, 230–32, 234; cabinet's responses to, 231–41, 243; Diefenbaker and, 7, 228, 230, 239–40, 241–42, 280; vs early discriminatory policies, 227–28, 230, 240, 241, 285; and emphasis on education/skills, 230–31, 238, 240; later points system, as legacy of, 243; and recognition of post-colonial world, 228, 239, 241, 242–43. *See also* Fairclough, Ellen, as immigration minister

Imperial Economic Conference (1932), 34

Imperial Oil, 212

India, 33, 97, 211, 214–16, 222, 284; Diefenbaker's visit to, 6, 26, 28, 30, 37; immigration from, 230, 241; independence of, 189; as member of ICC, 217, 218, 219–21; perceived communist leanings of, 30, 215; and South Africa, 8, 56, 192–93. *See also* Nehru, Jawaharlal

Indochina, 7, 217–22, 284; 285. *See also* Laos; Vietnam, ICC's work in

Indonesia, 27, 28, 29, 213–14, 222, 284

Ingram, Kenneth, 71–72

intercontinental ballistic missiles (ICBMs), 9, 10, 18n13, 125–26

International Control Commission (ICC): for Laos, 218–19, 221, 284; for Vietnam, 219–22, 284. *See also* Laos, ICC's work in; Vietnam, ICC's work in

Iran, 93, 95, 110

Iraq, 93, 95, 253

Irwin, Arthur, 172, 179

Israel, 72, 75, 88, 89, 240

Japan, 30, 95, 97, 274; Diefenbaker's visit to, 7, 214

Jockel, Joseph T., 15

Johnson, David, 90, 95

Johnson, Lyndon B., 4, 107

Johnston, J.B., 27

Jordan, 93, 95–96, 97

Jung, Douglas, 33

Kasavubu, Joseph, 199

Katanga (Congolese province), 203–4

Kennedy, John F., 103–15, 281–82; and Diefenbaker, 12–13, 18n6, 105–6, 107, 108–9, 110–12, 117n15, 133–34, 144, 150–53, 154; personality of, 105, 106–7; and preference for Pearson over Diefenbaker, 8, 13, 106, 113–14, 153, 275. *See also entry below*; Cuban Missile Crisis

Kennedy administration, 3–4, 8, 12–14, 15, 103–15; anti-communism of, 104, 108, 110; arrogance of, 104–9; attacks on/undermining of Diefenbaker by, 273–76; background of, 104; inexperience of, 107–8; and negative perceptions of Canada, 12–13, 103–4, 111–15, 169–70, 281–82; as non-consultative, 104, 106–9; and nuclear weapons issue, 103, 109, 112–15, 132–37, 258, 274, 282; press release by, as contradicting Diefenbaker, 3, 14, 103, 113–14, 115, 136, 155; toughness valued by, 18n6, 109–11

Kennedy, Joseph P. (Joe), 106

Kennedy, Robert F., 105, 116n6

Kent, Tom, 68, 77, 156

Kenya, 197

Khan, Ayub, 28, 31, 215. *See also* Pakistan

King, William Lyon Mackenzie, 27, 125, 237, 271, 276

Khrushchev, Nikita, 29, 95–96, 150, 260, 263

Killian report, on US defence, 125

Kohler, Foy, 105

Krishnamachari, T.T., 216

Kubitschek, Juscelino, 170

Lacrosse missiles, 10, 125, 126–27, 128, 146

Lafer, Horácio, 171–72

Lange, Halvard, 96
Laos, 209, 217–19, 220, 222; ICC's work in, 218–19, 221
Latin America, 7, 11–12, 14, 167–80, 283; and Canada's hemispheric relationships, 168–70, 172–73, 176–78, 180; Canadian diplomacy/ missions in, 171, 173–74, 175, 177, 178–79, 228, 280; Canadian visits to, 7, 169–70, 172–73, 283; and issue of OAS membership, 106, 169, 171–80, 274; military coups in, 179; and threat posed by Cuba, 167–68, 171, 174–80; US-Canada tensions over, 14, 107, 110, 168–69, 174–80. *See also* Cuba; Mexico
Laurier, Wilfrid, 78
Law of the Sea, UN Conference on (1958), 252, 253
Lebanon Crisis, 87–98; background to, 88; and British-US Middle East policies, 89–90; and British-US military plan, 89–97; Iraqi coup and, 93; Smith's role in mediating, 89–92, 94–97, 253; UN force sent in response to, 91, 92, 94–95, 253
Léger, Jules, 89, 90, 92, 94, 96, 198, 251
LePan, Douglas, 216
Lesage, Jean, 79
Liberal Party: and African decolonization, 188–89, 194, 204; and Asia, 209, 214–15, 217, 222, 284; as compared to Progressive Conservative Party, 4, 16–17, 46, 51, 87, 114, 277, 280; Eisenhower administration and, 87, 92; and election campaigns (1957/1958), 6, 76, 77–79, 271, 272–73; election victory of (1963), 3, 114, 124, 155–56, 273, 276; and "golden age" of foreign policy, 4, 5–6, 16, 25–26, 169, 250, 279; and immigration, 230–32, 236, 237, 243; issues inherited from, 9–10, 126–27, 230–32; and Latin America, 169, 177, 180; as passing Fairclough's

employment bill, 229; and "pipeline bill" debate, 78, 255, 271, 272; pro-nuclear stance of, 14, 127, 128, 135–36, 154–56, 263–64, 273–76, 277; and Suez Crisis, 5–6, 8, 27, 46, 68, 69–70, 73–80, 252, 255, 281. *See also* Pearson, Lester B.; St. Laurent, Louis
Lloyd, Selwyn, 92, 97
Lockheed F-104G (Starfighter) aircraft, 10, 12, 146
Lodge, Henry Cabot, 94, 259
López Mateos, Adolfo, 170, 171, 172, 174
Loufti, Omar, 90
Louw, Eric, 191, 193
Lumumba, Joseph, 256–57
Lumumba, Patrice, 109, 201–3
Lynch, Charles, 256–57, 275
Lyon, Peyton V., 17*n*3, 277

Macdonald, John A., 78, 155
Macdonnell, R.M., 90, 91
Macmillan, Harold, 28, 30, 87, 178, 239–40; Diefenbaker's relationship with, 18*n*6, 25, 27, 47–48, 50, 54–55, 58–59; and Kennedy, 38, 58, 135; and Lebanon Crisis, 91, 93, 95; and South Africa, 53–57, 59, 191–93, 281, 283–84; and UK's application to join EEC, 7–8, 35, 38, 45, 47–48, 52–53, 57–59, 280–81; "wind of change" speech by, 53, 54, 186. *See also* British-Canadian issues/ irritants; United Kingdom
Malaya, 191, 211; Diefenbaker's visit to, 6, 26, 27, 28, 29, 33, 34, 36–37; as preferred Canadian partner, 213–14, 222, 284
Malik, Charles, 88, 90
Maloney, Sean, 144, 149
Manion, John L. (Jack), 235, 245*n*52
Mao Zedong, 210, 211–12
Martin, Lawrence, 256
Martin, Paul, 177, 250, 258 Maud, John, 191
McDonnell F-101 Voodoo aircraft, 12, 133

McMahon, Patricia, 16, 144, 152, 249
McNamara, Robert, 12, 108, 114, 116n6, 133, 135, 155–56
McNaught, Kenneth, 239
Menzies, Arthur, 213, 215
Menzies, Robert, 54–55, 193
Merchant, Livingston, 13, 94, 96, 152–53, 218, 257; on Canada, 106, 109, 111, 113; and nuclear weapons issue, 142n85, 152, 275
Methodist Church, 229
Mexico, 169, 170, 171, 174; Diefenbaker's visit to, 7, 172–73, 283
Military Assistance Advisory Group (MAAG) (US), 219
Miller, Frank, 130–31, 134
Minifie, James, 70
Mitchell, G.D., 91
Mobutu, Joseph, 202
Mollet, Guy, 72
Moran, Herbert, 215, 261
Morocco, 197, 198
Mossadeq, Mohammed, 110
Munton, Don, 16
Murray, Geoffrey, 90–91

Nash, Knowlton, 20n37, 85–86, 105, 249
Nash, Walter, 36
Nassau Agreement (US-UK), 124, 135–36, 137, 154
Nasser, Gamal Abdel: and Lebanon Crisis, 88, 90, 92; and Suez Crisis, 71, 74
National Defence, Department of. *See* conventional forces/weapons; defence policy, in nuclear era; Harkness, Douglas; nuclear disarmament, *and entry following*; nuclear weapons
National Liberation Front (Algeria), 198
Nehru, Jawaharlal, 27, 32, 211; neutralist stance/perceived communist leanings of, 30, 215; on South Africa, 8, 56, 192–93. *See also* India
Nehru, R.K., 192, 193
New Democratic Party, 273, 276

New Zealand, 34, 38, 59, 211, 239; Diefenbaker's visit to, 6, 27, 28, 36
Newfoundland: storage of nuclear weapons in, 148
Newman, Peter C., 14–15, 144, 249, 277
Newsweek, 105, 112–13, 152, 275
Newton, Ted, 179
Nicaragua, 171
Nicholson, Patrick, 144
Nigeria, 283
Nixon, Richard, 167
Nkrumah, Kwame, 33, 52, 195–97, 207n41
Nobel Peace Prize, 156; as won by Pearson, 13, 78, 111, 153, 273, 275
Nolting, Frederick, 221
non-alignment, 188, 202, 218; Bandung Conference on, 30; Diefenbaker's suspicions of, 30, 283; and Lebanon Crisis, 91, 95, 97–98
Norstad, Lauris, 14, 127, 129, 135, 154–55, 156, 275–76
North American Air Defence Command (NORAD), 9, 15, 95, 125, 133, 252; planned test of, as scuttled by Green, 259–60; and requirement for consultation of Canada, 9, 145, 153; tensions with Kennedy over, 14, 38, 85, 153
North Atlantic Council, 123
North Atlantic Treaty Organization (NATO), 5, 28, 72, 79, 86, 93, 147, 154, 194, 283; and Algerian War, 198–99; and Berlin Crisis, 254–55; and Congo Crisis, 200–4; and conventional weapons issue, 123, 125, 127–30, 131–32, 135, 150; and Lebanon Crisis, 91–92, 95–96; and massive retaliation strategy (MC 14/2), 123–24, 125, 129; nuclear weapons for, 10, 12, 14, 112, 127–37, 150, 154, 156, 275–76
North Vietnam. *See* Vietnam, ICC's work in
Norway, 134; and Lebanon Crisis, 91, 96–97, 253

nuclear disarmament: Canada's history of ambivalence on, 125; DEA strategies on, 124, 126–30, 133; Green's advocacy of, 11, 110, 115, 124, 136, 148–50, 154–56, 173, 194, 258, 259, 262–64; Ireland's UN resolution on, 132; public opinion on, 10–11, 143–45, 146, 147, 150–52, 153, 155–57, 282. *See also entry below*

nuclear disarmament, Diefenbaker's changing position on, 143–57; and anti-nuclear movement, 10–11, 143–45, 146, 147, 150–52, 153, 155–57, 282; and election campaign (1963), 155–56; and eroding relationship with Kennedy, 144, 151, 152–53, 154; historians' views on, 144–45; and joint control/sovereignty issue, 13, 124, 143–44, 147–48, 149, 151, 154, 156; and Norstad's comments on NATO commitments, 154, 156; and Pearson's pro-nuclear stance, 154–56; as stated in Parliament, 126–27, 136, 146, 155

nuclear weapons, 123–37; DEA-National Defence split over, 10, 123–36; Diefenbaker government's changing policy on, 9–10, 12, 14, 15, 112, 126–27, 132–37, 145–46, 155–56, 282; joint control of, 13, 124, 135, 143–44, 147–48, 149, 151; and Norstad's comments on NATO commitments, 14, 135, 154, 156, 275–76; Pearson's willingness to accept, 14, 127, 128, 135–36, 154–56, 263–64, 273–76, 277; press commentaries on, 14, 19n26, 130, 275-76; Ritchie on, 273–74; storage of, 143, 148, 150; US responses to decision-making on, 103, 109, 112–15, 132–37, 258, 274, 282. *See also* Bomarc missiles; conventional forces/weapons; defence policy, in nuclear era; *specific weapons and aircraft*

O'Donnell, Kenny, 105, 116n6

O'Hagan, Richard, 114

Opération des Nations Unies au Congo (ONUC), 199–204, 283

Operation Pan America (Brazilian proposal), 170, 172, 176

Operation Skyhawk (planned NORAD test), 259–60

Organization of American States (OAS), 106, 169, 171–80, 274

Pakistan, 93, 189, 230; Diefenbaker's visit to, 6, 26, 28, 29, 31, 36, 37, 211, 215–16; Khan regime in, 28, 31, 215; as preferred Canadian ally, 214–16, 222, 284

Pathet Lao (Laotian communist movement), 217

peacekeeping, 123, 284; in Congo, 199–204, 205, 283; in Lebanon, 90–92, 94, 96; vs "muscular" peacemaking, 203–4, 205; in Sinai, 90, 94; Suez Crisis and, 68, 73–76, 199, 272

Pearkes, George, 9, 125–26, 127, 130, 131, 260

Pearson, Lester B., 4, 197, 250; changing views of on nuclear weapons, 14, 127, 128, 135–36, 154–56, 263–64, 273–76, 277; and election campaigns (1957/1958), 76, 77–79; election victory of (1963), 3, 114, 124, 155–56, 273, 276; Kennedy's preference for, 8, 13, 106, 113–14, 153, 275; as Nobel laureate, 13, 78, 111, 153, 273, 275; Suez Crisis peacekeeping solution of, 68, 73–76, 199, 272; as unable to win majority government, 3, 156, 264, 273, 276

Peru, 173, 178, 179, 184n43

Pickersgill, Jack, 82n15, 231–32

"pipeline bill" debate, 78, 255, 271, 272

Plumptre, A.F.W., 216

Poland: as member of ICC, 217, 218, 221

Polaris ballistic missiles, 10, 130–32;

Nassau Agreement on, 124, 135–36, 137, 154
Polymer Company of Canada, 172
Preston, Richard, 188
Progressive Conservative Party, 154–55, 266*n*8, 272; as compared to Liberal Party, 4, 16–17, 46, 51, 87, 114, 277, 280; Smith's ties to, 11, 96, 250

Quadros, Jânio, 177–78
Queen's Own Rifles, 74–75

Rahman, Tunku Abdul, 191
Rayburn, Sam, 107
Reid, Escott, 16
Richter, Andrew, 144
Ritchie, Charles, 90, 273–75; and Asia, 219, 222; and Congo Crisis, 200, 202; on Green, 259, 273–74; on Kennedy and his circle, 104, 105, 106, 108; and Lebanon Crisis, 89, 90–91, 95; on Smith, 251; on US attitude to Canada, 4, 274–75
Roberts, Charles, 105
Robertson, Norman, 89, 92, 212, 216, 219; and Congo Crisis, 200; and Latin America, 175, 180; and nuclear disarmament, 124, 129, 148–49, 273–74; and nuclear weapons issue, 124, 127–28, 129, 130–32, 134, 135; with Smith and Green, 251, 259
Robinson, H. Basil, 4, 249; on African politics/crises, 191–92, 200; on Diefenbaker-Eisenhower relationship, 85; on Diefenbaker-Kennedy relationship, 107, 109, 112; on Diefenbaker's Commonwealth experiences, 25–26, 28, 33, 56, 215; on nuclear debate, 145, 150; on Smith, 251–55
Ronning, Chester, 211, 218, 220–21
Roosevelt, Franklin D., 86
Rostow, W.W. (Walt), 12, 13, 104, 116*n*6, 153
Rostow memo, 12, 13, 153, 184*n*48

Rowe, Earl, 272
Royal Canadian Air Force (RCAF), 10, 124, 137*n*7
Rusk, Dean, 103, 104–5, 109, 111, 113, 114, 176, 218, 221–22, 263

Schlesinger, Arthur M., Jr., 104, 274
Sévigny, Pierre, 109, 177
Sharpeville Massacre, 53–54, 190
Shriver, Eunice Kennedy, 105
Simpson, Erika, 16, 144
Singapore, 27, 28, 34
Skybolt missiles, 108, 135
Smith, C.E.S., 235
Smith, Denis, 15, 249, 271
Smith, Rufus, 106, 221
Smith, Sidney, 10–11, 27, 217, 228, 249–51, 264–65, 280; and Berlin Crisis, 254–55; and PRC, 211, 216; and Commonwealth education initiatives, 253–54; Diefenbaker's relationship with, 11, 96, 252, 254–55, 284; Green's advantages over, 258–59; and Latin America, 168, 170, 283; and Lebanon Crisis, 89–92, 94–97, 253; Ritchie on, 251; sudden death of, 11, 148, 250, 255
Sobolev, Arkady, 94
Social Credit Party, 272, 273, 276, 279*n*2
Somoza, Anastasio, 171
South Africa, 187–88; as seeking to remain in Commonwealth, 53–57, 59, 190–93; withdrawal from Commonwealth by, 56, 193–94, 204–5. *See also entry below*
South African apartheid, Diefenbaker's stand against, 190–93, 204–5; evolution of, 34, 53–54, 190–91; as excluding sanctions, 175; immigration policy and, 228, 238; Nehru and, 8, 56, 192–93; as singled out by South Africa, 44*n*78, 56, 193; tensions with Macmillan over, 53–57, 59, 191–93, 281, 283–84; as urged by Bryce, 192, 193

South Vietnam. *See* Vietnam, ICC's work in
Souvanna Phouma, Prince of Laos, 217
Soviet Union. *See* Union of Soviet Socialist Republics
Special Commonwealth African Assistance Program, 188
Spittal, Cara, 28, 145
Spooner, Kevin, 249
Spry, Graham, 48
Sputnik satellite, 125
St. Laurent, Louis, 4, 47, 51, 69, 211, 213, 214, 250, 265, 276; and Africa, 33, 188–89, 194, 198, 204; and "pipeline bill" debate, 271, 272; and Suez Crisis, 6, 27, 46, 68, 72, 74–78, 252; policies of, continued by Diefenbaker, 16–17, 188–89, 204, 280, 284
Stairs, William, 187
Stalin, Joseph, 29
Starfighter. *See* Lockheed F-104G
State, Department of (US): and Canadian wheat sale to PRC, 213; and Eisenhower, 86–87; and Laos, 221–22; and Kennedy, 13, 110; press release by, 3, 14, 103, 113–14, 115, 136, 155; and Vietnam, 219
Stevenson, Adlai, 105, 109
Stevenson, Michael, 16
Strauss, Franz Josef, 129
Stuart, Douglas, 86
Stursberg, Peter, 72
Suez Crisis, 16, 71–78; Liberals and, 5–6, 8, 27, 46, 68, 69–70, 73–80, 252, 255, 281; Parliamentary debate over, 74–76, 255; Pearson's solution to, 68, 73–76, 199, 272; US role in, 68, 71–72, 74–76. *See also entry below*
Suez Crisis, anti-Americanism following, 3, 5–6, 8, 67–80, 281; and Canada's refusal to support UK, 5–6, 27, 46, 69–70, 72–76; and criticism/scrutiny of Canada-US relationship, 67–68, 70–77; and

Diefenbaker's election victories, 69–70, 75–80, 82*n*15
Sukarno, 213
Syria: as part of UAR, 88, 90, 91, 253

Taylor, A.J.P., 105
Taylor, Maxwell, 129
Tello Baurraud, Manuel, 171, 172, 173
Thompson, Robert, 276, 278*n*2
Toronto Association for Peace, 146
Toronto Committee for Disarmament, 148
trade: UK's EEC proposal on, 47, 48, 50–51, 57; US controls on, as affecting Canada, 79, 210–13; US embargo on, with Cuba, 11–12, 174–75. *See also entry below*
trade, Diefenbaker's keen interest in: with PRC, 79, 93, 210–13, 274; as promoted on Commonwealth tour, 28, 34–37; and proposed diversion to UK, 34, 49–50; as tied to aid, 36–37
Tremblay, Paul, 179
Trudeau, Pierre Elliott, 40, 265, 273
Trujillo, Rafael, 171, 175
Tunisia, 197, 198

Union of Soviet Socialist Republics (USSR), 29, 35, 88, 149; and Cuba, 98, 134, 108–9, 153–54, 186, 263, 276–77; and division of Berlin, 12, 129, 133–34, 136, 150, 254–55; military technology of, 9, 12, 125–36; planning for attack by, 10, 18*n*13, 123–37; world leaders' relationships with, 14, 30–31, 71, 178–79, 201–2
United Arab Republic (UAR), 88, 90, 91, 253
United Auto Workers (UAW), 79, 210
United Kingdom (UK), 45–59; application to join EEC, 7–8, 35, 38, 45, 47–48, 52–53, 57–59, 280–81; Diefenbaker's visit to, 27–28, 29–31, 35, 52. *See also* British-Canadian issues/irritants; Macmillan, Harold

United Nations Emergency Force
(UNEF), 91, 92, 200; in Sinai, 90,
94; and Suez Crisis, 72–77, 199,
272. *See also* peacekeeping
United Nations Observation Group
in Lebanon (UNOGIL), 91, 92,
94–95, 253
United States. *See* anti-Americanism;
British-US collaboration/cooperation;
Cuban Missile Crisis; defence policy,
in nuclear era; Eisenhower, Dwight D.;
Kennedy, John F.; Kennedy
administration; Laos, ICC's work in;
Lebanon Crisis; nuclear weapons;
Suez Crisis, anti-Americanism
following; Vietnam, ICC's work in
Universal Declaration of Human
Rights, 238
University of Toronto, 11, 96, 146, 250

Valluy, Jean, 129
Van Stolk, Mary, 146
Venezuela, 167, 171, 175
Verwoerd, Hendrik, 191, 193
Vietnam, ICC's work in, 219–22;
Geneva peace settlement and, 217,

220–21; Geneva truce agreement
and, 218–20; and history of US
military aid to South, 219–20; and
subversion/assassinations by North,
220–21; US-Canada tensions over,
108, 220–22
Vietnam, North (DRVN), 217, 219,
220–21
Vietnam, South, 219–21
Voice of Women (VOW), 148, 151, 282
Voodoo. *See* McDonnell F-101

Waldock, D.A.G., 130, 131–32
Warsak Dam (Pakistan), 215–16
Webster, David, 214
wheat, sale of, 172, 214; to PRC, 7,
209–13, 222, 274, 284; as tied to
aid, 36, 51–52, 215–17; US-caused
crisis in, 209–10
Wigglesworth, Richard, 260
Wigny, Pierre, 201
Wittner, Lawrence, 152
Woodsworth, Charles, 219, 221
World Council of Churches, 238

Zeiler, Thomas, 110